Quality Control
for Management

Quality Control for Management

Kenneth Kivenko

Prentice-Hall   **Englewood Cliffs, N.J.**

Prentice-Hall International, Inc. *London*
Prentice-Hall of Australia, Pty. Ltd., *Sydney*
Prentice-Hall Canada, Inc., *Toronto*
Prentice-Hall of India Private Ltd., *New Delhi*
Prentice-Hall of Japan, Inc., *Tokyo*
Prentice-Hall of Southeast Asia Pte. Ltd., *Singapore*
Whitehall Books, Ltd., Wellington, *New Zealand*
Editora Prentice-Hall do Brasil Ltda., *Rio de Janeiro*

© 1984 *by*

PRENTICE-HALL, INC.

Englewood Cliffs, N.J.

Library of Congress Cataloging in Publication Data

Kivenko, Kenneth
   Quality control for management.

   Includes index.
   1. Quality control.   I. Title.
TS156.K495   1984   658.5'62   83-26928
ISBN 0-13-745217-9

Printed in the United States of America

To my wife Marilyn and sons Leigh and Bram.

Acknowledgments

I owe thanks to a large number of people for advice, suggestions, comments, and technical assistance in the preparation of the manuscript. In particular, Erwin Spinner, Rene Lebeuf, Maxine Mani, Michael Galipeau, John Ackerman, Rolf Seiler, Ann King, Marina Harvey, Lionel Leville, and all of Canadian Marconi Company provided invaluable critiques, feedback, and support at numerous stages in the writing of the manuscript. Additionally, Henry Pukier of Organon Canada, Bill O'Flaherty of Sperry Gyroscope, George Laszlow of Canadair, and Pierre Dubois of Woods Gordon offered the benefits of their various experiences. The other people who assisted me number literally in the hundreds and are too numerous to mention individually. Accordingly, I thank them as a group and hope they will understand the limitations of space.

Kenneth Kivenko

About the Author

Kenneth Kivenko is currently Vice President of the Components Division of Canadian Marconi Company in Montreal. He has held positions in Quality Control, Product Assurance, and Operations Management. His present management role has allowed him the unique opportunity to apply his quality philosophy, principles, and practices directly to successful high growth businesses. The Division exports high technology components and sub-systems to a broad customer base in the United States and Western Europe.

Mr. Kivenko's responsibilities include product development, marketing, manufacturing, materials management, and quality control.

The author's professional experience includes two years with the Canadian Government Quality Assurance Branch and ten years with Canadian Marconi in quality engineering, reliability, environmental test, and quality management. He holds a degree in Electronics Engineering from McGill University as well as a diploma in management. He teaches Quality Control at Concordia University in Montreal.

Mr. Kivenko is a member of a number of professional associations including APICS, Sme-Robotics International, AIIE, ASQC, and the Quebec Order of Engineers. He is the author of *Management Work-In-Process Inventory,* Marcel Dekker, 1981 and has published in excess of 30 articles in numerous journals and periodicals on such subjects as product safety, quality cost optimization, procurement quality control, system availability, and quality's impact on business performance.

and approaches to recruiting, developing, and motivating QC personnel. It pinpoints techniques for increasing human performance (see Chapter 7).

In Chapter 8, modern quality management techniques from Japan, Europe, Canada, and the U.S. are detailed. Your on-the-job effectiveness will be increased multi-fold.

Chapter 9 provides proven review procedures and checklists for ensuring that new products don't bomb out in the factory. Of particular value is a Production Readiness Review procedure to assist production quality planning.

This book shows you how to apply contemporary statistical and quantitative methods to improve day-to-day quality management decisions. Perhaps more importantly, you'll learn strategies for *implementing* your decisions (see Chapter 10).

It reveals the cost, performance, and time benefits of computerized data processing, automatic test equipment, microprocessors, and word processors to the quality function. Clear guidelines and step-by-step case examples are set forth to help you use modern technology to reduce your quality costs (see Chapter 11).

It provides guidelines, procedures, checklists, forms, and case examples to evaluate your important outside factory—your vendors (see Chapter 12 on how to optimize the vendor/vendee relationship).

Chapter 13 presents proven procedures that can slash your quality costs and dramatically improve profits in your quality control program. And it also shows you how to audit, evaluate, and measure the performance of the quality function. Checklists, questionnaires, quality cost analysis—everything you need to know where you stand (see Chapter 14).

In summary, this book deals with a variety of quality problems and opportunities and provides solutions, ideas, helpful hints, and cautions in a clear, concise manner. Every aspect of QC from market research and product design, right through to customer use is addressed in pragmatic, meaningful terms.

Through the use of checklists, case examples, formulas, key ratios, practices, forms, charts, and references, proven techniques for reducing costs and improving product quality are presented. Each approach, however, is coupled to human factors because corrective action and change always involves people. The impact of poor personnel attitudes, training, and motivation is enormous and makes itself felt in poor workmanship, low productivity, high inventory, and customer complaints. This book also deals with topics such as personnel selection, promotions, excessive overtime, and supervisory techniques, directly aimed at the QC function.

Quality Control may well be the last frontier for profits. The dreams and promises of an effective industrial quality program have not yet been achieved with the possible single exception of Japan. These dreams can be made realities by employing generally simple, down-to-earth practices and disciplines, and keeping up-to-date with new techniques and equipment. Galloping inflation, rising interest rates, mounting energy costs, international competition, rapid technological change, and customer consciousness of quality and increasing government regulation dictate that industry take aggressive actions. The material provided in this book lays the foundations on which to build an efficient cost-effective quality program that will keep your firm healthy and competitive.

K. Kivenko

Table of Contents

1

Realizing the Full Potential of the Quality Program

The management of quality control is like the management of any function: 80 percent common sense and 20 percent theory and science. This book stresses the down-to-earth approaches to reducing costs and improving product quality while addressing the numerous available proven quality-improvement techniques and approaches. United States productivity, in most industries, has been declining relative to other countries for years (see Table 1-1).

Inflation, increasing government regulation, international competition, environmental considerations, energy shortages, and the rise in consumerism make efficient manufacturing essential for the 1980s and beyond. Quality control provides the last frontier for cost reduction and avoidance, decreased inventory, improved customer satisfaction, and increased sales. It will also help you avoid such disasters as:

- Expensive product recalls, typified by the auto industry.
- Safety hazards such as cargo doors falling off airplanes.
- Loss of market share due to the higher quality of imports.
- Excessive quality losses that ultimately lead to takeover, merger, or bankruptcy (e.g., Motorola consumer group).
- Costly product liability actions, typical of the home appliance industry segment.

PRODUCT	IMPORTS AS A PERCENTAGE OF TOTAL U.S. SALES	
	1968	1978
Video recorders	N/A	100%
Color TV	11.0%	27.1%
Autos	10.5%	17.8%
Steel	14.2%	16.1%
Trucks	<5%	8.8%

- Electrical system breakdowns that black-out major cities (e.g., the great New York City blackout).
- Hotel balconies that collapse due to inferior design quality, killing people and causing hundreds of thousands of dollars in property damage.

Any reputable manufacturer will find it an economic necessity to perform the basic QC tasks discussed in this book. It is only those manufacturers who adopt a "let the public be damned" attitude who do not find it necessary to perform the total quality job. In this day and age, this is getting more difficult to do. No longer does the principle of *caveat emptor* apply, but rather the rule is "let the seller beware." There are many instances where consumers have instituted successful lawsuits against manufacturers for inferior products. The increasing demand by the public for better-qual-

1

TABLE 1-1. Reasons for U.S. Productivity Decline

- Inadequate sensing of market changes (energy, consumerism, safety, quality)
- Tax measures that fail to encourage investment, risk, innovation.
- A nation that has faced the Vietnam War, Watergate, large-scale business scandals, serious drug problems.
- Large diversion of resources to national defense.
- A legal system that encourages product liability suits, large settlements, heavy fines.
- A de-emphasis of craftsmanship, product quality, reliability.
- Lagging investment in automation and plant modernization.
- Requirement for relatively short payback periods on investments.
- An apparent inability to recognize and react to foreign competition.
- A decline in the work ethic due to affluence, social security benefits, and unemployment insurance.
- Relatively poor union/management relations.
- Large wage and benefit increases without corresponding productivity increases.

ity products and international competition require that manufacturers develop full-fledged quality programs covering the entire spectrum of company operations (Figure 1-1).

> Quality Control is not just a little room adjacent to the factory floor. Quality Control is—or should be—a state of mind.
>
> Dr. Norihiko Nakayama
> President of Fujitsu America, Inc.

This chapter discusses product quality, identifies a myriad of cost and other benefits, defines fundamental control concepts, and explains top management objectives and concerns.

QUALITY: A CORNERSTONE FOR PRODUCTIVITY GROWTH

The impact of quality control on the financial performance of the firm can be enormous. Product quality affects such cost variables as:

- *Manufacturing Costs.* Among the manufacturing costs that can be avoided through a robust quality control program are:

  —Costs for labor to repair or reprocess products that did not meet acceptable performance levels the first time around.

  —Costs due to loss of product yield because a portion is defective and must be scrapped.

  —Costs for labor to sort and inspect product quantities that contain some "bad" and some "good."

  —Costs for downtime on equipment that cannot operate because incoming materials are unsuitable for further processing.

- *Inventory.* Interest costs on extra inventories that are maintained because of downtime, rejections, or unscheduled processing due to rework.

- *Wasted Capacity.* Low yields, high rework, and excessive repairs don't only cause production costs and work-in-process inventory to increase. The capacity wasted in rectifying faults could be available for productive uses. Often a planned plant expansion can be delayed simply by decreasing the amount of time spent doing things twice.

- *Accounts Receivable.* In cases where a defect is detected prior to payment of the invoice, a customer may elect to hold up payment until a correction is made. Tight money conditions may cause customers to use any excuse available to hold up payment, and poor quality is one of the best.

- *Returns and Allowances.* Costs incurred in remedying latent product defects—for example, warranty adjustments or recall and repair charges—inflate the allowance account, thus reducing net sales. Shipping and freight charges also increase, since the expense for returning defective products to the place of manufacture for repair is often borne by the manufacturer.

- *Selling Costs.* Extra effort that could be used for selling is diverted to such activities as investigating complaints, reporting defects, and pacifying irate customers, thus decreasing sales productivity and increasing selling costs.

- *Loss of Market Share.* Where product deficiencies reach the level of hurting a company's or product's reputation, prospective customers may turn to competitive products as they hear of problems from various sources. Thus, with increasing percentages of defective product to the user, there will be an increasing rate of sales loss (Table 1-2).

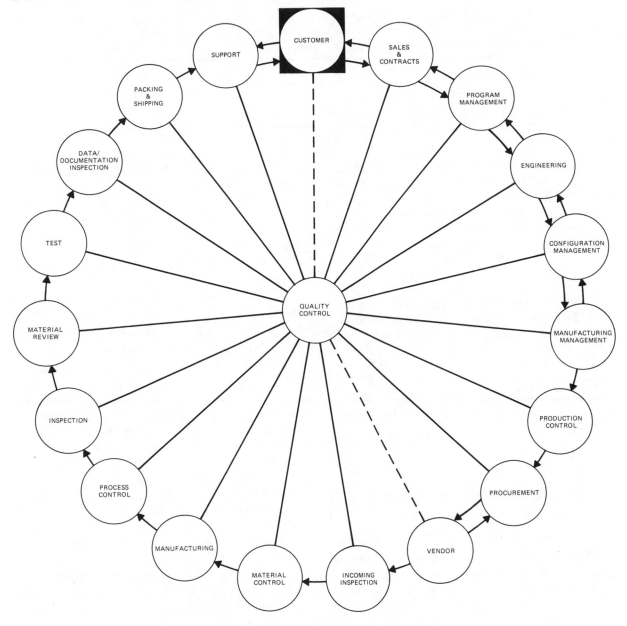

FIGURE 1-1. Quality Control Scope of Involvement
Courtesy of Canadian Marconi Company.

- *Product Liability.* Expensive product recalls and product liability suits cause severe financial damage to earnings. In extreme cases a company may be forced into bankruptcy. At the least, market share can be significantly eroded because of adverse publicity.

Here is a list of typical annual cost savings available when an effective quality program is in place:

- Elimination of machine oil leaks that contaminated machined materials. Regular mainte-

nance schedule was adhered to and normal seal repairs were made. *Savings:* $13,160.

- Clerical employees effected changes that reduced the shipping error rate by 50% and no packages were lost or misrouted. *Savings:* $32,-100.

- Elimination of failures resulting from mating flat ribbon cable to cylindrical connector. A metal guide was designed and new techniques were devised. *Savings:* $11,500.

- Reduction of receiving inspection and inventory costs. A diligent vendor certification effort

TABLE 1–2. Value of customer renewal rates. Quality contributes to higher renewal rates. Contrast an 80 percent renewal rate (with growth of an original sales dollar to $3.95) against a lot 60 percent rate (growth only to $2.43).

Selling Period	1	2	3	4	5	6	7
80% renewal rate	1.00	1.80	2.44	2.95	3.36	3.69	3.95
60% renewal rate	1.00	1.60	1.96	2.18	2.31	2.38	2.43

slashed incoming test costs and reduced inventory build-ups because of part shortages. *Savings:* $75,000.

- Reduced number of engineering changes. Implementation of design review processes reduced the number of engineering changes on new product releases. This resulted in decreased inventory write-offs of obsolete parts, less rework, improved field reliability, and better schedule performance. *Savings:* $96,000.

- Elimination of work delays caused by tool calibration procedures. New calibration procedures were established. *Savings:* $7,120.

WHAT IS QUALITY?

There are many definitions of *quality*. Here are five of the most common:

1. Relative excellence
2. Value for money
3. Conformance to drawings and specifications
4. Conformance to the purchase order
5. Fitness for intended function

Relative Excellence: This definition is more appropriate to handicrafts, works of art, and fruit and vegetables than to engineered products. It means that you do the best you can under the circumstances, grade the resulting products, and adjust the price accordingly. That doesn't seem to be what we are after.

Value for Money: You can buy a Model-T Ford in mint condition. It's a steal at $35,000. There's no doubt about its value for the money—to the right buyer. But, would you want to drive it back and forth to work? "Value for money" doesn't help us very much.

Conformance to Drawings and Specifications: That is certainly one of the best ways of measuring quality, but does it, by itself, guarantee user satisfaction? Only if the drawings and specs clearly and adequately provide for all those things that the user is entitled to expect, and nothing more. We

want to be an honest supplier—but not a nonprofit organization.

Conformance to the Purchase Order: That's what most incoming inspection is based on, isn't it? But it suffers from the same limitations as conformance to drawings and specifications. Do you know anyone who has seen the perfect purchase order?

Fitness for Intended Function:

—being what it is supposed to be

—doing what it is supposed to do

—whenever, and for as long as, it is supposed to do it.

This is what we're really after. But it involves a lot more than ganging up on the little guy that cuts the metal and inspecting his output.

Total quality is the sum of quality of design plus quality of each produced item's conformance to the design (see Figure 1-2). It is more efficient to deal with these two aspects of quality through the areas of the organization that bear specific responsibilities for one or the other of them.

Case in Point: A homemaker shopping for a dishwasher considered such features as capacity, ease of operation, power requirements, cleaning performance, and appearance. (These features reflect quality of design.) When the unit was installed, a banging noise was heard and the dishwasher failed to operate. The homemaker told her friends and neighbors that Product X was not a "quality" product. While the unit had all the required features (quality of design), it was not assembled properly in the factory, reflecting nonconformance with design requirements.

If we want to recognize and agree on quality in a specific item, we must be able to describe it. What do we have to take into consideration when

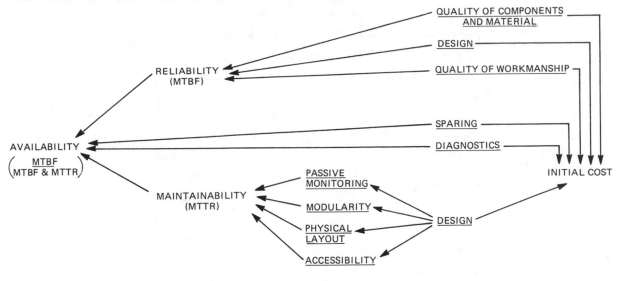

THE UNDERLINED ELEMENTS CAN BE CONSIDERED AS PARAMETERS OF A TWO VARIABLE FUNCTION (AVAILABILITY AND COST)

FIGURE 1-2. Minimization of Total Cost for Functional Products
Courtesy of Canadian Marconi Company.

we are specifying the *quality* of a product? Some of the design characteristics of a product that need to be considered include:

- Capability
- Availability
- Reliability (mean time between failures)
- Operability
- Maintainability (mean time to repair)
- Durability
- Safety
- Operating life

Assurance of quality depends on tangible evidence of adequacy for each of these characteristics.

Specifying product quality is quite a chore. Not only must we consider and balance out all of those characteristics, but we have to find out what the customer wants and is prepared to pay for and what is possible and practical with the money and time available. Then we make the necessary trade-offs (see Figure 1-3).

For engineered products, the maximum quality is fixed on the drawing board. Everything beyond that point is downhill unless proper controls are maintained. If we expect anything else we are not talking about production, we are talking about handicrafts.

WHAT DO WE MEAN BY "CONTROL"?

Control, used in the context of quality control, has a special meaning. Control of a dynamic system (that is, a system that operates over time and whose output depends upon the input) implies feedback of performance and a comparison of the output with a desired standard. Since comparison usually involves a difference between actual performance and some standard, such control is commonly termed *negative feedback control* (see Figure 1-4).

Control points are normally set up at strategic locations during the life cycle of a product. The usual control points are:

- During various stages of product development.
- On receipt from another company or operating division.
- Before a major or costly operation.
- Acceptance of set-ups tooling or special measuring equipment.
- Prior to an irreversible, nonrepairable operation.
- Before movement between departments or delivery to stores.
- After creation of a critical quality characteristic.
- Prior to sealing or other operation that would preclude later inspection (referred to as a *last point inspection*).

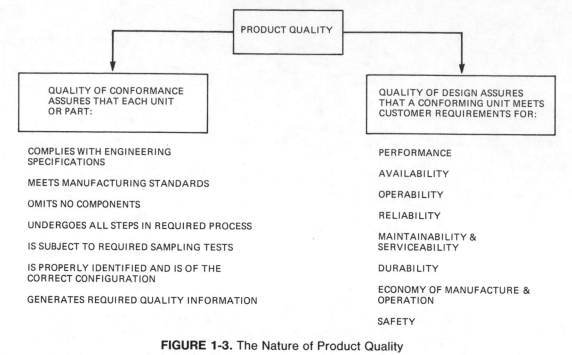

FIGURE 1-3. The Nature of Product Quality

- Before shipment to a customer or distribution warehouse.
- During the warranty period of product usage.
- At a customer interface after a product has been sold (e.g., complaint analysis, reliability measurement, safety evaluation).

The sensing device measures the specified characteristic(s) of the output, and this information is compared with the desired level. The resulting error signal, in turn, adjusts the operation of the controlled process.

The controlling system in Figure 1-4 is called a *closed loop* feedback system, with the lower loop being the feedback loop. Removal of this loop would change the system to an *open loop* system in which there is no interaction between the actual output and the desired output. The exercise of control by management is fundamental to the operations of any organization. Since effective organization of the efforts of many people requires that supervisory and management personnel be responsible for proper performance in their area, they must have a means of judging performance.

Management controls provide this ability. They take many forms, varying from a simple workplace meeting, periodic reports, and procedures to a complete management information system. Quality depends upon a full range of con-

trols that cover production, procurement, engineering, and management data.

This does not mean, however, that quality control will be the sole operator of a control point at any one area in the organization. Effective management policy has an important function in determining who shall primarily operate controls at any one point in the organization. Regardless of who performs the control process at any given point, however, it remains the responsibility of the quality control department to assure management that all controls connected with the problem of quality are in proper operation. If it is not the prime operator of a control of this kind, the quality function must occasionally sample or audit its operations. In other words, controls may not oper-

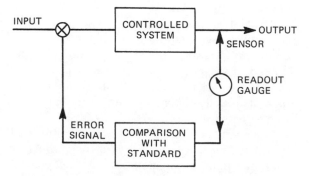

FIGURE 1-4. Block Diagram of a Control System

ate in total isolation and remain valid. They, in turn, must be controlled by audit.

Quality is never an accident.

These individual control loops are applicable in the product life cycle starting from product design right through customer use. Many feedback loops are multiple loops crossing several activities and processes. Modern quality control is not an after-the-fact activity; it is oriented toward improving, not just policing; preventing errors, not documenting them.

QUALITY STANDARDS PROVIDE A BASIS FOR *CONTROL*

Drawings and specifications provide a quantitative basis for acceptance for attributes such as functional requirements, dimensions, weight, purity, and marking. In some products (wine, food, decorations) esthetic characteristics are the *raison d'etre* of the product. In the jewelry, rug, textile, and furniture industries, appearance is the most important quality characteristic in the product. In other products, these characteristics are not so clearly vital, but may nevertheless determine the saleability of the product—either negatively (scratches on a new car) or positively (neatness of electrical wiring). Sensory standards such as taste, odor, workmanship, and appearance are subjective and are difficult to specify on engineering drawings. In order to provide control, however, a standard against which acceptance decisions can be made must be prepared. This is a management responsibility that is all too often abdicated.

The absence of an objective standard can cause unnecessary disputes between QC and other functions, lead to costly and highly variable accept/reject decisions, and decrease sales, either because of higher costs associated with unduly "tough" standards or low quality due to unrealistically lax standards.

In many ways, the lack of a standard can wreak more havoc on a firm's well-being than the lack of a quality policy.

Case in Point: A manufacturer of machine tools provided detailed engineering drawings defining dimensional, surface finish, and color requirements. Workmanship standards were left to "shop practices." These practices were neither complete nor adequate, and constant arguments between production and QC took place. The direct and indirect costs of wasted debates, discrepancy reports, and material review activity were significant.

To be effective, a quality standard must be:

√ technically attainable
√ economic with due consideration to yield and market factors
√ understandable by those who must comply with it
√ consistent
√ maintainable and stable
√ relevant to market
√ legal and comply with regulatory body statutes
√ consistent with personnel safety requirements

The delineation of sensory quality standards has been surrounded by confusion. The use of human beings as test instruments can always be relied upon to generate dispute and controversy. Unless an instrument can be devised to secure a measurement, test panels (human beings) and bonded samples must be used.

In the graphic arts industries, for example, it is common practice for the manufacturer to prepare samples for customer approval. Once approved, they become the agreed-on acceptance standard for many sensory qualities. Samples are also commonly used in the paper products and textile industries. It is normal practice to file copies of these samples with the pertinent written descriptions and orders.

If management or customers do not provide a suitable standard, the inspectors surely will. The standard chosen may be far from optimum, but be assured it will be established.

Quality standards can be established by taking the following eight-step approach:

1. Study the process yield at different quality levels.
2. Evaluate customer sensitivity to various standards.
3. Research competitor quality standards and/or industry practice.
4. Analyze above information.

5. Obtain management decision and approval.

6. Document the standard (master reference standard, certified test panels, photographs, physical samples, workmanship manuals).

7. Train production and quality personnel in the use of the standard.

8. Perform periodic audit to ensure effectiveness.

Observation: Quality standards can also be used (or misused) as nontariff barriers to trade. What often angers U.S. and European officials is not the marketing prowess of Japanese exporters, but the complex regulations that hamper foreign entrepreneurs in Japan. Examples abound. An American maker of aluminum baseball bats was developing a good market for his product until the Japanese softball association ruled that his bats could not be used in tournament play because the label stamped on them supposedly made them defective. Companies selling products in aerosol spray cans complain that their cans must be 25 percent thicker in Japan than anywhere else in the world. Moreover, the outfit that inspects the incoming aerosol products is a prime Japanese spray-can maker.

One reason that U.S. automakers in 1981 sold only 7742 cars in Japan (vs. Japanese car sales of 1.9 million vehicles in the U.S.) is a host of design and safety standards that force expensive changes in virtually every foreign-made car imported into Japan. During the year, General Motors sold a total of only 612 Cadillacs in Japan, partly because changes in such items as headrests, safety reflectors, and electrical wiring pushed the cost of the car to more than $40,000.

QUALITY CONTROL AS A WAY OF LIFE

Thus far we have talked mostly about quality control of manufacture, but the concepts of quality control are in fact quite universal in their applications. Thus, the same principles apply in many fields:

Office Work, Production Control, MIS, etc. The normal function of an office is to receive, process, and deliver information. Thus, the production planning department supplies information on machine loading. We still have an objective, which is to supply this information as cheaply as possible within the time required, with a minimum number of mistakes.

Material Control, Inventory Control, Stores, and Purchasing. The high cost of paperwork errors is not always evident. For example, take inventory records: Reducing errors here can be one of the most lucrative cost improvement programs you can undertake. The actual savings reported by companies always seems to exceed the clerical costs of straightening out the records.

Inventory records are not simply historical notations, useful only for preparing annual balance sheets, reports to stockholders, and tax returns. These are working control records for a major operating asset. If book inventories are overstated, you might run out of a raw material and shut the entire plant down, or else find that you can't ship the 100 finished units supposedly on hand for your customer because the phantom units exist only on paper. Similarly, understated records mean you are carrying more inventory than you know about. The cost of carrying this extra inventory may be 2 percent or more per month in your company.

Consider the other costs involved when unreliable records are maintained: Expeditors are added to the payroll; each foreman starts defensively hiding extra inventory that gets lost or dust-covered inside his own department; and the production planner must run out and count the inventory whenever she "really" wants to know how much there is for some important order. Resulting panics will probably have an adverse impact on product quality.

A worthwhile investment in good record-keeping is indicated. All errors, even clerical errors, cost money. Eliminate them at the start. The principles of QC can help.

The Service Departments. Quality control can be applied to plant maintenance, accounting, distribution, the retail trade, and so on. We can apply it to the delivery of letters and parcels in a town; it could be applied to your in-plant cafeteria.

Design. Design is a large field to which quality control principles can be applied. Design review, qualification testing, and first article inspection are some techniques that have been successfully applied.

It is quite difficult to think of any activity to which the principles of quality control cannot be applied. Some companies have already recognized its great and universal value by giving the quality control manager a seat on the board of directors.

THE QUALITY CONTROL SYSTEM

A system in business is a harness within which people work. A tangled harness reduces teamwork, results in people working at cross-purposes, and produces friction and wasted efforts.

Case in Point: The receiving inspection department of a medium-sized company decided, for budgetary reasons, to revert from 100 percent test to MIL-STD-105 attributes sampling of a certain part. When the production superintendent heard about the proposal she pointed out that the purchased part was from a small business concern with marginal quality controls and, more important, that the part was used in a nonrepairable potted subassembly. After further consideration, the receiving inspection supervisor agreed to search for an alternate means of keeping within his departmental budget.

The quality control effort must be an organized system for integrating the quality development, quality maintenance, and quality improvement efforts of the various groups in an organization so as to enable production and service at the most economical levels that allow for full customer satisfaction. A QC system consists of a set of procedures, tests, inspections, analyses, and audits, linked together in a rational manner in order to accomplish some set of organizational quality objectives.

High quality, after all, is not achieved by a few random management decisions but by a complex, all-encompassing, interactive management system that has the uncompromising long-term support of top management. The basis of this system is not simply an appropriate arrangement of people and machines. It is a way of thinking.

You don't inspect quality into a product, you have to build it in.
Before you build it in, you must *think* it in.

Checklist of Prerequisites for Quality Control System

In order to implement a cost-effective dynamic-feedback quality control system, the following elements must be in place:

√ Top management commitment authorizing the quality control system with continued support, interest, and leadership.

√ A documented quality system manual defining the various control loops from initial conceptual design to field product support.

√ Machinery and equipment capable of producing acceptable output product (or services). Proper maintenance and working environment is assumed.

√ Acceptable exogenous factors such as political stability, macroeconomic conditions, company cash position, and so on.

√ Measurement devices with sufficient accuracy and repeatability to obtain information about the product.

√ Knowledge of how to use the measuring equipment (usually achieved through formal or informal training).

√ Instructions on frequency of samplings and audits.

√ Instructions on the processing of measurement data. The timeliness of measurement data must be stressed because delays in the feedback loop decrease control effectiveness and lead to instability of the system. There also is a requirement for coordination of information flow and data processing to supply all individuals in the organization with appropriate information for control purposes.

√ Specifications and standards for comparison with actual performance.

√ Instructions concerning the error magnitude at which action must be taken (e.g., operating parameters adjusted) and what that action should be.

√ The means to take corrective action and to measure the effectiveness of that action.

√ Instructions for the disposition of unacceptable parts.

√ Periodic checks on the status of the quality control system itself. It must be audited at intervals to ascertain that all control loops are functioning properly. While it is true that a failure in the quality control system eventually will result in a disturbance in the output quality of the firm, there usually is a considerable delay before the change becomes apparent. Moreover, top management may be the first to detect such disturbances—an unhealthy situation for those responsible for the quality control system management. Failures must be detected and corrected before output quality is adversely affected.

WHAT TOP MANAGEMENT EXPECTS FROM QUALITY CONTROL

Each person in top management has personal goals and corporate objectives. The personal goals typically include job satisfaction, personal growth, wealth accumulation, stature, and power. In order to reach these goals, corporate objectives in the areas of sales growth, market penetration, new products, profitability, and return on investment must be achieved. Top management thus expects the quality control function to help achieve these sometimes opposing primary goals. It is important for the QC manager to know and fully comprehend these goals and the changes they undergo with changes in management and corporate policy, whether written or unwritten. He or she must understand these factors in both top management and shop floor terms and act accordingly.

Pitfall to avoid: A QC manager of a chemical company provided a comprehensive report to top management on a monthly basis. The report was lengthy, full of technical jargon and mathematical detail. As a result it was promptly discarded and a vital communication link broken.

Indirectly and implicitly these primary goals have a secondary but vitally important dimension. Top management does not want to be embarrassed by a product recall. It does not want to suffer huge quality losses that make the firm ripe for a takeover and/or their positions uncertain. Senior management is not keen on receiving a constant flow of customer complaints, accusations of fraud, or product liability claims. Top management wants orderly growth without the major disruptions that inadequate quality control can cause. In short, management expects quality control to help minimize the risks of doing business in a complex world; it does not like surprises. As the controller of a huge multinational once said, "May all our surprises be pleasant ones."

Given these considerations, one can prepare a list of general things top management wants from quality control. They include:

- Increasing sales by consistently maintaining the desired level of product quality.
- Enhancement of the firm's image by widely publicized superior-quality achievement and recognition.
- Reliable delivery schedules because of the elimination of unplanned "quality problem" bottlenecks.

- Minimization of customer complaints, high accounts receivable, debit memos, and warranty claims.
- Expanding market share by building a reputation for a safe, quality product.
- Optimizing profits by controlling scrap, rework, repair, and sorting.
- Keeping piece-part and work-in-process inventory in check by standardization, vendor control, defect prevention, corrective action, salvage control.
- Assisting purchasing in getting on-time deliveries, cost reduction and vendor development.
- Assuring that new products will have a minimum of quality problems and will be readily approved by customers, regulatory bodies, industry groups, and consumer associations.
- Developing harmonious, profit-oriented relationships with other functions throughout the corporation.
- Running a lean, cost-conscious, pragmatic, high-integrity, and competent quality control department.

A quality program has utility only for what it can accomplish in achieving product quality at the right price.

THE ROLE OF QUALITY CONTROL

A QC program is an integral part of the overall company business plan (Figure 1-5). It is not and

FIGURE 1-5. Interaction of Quality with Other Key Company Areas of Concern

cannot be independent or isolated from the mainstream of business activity. Table 1-3 shows the role QC has to play during the product life cycle and could serve as a basis for defining the key elements of a modern industrial quality control program. The table also shows which functional organizations impact quality of design and quality of conformance at each stage of new product generation. It should be clear that virtually every function directly or indirectly impacts product quality. This is perhaps one of the strongest arguments for wanting QC to report to general management because it permits QC to actively participate in the formulation and accomplishment of company goals and cost objectives. The best way to reduce the cost of quality problems is to prevent them in the first place. Reworking defective goods or tossing them out is always expensive. A well-conceived defect prevention-oriented QC program is the key to success.

It is valuable to get a feel for the distribution of quality costs for different industries. Table 1-4 summarizes the results of a 1976 survey of readers of *Quality* magazine. Remember that the figures have neither been adjusted to compensate for differences in manufacturing technology or accounting practices nor have they been audited for veracity. One may assume that they represent *minimums*. It is interesting to note that the same survey revealed that those firms with formal QC programs had total failure costs (as a percent of net set billed) of less than half of those with informal QC programs. Further, these costs at best count the measurable quality costs but do not include the hidden costs of the disruptions, excess inventory, or opportunity losses caused by poor or nonuniform product quality.

Regulatory Agency Requirements: They're Everywhere

State and federal regulations can affect many quality control operations. Many requirements, such as those related to the purity of food and drugs, package content identification, and safety features are imposed for the economic or physical protection of the consumer. Additional restrictions are imposed for other purposes. For example, the alcohol content of all liquor is closely controlled for tax purposes.

Similarly, for pharmaceuticals sold in the U.S., companies must meet the standards of the United States Pharmacopeia and the *Current Good Manufacturing Practices* as described in the Code of Federal Regulation, Title 21. Quality standards in Canada recognize international compendia such as USP, British Pharmacopeia, Codex Français, or the European Pharmacopeia.

Some products require approval of their design and construction by some regulatory or other independent agency. Underwriter's Laboratories for electrical appliances, the Federal Communications Commission and their counterparts in foreign countries for two-way radios, and the Federal Aviation Administration for aircraft are a few of the agencies. All pertinent agency requirements must be planned for, as frequently a product needs approval for more than one.

The quality organization is often involved in the testing and certification aspect of the product approvals effort as well as assurance of proper marking or placarding of the approved product; but, regardless of which organizations do what, the resulting "seal of approval" becomes the basis for customer acceptance of the product as a saleable item.

An important consideration is that a product, to be accepted in the marketplace, must reflect at least the same level of performance, durability, and safety as the test samples on which agency approval was granted. Even if the agency does not regularly monitor this continuing level of performance, the company has both the legal and ethical responsibility to assure itself that its ongoing production output conforms to applicable specifications.

A manufacturer that conducts new product programs in a manner that obtains the required product approvals will achieve marketability of products in a technical sense, and will minimize certain types of product liability exposure.

Noncompliance with government regulations can result in heavy fines and, in extreme cases, a company can even be forced to discontinue producing an item. These types of actions also cause indirect losses to the company in its sales of other products because of the bad publicity.

The quest for a cleaner environment adds more restrictions to prevent the discharge of smoke and industrial waste from industrial plants. Energy conservation places restrictions on plants and production processes. These types of regulations impose additional costs on manufacturers and create problems (and opportunities) for quality control.

TABLE 1–3. Functional Responsibilities in Product Planning, Design, and Production

P: Prime Responsibility
C: Contributing Responsibility

	GM	Mktg	Engrg	Mfg	Finance	QC
A. Product Planning Phase						
1. Establish business scope, objectives, and strategy.	P	C	C	C	C	C
2. Identify market needs and business opportunities.		P	C	C	C	C
3. Prepare Product Business Plan (market study, pilot marketing, sales forecast, cost analysis).		P	C	C	C	C
4. Prepare Product Program Schedule.		P	C	C	C	C
B. Product Design Phase						
1. Prepare and issue Product Design Specifications.		C	P	C		C
2. Prepare Development Authorization.			P	C	C	C
3. Establish design, process, and test specs.			P			C
4. Approve vendors.			C	C		P
5. Evaluate material component selection.			C	C		P
6. Conduct Design Review.		C	P	C		C
7. Establish release criteria.		C	P	C	C	C
8. Establish process capability.			C	P		C
9. Establish quality planning.			C	C		P
10. Conduct preproduction run.			C	P		C
11. Prepare and issue Product Release Report.		C	P	C	C	C
12. Issue process and test specifications.			P	C		C
13. Prepare commercial-specification release sheets.		C	P			C
14. Prepare appropriation and procure manufacturing tooling and test equipment.			C	P	C	C
15. Install equipment and establish production.			C	P		C
C. Production Phase						
1. Establish Manufacturing Production Plan.				P		C
2. Issue Manufacturing Specifications.			C	P		C
3. Establish methods and manufacturing standards.				P		C
4. Establish Cost Improvement Plans.	P	C	C	C	C	C
5. Redesign product for cost, ease of manufacture, and quality improvement.			P	C		C
6. Process customer orders.		P	C	C		C
7. Analyze customer returns.		C	C	C	C	P
8. Measure and report compliance with quality policy.		C	C	C	C	P
9. Measure and report compliance with product quality plans.		C		C		P
10. Evaluate business performance.	P	C	C	C	C	C

TABLE 1-4. Formal QC Program-Quality Costs (percent of net sales billed)

Category	SIC Number	Responses	Total Quality Costs	Prevention Costs	Appraisal Costs	Internal Failure Costs	External Failure Costs
Furniture and Fixtures	25	2	2.45	0.36	0.97	0.86	0.55
Chemicals and Applied Products	28	2	4.81	0.68	1.11	2.03	1.00
Rubber and Miscellaneous Plastic Products	30	1	14.70	0.40	2.30	9.50	2.50
Primary Metal Industries	33	4	6.11	0.40	1.47	2.98	1.28
Fabricated Metal Products	34	7	5.09	0.51	1.67	1.90	0.77
Machinery Except Electrical	35	26	4.43	0.49	1.05	1.76	1.14
Electrical and Electronic Equipment	36	32	5.94	0.90	1.75	2.07	1.21
Transportation Equipment	37	10	3.79	0.34	1.76	1.29	0.50
Instruments and Related Products	38	16	7.27	1.20	2.12	1.78	2.15
Miscellaneous Manufacturing	39	5	3.71	0.33	1.10	1.72	0.57
Grand Total		105	5.8	0.6	1.5	2.5	1.2

(Reprinted with permission from *Quality*, June 1977, a Hitchcock Publication).

QUALITY MANAGEMENT TASKS

The goal of senior management is to manufacture a product into which quality is designed, built, and maintained at the most economical costs that allow for full customer satisfaction. In broad terms, this goal translates into the following general quality control tasks:

1. Participate in design reviews, reliability analysis, environmental testing and other defect-prevention tasks.

2. Help create a quality environment and culture.

3. Keep within operation costs established by budgets and estimates.

4. Acquire adequate personnel, equipment, and facilities to perform professional quality control work.

5. Establish accurate, adequate, and economical measuring techniques and equipment for control of product quality.

6. Control purchased material quality as specified in engineering drawings, documents, and purchase orders.

7. Measure product quality through process eval-

uation, product inspection/test, packaging inspection, and audit.

8. Diagnose quality-inhibiting situations and conditions and identify the underlying causes.

9. Feed back quality information to organizational groups and vendors requiring this knowledge.

10. Initiate corrective action to eliminate poor design, material, processes, and workmanship.

11. Collect quality data to assist in analysis and prevention activity.

12. Promptly respond to customer complaints and queries.

During the 1976 ASQC annual Technical Conference in Toronto, attendees were requested to fill in a survey questionnaire regarding the effectiveness of major quality program tasks on product quality (fitness for use). Respondents were told to assume that all tasks were professionally accomplished. Over 200 forms were completed.

It was assumed that responses would vary, depending on product complexity and maturity, contractual provisions, manufacturing volume and rate, industry practices, customer, intended use, and other considerations. Surprisingly, there was a high degree of uniformity of responses. The results are summarized in Table 1-5.

The survey took into account not only effectiveness but cost-effectiveness. The measure of cost-effectiveness was return on investment (ROI). Failure Analysis, Material Review, and Corrective Action was the only task to have the highest rating in both categories. On the other hand, Analysis was the only task to have the lowest rating in both categories possibly because of the relative lack of success of these techniques to predict product problems/failures. The survey would appear to confirm that Pareto's Principle applies to quality program tasks as well as to a variety of industrial problems.

PRAGMATISM IN QUALITY CONTROL

The quality function must be innovative, be sensitive to the needs of other functions, know the company's business position and aims, be cost-conscious, be aware of market needs, and be responsive to internal and customer requests for action or information. It must be willing to take risks, aggressively participate in hard-nosed business decisions, manage its own budget care-

fully, and operate at a down-to-earth level. This type of pragmatism can manifest itself in many ways.

Case in Point: A routine review of nonconforming material discrepancies indicated chronic inadequate-plating thickness on a certain part. The problem was apparent on parts from all three approved vendors. Further investigation by QC revealed that engineering had over the years given suppliers verbal waivers against the specification. An engineering change relaxing part tolerances was prepared, thus saving inspection and purchasing time and money. The offending engineer was politely informed of the problems caused by uncontrolled waivers and drawing changes. She is now a model of disciplined engineering.

Case in Point: A firm with a comprehensive environmental-simulation laboratory experienced a four-month period of extremely low loading. The alert QC manager took on outside test jobs during this period and grossed $50,000, of which $20,000 was net profit.

Case in Point: A source inspector on a routine visit to an out-of-town supplier hand delivered an important proposal to a nearby potential client. While with the supplier, he expedited some parts on behalf of production control. On his return to his factory he brought back some desperately needed parts. Total QC involvement leads to sensible quality control and acceptance by other functions.

THE BAKER'S DOZEN—POINTERS FOR ECONOMICAL QUALITY CONTROL

The quality manager who heeds the advice implicit in the thirteen items listed below has a high chance of success.

1. *Pareto's Principle:* Put your quality efforts into projects with the greatest returns.

2. *Second Law of Thermodynamics:* Systems require constant maintenance otherwise they degenerate to their lowest energy state (chaos).

3. *Operator/Management Controllable Ratio:* 30%/70% —Before assigning defect causes to shop floor

TABLE 1–5. Results of QC task effectiveness survey.

QUALITY SURVEY QUESTIONNAIRE

Quality Control Tasks	EFFECTIVENESS RATING					R. O. I.			Comments
	1	2	3	4	5	Lo	Med	Hi	
	Lo				Hi				
Planning Tasks									
Quality Program Plan				√				√	
Specification Review				√				√	
Application/Environment Analysis			√					√	
Process Capability Studies			√				√		
Design Standards		√				√			
Measuring Equipment Design			√			√			
Analysis (Tolerance, Reliability, FMEA, etc.)	√					√			
Appraisal Tasks									
Design Review				√				√	
Part/Vendor Approval(s)			√				√		
Qualification/Development Tests				√				√	
Production Tests and Inspections			√				√		
First-Article/Piece Evaluation			√					√	
Special Tests, Product Audits			√				√		
Hardware Support Tasks									
Purchasing/Vendor Control			√					√	
Material Handling and Storage Control			√				√		
Calibration		√				√			
Quality Standards			√				√		
Special Process Controls			√					√	
Packaging and Shipping Inspection		√				√			
Configuration Control					√	√			
Failure Analysis, Material Review, and C/A					√			√	
Customer Liaison				√			√		
Tool Proofing		√				√			
Administrative Support Tasks									
QC Manual and Procedures			√				√		
Data Collection and Analysis/Quality Costs				√		√			
Statistical Techniques			√					√	
Quality Records, Shop Travellers, etc.				√		√			
Quality Program Audits			√				√		
Personnel Motivation and Training				√			√		
Work Instructions					√			√	

personnel remember the odds are its management's fault.

4. *Murphy's Law:* If it can go wrong it will. Quality practitioners will need no further explanation.

5. *Knowledge × Skill* = Ability
Attitude × Work Situation = Motivation
Ability × Motivation = Human Performance

6. *An Ounce of Prevention Is Worth a Pound of Cure:* Quality prevention tasks have a very high return on investment.

7. *Don't Do Effectively That Which Shouldn't Be Done at All:* Don't collect quality data you don't use; don't perform useless tests; don't overspecify tolerances, etc.

8. *Don't Make an Enemy When You Can Make a Friend:* The QC function needs all the friends it can get.

9. *Parkinson's Law:* Quality staff can easily grow to fill the space available; watch the headcount very carefully.

10. *When You're Talking, You're Not Learning:* QC people should take special note.

11. *Failure Is an Orphan; Success Has Many Fathers:* Don't expect glory; prepare yourself for a career as a professional scapegoat.

12. *When You Cannot Measure It, When You Cannot Express It in Numbers, Your Knowledge Is of a Meager and Unsatisfactory Kind:* Lord Kelvin's profound observation provides the foundation of modern quality control.

13. *Haste Makes Waste:* As old as time itself but still as true as ever.

REFERENCES

Athos, A. G. and R. T. Pascale, *The Art of Japanese Management.* New York: Simon and Schuster, 1981.

Beach, N. F. "Management and Quality Control." *Industrial Quality Control,* April 1966.

Crosby, P. B. "Quality and Management Style—What Is Japan's Secret to Industrial Success?" *Quality,* June 1980.

Fiegenbaum, A. V. *Total Quality Control.* New York: McGraw-Hill, 1961.

Fyffe, D. E. "Control Concepts and the Q.C. System." *Quality Progress,* Nov. 1968.

Juran, J. M. "The Two Worlds of Quality Control." *Industrial Quality Control,* Nov. 1964.

MIL-STD-109B "Quality Assurance Terms and Definitions." (U.S. Military Standards).

Safiuddin, M. "Systems Analysis." *Machine Design,* Jan. 11, 1973.

"System and Order." *Royal Bank of Canada Monthly Letter.* May 1971.

2
Organizing Quality Control as a Profit Center

Organization strongly influences which quality standards and economic objectives can be met and maintained by a company. The organization of such departments as design engineering, manufacturing and marketing, as well as quality departments, greatly influences product quality. For example, the organization of design groups must provide for all design activities necessary to meet quality objectives. A drawing control function is needed in most instances to ensure that all released drawings incorporate the latest changes and are properly distributed to relevant groups. A design checking function is needed to preclude miscellaneous drawing errors. Qualification and design proofing tests are also required to ensure design integrity.

The challenge to management is to apply the various modes and designs of organization in order to maintain the maximum return on the total resources available in the organization. An organization, like any dynamic system, is invested with frictions. The primary objective of the QC executive in defining an organization is to establish a structure through which quality objectives can be satisfied with minimum energy dissipated in overcoming organizational frictions. The organization must be streamlined and be able to sense and respond to changes quickly. Continuous emphasis must be placed on the QC organization as a company grows (or retracts) and matures.

Lines of authority should be made clear in an organization. Quality work can best be accomplished in an organization in which responsibilities are precisely outlined and orderly procedures prevail.

Organization can be defined as:

> A system of authority, responsibility, and communication relationships with provisions for structural coordination, both vertically and horizontally, facilitating the accomplishment of work and objectives.

Improved organization and control of the quality function has the following benefits:

1. Improved company return on investment through better quality, less scrap and rework, and improved sales.
2. Enhanced customer satisfaction.
3. Greater emphasis and concentration on quality cost-reduction opportunities.
4. Identification and resolution of conflicting management objectives.
5. Development of better production plans.
6. Improved operating controls.
7. Reduction of costs associated with supporting redundant quality control procedures and systems.

Avoid the "policeman" image—build solid interdepartmental interfaces. An effective QC organization will promote sound interdepartmental relationships. Good interfaces with other functions in the company result in improved understanding of each other's problems and needs. This

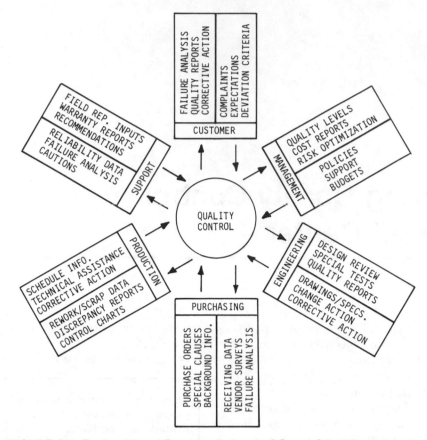

FIGURE 2-1. Reciprocity of Services Between QC and Other Departments

improved understanding promotes a cooperative attitude and better communication, which in turn reduce conflicts, delays, and wasted effort. When problems arise, they can be settled more quickly and with fewer political repercussions from other departments. Remember that there is a great interdependency among departments—QC is not an island (see Figure 2-1).

The QC manager can help achieve good interfaces with other departments by:

- establishing an organization and staff that are congruent with company objectives and management style.
- using defect information with discretion.
- offering to help solve quality problems.
- fraternizing with other department heads and discussing general topics of interest to the company.
- providing good service to user departments.
- providing assistance whenever possible.

Case in Point: The designer of a new product was experiencing some difficulty because of his limited knowledge of statistics. A quality engineer heard of the problem and offered his services. The engineer's problem was soon solved and a very strong bond between the two individuals developed.

- communicating, discussing, and mutually agreeing on quality requirements prior to implementation.
- avoiding win/lose confrontations.
- demonstrating flexibility and understanding.
- being quantitative, fair, and unbiased in decision making (e.g., material review).
- encouraging the staff to maintain good interdepartmental relations.

INSTRUMENTS OF ORGANIZATION

There are many devices used by managers of larger organizations to control the operations of the business. Many of these, when viewed in context, are actually instruments of organization. A review of some of the more important ones serves to illustrate the real scope of the organization function and can lead to the identification of the source of some real organizational problems.

The Organization Chart

The organization chart defines the formal structure of the organization. It identifies which positions have authority over which subordinate positions and generally identifies the flow of authority, responsibility, and accountability from the top to the bottom of the organization. The mental image we tend to carry of the organization chart as the total and all-encompassing symbol for organization is completely inadequate. It certainly does not define the scope or nature of the authority possessed by any position or the nature of the responsibilities it bears. In addition, the organization chart communicates nothing of the responsibilities for horizontal communication throughout the structure. And yet, the quality of the horizontal communications in an organization is frequently a necessity to the successful achievement of common objectives. This, then, reduces the organization chart from its position as the essence of organization to its more practical role as an instrument of organization.

Policy

The policies of an organization are instruments of direction that establish guidelines and constraints. But they are also instruments of organization in that they impose responsibilities on the functions of the enterprise. They also assist in structural coordination because the requirements established by quality policy serve to harmonize the work of the individual units in the achievement of objectives.

Procedures

Procedures establish standardized methodology in and among elements of an organization. They further define authorities, responsibilities, accountabilities, and communication relationships, and they provide for vertical and horizontal coordination of the structure. Procedures are a very important instrument of organization.

Note: Sometimes policies, procedures, and organization charts fail to pinpoint quality authority and responsibility. One sure way to find out if you are accountable for some decision is to reflect on the case of the army general who had just won a major battle. A newspaper reporter asked: "General, do you feel that you were responsible for this impressive victory?" "Well," said the veteran military man, "I don't know, but if I'd lost the battle, I'd be peeling potatoes in Kansas."

Audit

Operational, quality, and product audits help determine if control systems are working as desired. Audits are also effective in uncovering duplication of effort, voids in control, and communication blockages.

Individuals

While rarely discussed, an individual's strength of character, unique technical skills, or political influence may cause the authority relationships to be quite different from those defined in organization charts.

> *Case in Point:* A highly talented failure-analysis engineer in the auto industry commanded more influence than would be indicated by inspection of the organizational hierarchy. His technical skills were utilized by production personnel to such an extent that a type of dependence developed. His "recommendations" for disposition of nonconforming material and corrective action were unchallenged and rapidly implemented.

Facilities

Facilities include a broad range of systems such as telephones, technical library, computer-based information systems, in-plant transportation systems, in-plant mail systems, and even public transportation facilities such as airplanes and trains. It is not unrealistic to count these facilities as instruments of organization. Reflect on the impact on industry and business if these facilities were suddenly to vanish. The facilities available for rapid communication make it possible to decentralize organization, both physically and functionally. Without these facilities, it would be impossible to do so.

> *Case in Point:* A multinational U.S. electronics corporation with six operating divisions experienced a problem with the testing

of complex integrated circuits. A cost/benefit analysis revealed that the only cost-effective approach was to automate the testing process, but no one division could afford the costly equipment by itself. The solution was to set up a central test facility that would service all divisions. The test establishment became a corporate service and reported to the corporate director of quality. The resulting benefits:

- automated test equipment could be justified because of the higher volume of parts. Unit test costs dropped from five cents to two cents—a 60 percent saving.
- productivity was improved because of better workload balancing among employees.
- the receiving cycle time was reduced from two weeks to four days.

The analysts did note, however, that these benefits were possible only because of the similarity of components used and the willingness of the various division heads to have a centralized facility.

Committees

It is generally agreed that committees do not properly make decisions in an organization because committees cannot realistically be held accountable. Also, committees tend to be instruments of compromise and therefore are not effective decision-making bodies. However, committees can perform a valuable horizontal coordination function and provide a forum for airing different points of view. Committees can confer, deliberate on questions, and coordinate the activities of multiple functions in carrying out management directives.

> The efficiency of a committee meeting is inversely proportional to the number of participants and the time spent on deliberations.

Job Descriptions

A job description defines an array of tasks that have been accumulated into a standard job. For example, the task of apportionment, reliability prediction, parts qualification, and failure analysis can be expected to be performed by a single individual in a job that we might title "reliability engineer." Job descriptions, therefore, perform the organizational function of specializing labor and defining responsibilities.

Position Descriptions

Contrary to common assumption, the terms *job description* and *position description* are not interchangeable. While a job may have several incumbents (say, a quality engineer's), a position has only one incumbent. For example, a particular position may have responsibilities assigned in addition to those contained in the job description. Position descriptions, therefore, are instruments for the definition of authority, responsibility, and communication relationships, and they further facilitate the specialization of labor.

ORGANIZING FOR CONTROL OF QUALITY, OR, WHO DOES WHAT?

The best organizational form for quality control depends on company objectives and size, management policies, organizational culture, nature of product and industry, number of products, and even to some extent on certain individuals.

The quality system involves more than inspection and test in the manufacturing phase. Every department has a responsibility for assuring that the customer's quality requirements are met. The responsibilities for quality must be clearly assigned. Quality is everyone's responsibility, but unless every department fully understands what is expected, quality is likely to suffer. Each person is apt to assume that someone else is taking care of the problems. The responsibilities for quality assigned to each department and function vary from company to company. Most frequently, however, the responsibilities are assigned in the following way:

Marketing

- Liaison with customer.
- Determine the customer's quality requirements and acceptable quality levels.
- Assure that the product quality requirements and any quality system requirements are defined clearly and completely.
- Investigate the customer's opinion of the product quality and performance.

- Continually report this opinion to the departments concerned.

Marketing Objective: Increase market share and sales by satisfying customer needs. That is, through market research, direct sales, advertising, promotions, trade shows, and the like, identify customer product and service requirements.

Engineering

- Design quality and safety into the product or service.
- Design products that comply with the customer's quality requirements while utilizing an optimized material/manufacturing process.
- Prepare specifications that accurately define these requirements.
- Prove-out products prior to production release.

Engineering Objective: Design safe, reliable products. That is, by using minimum development funds and time, translate marketing-defined needs into a physical product or service.

Manufacturing

- Critique drawings or specifications that would be too expensive or impractical to meet.
- Provide facilities capable of meeting the quality requirements.
- Manufacture and deliver products that comply with the drawings and specifications developed by engineering.

Manufacturing Objective: Optimize the costs of the production process. That is, convert components and raw material into a finished product, meeting engineering and schedule requirements at the lowest practical cost.

Purchasing

- Select and/or develop vendors who are capable of complying with quality requirements on a competitive basis.
- Keep vendors informed of current quality requirements.
- Work with vendors to correct quality problems.
- Assure material is transported safely and economically.

Purchasing Objective: Optimize the cost of the buying process. That is, at the lowest practical cost, select suppliers and place orders that will result in the most favorable balance of price, quality, and schedule performance for parts and material required in the production process.

Inventory Control

- Use standard parts to greatest extent practicable.
- Identify unusual material issues due to rejects.
- Maintain adequate supply of parts and materials.
- Properly store materials to prevent degradation and/or loss.

Inventory Control Objective: Optimize the costs of having, not having, and controlling inventories. That is, at the lowest practical cost, achieve the most favorable balance between the cost of carrying inventory and the cost of having stockouts.

Controller

- Keep management informed about the costs of quality.
- Provide cost breakdowns so that problem areas can be identified and corrective action justified.
- Implement cost collection system and internal control procedures.
- Provide accurate data on costs generated by in-plant operations and on those generated by returned material and product warranties.

Financial Objective: Measure cost performance so that operational personnel and management may be appraised of financial position and potential problem areas in a timely manner.

Personnel Relations

- Recognize the impact of the human factor on quality.
- Develop and implement recruiting, selection, placement, training, and upgrading procedures that will result in a work force capable of meeting quality requirements.
- Communicate regularly to employees on the need for, and the importance of, working to quality standards.

Personnel Objective: Negotiate with union or associations, keep personnel records, deal with specialized employee problems, maintain employee benefits system, and act as communication focal point for company on general issues.

If there is one weakness in the quality system, it is usually a deficiency in the integration of the elements and their subelements into a working whole.

Case in Point: An inward-looking manager was assigned responsibility for the QC department. He immediately instituted certain changes and focused his attention on his own people and organization. He did not develop contacts or communication lines with the managers of other departments. When these other groups complained about the changes in QC policy and practice, he ignored them or argued things were okay as they were.

After six months, the managers of manufacturing and materials pressured the division vice president to have him reassigned. A new manager was brought in to straighten out the interface and communication problem. His interest in other parts of the company as well as his department resulted in much better relations, and the complaints ceased.

Since different organizations view quality in the light of their own objectives, an organization structure that does not provide proper check and balance among sometimes-conflicting objectives will cause one or several to be undesirably subordinated. The objectives of successful quality control can be easily subordinated to those of production and procurement in the manufacturing and purchasing departments. Also, excessive costs of supporting redundant and unnecessarily divergent quality control functions within departments can detract from the basic objective of integrated quality control. Tables 2-1 and 2-2 provide a framework for examining your quality organization.

QUALITY PROGRAM MANAGEMENT

Typical management studies are technique-oriented and deal with theoretical solutions to hypothetical problems. If you have been struggling for years with the same quality problems of excess scrap, customer complaints, the high cost of quality control, and poor interdepartmental relation-

ships, it is quite likely that attempts at improving quality costs have dealt with symptoms of a more fundamental problem of organization and assignment of responsibility.

U.S. Military Specification MIL-Q-9858A "Quality Program Requirements" provides one of the most succinct set of criteria for a quality program organization:

"Organization. Effective management for quality shall be clearly prescribed by the contractor. Personnel performing quality functions shall have sufficient, well-defined responsibility, authority, and the organizational freedom to identify and evaluate quality problems and to initiate, recommend, or provide solutions. Management regularly shall review the status and adequacy of the quality program. The term "quality program requirements" as used herein identifies the collective requirements of this specification. It does not mean that the fulfillment of the requirements of this specification is the responsibility of any single contractor's organization, function or person."

Many departments contribute to the quality effort. Their actions, together with those of the quality control department, constitute the total quality program. These facts, however, necessitate the assignment of responsibility for quality coordination and management to a particular organizational component (e.g., the quality control department).

As a minimum, a quality organization must have the capability of implementing and influencing overall quality policy, interfacing with higher management, production, marketing, and engineering; controlling output quality; recommending corrective action, and measuring quality status and improvement. Any organizational form that has these capabilities is an acceptable form. The key point to realize is that the quality control organization must be capable of meeting the quality system specifications imposed on it. As business needs change, so will organizational structures and relationships.

Changing things is central to leadership, and changing them before anyone else is creativity.

TABLE 2-1. Checklist for Evaluating or Designing an Effective QC Organization

---

√ Provides effective management of quality consistent with overall needs of company, product, and customer.

√ Bears evidence of top management support.

√ Provides adequate independence of critical functions; for example, quality control does not report to manufacturing.

√ Has a well-defined hierarchy and identification of responsibilities.

√ Is adequately staffed to accomplish its mission.

√ Is logical in its design; for example, related functions are under one manager.

√ Is as simple as possible in terms of the business environment and product lines.

√ Provides design growth potential without requiring a major restructuring when minor changes are needed.

√ Provides for lateral, vertical, and diagonal communication.

√ Ensures that authority is properly delegated and distributed.

√ Does not have voids or gaps; for example, all quality program elements are allocated.

√ Makes sure that it is amenable to change when conditions or performance indicate deficiencies; for example, deletion or addition of functions can be readily accomplished.

√ Ensures that corrective action recommendations will receive a fair hearing.

√ Identifies whom to go to if quality problems need resolution and cannot be worked out at lower levels.

√ Defines functions, work scope, and mandate.

√ Minimizes levels of management and hence barriers to prompt communication.

√ Avoids blowing marginal functions out of proportion into separate groups, branches, or departments.

√ Minimizes overlap and duplication of effort.

√ Has optimized span of control.

√ Provides for regular review and audit.

LOCATION OF QUALITY CONTROL WITHIN THE TOTAL ENTERPRISE

There are a number of factors that determine where QC should report within the company. Among the major factors:

TABLE 2-2. Organizational Pitfalls

There are several deficiencies to watch for when designing or changing a QC organization. These include:

● Lack of consideration of interfaces with other departments, customers, and government.

● Superficial top management support and interest in organizational changes and lack of follow-up to make sure they are working.

● Lack of clear-cut responsibilities and authority assignments.

● Fundamental quality objectives not thought through.

● Lack of recognition that quality organizations must be tailor made and not carbon copies of other companies.

● Too many supervisors with near-equal power and no one manager with enough to make timely decisions and to see that they are implemented.

● Too many layers of management that prevent information from going up or down the hierarchy without getting lost or distorted and slowing down responses to new objectives and instructions.

● No operating charters developed for each major quality function.

● Work packages not defined and organized in a systematic and congruent way.

● Span of control too great. A maximum of five is often given in the literature. However, it depends on the situation and more than ten people may be effectively managed in certain cases.

● Duplication of effort among the various QC functions (e.g., between quality and reliability engineering).

● Frequent organizational changes without significant improvements in performance or efficiency.

● An attempt to force fit functions into blocks without consideration of individual managerial capabilities.

● Absence of quality planning/engineering function.

Organizational Level at which Management Wants Trade-off Decisions Made

Business organizations are concerned with three main parameters of operation—quality, cost, and schedule. It is inevitable that these parameters come into mutual conflict. A defective lot of material is produced. Management must decide whether to ship the lot and thereby subordinate the quality considerations to those of cost and schedule, or to scrap or rework the lot and thereby subordinate cost and schedule to quality. This decision will be made; it cannot be avoided. The court of last resort for this decision is the lowest common denominator in the management chain of the contending functions. If, for example, the manufacturing department is convinced that the material must be shipped and the quality control department is convinced that the material must be withheld, the final decision will be made by the lowest level of management having common authority over both the manufacturing and the quality organizations. If quality control reports to the manufacturing manager in parallel with the production superintendent, that decision will be made by the manufacturing manager. Senior management should require that the quality organization report to the level of management where this decision is properly made.

> It's best that the King's food taster reports not to the chef, but to the King.

The Impact of the Quality System Failure

The level at which management wants trade-off decisions made will usually be dictated by the impact a failure in the quality system will have on company operations. However, there is sufficient distinction between these two considerations to warrant their separate discussion. In some businesses a breakdown of the quality system that results in the delivery of goods that do not meet specifications will have little or no impact on operations. This is most true in the case where engineering specifications are established to facilitate production but are of little consequence to the ultimate buyer and to the success of the product in the field. In these circumstances a breakdown of the quality system can at worst result in a temporary increase in quality costs. Under these circumstances it is not inappropriate for the quality organization to report to the manufacturing manager. The manufacturing manager can be held totally accountable for cost and schedule. Any failure of the quality system which results in an

increase in costs will be laid at his doorstep. In fact, if he is to be held accountable for cost and schedule, then he should be given control of the quality organization, since quality control is really a service organization to him. Under other circumstances, however, a failure of the quality system might result in the destruction of a major portion of the business, of perhaps the corporation itself.

Examples of this degree of sensitivity might be found in the aerospace or pharmaceutical industries or certain civil engineering operations. A gross failure in the quality systems of any of these businesses could result in catastrophies of such a nature as to threaten the very existence of the enterprise. Here, it would be reasonable for management to conclude that the head of the quality organization should report very high in the organization to provide maximum protection for the company's processes.

Type of Market/Customer

In a situation where there are relatively few sellers and relatively many buyers, the policies of individual customers rarely have an effect on the organization. However, in those cases where there are many producers and few buyers or where the buyers are represented by an institutional or a governmental agency, then customer policy becomes very important. While the classic examples in this area are businesses under contract to the Department of Defense, the same situation exists in organizations doing business under the purview of government regulatory agencies or certain consumer organizations.

The Extent to which Quality Control Represents the Company to the Customer

If the quality control organization operates strictly within the boundaries of the company with no direct customer contact, then this is not a consideration. In a number of industries, however, quality control directly interfaces with customer representatives and is responsible for maintaining effective working relationships with the customer. In some businesses the quality organization actually performs certain field service functions such as answering customer complaints, determining liability for product failures under warranty clauses, or servicing products in the field. It is generally true that the greater the extent that the quality organization represents the company to the customer, the higher the quality organization will tend to be located within the organization.

Number of Functions Included

The range of activities performed within the quality organization may indirectly dictate its location within the business. The number of interfaces with other organizations is often implied by the number of functions within quality control. For example, a quality control group composed only of inspection activities is apt to have interfaces only with manufacturing. However, an organization composed of inspectors, testers, reliability engineers, procurement, quality assurance, and laboratory personnel is apt to have interfaces with the manufacturing, purchasing, and engineering organizations, and with suppliers. The need to maintain effective relationships across this broad range of interfaces often makes it desirable that the manager of the quality control organization be at the same organizational level as the managers with whom he or she must work.

Management Philosophy

The organizational concepts of senior management often play an important role in QC organization. Some corporations believe in decentralization to the greatest extent possible so that each basic work group can be held accountable. Other leaders of industry may deliberately downplay the importance of quality and instead stress price. Conversely, management may want to stress quality in the corporate image and public relations effort so that QC would be in a position of high visibility. Cultural factors may also influence the location of the QC department.

INTERNAL ORGANIZATION OF QUALITY CONTROL

There are five major factors which directly impact the internal organization of quality control:

Technological Considerations

Perhaps the most common form of organization in industry, the classic functional organization, is formed by grouping common technical skills into departments that can be managed by a single individual. In a quality organization all inspectors may form the inspection department; all quality engineering personnel and statisticians may form a quality engineering department; while metallurgists, physicists, chemists, and other laboratory personnel may be gathered into a materials and processes laboratory function.

Organizations with which Quality Control Interfaces

The quality organization in most industries is fairly complex and represents a range of technologies. This fact forces the quality organization into interfaces with a number of other organizations. If those interfaces are indeed critical to the successful performance of the quality control organization, they should be considered in the organizational scheme and the form of the organization should be designed to maximize the efficiency of those interfaces.

Functional Relationships

It is generally accepted that there are two organizations existing within any enterprise. The first is the formal organization (reflected by organization charts) established by management; the second is an informal organization dictated by the way in which people naturally tend to work. In its extreme form, the informal organization is staffed by the natural leaders and manned by the natural followers, and it may have little or nothing to do with the formal organization. There is apt to be maximum organizational efficiency when the formal organization and the informal organization are as similar as possible to one another, that is, when it has been organized along the lines that people naturally tend to work.

Size

While there are relatively few organizations today that organize strictly on the basis of size, it is a consideration at some level of almost every organization. An organization where size alone determines the internal organization would be one with a large, undifferentiated work force. In this form of organization the total number of workers are divided by the ideal size of the work unit. At the next level it is determined how many first-line supervisors a second-line supervisor can reasonably be expected to supervise, and so on until the total work force is divided and structured. As the total work force expands or contracts, the number of leaders and levels of management are added or subtracted as dictated by the ideal size of the work unit.

Geographical Decentralization

Geography may make it impossible to optimize the size of the work unit. Branch plants and certain industrial operations (such as those dealing with explosives) require physical separation of processing areas to avoid the possibility of sympathetic explosions in the event of an accident. In these situations, it is common to have supervision assigned by location or building, for example. Organization by shift is another version of such decentralization.

WHAT ARE THE QUALITY CONTROL FUNCTIONS THAT MUST BE ASSIGNED?

The internal functions of QC vary greatly depending on a wide range of factors. Normally, however, the following functions must be assigned:

- Reliability, safety, and maintenance engineering
- Quality engineering
- Product inspection and test
- Test laboratory
- Failure analysis
- Procurement quality control incoming inspection
- Quality administration, budget control
- Policy and procedure generation
- Calibration laboratory, equipment maintenance
- Tool proofing, setup control
- Software quality control
- Invoice and shipping inspection
- Process control
- Components engineering
- Product and procedural audit
- Material review
- Measuring equipment design and certification
- Information systems, quality records

ASSIGNMENT OF ACTIVITIES TO INTERNAL ORGANIZATIONAL FUNCTIONS

While it is true that the assignment of the majority of the people is rendered obvious by the definition of the internal QC organization, the assignment of the majority of the activities is not so obvious. There are several criteria to be considered in the assignment of activities to major organizational functions.

Assignment by Similarity

Assignment by similarity is the most common form of activity assignment. It identifies the major distinguishing characteristic of the activity to be assigned and identifies an organization where that same characteristic is predominant. This principle would then suggest that the shipping inspection function be assigned by product inspection because there it finds the greatest similarity with the other activities.

Assignment by Association

This criterion suggests that an activity should logically be assigned to the manager who uses that activity the most, that is, the manager whose operations most depend upon the proper functioning of the activity in question. Application of this criterion to the function of material review, for example, would suggest that it be assigned to the chief inspector since the inspection department submits materials to material review and is responsible for assuring the proper execution of material review dispositions. In other words, the material review activity generally has its most intimate association operationally with the inspection department.

Assignment for Competition

This criterion holds that some desirable functions may be suppressed because the manager to whom they are assigned either fails to understand them or disagrees with their development. As a result, the development of these activities is suppressed and the separation of these activities from that manager will allow them to flourish.

Case in Point: A former quality audit manager was assigned the responsibility for running the failure analysis laboratory. The laboratory was equipped with state-of-the-art test equipment and staffed by highly technical engineering specialists. The manager could not relate to their needs or understand the significance of their reports. The lab was subsequently transferred to the reliability engineering manager.

Assignment for Suppressed Competition

This criterion is exactly the opposite of the previous one. It suggests that some functions are naturally competitive with one another. A great deal of organizational energy may be dissipated in the course of this competition. It suggests that assignment of these activities to the same manager will encourage cooperation, or at least suppress outward competition between these organizations. For example, the reliability and quality engineering departments usually cross each other's trails as they go about their business. This happens because they are in the same business: that of preventing failures. Combining them at least permits the saving of one manager and possibly a few supervisors. The quality engineers benefit from being exposed to engineering analysis, design review, and qualification testing; the reliability engineers learn from living close to real-world production and procurement problems. Competition and conflict are minimized under such a structure.

Assignment for Coordination

This criterion recognizes that timing and integration between activities are critical to the performance of certain operations. For example, an inspection audit activity that is designed to measure the effectiveness of the inspection decision requires that products be checked after they have been inspected but before they have been returned to manufacturing. These products are then reinspected by the audit activity. If this is to take place, timing and integration between audit inspection and the regular inspection activities are critical. Assignment to effect coordination would suggest that the two activities should be given to the same manager so that he or she might effect the required timing and integration. An exception to this assignment would be one in which a conflict of interest might be established.

Assignment for Check and Balance

This criterion implements the principle of checks and balances. It suggests that an activity that is established primarily as a check on another activity should normally be assigned to a different manager. It is the application of this principle that results in audit personnel not reporting to the chief inspector.

It is generally impossible to simultaneously satisfy all of the above criteria. For example, assignment by similarity, assignment by association, and assignment to effect coordination would all suggest that the inspection audit activity be assigned to the chief inspector. However, the principle of check and balance suggests that they not be. Therefore, it is of critical importance that the manager, in organizing, identify the relative importance of the satisfaction of these various criteria and organize to satisfy those that are most important in the particular business and operating environment. Figure 2-2 depicts the quality organization that one might find in a high-technology company.

DECENTRALIZED QUALITY CONTROL: INTERESTING—BUT LOOK BEFORE YOU LEAP

Centralization is based in part on the premise that those who produce do not have time or cannot be trusted to evaluate the quality of the product they have produced. Management here believes that quality control must be independent and report directly to them because production should not be allowed to influence quality decisions.

In sharp contrast to the centralization approach, one can hypothesize that human beings take pride in the quality of their work and can be motivated to exercise self-control. A quality control setup based on this suggests generating quality consciousness at all levels by placing responsibility where it truly belongs. For example, the production person is informed that not only is he responsible for the quantity produced and scheduled, but also for the quality of goods manufactured. He is encouraged to organize his own quality checks with his operators and supervisors. If this is not possible, he can be assisted by quality assessors who evaluate quality and report nonconformances directly to him. He decides when to stop the processes and when to leave them alone,

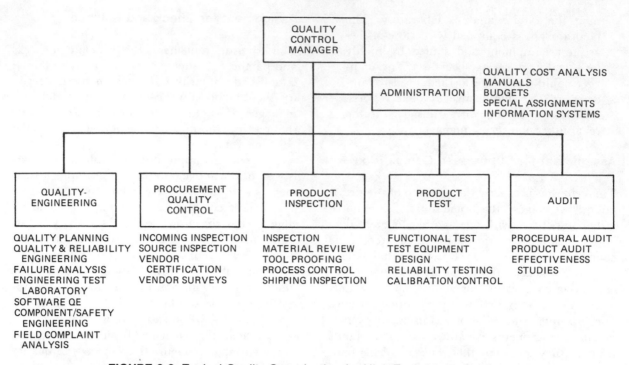

FIGURE 2-2. Typical Quality Organization for High Technology Company

what goods should be sent to the assembly lines or to customers and what should be quarantined for 100 percent inspection.

In this way the production person is made conscious of the fact that quality is his or her business and no one else's. The impact of this policy is felt at all levels of production management from operators to production department heads. Ideally, the evaluation feedback and action part of quality control should be organized at the operator's level for maximum effectiveness. Thus, a climate is created to generate overall quality consciousness in the plant. Since he or she is directly in touch with each process, the production person has the knowhow to take remedial and preventive measures and comes up quickly with process innovations to improve quality levels. Under decentralized quality control, only procedures, instructions, and systems of real utilitarian value to the shop floor person survive. Inspectors directly under production carry out work considered most useful, and all superficial activity ceases. They have a sense of belonging to the production group with all the growth opportunities available in the production channel.

The same type of organization could also be applied in procurement, for example. A procurement quality control (PQC) staff would report to the purchasing manager. By controlling vendor survey and incoming inspection he or she could be held fully responsible for vendor performance and the total cost of purchasing. Drafting office checkers very often report to the manager of the drafting office, but the general approach has not caught on with other functions.

Cautions: There are numerous cautions and pitfalls to avoid when considering a decentralized quality organization:

- When quality control is decentralized, the systems approach becomes difficult if not impossible to implement.

- The department heads may not be capable of or interested in managing a quality control function, or may be diverted by day-to-day problems.

- Incentive pay systems may fail to consider the impact of product quality.

- Quality training and professional development may be suppressed.

- Interdepartmental quality problems may not be evident or attended to. (Quality control is a complex, dynamic *system*.)

- A noncentral organization may not be compliant with government or contractual requirements.

- Decentralization may increase vulnerability in product liability cases.
- The overall integrated quality picture of the firm may not be evident.
- A costly audit function may have to be set up.
- Decentralization may cause customer quality queries, complaints, and corrective action requests (CARs) to get lost in an organizational swamp.

MATRIX MANAGEMENT ORGANIZATION AND QC

The matrix organization depicted in Figure 2-3 evolved to respond to heavy planning and reporting requirements, handle widely differing contract provisions, control complex product quality and reliability, liaise with sophisticated customers, and properly control project costs and schedules.

This matrix management structure involves placing a program/product manager (PM) in charge and providing him or her with full- or part-time functional specialists. This structure has proven to be adept at handling one-time undertakings that are:

(a) definable in terms of specific goals

(b) infrequent, unique, or unfamiliar to the present organization

(c) complex with respect to interdependence of detail task accomplishment

(d) critical to company operations

In order to interface properly with the PM, the quality control department establishes a program product assurance (PPA) section that can provide functional quality representation on the program team. The PPA coordinator (generally a quality engineer with management skills) in turn selects representatives from other product assurance sections and is given the responsibility of overall quality management on the program/ project. (See organizational structure depicted in Figure 2-4.)

Not all functions can be integrated into program teams. Normally, purchasing, shipping, special processing areas, and fixed facilities such as environmental chambers, failure analysis laboratory, and incoming inspection would continue to be run by functional management because of extraordinary personnel skill requirements, and expensive test equipment. Similarly, quality information (inspection reports, failure reports, quality loss data) would be forwarded to a centralized processing unit.

The benefits of the matrix structure on the quality control function are many:

- The matrix approach permits each function to clearly see its contribution in relation to pro-

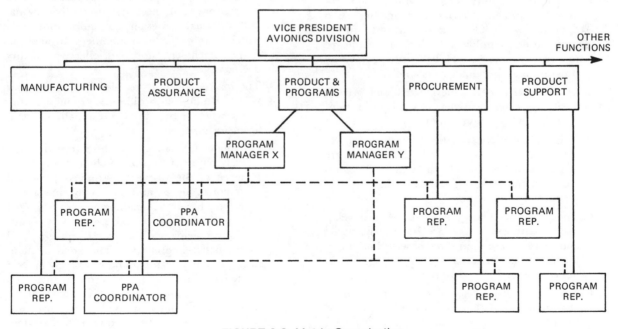

FIGURE 2-3. Matrix Organization

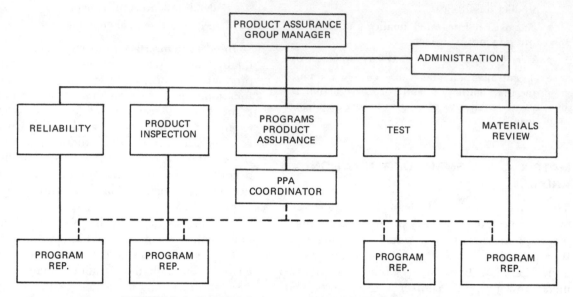

FIGURE 2-4. Product Assurance Matrix Organization

gram goals and to other organizational units. A high level of motivation is thus achieved with a corresponding sense of personal responsibility and commitment.

- Program-assigned personnel develop professionally at an exceedingly fast rate. QC personnel in particular typically become more cost conscious, innovative, efficient, and broad-minded.

- The added visibility of an individual's performance permits early recognition and increased opportunity for advancement. In order to ensure proper employee evaluation, employee progress reviews should be jointly signed by program and functional personnel.

- Quality personnel achievements and growth create a greater awareness of the contributions that the QC function can make.

- Defect-prevention activities such as design review, prerelease testing, and parts control are achieved with relatively little difficulty compared to the results obtained under a purely functional organization.

- The program concept itself seems to develop people with goals that are less differentiated and more diffuse than those observed in purely functional organizations. This is particularly noticeable for PPA coordinators.

- Traditional conflicts between manufacturing and quality function are virtually eliminated except for those based on purely technical considerations, which are subject to resolution by

logic, the laws of nature, and testing. Conflict resolution is more open and direct under the program structure.

- The PPA coordinator, when accepted as a program team member, will be able to influence other program team members and instill a high level of quality consciousness, leading to an immeasurable long-term beneficial effect on a company's quality attitude.

- The close physical proximity of team members, various program meetings, and other formal and informal program communication networks permit QC team members to make informed technical and cost-effective quality decisions.

- The matrix concept provides a relatively easy way of dealing with differing product quality levels, whether they are contractually or management imposed.

- Functional QC supervisors find that they are actively required to provide the benefits of experience to their program-assigned personnel on major problems and on new business. Furthermore, functional management is expected to transfer information (failure analysis results, vendor problems, special process problems, and so on) between programs. The areas of planning, personnel training and development, cost reduction, automatic test equipment, and operating procedures can be given more attention by functional management because they are freed from a large fraction of their former activities.

Cautions: Along with the many benefits derived from program management come some problems requiring careful management attention:

- The problem of defining the relative quality authority between the program manager and product assurance is a major one. Figure 2-5 shows how differences of opinion can be referred to the relevant functional organizations and resolved through the hierarchy.

- The generation of "special" QC procedures on programs can play havoc with standard operating procedures. Because these special procedures are generally more efficient for a particular program, a divisional quality policy manual must be established with programs left the responsibility for determining how control policies should be met. All special procedures should be released through a central QC administration for control purposes.

- Less qualified or inappropriately placed personnel are readily identified by the program and placed under great emotional strain by the high performance requirements, schedules, and other pressures. Such cases are usually rare enough so that each can be satisfactorily resolved by appropriate management action.

- Interprogram communications can be a serious factor if duplication of effort is to be avoided, effective corrective action implemented, and technology transfer accomplished. Program status reporting and a quality alert system help, but this particular area is one of functional management's key responsibilities in a matrix structure. A strong functional management must additionally ensure that the stability of the organization, long-range planning, and personnel growth are not seriously impaired because of short-term program objectives.

- The possibility of the program concept unconsciously "contaminating" the thoughts of program-assigned quality personnel should not be overlooked. This is best controlled by sound personnel selection, close functional management contact with their program representatives, and continuous quality auditing by an independent authority such as a corporate or divisional audit group.

- Because the duration of a program is reasonably well defined, it is to be expected that program personnel will come to anticipate their next assignment toward the end of a program. This can result in reduced efficiency and divided allegiance as quality engineers and other key personnel look to others outside the pro-

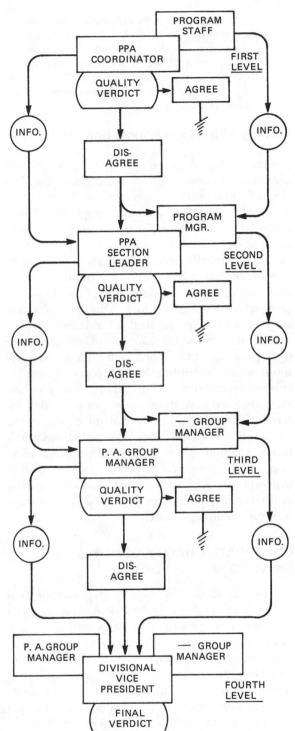

FIGURE 2-5. Quality Conflict Resolution Flow Chart Courtesy of Canadian Marconi Company.

gram environment. Management must counter this natural tendency by a potent company sales policy that has provided new projects for key personnel. Whether or not the sales effort is successful, management must follow a basic rule of conduct—that of letting people know where they stand.

Dealing with Interdivisional Shipments

Interdivisional shipments in large corporations sometimes involve a lot of unnecessary duplication of effort and costs related to surveillance, material review, and incoming inspection. Interdivisional rivalry and one-upmanship can be as fierce as or worse than company-to-company relations. A mutually acceptable interdivisional QC agreement can define working ground rules and establish divisional responsibilities for major aspects of a program/product. This type of agreement places a great deal of reliance on the generation and maintenance of a single corporate QC program plan for each major product line/contact describing the total company quality control contribution. This plan constitutes the most detailed task description against which internal funding for quality control efforts in the various operating divisions is provided and monitored. The main point is to establish communication and cooperation and minimize the expenditure of effort to meet company quality and reliability goals. See Table 2-3 for a sample interdivisional agreement.

CORPORATE QUALITY CONTROL: WHAT TO WATCH FOR

Up to the 1950s, the typical large corporation consisted of numerous plants, perhaps spread in a few countries. During the 1960s and 1970s the multinational conglomerate came into being. Companies such as Exxon, ITT, RCA, Litton, and General Electric fit this description. These corporations are not limited to a line of products or even a group of related products. Such a corporation might have electronics, car rental, insurance, and newspaper divisions and operate in the U.S., Canada, United Kingdom, France, Taiwan, and several South American countries. Organizationally this has led to the development of executive vice-presidents of finance, industrial relations, and operations. Several corporations have installed a corporate QC function reporting to the

TABLE 2-3. Sample Interdivisional Quality Control Agreement

1.0 *Purpose*
This document defines the terms and conditions of the Specialized Component's and System Division's agreement regarding delegation of quality control and acceptance authority by the Systems Division. This would permit direct shipments between the divisions without incoming inspection.

2.0 *Scope*
This document applies to all material produced and accepted by the Specialized Components Division (SCD) in satisfaction of Systems Division work authorizations. This agreement shall in no way affect the requirement for SCD to deliver acceptable hardware and services.

3.0 *Applicability*
Unless otherwise specified on work authorizations or related documents, this procedure shall be in effect. In all cases, work authorizations shall take precedence over this document.

4.0 *General*
In order to avoid duplicate inspections and increased costs, the Systems Division is willing, in so far as practicable, to utilize the quality controls established by SCD. This principle is valid to the extent that SCD maintains a documented quality system acceptable to Systems Division whose adequacy is periodically verified.

5.0 *Requirements*
The SCD agrees to comply with the following conditions at no increase in price so long as this agreement may be in effect:
1. To maintain a quality system in accordance with Corporate Specification XXXXX.
2. To permit periodic audits of this quality system by the Systems Division.
3. To provide evidence of product acceptance with each shipment.
4. To maintain adequate quality records.
5. To comply with Systems Division Procurement/Materials Management requirements regarding invoicing, identification, packaging, and delivery.
6. To be responsive to Systems Division Corrective Action Requests.

6.0 *Defective Material*
Systems Division retains the right to return rejected lots for 100 percent inspection at no additional cost. Because of schedule requirements, Systems Division may decide to rework/repair defective material and charge the additional costs incurred to SCD.

7.0 *Agreement Termination*

This Agreement shall cease to be in effect when (a) the requirements of para. 5.0 are not satisfied and no corrective action can be agreed upon, or (b) either party wishes to withdraw providing that at least six months advance notice is given.

8.0 *Special Requirements*

The following requirements are considered special and do not form part of this Agreement:

1. Customer Source Inspection
2. Material Review Delegation (PMR and MRB)
3. Traceability Requirements
4. Measuring Devices Certification
5. Material/Process Certification
6. Data packages other than 5.0(3) and (5)
7. Tool Inspection and Proofing
8. First Article Inspection
9. Personnel Certification
10. Qualification Tests

The above requirements may be imposed via the appropriate work authorization or as mutually agreed in writing between the applicable Systems Division and SCD.

9.0 *Reservations*

Systems Division reserves the right to process material through incoming inspection as a product audit activity or when material quality is suspect. This agreement in no way limits the rights of the Systems Division to reject any and all material found to be unsatisfactory in meeting the requirements specified in applicable drawings, specifications, and standards.

---

president (Figure 2-6), but few have been successful.

Duties

In order to be useful and cost effective the role of the corporate QC office must be clearly defined and understood. The duties that have resulted in net benefits usually include:

- development of corporate quality policies
- initiation of QC training courses
- evaluation of new measuring equipment and automation
- providing specialized consulting services usually of a management nature
- serving on government and trade committees
- coordination of quality cost programs
- chairing corporate quality council meetings where common problems are discussed

- setting quality improvement objectives for divisions
- preparing executive reports on quality, reliability, and safety matters
- assisting with proposals
- auditing division/plant quality control practices
- identifying personnel for promotions
- initiating quality circle programs

One can imagine the enormous challenge and responsibility of the corporate QC function. While the financial function can look at everything in dollars and cents, quality control programs depend on the nature of the product, the market served, and a host of technological factors.

Case in Point: A large conglomerate acquired a medium-sized manufacturer of ball point pens. The typical price was 39¢, compared with the unit price of $500, which was typical of the products of the parent company. The introduction of stringent quality controls and reporting systems nearly bankrupted the firm within its first year under the new management.

Management Traits

Installing a corporate QC program requires considerable thought, imagination, and planning. It requires tact, diplomacy, and common sense. A corporate QC manager must be sensitive to divisional management goals. He or she must not impose rigid practices on business units that would not find them profitable. Standardization procedures must be cautiously applied and not force-fitted. Unilateral actions must be avoided like the plague. Corporate QC management must be aware of the political factors involved in complex organizations. Some additional cautions:

- Tailor quality requirements and improvement plans to division's needs, objectives, and stage of development.
- Keep in close communication with division and plant managers.
- Recognize cultural, social, and linguistic differences in different countries.
- Get adequate budget funding from corporate management; don't become dependent on divisions.
- Don't try to do too much too soon; concentrate on the most rewarding tasks first.

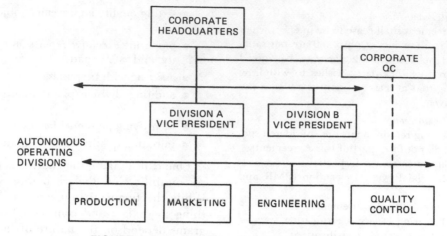

FIGURE 2-6. Multidivision Quality Organization

- Give credit to divisional managers and quality control personnel when appropriate.
- Keep paperwork and bureaucracy to an absolute minimum.
- Avoid comparing one division or company to another.
- Greet each success with praise and appreciation; each failure with an offer of support and assistance.
- Keep the program practical and cost sensitive; avoid philosophy.
- Don't act like a "Super QC" practitioner because of corporate assignment.

- Be quantitative and objective; don't be subjective and unduly hasty in making assessments.
- Develop good relationships with division QC managers.
- Remember that division managers have a profit and loss (P & L) responsibility and are driven by programs and tasks that relate to financial return.
- Recognize that division managers are autonomous and politically powerful; corporate QC will, in the end, derive its influence from professional competence, management capability, and communications skills.

REFERENCES

Clark, T. "Manage Every Product Contract with a Program." *The Electronic Engineer*, Dec. 1968.

Crosby, P. D. "Cutting the Cost of Quality." Industrial Education Institute, 1967.

Gronseth, J. R. "Promoting Effective Coordination among Marketing, Engineering and Manufacturing." *Engineering Digest*, Oct. 1977.

Hevesh, A. H. "Practical Quality Assurance in Multi-Divisional Programs." *Quality Progress*, April 1968.

Juran, J. M., and F. M. Gryna. *Quality Planning and Analysis*. New York: McGraw-Hill, 1970.

Kiesell, R. M. "What's New in Quality Assurance Management." *Quality Progress*, April 1968.

Kivenko, K. "Program Management and the Product Assurance Function." *Quality Progress*, Dec. 1971.

Ouchi, W. G. *Theory Z*. New York: Avon Books, 1981.

Steiner, G. A., and W. G. Ryan. "Industrial Project Management." New York: MacMillan, 1968.

Stewart, J. M. "Making Project Management Work." *Business Horizons*, Fall 1965.

Walker, A. H., and J. W. Lorsch. "Organizational Choice: Product vs. Function." *Harvard Business Review*, Nov.–Dec. 1968.

3

Reducing Quality Control Costs

The costs and controls to be discussed in this chapter permeate the entire quality cost structure and, as such, can have a major impact on the total cost of economical quality control. These costs relate to measuring equipment, paperwork, personnel, procurement control, information systems, and a host of administrative expenses. Control of these costs may well determine the viability of a particular quality program. This chapter details the ways and means for running a lean, efficient quality control operation.

USING THE BUDGET PROCESS FOR COST REDUCTION

The planning phase of the annual budget process provides the main opportunity for increased efficiency. It is during this phase that past practices are re-examined, ideas for change are considered, and opportunities for breakthrough are seized. This is the *cost reduction* phase of budgeting. The typical budget review and approval process is shown in Figure 3-1.

ZERO-BASE BUDGETING

The usual method of budgeting is to review the various elements of existing projects and estimate the funds that will be necessary to maintain those activities over a projected period of time. Spending is increased as new projects are brought on line during the budgeting period. At the end of the period, the cycle begins again with new analyses and estimates and, usually, further increases in spending.

Implicit in this method of budgeting is the assumption that current projects should be continued—that such projects are necessary and are being performed as efficiently as possible. In practice, this assumption may lead to a continuation of projects that should be terminated, resulting in a constant accumulation of activities and a steadily rising level of spending. What is needed is a method for justifying any spending, not just increases in current spending. This method is ideal for the quality function, which sometimes gets bogged down in tradition.

Zero-base budgeting (ZBB) provides an analytical framework for evaluating projects and activities in terms of overall program planning and requests for funding. Its principal objectives are to:

- Involve managers at all levels in the budgeting process.
- Justify funding requests for existing projects and activities as well as for new ones.
- Focus the justification process on the evaluation of discrete, well-defined units of activity.
- Establish objectives against which subsequent accomplishments can be measured and evaluated.
- Analyze the probable effects of different budget amounts or performance levels on the achievement of objectives.
- Provide a credible rationale for reallocating resources.

With ZBB, each manager must justify his or her entire budget from scratch (hence, *zero-base*). To accomplish this, the quality manager must assess the benefits gained from on-going operations,

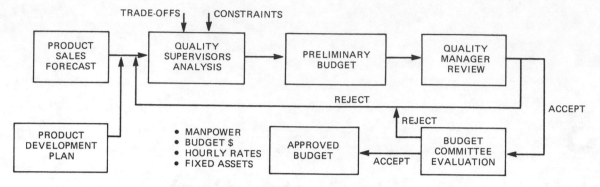

FIGURE 3-1. The Budget Flow Process

as well as the need for additional funds. This requires that all QC activities be evaluated in terms of discrete, well-defined "decision packages" and ranked in order of importance.

The first step is to determine the lowest level in the organization or department at which cost data are maintained and budget decisions made. This *decision unit* might reside at the first-line supervisor level or the division director level, depending on the nature and size of the organization. Once this level is identified, *decision packages* are developed within each decision unit to provide a basis for making funding decisions. These decisions comprise the operating budget for the manager's area of responsibility.

Each decision package specifies a certain level of effort for executing a particular function. Each package is incorporated in a report that consists of the following elements:

- purpose of the function, including specific objectives
- consequences of not performing the function
- alternatives: different ways of performing the same function
- costs of performing the function and the benefits expected

Determining which functions should serve as the basis for decision packages is not always easy. There are no simple rules. The aim is to earmark functions that are important enough to have a direct impact on budgeting. Selection will depend on the type and size of the organization, as well as the type and complexity of the projects and tasks performed.

One of the best reasons for developing decision packages is that the manager is forced to evaluate the organizational structure in terms of the interrelationships among activities and organizational units. This evaluation will identify people, projects, and services provided that will allow the manager to specify how he wants his activities structured for budget-decision purposes.

Each decision unit includes a *minimum-effort* package for each function within the unit. The operating manager specifies a reduced level of effort in the present budget period. This is then projected as the minimum level of effort for the next budget period.

Usually a ceiling is established, and packages are prepared at specific levels of effort from the minimum (say, 80 percent of present budget for that function) to the ceiling (perhaps 115 percent of the present budget). The ceiling is based on an estimate of the funds that will be available for the next fiscal year. Since this level is the maximum likely to be approved by top management, packages should be developed and rated only to the ceiling level. Packages that would require funding beyond the current budget amount would have to be justified in terms of the increased results that are envisioned.

By analyzing and comparing decision packages, realistic trade-offs can be made between functions. Decision units with increasing workloads that justify increased funding might be favored at the expense of others that have decreasing workloads and can get along with reduced funds. Thus, funding is constantly redistributed according to the recommendations and evaluations of the managers who are responsible for results.

It is a rare implementation of ZBB that does not result in a significant shift in the allocation of available quality resources, usually toward prevention activities.

Caution: Although advanced techniques such as ZBB are designed to provide rational budgeting decisions, managers will not always agree as to what is rational. It should be expected that those who use the method will try to find ways to favor the projects they think are important, and stymie those they think are unworthy or unnecessary.

PREPARING THE QUALITY CONTROL BUDGET

Regardless of whether traditional or advanced budgeting procedures are used, the end result is budgets for various cost elements. Experience has shown that the direct labor portion of the budget is relatively easy to predict using historical ratios such as production to inspection, incoming inspection as a percent of purchased material dollars, or total QC department costs as a fraction of total production cost of sales. The overhead portion of the budget requires by far the greatest attention. Don't let fat creep in. Pay heed to Parkinson's second law:

Expenditures rise to meet budget.

Here are ten key cost overhead elements in the quality budget and ideas on how to keep them in line:

1. capital equipment
2. equipment maintenance and repair
3. calibration
4. communications
5. quality information system
6. materials and supplies
7. travel
8. education and training
9. space
10. miscellaneous

Capital Equipment Requirements

Capital equipment depreciation has always been a significant part of the quality budget. With increasing capital constraints and rapidly changing technology, renting rather than buying measuring equipment can often bring direct savings. For short-term needs (seasonal job, short-term contract, or fill in), rent it. When you're finished, send it back. Rented instruments usually can be returned at any time and replaced with later models. You can try out new instruments—see if they fit your operation before buying them. Rented instruments never sit on the shelf collecting dust and eating up your capital. Remember: Profits are generated by instruments in use, not by idle instruments. Renting eliminates large capital cash outlays. Renting also cuts taxes—payments are deductible operating expenses that produce sizeable after-tax savings compared to capital equipment—you buy only for relatively long-term requirements, rent for short-term needs.

Caution: Watch out for rental period versus purchase option. Renting for too long may be too expensive.

Another possible method of reducing costs is through the subcontracting of testing, inspection, or analysis. There are independent laboratories offering their facilities for testing (physical, functional, environmental, etc.) just about any component or product. For some complex tests, they may be expensive, but they represent the only alternative to the small firm that lacks the facilities to do its own testing. They can also absorb routine or overflow work from in-house labs. If the routine testing service is nearby and it is familiar with a company's needs, it can generally give results quickly, even though special equipment or fixturing may be required. When the problem involves a new MIL-SPEC test procedure, for example, results will come sooner with the help of someone farther up on the learning curve. A final reason is the need for part-time expertise, for example, when a company has only a temporary need for a metallurgist or a design analyst in an unusual specialty. By borrowing the talents and experience of a testing firm's engineers only when they are needed, the cost of training someone and then using that person only part-time is eliminated. A side benefit of using an independent test lab is the lab's impartiality in product liability areas, provided that it is a reputable agency.

Note: Don't forget government labs—they are usually well equipped and staffed. Prices are competitive or even free depending on circumstances.

Observation: In some industries, laboratories must be government approved or at least carefully evaluated by the company intending to subcontract testing. For instance, in the pharmaceutical industry, a "new" vendor such as a contracting lab must first be validated by an inspection using, say, spiked samples.

Equipment Maintenance

Money to maintain all the necessary physical equipment of the quality department is another significant budgetary item. Past records of repair service invoices, converted to averages (adjusted for inflation) and multiplied against the unit count will give the dollars planned into the budget.

Work done in-house as well as outside repair work on test, analysis, and data processing equipment are considered in the cost of keeping the department's physical assets in shape. Though this should be a constant effort, budget time seems to be an appropriate spot to review which units are under service contracts. Are some up for renewal? Is it still worthwhile? It's also a good practice to review the equipment inventory list to see if some measuring equipments have reached the point of noneconomical repair or simply will not be used because of changes in technology, product mix, or workload.

Caution: Planned new equipment should not be figured at the same rate as the present year, since at least some part of the initial year is generally covered by guarantees or warranty. Additionally, one should always check on this protection point regarding proposed capital equipment purchases. It could make a big difference in your repair budget.

Maintenance costs can also be reduced by equipment standardization.

Case in Point: Over 100 pieces of "ph" measuring equipment of nine models were used by a $450 million French chemical supplier. After careful analysis, it was established that this could be standardized to four models from two suppliers. The result was decreased maintenance costs because reasonable spare parts could be stocked, ph meters could be interchanged while waiting repair, and spare part prices fell because of increased purchasing volume. Annual repair charges were reduced 12 percent.

Observation: When large quantities of measuring equipment are in use, it may be more economical to employ your own maintenance technician than to send it to a calibration service vendor or manufacturer for repair.

Calibration

Calibration of inspection and test equipment is a necessary part of the appraisal function. However, calibration costs can quickly run out of hand unless appropriate controls are imposed. For instance, many companies calibrate equipment on a fixed interval basis. Intervals based on usage or calibration test records usually yield more reliable equipment at lower cost. Substantial savings can also be achieved by performing limited calibrations.

Case in Point: A small Chicago relay manufacturer was required to perform a special test. In this case a $\pm 0.1\%$ meter with a 150-volt AC range was used in the special test to measure 115VAC at 400 Hz. Elimination of all other voltages and frequencies greatly reduced calibration time and a $2500 per annum cost saving was achieved.

Multimeter and power supply meters are examples of items that are intended for monitoring/indicating rather than actual measurement. Such instruments require regular maintenance but need not be calibrated. A decal label stating "Not To Be Used for Acceptance Purposes" and good test procedures provide adequate control over possible misuse. Finally, calibration costs can further be reduced by not calibrating surplus instruments in inventory until they are actually required. If these controls are implemented, savings of 20 to 30 percent can be expected.

Communication Expenses

Don't take a trip if a long-distance call will do. Don't make a call if a letter will do. Are all phone lines currently in use really required? Would extensions, which are cheaper, be adequate?

Case in Point: One large corporation got into the habit of sending out teams of quality and other personnel to suppliers every time a supplier had a quality problem. During an economic downturn, the company examined this practice and found that most trips were not necessary and could have been adequately handled by long-distance calls or Telex. In fact, in some of the cases, faster corrective action would have been obtained if the vendor had seen how his component was used and handled at the buyer's plant.

Information Systems

This area can represent a gold mine for cost reduction. Have you recently reassessed the need for all the pieces of paper pushed out by the computer? In medium and large companies, the information explosion seems sometimes to be based on the principle, "What else can we find for our computer to process?" Indeed, many reports are never read and, because of their sheer volume, are counterproductive in that they can discourage the use of truly valuable reports.

Case in Point: One large telecommunications manufacturer issued a weekly scrap loss report to more than fifty people of which possibly only seven or eight have a real interest and two or three people could effect action. After a consultant reviewed the firm's information needs, over $10,000 was saved in clerical costs, computer time, and paper.

Reports can be useful, but they must provide analyzed information in a timely manner to those who need and will use the information. Since data processing costs are closely related to the volume of data processed, the number of reports, and the number of copies per report, the opportunities for substantial savings are abundant.

Materials and Supplies

This cost element can include everything from pens, rulers, and templates to material samples for QC evaluation. An aura of cost consciousness should permeate the QC department to prevent frivolous use of expendable items. Usage records should be maintained and appropriate norms established.

Caution: In most industries this segment of the budget will be relatively small. Don't nickel and dime quality engineers or other professionals for such day-to-day items as pencils, graph paper, and writing pads. Besides, it consumes time and administrative effort to control these items.

Travel Costs

Travel may be a substantial figure in the QC budget, depending on the type of business you are in. Most of these dollars will be spent on the two ends of the manufacturing cycle—start and finish. Supplier contacts, either survey or problem-solving, are difficult to estimate. However, the best gauge of activity in this area is the expected new-products schedule balanced against the condition of your vendor rating list. A substantial increase in new parts to be acquired over the next year, or the requirement that you should be finding some better sources, will dig deeply into this account and should be financially planned.

If a complex product (or line) is being purchased from another firm, expect extra travel cost while familiarization occurs with the selling firm over quality procedures, requirements, and test methods.

On the other end of the cycle, "selling" the quality of the product or investigating field problems also takes transportation. Additionally, many government procedures include periodic conferences in distant cities or witnessing on-location qualification tests.

With increasing energy costs, both air fares and car rental costs have escalated. Accordingly, travel costs must be controlled. Figure 3-2 shows a form used to authorize travel, its mere existence can sometimes eliminate marginal trips that might otherwise have been taken. This is one form that just may be cost effective.

Another ripe area for travel cost reduction is the vendor survey. The vendor survey is a basically sound idea that has been run into the ground. Restrict surveys to major subcontracts and engineering critical parts and avoid excessive concentration on procedural detail. Consider using commercial vendor evaluation services/data banks, especially where geography (distance) is a factor. A simple phone call to existing vendor customers can sometimes provide all the information you need.

Education and Training

Conferences and training are likely topics for a large cut during the budget-review cycle, because

XYZ CORPORATION
           TRAVEL REQUEST

		DATE OF ISSUE	
NAME	IBM NO. CC	DEPARTURE DATE	RETURN DATE
TRAVEL TO		MODE OF TRAVEL ☐ AIR ☐ PRIVATE CAR	☐ OTHER _____
PURPOSE OF TRIP		SITE VISITED	
		TEL. NO. (BUSINESS)	TEL. NO. (HOTEL)
PURPOSE OF TRIP		SITE VISITED	
		TEL. NO. (BUSINESS)	TEL. NO. (HOTEL)
AIRFARE	CASH	TRAVELLERS CHEQUE ☐ PER DIEM ☐ AT COST	PER DIEM RATE	CHARGE NO. LABOR	CHARGE NO. EXPENSES
PREPARED BY DATE	APPROVED BY DATE	APPROVED BY DATE	APPROVED BY DATE

FIGURE 3-2. Travel Request Form
Courtesy of Canadian Marconi Company.

the quality group generally requests far above the company per capita average. This is attributed to two factors: the rapid growth of the profession and the diversity of skills required.

The quality profession is among the most changing and fluid of the engineering-oriented careers. To stay up to date, the QC person must meet with contemporaries more often, attend more courses, buy more books, and gain more immediate knowledge than virtually any of his or her peers. Set goals for the department. Decide how much training is absolutely essential and base your cost estimate on it.

Space

Many corporations assign a cost-per-square-foot charge to using departments and this must be included in the QC budget. Anything that con-

serves space utilization will bring down this charge. Neat, moderate height racks for storing test equipment, open office areas, industrially engineered floor layouts (for incoming inspection, especially), well-planned test setups, conveyor systems, efficient record-storage systems (such as microfilm) and shift work all act toward cutting down QC space needs. When performed on a plant-wide basis, such attention to detail can sometimes eliminate or delay the need for a costly plant addition or expansion.

Pitfall to Avoid: Don't forget the costs of moving, space rearrangement, or test facility installation.

Miscellaneous

The miscellaneous category should actually be avoided whenever possible as it typically ends up being a center of uncontrollable costs. Have miscellaneous or contingency accounts been examined? Some departmental supervisors use these "slush" funds to cover up poor planning or to perform unauthorized side projects.

Caution: Often forgotten is the cost necessary to cover *unplanned manloading*—special help utilized during vacations and leaves of absence, and replacement time for personnel losses. Generally, the company's budget committee, which may consist of a single person or a group, has standard figures to cover this. Newspaper ads, agency fees, and other recruitment expenses must also be factored into the budget.

CLASSIFY EMPLOYEES AS DIRECT LABOR

To be classified as direct labor, an employee should by definition be able to meaningfully charge his or her time to specific pieces of work. This is certainly possible for incoming inspection, assembly inspection, product test, and final acceptance. The writing of generally applicable QC policy/procedures, systems audits, and process analysis typically cannot be included as direct labor and hence are indirect labor and part of overhead expenses.

To the extent that it is practical to achieve, this categorization will improve the cost visibility of the quality function, increase the cost consciousness of QC department supervisors, and reduce the stigma of quality control as an overhead or "burden" function.

Case in Point: A QC manager, unaccustomed to rigid cost controls, routinely sent her procurement quality control (PQC) people on vendor visits of marginal value. The costs incurred were significant, as they included employee wages, airfare, hotel accommodation, and car rental. Two months after converting PQC to direct labor, a production manager queried the excessive costs as reported on the company's job costing system. After intensive discussion, it was agreed that future vendor trips would be jointly agreed to by QC, procurement, and production in advance.

It is also important to judiciously allocate general quality control overheads to various direct labor cost center budgets such as test, incoming inspection, quality engineering, or product inspection. Some logical process of allocating overheads such as by the number of people, floor space utilized, or even by capital investment employed can be used. More often than not the first cut at allocation will yield "good" hourly rates for some cost centers and "bad" hourly rates for others.

Case in Point: The quality engineering cost-center hourly rate turned out to be $22.50 per hour after prorating overhead costs on the basis of headcount. Since the design engineering rate was $21.75 it was felt that the rate should be reduced to $20.50 to make it more "saleable." The residual unallocated overheads were shifted to the forty-two person test department, which could more readily absorb the costs without upsetting user departments (this technique may not be permissible on some government contracts).

LET RATIO ANALYSIS POINT THE WAY

Ratios are the most commonly used management control tools for goal setting, trend monitoring, and performance measurement. They are easy to compute; they graph nicely; they become a common language among divisions, groups, and departments; and they put large and small groups on a common basis. Unfortunately, ratios are frequently misused because of a lack of understanding. Because they appear conceptually simple, the reader does not concern himself with the elements that make up the ratio. An understanding of the elements and their characteristics, and thereby the use of ratios from which to draw operating conclusions, can be a very powerful quality management tool.

Another point worth noting is that overall ratios are dangerous as averages in that they may hide a great deal that may be of significance. Often, the responsibility for the various segments of production is divided organizationally, and quality ratios that ignore this fact are of questionable value. No single person is accountable for performance, and management action cannot be properly directed. Structure your ratio analysis and performance reporting according to at least two criteria:

1. quality accountability (organization)
2. availability of data from the quality data collection system

If significant product-line differences exist or your management is product-line oriented, additional stratification may be necessary and desirable. Often inherent in this situation, however, is the fact that a significant portion of processes are common to more than one product line. Computation of ratios by product line may be impractical or at best arbitrary, since quality performance would be assigned or allocated to product-line categories on a basis that is itself arbitrary. A practical solution to this dilemma is to control processes as a total and to monitor finished goods by product line.

By using historical information based on as long a period of time as you can go back, you can determine what your various quality ratios have been. Once this is done, you can adjust this to what you want as a future target. You can make it higher or lower than your historical records, based on what you feel you can do and want to do in the future. The ratio that you choose to use is basically an estimate based on your knowledge of the situation and your goal. If appropriate ratios can be agreed upon between production and QC, they provide a target or goal to work for and, if there is agreement between the groups, it can support better relations and goal congruence between the groups.

Pitfalls to Avoid:

1. Ratios work best when your situation is fairly level and your working inventory is neither increasing nor decreasing sharply. If you are either increasing or decreasing sales significantly, ratios tend to distort the targets in the present period.

2. Quality cost comparisons between companies are always dangerous. Differences in size, accounting treatment of costs, fraction of items purchased versus fraction made-in-house, and other factors tend to distort quality ratios.

3. Look out for changes in the level of automation. If production automates significantly their costs will be reduced. Unless QC makes similar changes, all ratios will be thrown out of whack.

Case in Point: The incoming inspection supervisor of a multidivisional producer of oil rigs presented his budget based on a 3.75 percent cost of incoming inspection. The quality manager rejected the proposed budget because it was excessive. The reasons:

(1) A new coordinate-measuring machine installed at incoming inspection was slashing inspection times of mechanical parts by 50 to 80 percent.

(2) The previous year's data was based on the receipt of many small individual lots with correspondingly high inspection set-up costs. The production plan for the coming year provided for fewer supplier shipments but significantly larger lot sizes.

(3) A large fraction of the previous year's costs were due to sorting. Recently introduced policies on inventory stocking and billing vendors for parts screening should have reduced the projected incoming inspection ratio.

(4) About 15 percent of the parts were added to the firm's vendor certification program and hence would receive greatly reduced inspections.

(5) The historical ratio had been based on standard material costs, but the company had now reverted to an actual cost system. A restatement of the prior data resulted in a reduction in the ratio.

After considerable discussion, a figure of 3.15 percent was agreed upon.

Some ratios that are useful during the annual budget process are shown in Table 3-1.

KEEP AN EYE ON BUDGET VARIANCES

To succeed at cost control, one must constantly compare actual costs incurred to budget. This applies particularly to functional expenses (cost center overheads). The evaluation of cost variances can be time consuming, so the largest variances should get the most attention. The discoveries can be very illuminating:

- Excess overtime and idle time: This was traced to a product line that exhibited poor production control. Seventy percent of the QC costs were incurred in the last two weeks of the shipping month; idle time was incurred in the beginning of the month.

- Over-budget purchased materials: A $250 Polaroid camera was inadvertently keypunched in as $25,000.

TABLE 3-1. Some Helpful Ratios

1. *Quality control costs to production cost of sales.* This ratio is particularly useful in detecting intermediate- to long-term cost trends.

2. *Square feet per employee.* The more square feet per QC employee the less likelihood that everything is optimized. Acceptable norms are available in industrial engineering handbooks.

3. *Inspection to assembly direct labor.* This ratio is fairly stable but can be misleading if there are significant changes in product mix, make/buy policy, or degree of automation. A typical figure in the electronics industry would be in the 1:10 to 1:15 range.

4. *Warranty as percent of sales.* Very useful, but use carefully if you are introducing an unusual number of new products.

5. *Cost center overhead rate.* The higher the rate, the more suspicious you should be. Year-to-year figures are instructive.

6. *Direct to indirect labor ratio.* Indirect quality staffers should always be viewed with a critical eye.

7. *Incoming inspection as a percent of material inspected.* An excellent tool for budgeting and controlling incoming inspection or PQC. Watch out for distortions caused by the receipt of high-value items such as computers or peripherals.

8. *Percentage increase on QC costs divided by increase in sales.* Inflation should tend to cancel so that a ratio of greater than 1.0 needs reassessment. This ratio is, however, unreliable if product inventory fluctuates significantly.

- High depreciation charges: A coordinate-measuring machine was incorrectly written off over three years instead of seven.

- Excessive direct labor charges to overheads: Investigation revealed a mild downturn in work, so test technicians could not charge full time to authorized jobs.

- Large variance in Xerox costs: Accounting erroneously double charged QC.

- Major increase in books and publications account: Seven senior QC people bought the same $35 statistics handbook.

- Incorrect allocations from plant engineering: The charge for space did not match the actual space utilized by the reliability test laboratory.

- Over-budget indirect labor: A quality engineer was incorrectly classified as indirect labor by the personnel department.

- Unusual travel expenses: Four QC supervisors attended an out-of-town zero-defects seminar.

APPROVALS: KEEPING A TAB ON COSTS

Like purchasing, manufacturing, or marketing, QC management must control who is authorized to approve certain cost-related activities. Without a set of basic controls, some very embarrassing things can occur. Some of the most critical decision areas involve:

- QC cost estimates for proposals: These would normally be approved by the QC manager, prior to transmittal to product costing or pricing functions. Their potential impact on the firm can be significant, as quality costs in some industries are a major fraction of total factory cost.

- Capital equipment additions: Appropriations generally require top management approval of the proposal submitted by the QC manager. These appropriations must be professionally prepared because they directly reflect on the planning and analytical skills within the QC department.

- Employee requisitions: Depending on company size, the acquisition of additional personnel may be delegated to the next level of supervision below the QC manager if within current authorized budget limits.

- Purchase requisitions: Depending on dollar value, contractual complexity, contract currency exchange risks, and the like, the QC manager or his or her immediate manager may want to sign some requisitions.

- Travel requests: The QC manager may typically delegate this, but overseas travel or trips of greater than one week duration should be controlled by senior management.

- Employee progress reviews: This is highly dependent on company organization structure but the QC manager should, as a minimum, review progress and salary of all key QC personnel at least annually.

- Expense accounts: QC supervision may be delegated authority up to some dollar limit. Company ground rules for preparing expense accounts should be distributed to all those who are expected to incur travel or entertainment expenses. A frivolous attitude here can severely undermine cost consciousness—a valuable QC attribute.

- Overtime: This is normally controlled within budget limitations by QC supervision. Overtime is a closely watched parameter and is usually an indicator of some planning breakdown. This is one potential problem area that a QC manager can live without.

- Test reports: A poorly prepared report can immeasurably hurt the quality control image within the company. Deficient reports submitted to customers can hurt more than image—they can necessitate costly rewrites and lose sales. All reports sent outside the QC department should, as a minimum, be approved by QC supervision.

PARTS EVALUATION COSTS AND TIME CAN BE CUT

In order to design, develop, and produce modern, complex hardware systems with some assurance that they will have adequate reliability to perform as required, the individual reliabilities of the piece part requires subjecting the part to environmental and load conditions which simulate those to be experienced by the part in actual usage. This method of obtaining reliability data can be expensive and time consuming, especially when tests are duplicated by separate companies designing similar equipment that use identical piece parts. To eliminate costly duplication of parts testing and reduce the cost to the government of military and space equipments, the Government-Industry Data Exchange Program—GIDEP—was established. One $40 million division of a Canadian electronics firm claims yearly savings of nearly $100,000.

Previously restricted to government activities and contractors, the program is now available free to any activity generating and using this type of data exchange.

The technical data bank includes information on parts, components, materials, manufacturing processes, calibration procedures, and related technical test data. The test data are primarily results from environmental testing as conducted by participating contractors, associated subcontractors, and certain activities of the government agencies who are engaged in design, development, and production of military and aerospace equipment for the government. GIDEP also provides general technical reports and documents of particular significance to parts application, contractor-generated reliability specifications, in-process parts testing activity, and related documents. The

calibration procedures are the results of technical reports prepared to calibrate the instrumentation required for the attainment of repeatable, accurate test results.

GIDEP offers you:

- Savings in time, effort, and manpower
- Common technical information interchange
- Get to know a lot of people with similar problems
- Four major data interchanges
    (a) engineering
    (b) failure experience
    (c) reliability/maintainability
    (d) metrology/calibration
- Parts and components information for all disciplines
    (a) environmental
    (b) design
    (c) engineering
    (d) quality
    (e) safety
- No cost participation

To contact GIDEP, write or call:

Government–Industry Data Exchange Program (GIDEP)
Officer in Charge
GIDEP Operations Center
Corona, California 91720
(714) 736-4677

FORMS CONTROL CAN INCREASE PRODUCTIVITY

It should be recognized that QC people spend nearly half their time with requirements that are not hardware. In other words, you are spending half your appraisal budget on paper shuffling. A count of all the forms and instructions QC people must handle, plus the time necessary for obtaining prints and specifications (and sometimes test equipment) will show you the accuracy of this statement. Government contracts, by nature, require much more paper. But many "company only" forms can be combined easily or eliminated. Many of the reasons for their existence are lost in the past. Forms should be rigidly controlled and completely reviewed and analyzed regularly. If acceptance people only record information vital to someone, they can typically increase their time usage by very significantly.

Table 3-2 is a forms evaluation checklist. It will

TABLE 3-2. Forms Evaluation Checklist

√ Does a repetitive need for the form exist?

√ Does the volume justify the generation of a form?

√ Is the need long-term or merely for the duration of a specific project or contract?

√ Will the form improve data collection of quality data?

√ Is the data captured by the form essential and relevant to increasing product quality or yield?

√ Does a similar form already exist in another department or division of the company?

√ Is the cost of the form (design, administration, printing, data processing, filing, and storage) less than the expected benefits?

√ Can two or more existing forms be combined (for example, a nonconforming material report and a material review board [MRB] form)?

√ Will the form simplify data collection, reduce errors, and eliminate repetitive entries?

√ Can the required data be entered directly on a terminal keyboard or read by a bar code reader?

help you decide whether or not a form is really needed.

OVERREACTION CAN INCREASE COSTS

Overreaction to an inspection escape is equivalent to the overreaction of production management to an inventory stockout (parts shortage). Typically, a defective item that has escaped detection by inspection, particularly if it has been picked up by a customer, leads to a tightening of all process controls, additional test procedures, and more intensive final inspection. Most of the time these added costs are an appeasement rather than a hard-nosed professional quality decision. Escapes do offer an opportunity to validate one's QC program and should be thoroughly and objectively investigated. It is, however, not appropriate to look for scapegoats or add unnecessary tests.

The management of QC involves the management of risk—be it sampling error risks or the risks of abbreviated testing—and cost. Effective QC program plans should not be shelved because of one possibly isolated incident. Where safety, performance, or other critical functions have been compromised, corrective action must be taken,

otherwise the QC manager should stand firm to prevent undue inflation of quality requirements and costs.

Keep cool when an inspection escape occurs. The hasty introduction of a costly test may not be worth the small risks involved in the long run.

Note: The justification of certain tests or procedures cannot be left up to only QC personnel. There may be a valid reason for a certain test, but the logic may be lost in time. Hence, a new QC person may judge it unnecessary and run into trouble. *Lesson:* Issue with the product profile the reason for each test.

COST-JUSTIFY CAPITAL EQUIPMENT ACQUISITION

The cost of quality control can frequently be reduced by the acquisition of labor-saving equipment. However, like all capital equipment, the capital outlay must be matched by economic and/or other benefits. The justification must be sufficiently detailed if prompt management approval is desired. Additionally, senior management often evaluates QC management by the quality of its capital appropriation requests. Table 3-3 provides a checklist to ensure that key factors have been considered.

The basic outline of a cost justification for QC capital equipment should contain the following elements:

1. Purpose (cost improvement, replacement, expanded capacity, technological need, environmental/regulatory).

2. Scope and summary of project (including purchase price and timing of expenditures).

3. Description of project including current practice, benefits of the new equipment, workload forecast (based on budget and five-year plan), expected annual cost savings (if applicable), expected annual operating costs, and installation expenses if significant.

4. Economic analysis using one of several quantitative techniques that consider the time value of money.

5. Conclusion, including an impact statement if appropriation request is not approved.

In preparing cost-benefit analyses, the following cautions should be observed:

● The equipment price should be based on a firm supplier quote with as long a validity period as

TABLE 3-3. Capital Equipment Guide Questions

1. Has all reasonable alternative equipment, including refurbishing existing machinery, been considered before selecting the chosen item?

2. Have quoted performance specifications been checked by independent tests or liaison with current users? How long has the machine been on the market? What are the limitations and soft spots of the machine?

3. Has equipment size and shape been considered from an operations point of view?

4. Does the unit require modification to operate on local electrical power? Is Underwriter's Laboratory approval required before installation? Does the unit comply with local and federal health and pollution control regulations?

5. Is the selected vendor reliable and geared to providing adequate after-sales service? Is quoted delivery time acceptable and realistic?

6. Have all appropriate options been considered? Does the machine have modularity of design to permit future growth? Is other ancillary equipment needed if the machine is acquired?

7. Is the work capacity of the machine consistent with current and forecasted workloads and other equipment planned for acquisition?

8. Are specialized sole source or costly materials or fuels required to utilize the machine? Are the terms of the licensing agreement (if any) acceptable?

9. Does the equipment require air conditioning, clean-air control, unusual water and air supplies, extraordinary foundations, etc.?

10. Are adequate supplier training, operating and maintenance manuals, and other key documentation available?

11. Is the equipment physically and functionally designed for servicing and maintainability? Are critical spare items such as computers likely to be available during the useful life of the equipment?

12. Are uptime guarantees and warranty provisions adequate? How much will an annual service contract cost?

---

possible. A price contingency may be included but should be explicitly identified.

- The project cost must include exchange, duty, freight, taxes if applicable, and installation and other expense costs. The salvage value of any surplus equipment should be noted but deducted from the capital cost of the project only if this is standard company policy.

- The claimed labor savings should be based only on variable costs. Fixed costs by definition will not be saved if the project is undertaken.

Note: Complex measuring equipment may have a significant learning curve associated with it, that is, the cost of learning how to use it.

- Ongoing maintenance, spares, and calibration costs should be considered in the analysis. Calibration is a very significant factor for QC measuring equipment.

- The economic life of the project must be consistent with changing technology trends and utilization rates. Company depreciation policy should also be used as a guide, since this is based on experience and business considerations. Some items of test equipment probably will be obsolete within three years.

- The basis for the claimed savings must be supported by analysis, accepted time standards, or other professionally recognized quantitative methods. A conservative approach is preferred since QC just cannot afford a political "white elephant."

- Any external financial assistance should be factored into the analysis (contract funded, federal tax exemptions, grants, and so on).

- The possibility of leasing the equipment should be considered because, under certain conditions, the tax advantages can be significant. The accounting department should be consulted when performing a lease/buy analysis.

> "If you need a piece of equipment but don't buy it, you pay for it even though you don't have it."
>
> Henry Ford

PHOTOGRAPHY CAN SLASH DOCUMENTATION COSTS

The old Chinese expression, "One picture is worth a thousand words," must have been written for quality control. Cost savings abound in a wide range of application areas, including:

- *Discrepant purchased material:* A single photo will eliminate a vendor's natural tendency to doubt incoming inspection results.

- *Failed parts analysis:* Color and/or black-and-white microphotos provide convincing evidence of failure mechanisms.

TABLE 3-4. Sample Capital Appropriation Request

To: Mr. U. R. Boss
From: Q. Manager
Subject: Acquisition of Alpha Corp. model 123 coordinate-measuring machine

Introduction and Purpose of Machine

Present requirements for competitive production of mechanical parts to high standards of precision necessitate that the quality control function keep up with the demand for greater inspection throughout.

As machined parts are becoming increasingly more complex with more features and tighter tolerances, conventional measuring techniques such as surface plate and height gauge methods are too costly, too slow, often inaccurate and error-prone, and therefore inadequate.

To achieve increased productivity at reduced costs with faster turnaround time of manufactured mechanical parts, it is proposed to purchase the model 123, computer-assisted three-axes coordinate-measuring machine (CMM).

System Description

The model 123 will cost $55,000 including all necessary probes and options. The F.O.B. point is our dock. Lead time is three months. The model 123 is a three-axes (x,y,z) coordinate-measuring machine (CMM) that is capable of measuring a number of dimensional parameters.

Characteristic data is obtained via the three-dimensional touch-signal probe that registers a point of measurement whenever and wherever the probe touches the work piece with ±0.0002″ (maximum error) repeatability.

The system's controller is the HP9825S desktop computer.

Alpha has developed a proprietory and an advanced operating system software package that optimizes and interfaces the model 123 CMM with the HP9825S computer. For this reason, the CMM must be bought as a complete system.

An easy-to-learn-and-use high-level programming language (HPL) ensures that no special programming skills are required to operate the CMM efficiently and effectively.

The ability to copy the entire contents of memory, including all programs, data, flags, special function keys, etc., onto the tape cartridge allows the user of the CMM to return to the identical operating environment at a later time, thus only once must a program for a specific part be generated.

The live keyboard of the HP9825S permits one to perform calculations, execute subroutines, list the current program, and examine or change program variables while a program is running.

The Alpha 123 coordinate-measuring machine also has the ability to register instantaneously a number of dimensional parameters, such as:

automatic plane alignment

automatic axis alignment

X-Y-Z coordinates

X-Y-Z coordinates from an imaginary datum point

polar/cartesian conversion

metric/inch referencing

Also included with the Alpha CMM system is a complete set of three-dimensional touch-signal probes.

Competition Comparison

An analysis was made comparing the Alpha coordinate-measuring machine with three other vendors. Whereas measuring capacity disqualified the Beta unit, price disqualified Pi and Omega CMMs.

TABLE 3-4. Continued

Specifically:

Measuring Capacity:	Alpha	Beta	Pi	Omega
	X Y Z	X Y Z	X Y Z	X Y Z
	28×24×18	24×22×18	13×24×16	18×28×28
Approx. Price	$55,000	$58,000	$60,000	$75,000
Field Service Available	Local	N.Y.	L.A.	Boston

The comparisons showed that overall the Alpha CMM is the best buy.

Highlights of Advantages of Coordinate-Measuring Machine

- Dramatic time savings are achieved with CMMs over traditional surface plate inspection. Typical ratios are 1:10.
- Better utilizing of manpower—low-skilled personnel can be used to perform complex inspection work due to sophisticated computer software assisting in the inspection task.
- Reduced need for complex holding fixtures that are expensive and time-consuming to manufacture.
- Errors because of human factors are reduced to a minimum, as speed, accuracy, and repeatability are a function of the CMM.
- The CMM can be used as a tool in dimensional-defect analysis.
- Complex mechanical engineering developments can be proofed-out easily and efficiently, therefore reducing development time.
- Vendor-supplied critical mechanical parts can be inspected quickly, therefore reducing time of disposition of incoming material.
- Reduction of many dedicated functional gauges that can only check one part or feature individually.

Return-on-Investment Justification

Mechanical parts incoming inspection and the "first-off" piece inspection areas can be singled out as those areas where inspection throughput is of the greatest importance; these two inspection areas directly influence the production flow and the manufacture of mechanical parts the most.

For instance, a complex part, such as a casting that is bought from an outside supplier, must go through incoming inspection. There, all drawing specifications and dimensions must be verified. As the complexity of the part increases, the inspection time increases proportionally. This then has a direct impact upon the entire delivery schedule of the part.

Considering the manufacture of a new part made on any numerical-controlled (NC) machine, it is self-evident that all errors must be detected immediately. Any error passed by at this stage has grave consequences since we are producing nonconforming parts *en masse*. Speed is of the essence so as to minimize NC machine downtime.

Here again, conventional inspection techniques are not adequate as they are slow, error prone, and costly, whereas a computer-aided coordinate-measuring machine is fast, and easy to operate.

(A) It is anticipated that 2000 castings per year will be processed through incoming inspection. In favor of conservatism only 15 lots of 50 castings (750 castings) are considered complex enough to warrant the use of the CMM. To each of the fifteen lots, sampling plan "MIL-STD-105D Inspection Level II" with an AQL of 1.0 must be applied. This determines the total number of castings per lot that must be inspected 100 percent for all dimensions.

Applying the above plan gives the following:

TABLE 3-4. Continued

(13 castings/lot) (15 lots/year) = 195 castings/year
that must be inspected 100 percent.

Using conventional inspection techniques requires on the average five hours inspection time per casting, or:

(195 castings/year) (5 hours/casting) = 975 hours/year

Using the CMM requires on the average 1 hour inspection time. *Note:* This includes any programming that may be required, or:

(195 castings/year) (1 hour/casting) = 195 hours/year

Net savings/year = (975−195) ($11.01*) = $8588

Note: * $11.01 rate/hour = $8.74 basic rate + 26% employee benefits.

(B) We presently utilize five NC machines on a twenty-four-hour-a-day basis. In order to allow for set-up time, maintenance, unscheduled idle time, etc., assume that all machines operate at 60 percent efficiency.

This gives (5 NC machines) (24 hours) (0.6 loading) (5 days) = 360 hours/week.

The average inspection time for tape proofout of the first-off piece using conventional inspection techniques is 26 hours/week.

Utilizing the CMM requires 5 hours/week of inspection time. *Note:* This includes all programming time.

Net savings of inspection time/week = (26 hours − 5 hours) = 21 hour/week or
(50 weeks/year) (21 hours/week) = 1050 hours/year

Net savings/year = (1050 hours/year) ($11.01 rate/hour) = $11,560

Total net savings/year = ($8588 + $11,560) = $20,148

Conclusion: Using a four-year economic life, the discounted cash-flow rate of return is 17 percent. Since this is within the acceptable band of rates of return set by management, it is highly recommended that we proceed with this appropriation. If the five-year sales forecast is substantially correct, the cost savings and ROI will be further increased.

Q. Manager

- *Measurement setups:* A photo can simplify repeating the setup and slash narrative writing time.

- *Acceptance standards:* Close-ups may be needed, but they can be very useful in subjective areas such as soldering, appearance, color, particle contamination, and so on.

- *Training:* Photos can be an excellent, relatively inexpensive training aid.

- *Qualification test:* Photographs of setups, real-time vibration, post-test appearance, etc., offer firm, visible documentation of test results and validity.

- *Discrepancy reporting:* Marked up photographs can simplify discrepancy reports and provide clearer guidance on required rework/repair actions.

- *Inspection work instructions:* 35mm slides keyed to taped instructions can help ensure error-free, consistent inspections.

- *Shipping damage:* Photographic documentation of items damaged in transit can streamline claims against carriers.

- *Documentation of completed work:* Photos can be used to document such varied requirements as modification implementation, warranty repairs, and change incorporation.

AVOID UNNECESSARY QUALITY REQUIREMENTS

Unnecessary quality control requirements can add up to high product costs. A seemingly harmless tightening of a tolerance can sometimes increase manufacturing and quality control costs exponentially. Therefore, great care is needed to avoid unnecessary requirements. To minimize these costs, follow these practices:

- Be sure that all specifications are really needed to satisfy the customer.
- Identify those specifications and standards that account for the greatest costs. Look at these requirements for reducing labor and material costs.
- Periodically examine inspection/test stations to ensure that they are still fulfilling their original hoped for benefits.

> Don't do effectively that which shouldn't be done at all.

- Minimize duplication of tests. If the sole reason for duplication is distrust, something is really wrong in your plant.
- Have vendors send you properly inspected components. Don't let your incoming inspection become their final inspection. Make sure your vendors understand that you mean business.
- Use material review decisions to ferret out potentially "overspecified" product requirements.
- Verify that a change in the specification doesn't create additional manufacturing and inspection problems.
- Find out if changing a tolerance for one operation will make a following or preceding operation easier and cheaper.

Remember that having requirements to create an excellent product is good, but setting standards for perfection can lead to excessive costs, delays, and reduced competitiveness.

EFFICIENT USE OF PERSONNEL RESOURCES

Your people are your most important asset—use them efficiently:

- The difference in salary between a quality engineer and a quality technologist or technician can be very significant. Since salaries and wages are usually the biggest single item in the quality budget, it is wise to verify that you have the correct mix of skills. This is a common industrial problem that quality control management must periodically address.

Case in Point: A high technology aerospace firm performed a survey to determine how effectively the skills of engineers were being used in quality engineering activities. It was found that quality engineers were spending only 40 to 50 percent of their time on engineering-level tasks; the remainder of their time was spent on tasks that were well within the capabilities of quality technicians. After appropriate job design techniques were applied, the amount of time spent on tasks requiring their expertise increased over 75 percent. Care must be taken, however, to include in the job those tasks that are potentially motivating to quality engineers.

- Don't force someone to sit and stare at the bottles or boxes passing by. Get a photoelectric cell, x-ray scanner, or automatic check-weigher. It's more reliable and less expensive. Low-grade inspectors using modern measuring equipment can slash QC costs. Test thickness from one side: Use ultrasonics. Test heat from afar: Modern sensing guns make this easy. Optical scanners can detect holes, control coatings, and more.
- Use the right tools. Optical comparators, accurate gauges, and automatic tramp-metal detectors beat spot-check inspections every time. Take a tip from the medical labs: Tests that previously took days now take minutes because of computerized testing routines.
- Don't take on tasks for political reasons or because they sound good. Keep your people working at productive QC activities.

WORK SAMPLING CAN REDUCE LOST TIME

How much time do your inspectors spend inspecting? How much time do they spend on clerical work, walking, or in just plain idleness? *Work sampling,* a tool that has been used by industrial engineers for years, can help you find out. The technique is based on sampling theory—an appropriate and randomly chosen sample will tend to have the same distribution pattern as the population from which it is drawn. In other words, over a sufficiently large sample, the percentage of time a person or machine is observed to be working, idle, or in any other specified activity or condition tends to equal the percentage of time spent in that activity or condition in a normal working day. Hence, work sampling is simply a series of random observations taken over a period of time, after which the sums of similar observations are compared to the total observations.

Most inspectors are required to do more than just inspect. To learn what an inspector does with his or her time, you might have such recognizable elements of activity as inspecting, waiting for work, marking pieces, clerical work on inspection records, material handling, and idle or personal time. Perhaps you want to know how much time a person spends at the bench, the optical comparator, on a surface plate, or at a coordinate-measuring machine.

However you classify activity elements, do it carefully. Take a short study for a day or two to work out the bugs. Where possible, take advantage of existing classifications such as accounting codes or job evaluation descriptions for different activities. Usually five to ten categories are sufficient. Limiting the list will make the study easier and more reliable.

A quality control engineer familiar with the operation but not connected directly with it would make an ideal unbiased observer. Review the elements and make sure he or she can recognize them on sight and without hesitation. If two or more observers cover the same area, be sure they identify the same element by the same name.

Case in Point: The test department in a medium-sized minicomputer firm was experiencing an unusually high waiting-time cost. After work sampling, it was found that a certain high-speed oscilloscope was in short supply. The purchase of three such pieces of test equipment for a grand total of $45,000 virtually eliminated the waiting-time problem. The ROI on the project was 34 percent and test cycle time was reduced by one-and-a-half days.

If desired, the time spent on various elements can be used to establish time standards for each element, giving you a handle on your department's operating efficiency. For instance, suppose inspection activities are confined to three elements. The work sampling shows element 1 takes 35 percent, element 2 takes 25 percent, and element 3 takes 40 percent of available time. Allowing thirty minutes a day for personal time (coffee break, personal needs), there is remaining a total of 450 minutes working time per day. Per element, this is 157.5 minutes, 112.5 minutes, and 180 minutes. Divide these values by the number of unit tasks accomplished and you have a workable time standard without using a stopwatch study, but it is close enough to give you data for a routine report on operating efficiency.

Efficiency is merely output hours (determined by the quantity of work accomplished) divided by input hours or hours available (allowing for personal needs). Also, knowing the standards and production schedules, you have the ingredients for computing manpower needs.

The procedure for performing work sampling is as follows:

1. Define the study's objective—for example, to determine personnel time utilization, test equipment utilization, or set time standards.

2. Set measures of production for correlation with study results and collect data on production or work rates for each day of the study.

3. Prepare definition of each element to be studied.

4. Do initial statistical work—for example, estimate percent of each work element.

5. Let management and others know what is being done and select and train QC engineers or other personnel.

6. Create form for recording information on study and collect data.

7. Make required number of random observations based on statistical criteria available in industrial engineering handbooks.

8. Evaluate study results.

9. Prepare a report, present results, and recommend corrective action.

Caution: It will not take people long to realize they are under direct observation, and this will raise many questions in their minds. If they fully understand what you are doing you may lose some accuracy, since a few people will pretend to be busy when you approach. On the other hand, full cooperation is always valuable, and most people will cooperate when they do understand. Whatever you do, don't try to deceive people. This is poor personnel relations and can backfire with disastrous results.

VALUE ANALYSIS

Value analysis involves examining a product or operation to eliminate any cost elements that are not essential to the effectiveness, utility, or marketability of the product or operation.

For a product, this involves simplifying the design, substituting lower-cost materials, improving reliability or durability where the company is subject to warranty costs, or eliminating unneeded parts. Value analysis is an engineering discipline that provides required functions at minimum cost with no degradation in required performance or quality.

When applied to QC operations, value analysis can provide ways to eliminate unneeded or expensive steps that do not contribute worthwhile benefits. Quality control is typically a ripe area for such an analysis. As a result, the QC manager can implement changes that speed up work, eliminate paperwork, and simplify procedures. Thus, value analysis can be an effective aid in deciding how to lower QC department operating costs.

Case in Point: A large Japanese manufacturing firm performed a major value analysis of a stereo system intended for the mass consumer market. The quality control department shaved off 9 percent of the factory cost by taking the following actions:

- reduced inspection and tests by 16 percent
- recommended the utilization of looser tolerances on several parts
- suggested a change in processing that increased yield and eliminated two production operations
- identified eight parts that could be purchased as standard catalogue items rather than custom parts
- acquired an automatic circuit board tester that had a payback period of one year.

Caution: An aggressive value engineering team can sometimes get carried away. Beware of product or processing changes that will adversely impact product integrity. QC must check out value engineering changes prior to full-scale introduction and advise designers of any pitfalls or deficiencies. The purpose of value engineering is to launch an organized attack on unnecessary costs and eliminate them. A company with an energetic quality control function ensuring the quality of its products and a diligent value engineering function, minimizing the cost of its products, will prosper because quality control and value engineering truly are partners for increasing productivity.

CONSIDER MICROFILM: SAVE SPACE AND REDUCE COSTS

Quality control generates and uses voluminous data such as inspection records, final test data, quality standards/specifications, and nonconforming material reports. This data must be readily retrievable and stored for considerable periods of time. When one considers product liability and regulatory-body requirements, the storage period can sometimes exceed fifteen years. *Microform*—a general term that includes the more commonly known term *microfilm*—systems, because of the space savings provided, have become relatively common in business, primarily for engineering drawings but quality control applications abound.

The purpose of microphotography is to preserve records, to reduce the space required to store voluminous data, and to facilitate the rapid retrieval of records at a reasonable cost.

The advantages of using a microform (microfilm, microfiche, aperture cards, film jackets) system are:

1. In the area of compactness, a 16mm roll of microfilm can contain 2000 to 3000 images, thus drastically saving floor space.
2. Documents can be reduced to a uniform size.
3. Files are more compact and more easily controlled.
4. Satellite and disaster files are more practical.
5. Costs are reduced (for example, documents may be studied on microfiche without requiring normal size prints).
6. Microform files can be updated faster and more easily than standard-sized ones.
7. When handled properly, microform also provides a durable storage medium superior to ordinary vellum or paper records.
8. Duplicates or enlargements can be made, depending on need. Enlargements of drawings, for example, may be useful in preparing inspection work instructions.
9. Automated file operations can be more readily accomplished.

Microform viewers are available for microfilm, microfiche, and aperture cards. Viewers without hard-copy capabilities are relatively inexpensive and allow the operator to insert the microform and obtain an enlarged image on a screen for study and examination. The limitation of this device is that it does not produce a hard copy. When copies are not required, this equipment has the advantages of low cost, small size, low power consumption, light weight, and portability. If hard copy is desired, the operator must take the microfilm to the reproduction facility or send it to a vendor that has the equipment for converting microform into hard copy.

The use of microfilming is cost effective when floor space is at a premium and documents are to be retained for several years. Microfilm is also cost effective when a disaster file must be maintained as a backup for the master file.

CUT THE COST OF APPRAISAL

The measurement technology field is exploding with new instruments that are more productive, more capable, more flexible, and more precise. With the many changes they must face these days, being aware of what is available is not always very high on management's priority list. Even for a task force with this as their primary responsibility, it would be a formidable challenge. Dedicated professionals in many disciplines are interested in and make note of advancements in measurement that come to their attention. Time, however, does not always allow adequate communication between individuals and groups on this topic.

With some exceptions, being aware of currently available measurement instrumentation is not a clearly assigned responsibility. All too often information is unequally spread across many disciplines and is supplied on a partisan basis. Each group may have a different characteristic that they feel should be their major concern.

Individual test technicians become experts in the major drawbacks of their instruments. In manufacturing, the feeling is often that if making the measurement cannot be avoided, a more productive operator-instrument system should be sought. The people responsible for repair and calibration are those most likely to be concerned with reliability, ease of repair, and parts availability. Others will be more interested in reducing the potential for operator error and making sure that measurements are accurate. Whoever is responsible for the affected budget will most likely want to know more about price alternatives. The exact

pattern of interest variation may differ from company to company; however, several points of view can be expected.

In many cases taking advantage of the latest measurement technology can mean astounding improvements in productivity. These improvements may come directly from automation, a reduction in operator involvement, faster operation, or less downtime. Indirectly, significant improvements in process control may evolve from greater capabilities, flexibility, and/or accuracy. For example, scrap, rework, and warranty costs may be reduced.

When is a company taking full advantage of this potential? Perhaps a checklist similar to the one that follows might assist in evaluation:

√ Is current measurement technology information available to and disseminated among employees and managers?

√ Do test equipment suppliers have an opportunity to make in-house presentations to users and management?

√ Is there an individual or task force that addresses the productivity improvement potential of new test and measurement instrumentation?

√ Are new instrumentation procurement decisions made by an individual with a narrow range of concerns, or is there input from all points of view?

√ Do personnel attend trade shows where there are large numbers of exhibitors of test and measurement instrumentation? This would allow evaluation of a large number of instruments in a short time.

√ Are measurement technology texts, periodicals, reports, and literature acquired and made readily available to personnel?

√ Is membership in societies related to measurement and automation technology encouraged?

√ Does updating test and measurement facilities play an integral part in intermediate-range plans and forecasts?

√ Is the economic success/failure of test and measurement instrumentation regularly measured and reported?

√ Do shop floor personnel have an opportunity to air their views concerning existing equipment?

LOOK INTO NONDESTRUCTIVE TESTING

Nondestructive testing (NDT) is testing without destroying the workpiece. The American Society for

Nondestructive Testing Inc. (ASNT) is more specific. "NDT is the examination of an object or material in any manner which will not impair its future usefulness. The purpose of the test may be to detect internal or external flaws, to measure geometric characteristics, to determine material structure or composition, or to measure or detect some of the object's or material's properties."

NDT can play an important part in reducing manufacturing and QC costs by detecting defective materials and parts before costly machining or processing is applied to them. Many materials and processes related to welding, brazing, bonding, forming, felt metal brazing, and the joining of different metals are being nondestructively inspected to determine the effectiveness of processes. NDT tests have often disclosed built-in problems related to new processes and materials.

Another major area where NDT has played an ever-increasing part in cost reduction and increased reliability is in the inspection of equipment being overhauled or tested at the place of installation. The purpose of the NDT test may be to detect internal or external flaws in parts or equipment, to measure thickness of materials, to determine material structure or composition, or to measure or detect any significant change in the equipment that could cause failure at a later date. These types of tests have been carried out in refineries, gas and oil pipelines, heavy industrial machinery, and other areas where it is less expensive to carry the tester to the equipment than move the equipment to the testing area.

There are many excellent nondestructive testing methods currently in use. These methods include radiography (x-rays), magnetic particle, eddy current, ultrasonic, and dye penetrants. New techniques are being studied, such as neutron radiography, color radiography, flash radiography (pulsed x-rays), holography, liquid crystals, and infrared-thermal techniques.

Will NDT-based in-process inspection or process control pay off for you? The answer really depends on the cost of not having it now.

Case in Point: In a weapons plant a $7500 ultrasonic system is used to examine the internal structure of steel plate just prior to a heating and severe ring-forming operation. The reason is to sort out material that wouldn't withstand the process without delamination. The ring-forming operation

costs $500 per part, so every piece of metal that fails during rolling means $500 worth of labor and machine time is lost. In the first four months, the ultrasonic system detected the tiny failure-causing flaws in fifteen pieces of metal before processing. The system has paid for itself within four months!

Each application needs to be evaluated individually. There are almost as many reasons for adding in-process NDT to a process as there are applications. Here are six principal reasons why NDT has been integrated into processes:

- *Increase product yield.* By removing unpassable product or sensing a problem early enough to correct a process, the effective capacity of a particular process can increase. Several producers have been able to classify products more closely and get premium prices for top-of-the-line goods.

- *Save on raw materials.* Faster response made possible by in-process NDT can reduce the need to "throw in a little extra just to be safe." Because the process can be controlled while the material is moving through it, process settings can be based on the average rather than the worst-case condition. In a galvanizing line, for example, a common practice was to lay the zinc on thickly in the middle of the sheet in order to be sure it was thick enough at the edges. Now, with NDT, control flow is increased at the edges and cut back toward the middle. Result: Less zinc is needed to provide a more uniform coating.

- *Less wasted production.* By weeding out the unpassable stock or adjusting the process downstream to make good product from out-of-spec material, the effective capacity of a plant is increased without a large capital expenditure.

- *Less danger to equipment and personnel.* Variations in starting stock can cause breakdowns of processing equipment and danger to personnel. Very often adding an NDT-based sensing element upstream can detect and either correct the condition or segregate out the faulty goods before they cause any harm.

- *More efficient production.* The limiting factor in establishing overall processing speeds is often a margin for error in one aspect of the process—the risk of underfillings, the need to add more heat because a small fraction of the material will need it, or slowing down so the worst-case material can be processed into good product. An in-process NDT system can either segregate out the worst-case material or allow the process to run more efficiently most of the time and compensate for the problem when it's on the line.

- *Better management information.* Measurements taken in the process of operating can give management valuable information about reject rates, sources of problems, and quality of material from different suppliers. If a computer is involved, this information is available as part of the process control function. The management information package is simply a matter of programming.

NDT technology is becoming more accessible and affordable to smaller manufacturers. Today, some equipment can be size-matched to an application. Several firms market magnetic particle units in portable, semimobile, and fixed configurations and modular fluorescent systems that can be geared to end-user needs. Portable ultrasonic flaw detectors cost from $3000 to $5500. Large units, which do not operate on batteries and are usually cart-mounted, cost from $6000 to $20,000. Portable ultrasonic thickness gauges cost from $1000 to $2500. Complete systems start from $10,000 to $20,000.

The quality manager must look at NDT for cost reduction. Any time you can reduce inspection costs or warranty costs you are increasing profits. The idea is to build quality into the product rather than inspect for quality at the end.

MEASURE INSPECTOR OUTPUT

At times, complaints are received from other operating departments that quality control is not "inspecting fast enough" and the backlogs at the inspection stations are too large. In evaluating the problem, sometimes it is noted that the actual output per man-hour of the inspection department has declined without the knowledge of the inspection supervisor or quality control manager. As a result, it is highly desirable for the department to measure the output per man-hour for each major inspection station to determine whether or not the inspection efficiency is declining, remaining the same, or improving. There are two basic computational techniques for computing output.

(1) Output per Man-Hour =
$$\frac{\text{Number of Lots Inspected}}{\text{Total Number of Man-Hours Worked}}$$

Case in Point: To demonstrate this equation, consider a five-person receiving inspection department. During a given week, four of the people worked each day, eight hours a day. The fifth was absent one day in that week. Thus, the total number of man-hours worked in the receiving inspection department can be determined as follows:

4 people × 5 days × 8 hours = 160
1 person × 4 days × 8 hours = 32
Total Man-Hours = 192 Man-Hours

If the Receiving Inspection Department inspected a total of 250 lots during the week, the output per man-hour would be:

$$\text{Output per Man-Hour} = \frac{250 \text{ Lots}}{192 \text{ Man-Hours}}$$
$$= 1.30 \text{ Lots/Man-Hour}$$

If this computation were performed in each preceding week, the supervisor can then determine if a detrimental trend in output is occurring. When this output per man-hour is plotted on a time-phased chart, the decline in output can be readily noted.

Pitfall to Avoid: This statistic can be very misleading if lots are of varying sizes or of significantly different inspection complexity. If sampling is employed on some lots and not on others, this can also distort the ratios. Generally speaking, output per man-hour is a macrostatistic indicating gross department performance.

(2) Unit Test Time = $\dfrac{\text{Number of Hours Worked}}{\text{Total Number of Units Tested}}$

This statistic is used when information on specific part numbers is required. Care must be taken to isolate out setup and troubleshooting time from test time. Poor product quality can also reduce this ratio, but it does not necessarily mean that test technician productivity is declining; it simply means yield is low.

Observation: Inspection productivity is greatest when there is a visible backlog of work. When units are not on the shelf, ready for inspection, you can expect unit inspection times to climb. The only way to avoid this syndrome is with a believable production control system.

Several actions can be initiated to improve output per man-hour for any given test/inspection station. These are:

- Establish a goal level of output.
- Isolate products and tasks that require long inspection or test durations (say, longer than one hour) or areas with heavy backlogs.
- Establish improved gauging/testing to speed up high volume or time-consuming inspection items.
- Reevaluate the inspection/test procedure.
- Utilize reduced inspection (reduced sample sizes) where practicable.
- Reduce duplication of inspection—vendor inspection versus your receiving inspection through certifications.
- Employ more effective work scheduling.
- Employ retest matrices—a retest matrix is simply a matrix showing where to recommence testing, if a failure has occurred and been repaired. It obviates the need for a complete retest.

Case in Point: A complex functional assembly used in hydro-generating stations experienced a high test cost. Investigation revealed that each time a failure occurred, the test technician retested the unit completely even though the failed circuit would have no effect on prior test results, which were acceptable. The quality engineer prepared a matrix showing technicians where (which paragraph number of the acceptance test procedure) to recommence testing after a particular subassembly failure was repaired. Test costs were reduced 20 percent.

COST REDUCTION CHECKLIST

There are innumerable ways to reduce operating and production costs or to increase efficiency. These techniques are usually based on one or a combination of the following actions.

1. Reduction in energy, materials, parts, or space needed.
2. Elimination of an operation, paper work, condition, or part.
3. Rearrangement of steps in an operation to increase efficiency.
4. Acceleration of an activity or operation by using improved systems, equipment, or procedures.
5. Substitution of a new technique, part, material, or person for another.

The checklist in Table 3-5 illustrates the preceding techniques for reducing costs.

TABLE 3-5. QC Cost Reduction Idea Checklist

1. Can you share test equipment with other departments, divisions, or local firms?
2. Can you reduce the number of reports produced and distributed?
3. Can you reduce document storage costs by microfilming, using a low-cost document center, or renting a remote or inexpensive storage building?
4. Can you effectively use programmable calculators or microcomputers to ease "number crunching" routines?
5. Can you reduce personnel turnover by some relatively inexpensive technique, such as more recognition of good work performed and attention to people's feelings?
6. Can you simplify or use surplus parts and materials to fabricate special test and inspection fixtures?
7. Do you have on-line video displays for frequent and immediate access of design, status, yield, or cost information?
8. Do you use part-time help to do routine work and reduce overhead expenses?
9. Do you maintain close ties with local schools and colleges for obtaining part-time help and new permanent people with minimum hiring costs?
10. Do you have an active campaign to obtain quality cost reduction ideas from the staff?
11. Do you have a file of standard QC write-ups for use in new proposals so that they don't have to be rewritten?
12. Do you set up mutually agreed-to objectives with your staff?
13. Can you utilize commercially available computer software packages for reliability or other analyses?
14. Are inspection points located to maximize the return on dollars spent for inspection?
15. Are inspection stations and methods engineered for the most efficient work accomplishment?
16. Could inspection and test record and data reporting functions be more efficiently performed using the computer or other modern data-handling devices?
17. Can nomographs, charts, or tables be used to reduce administrative burden on inspectors?

TABLE 3-5. Continued

18. Do you use flexible work schedules to reduce turnover, absenteeism, and tardiness?

19. Can a technical consultant be beneficially employed for certain special problems?

20. Do you constantly evaluate new measuring equipment to determine whether it is faster and more economical than existing equipment?

21. Can you rearrange measuring equipment to allow one inspector to utilize two or more machines or perform off-line tasks?

22. Could statistical quality control techniques be profitably used?

23. Could tests now being performed by outside laboratories be performed at less cost in-house or vice versa?

24. Could some tasks now being performed by highly paid inspectors or technicians be performed by lower-classification employees?

25. Can available training films be used to reduce quality control training costs?

REFERENCES

Broach, W. H. "Instrument Renting, Pros and Cons." *Electronic Instrumentation,* Feb. 1972.

Burroughs, K. "What You Should Know About Zero-Base Budgeting." *Machine Design,* May 11, 1978.

Crosby, P. B. "Cutting the Cost of Quality." *Industrial Education Institute,* 1967.

Conet, J. J. "Improving the Management of Quality Cost." *ASQC Technical Conference Transactions,* 1968.

King, W. D. "The Six Phases of Cost Reduction." *Business Horizons,* Aug. 1973.

Kivenko, K. "Testing Electronic Products Automatically." *Automation,* Nov. 1973.

Manske, F. A. "Cutting Costs—The Plan, the Attack, the Follow-Up." *Supervisory Management,* July 1970.

McMullen, J. W. "Quality Budget Control." *Industrial Quality Control,* May 1965.

Pyzdek, T. "Impact of Quality Cost Reduction on Profits." *Quality Progress,* Nov. 1976.

Randal, A. B. "Merits and Scope of Cost Reduction." *Engineering Digest,* May 1969.

Sprow, E. E. "Let Someone Else Test It." *Machine Design,* Feb. 8, 1973.

"Guide for Reducing Quality Costs." ASQC, 1977.

4

Cost-Effective Communication Techniques

Product quality characteristics are formally communicated to employees by means of drawings, specifications, and process documents. With the increasing use of computers, these written documents have been replaced or supplemented with magnetic tape, paper tape, or punched cards that control machines or processes. However, in order to control quality effectively it is also necessary to communicate to employees a wide range of other requirements that directly impact quality throughout the corporation (Figure 4-1). This communication normally takes the following forms:

- quality policies
- procedures
- quality standards
- work authorizations
- product quality program plans
- inspection work instructions
- monthly quality status reports
- meetings

The source of many industrial problems is breakdown of communications. Figure 4-2 demonstrates that information must be known to both the operator and the managerial/technical staff to be practiced. The idea is to move from categories B, C, D, and E to A.

Pragmatic application of the communication tools provided in this chapter will improve employee attitudes, decrease scrap and rework, and reduce wasteful organizational conflict.

SET COST-EFFECTIVE QUALITY POLICIES

The operation of the quality system must have a foundation. Quality policies formalize the QC activity, provide direction and broad goals, and determine the framework and constraints under which the QC function must work. Policy, well stated and well communicated, speeds up administrative action and reduces conflicts.

There are twelve key characteristics of policy (and of policy statements):

1. Is what management wants.
2. Does not tell how to proceed.
3. Reflects broad decisions.
4. Helps operating people make sound decisions in accordance with company goals.
5. Brings consistency into the operation.
6. Provides fair treatment to all people.
7. Points all parts of the total action in a single direction.
8. Provides a definite objective.
9. Relieves top executives from the job of making routine decisions.
10. Can be applied in most similar situations.
11. Answers the "what-to-do" part of a question.
12. Can be applied to many, rather than to one, situation.

Pitfall to Avoid: A quality policy should not be:

- how the quality control department functions.
- the personal views of quality and reliability organization managers.

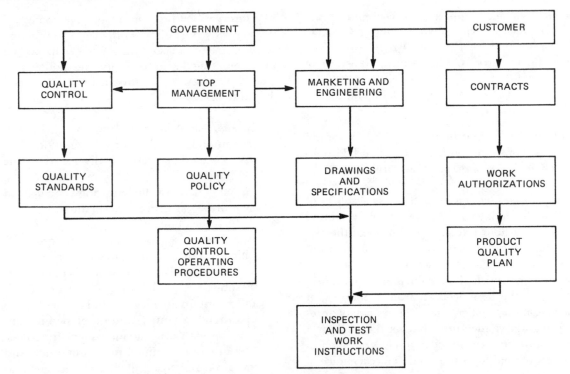

FIGURE 4-1. Hierarchy of Quality Communication Documents

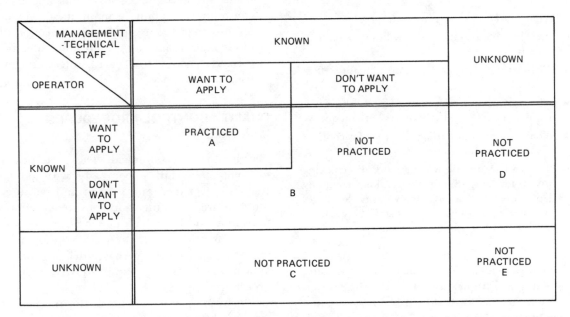

FIGURE 4-2. Many quality problems are communications problems. Area C, for example, shows that if information is known to management but not to the operator, the technique is not practiced.

- an unintended support to the concept that any individual or department within the company is solely responsible for quality.

- a quality control department propaganda handout to appease customer survey teams.

- a manual of procedures, standards, and/or detailed plans and objectives.

Quality policy cannot be prepared in a vacuum. It must be consistent with other established policies such as advertising, pricing, purchasing, public relations, and warranty.

A *policy statement* can be defined as a course of action to be followed consistently under stated conditions without reference to higher authority. A simple policy statement provided a foundation for a multimillion-dollar wood stove business: "You must be satisfied, or your money back."

Policy is the best decision from a number of choices. Quality policies form a system of integrated regulative measures that set the tone for a firm's approach to product quality. Very often a good deal of analysis is required before a choice of policy can be made. Fundamental questions must be answered:

- What markets do we intend to serve?

- How much are customers willing to pay for "quality"?

- Within these markets, how does quality affect income?

- What standards do we need to establish—quality leadership, competitiveness, or adequacy?

- What internal standards will we set for conduct of the quality function?

- How will we divide up the work of achieving fitness for use among the various company departments, among the various levels of supervision, between line and staff, between supervisors and nonsupervisors, between the company and its vendors?

Quality policies are the vehicles for responding to these important questions. Clearly, this is a job for top management aided by a business-oriented quality professional.

The content must be chosen to fit the individual company needs. Do not try to follow point by point the outline of another firm's policy. Decide first what is important for your company to state in writing, and then use other policies as a guide to the format.

Observation: It is useful to give some of the reasons why the policy is important to the organization. These "reasons why" can help people at the operating level to apply the policy intelligently. Quality policy statements can sometimes be quite brief.

Case in Point: A large multinational with several autonomous divisions operated in business areas that were so diverse that the 135-page corporate quality manual was discarded in favor of the following statement in each division's procedures manual:

"It is the policy of Company ABC to provide products, services and/or processes which will meet with our customer's quality requirements. To implement this policy, it is the objective of this Company to establish and maintain an effective and efficient quality program planned and developed in conjunction with other management functions. The program outlined in this manual, and the associated procedures, are designed to ensure that our customers' quality requirements are recognized, and that adequate control of this quality is maintained. Means are provided to ensure prompt detection of discrepancies and for timely and effective corrective action in all areas affecting contract performance."

QUALITY CONTROL PROCEDURES MANUALS

Because it is not economically feasible or practical to completely staff a company with only extremely clever men and women and because we must ensure continuity and consistency of operations in a world in which moving from job to job has become the accepted norm, we must provide operating personnel with guidelines, be they known as directives, administrative orders, or procedures.

Operating procedures persist for the same reason that human beings persist—because no one has yet figured out a way to get along without them. Procedures are written when the complexity of an operation or nonuniform application of a solution to a problem would prove uneconomical. To this end, most organized quality control programs require a procedures manual.

The quality manager's objective must be to interest and even excite employees about quality. To do this, the subject must be presented as something worthy and unique and, above all, something that involves everyone in the organization. If correctly designed, it can effectively present to the reader the full picture of total quality control.

Some of the benefits and characteristics of documented procedures are summarized below:

- Procedures are a means for management to describe in writing and in a readily accessible manner their required modes of operation.

- Procedures are not static things; they must be continuously adjusted in a controlled manner to meet changing times and conditions.

- Procedures are a reasonably simple vehicle for defining and standardizing proven methods.

- Operating procedures define how policy requirements are to be implemented in terms explicit enough to be clearly understood by employees, yet general enough to encourage professional approaches to assigned tasks.

- Procedures are a means of establishing continuity of operations when personnel changes occur and as a training aid for new employees.

- Procedures prevent "subject-to-change-without-notice" situations. This is particularly important in large, interdependent multifunctional organizations.

- Procedures provide a written standard to which operations may be audited.

- Procedures act as a ready reference.

- A QC procedures manual allows people to see their own responsibilities defined and interrelated with the roles of others.

- Another major value of a quality manual lies outside of one's own company. We have now fully entered the era of suppliers' quality assurance. Companies are required to give an account of their quality control organization and procedures to their customers so that a customer can determine the degree of confidence that can be placed on the supplier. The QC manual is an excellent vehicle for this purpose.

Bonus Benefits:

1. The fact that one is able to produce a manual to give visiting customers to read is a great time saver for quality managers.

2. A first-class QC manual in the hands of a sales department can be extremely effective. Sales can not only sell the product, they can also sell

the care and attention that will be associated with its manufacture. This is an important aspect that is often neglected.

ESTABLISHING A MANUALS PROGRAM

Before setting up a manuals program it is essential that certain factors be considered, for example:

- company size
- type of organizational structure
- type of industry: military, commercial, consumer market, high technology market
- available funds
- type of manuals: policies, procedures, instructions, or all three
- nature of product (unit price, sales volume)

In a complex organization consisting of a corporate group and several operating and staff divisions, it may be necessary to have a corporate quality policy in response to which the operating divisions would generate procedures. A further subdivision of procedures is the detailed work instructions that define and describe the steps to be taken in performing specific activities—how the job is done. Large companies may have three or more types of manuals; smaller companies may incorporate policies, procedures, and instructions in a single manual.

The manual being designed for a quality control program involved with U.S. military contracts must of necessity meet the requirements of specification MIL-Q-9858A, "Quality Program Requirements," or other equivalent document. In such cases, other support manuals may also be required, for example, quality standards manuals describing technical know-how on acceptance criteria for workmanship. On the other hand, in a small business in which good communications, a family spirit, and little or no staff turnover exist; where the chief quality control inspector is the owner, it is unlikely that a complex system of manuals will be needed. There may, however, be work instructions on important items and quality directives issued in memo form as the need arises.

The idea is to have a working, well-thumbed manual that permits employees to know what is expected of them. If the manual only comes out to settle arguments, you'd better take a cold, hard look at it.

Since the quality control department needs the

recognition and support of everyone to make the manuals accepted and therefore successful, it is mandatory that any manuals program have the full backing of top management. Top management speaks and understands in terms of dollars. The goal must be to show how good quality management, supported by clear-cut aims and objectives, and refined systems and procedures can save money. Since the funding of a manuals program will be of interest to the financial officer, the quality control department must be prepared to show why such a program needs to exist. Evidence can be gathered by monitoring failure costs in a small section, and, after sufficient information has been obtained, instituting some procedures and work instructions. A graphical representation of subsequent reduction in failures can be made. These figures will be more meaningful to the financial executive if shown as returns (reduction in failure costs) on investment (cost of producing procedures and instructions).

Caution: Do not allow yourself to become entangled in a hierarchy of manuals that you justify as a reason to keep an oversized writing staff employed. Let the economically justified manuals program determine the size of the staff.

> Procedures expand in proportion to the resources available.

If you have more procedures than absolutely necessary, you also have unnecessary expenditure of time and labor, an ever-increasing workload, and built-in booby traps in which customer and company auditors will have a field day reporting inadequate implementation of procedures.

Defining Responsibility for the Manuals

The preparation, coordination, and maintenance of quality control manuals should be the responsibility of a quality administration staff function reporting to the quality control manager. In cases where one or two types of manuals—say, a policy manual and an operating procedures manual—are required, a part-time writer with editing ability is necessary. Support people—a good typist and an illustrator (borrowed from the drafting office) for technical sketches or flow charts—can be a decided advantage.

For input material, harness your manual users' know-how. Allow them to fully participate in developing your procedures. Production personnel, who will be the most affected by quality procedures, will be more anxious to assist in implementing a manuals program that they have helped to create.

Effective Approaches and Techniques in Writing Procedures

An organized five-step approach to the development of a procedure can be summarized as follows:

1. *Problem definition:* The problem is clearly defined and objectives of the system to be developed are written.

2. *Preliminary survey:* All facts pertaining to the present system and procedures are gathered and analyzed. Facts are evaluated to determine whether:
   a. all activities are necessary and productive.
   b. flow of information is logical, direct, and controlled.
   c. all procedures are simple and easy to follow.

3. *Design:* The new or revised system and procedures are developed to accomplish the specified objectives. Each new procedure must be challenged from an effectiveness, cost, and time point of view.

4. *Implementation:* This includes:
   a. developing and writing the detailed standard instructions required to accomplish the procedures.
   b. validation of procedures.
   c. training operating personnel in the system and procedures.
   d. installing new or revised methods and debugging as necessary.

5. *Audit:* The new system is checked to determine that objectives are achieved.

In preparing manuals, think of the life cycle of the product—where it starts and ends before reaching the customer. The quality control manual should follow this cycle by taking into consideration those factors that can adversely affect quality, and by dwelling on the checkpoints necessary for material and paperwork flow, to assure adequate controls.

It is also necessary that organization charts and departmental responsibilities be included (usually in the front of the manual). Every worker likes to know where he or she fits into the company structure. It also gives one a better perspective of the over-all company picture, and how the functions in different departments fit together.

Layout, Content, and Style

Design a procedure page most suited to your company's needs. The page should be simple in its layout, and must bear such information as: effective date, procedure number, subject title, page number and revision code.

The basic content of any good procedure should include the following sections:

- purpose of the procedure
- basis of the procedure, including a statement of the fundamental principles upon which the procedure is based
- scope of the procedure
- responsibility for administration and performance of the procedure
- reporting relationships
- detailed instructions arranged in outline form for ease of reference and maintenance
- exhibits, flow charts, decision tables, and forms used with the procedure
- approval of the procedure by the affected department managers

Double- or one-and-one-half-spaced lines are easier to read. Number paragraphs and subparagraphs for quick reference. Underline headings for emphasis, and avoid getting involved in "sub-sub-sub-sub- . . . paragraphs"; by this time your reader will have forgotten what the main subject was about.

Pitfall to Avoid: The extent and nature of procedural coverage will vary from company to company. The content of QC manuals has been well covered in the literature.

Pitfall to Avoid: Some areas that are consistently inadequately covered or not mentioned at all include:

- evaluation of customer requests for quotation
- quality planning
- design and producibility reviews
- certification of special test equipment
- personnel training and certification
- packaging and shipping inspection
- handling of field product failure information
- customer accommodation and assistance

Since the quality control manual will have several unit procedures, a table of contents is necessary in which the titles, procedure numbers, effective dates, and revision status are identical to those appearing on the individual pages of the manual.

Each procedure must clearly define how things are to be done and by whom. Required action at group interfaces must be clearly described. Use language that is clear, concise, and easily understood by the operating personnel. The key is to *communicate.* Flow charts, not necessarily applicable to policies, are extremely useful for writing procedures; they can summarize a few pages and many words into a meaningful one-page picture (see Figure 4-3). They are especially useful for describing procedural systems that cross departmental boundaries. Include replicas of forms that are used in the quality program and called up in the procedures.

A manual should not exist merely to satisfy a customer requirement or so that the quality manager can demonstrate his or her prowess at writing. The manual is successful when those assigned copies of the manual keep it where it can readily be reached, if they pencil in additional notations

---

MEMORANDUM
September 18, 1984
To: Jane Doe
Subject: Quality Control Manual

Please find attached a draft copy of a new quality control procedure, for your review.

Please read it carefully, paying particular attention to the areas under your jurisdiction. There are some areas where a difference exists between what we are doing now and what we plan on doing as described in the text. The reasons for the changes were explained to you at the September 16 briefing.

When you are finished, pass along the document together with this memo to your other supervisors for review.

Please forward your comments to me no later than October 18. We will discuss your comments and concerns, if any, with you prior to release.

Quality Control Manager
R. J. Sweeney

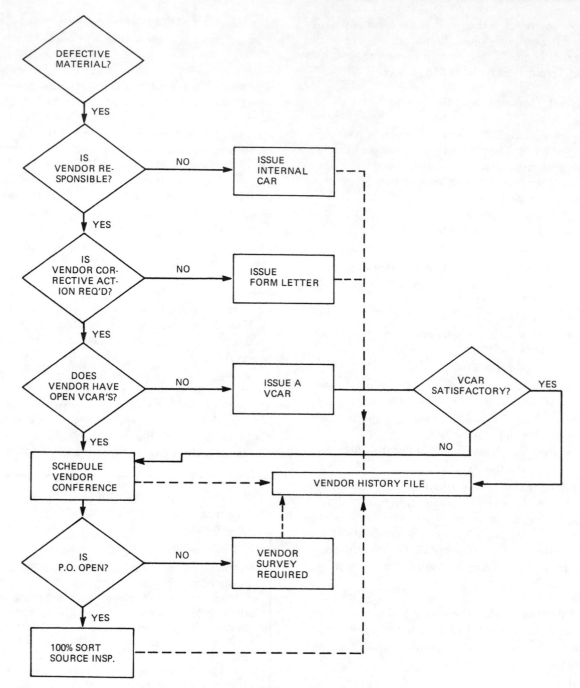

FIGURE 4-3. Vendor Corrective Action Flow Chart
Courtesy of Canadian Marconi Company.

when applicable, and if errors are promptly corrected.

Approval of Manuals

The individual quality procedures must bear the approval of the quality control manager, or representative, and/or the section heads reporting to him whose responsibility it will be to implement certain aspects of the quality program. It is crucial to have the concurrence of other affected department heads.

Printing and Distribution of Manuals

A large, heavy manual may put off readers to the point that they won't refer to it when they should. Use sturdy, attractive binders, with twelve to nineteen rings to avoid the tearing of pages that usually results from almost-continuous use. Binders are available in a choice of colors and may be imprinted with the company name and logo. In addition, paper must be capable of withstanding the wear and tear of every day usage. The typing and page collation would normally be done by the departmental secretary. Make sure that the typography of the finished product is attractive and readable. The quality manager should personally proofread each page. Avoid printing on both sides of the page; it is an expensive proposition, because changes cannot be readily incorporated without affecting both sides of the page. Individual procedures should be collected together in a leatherette or vinyl binder.

Policies should be distributed to top management and departmental heads; operating procedures to departmental heads, supervisors, and lead hands, where they must be made readily available to operators and inspectors.

It is important to assign a serial number to each manual and a record kept of each person receiving a copy. The task of making revisions then becomes fairly simple. Each recipient receives a copy of a revision page, which describes exactly what changes have taken place, and any modified or added pages.

Program Control and Follow-Up

Quality policies, once published, are relatively stable. Procedures, on the other hand, require modifications during implementation for many reasons: changing conditions or organizations, discovery of better methods, and unforeseen snags (see Figure 4-4). There is always the possibility that workers will find a different method, not intended by the released procedures. The target, therefore, should be to proceed with implementation and then follow up by means of quality audits, which ask the questions:

- What is the state of the quality program?
- Are the procedures effective?
- If not, why not?
- Is change necessary?
- Do personnel understand their responsibilities as written into the procedures?

This information must be fed back to supervision and management as well as to the procedure writer/coordinator, who needs to reassess the released procedure, discuss the implementations with the using areas, and decide whether or not revisions to procedures are required. The procedure/coordinator must also ensure that, at all times, the objectives of policies are being realized, regardless of the change in method of achievement.

> Bad procedures are more likely to be supplemented than repealed.

QUALITY STANDARDS: THE FOUNDATION OF CONTROL

Every moment of every day, we are surrounded by standards. The roof over our heads and the walls around us are supported by beams and joists of standard width and thickness; we wear clothing of standard sizes from our hats to our shoes. Standards govern the design and performance of the things we use: furniture, utilities, appliances, tools, and vehicles. There are even standards to monitor the cleanliness of the air we breathe. We eat food that must meet certain standards before it may be sold.

If standards are important to our individual lives, they are absolutely vital to our society. Without standards of measurement, there would not only be no commerce, but no science and no industry. Similarly, quality standards are funda-

PROBLEM	POSSIBLE CAUSES	INVENTORY OF SOLUTIONS
NOT FOLLOWED	OVER CONTROLS	REDUCE SCOPE OF DOCUMENT
	NOT AUDITED OR ENFORCED	SET UP PERIODIC AUDIT, REVIEW NEED
	DIFFERS FROM MANAGEMENT PRACTICE	CHANGE DOCUMENT (OR MANAGEMENT PRACTICE)
	NOT NEEDED	DELETE
	USER UNAWARE OF EQUIPMENT	THINK DISTRIBUTION LISTS THROUGH CAREFULLY
INCORRECTLY APPLIED	OVER CONTROLS	DELETE DOCUMENTS OR SELECTED PARTS
	AMBIGUOUS	REWRITE AND CLARIFY
	INSUFFICIENT TRAINING	PROVIDE NECESSARY TRAINING
	TOO COMPLEX	SPLIT INTO SEPARATE DOCUMENTS, RE-THINK APPROACH, REWRITE
INEFFECTIVE	CONCEPTUALLY WRONG	RE-EVALUATE
	NOT PROPERLY COORDINATED	DISCUSS WITH OTHER FUNCTIONS AND CORRECT DOCUMENT
	CHANGES NOT CONSIDERED	ENSURE EFFECTS OF CHANGES ARE INCORPORATED
	SUPERVISORS DOWNGRADE IMPORTANCE	INDOCTRINATE DEPARTMENTAL SUPERVISION
	TOO VAGUE	CLARIFY AND FILL IN DETAILS AS REQUIRED
	ADVERSE SIDE EFFECTS	USE SYSTEMS APPROACH
RESISTED	OVER CONTROLS	DELETE DOCUMENT OR SELECTED PARTS
	USERS NOT CONSULTED	REWRITE AFTER DISCUSSION WITH USERS
	DEHUMANIZES PERSONNEL	REWRITE OR DELETE
	DIFFERS FROM COMMON SENSE	DISCUSS WITH OPERATING PERSONNEL AND REVISE
	NOT MUTUALLY AGREED	ENSURE APPROVAL OF ALL AFFECTED ORGANIZATIONAL UNITS
INEFFICIENT	TOO COMPLEX, BUREAUCRATIC	FIND BETTER WAY, REVIEW FORMS, STREAMLINE, GET MIDDLEMEN OUT OF THE ACT
	TOO COSTLY	ASSESS COSTS AND BENEFITS
	TOO MANY CHANGES	DELETE AND DELEGATE AUTHORITY

FIGURE 4-4. QC Managers' Policy, Procedure, and Instruction Troubleshooting Tree

mental to the success of a quality system. Without a standard to compare against, we don't even know when we are out of control.

The initial step in eliminating the source of defects often calls for providing a control point where the defect makes its appearance. In nearly all cases, the starting point for work is with the standard that must be used. Sometimes, however, we find that no standard is actually defined. In these situations, individual judgment is the criterion for the operation. If the operation is sensitive to the differences in the ways the operation is performed by different operators, or even from time to time by any one operator, this is often the reason why the results fail to conform to a satisfactory product or situation. At other times, we may find that current standards are no longer valid because of a change in the process or in the end result requirements. A third major possibility may be that the present standard is too complex or is not easily understood.

There are two major applications of standards. One of them relates to how the job should be performed. This is a *process standard* and is usually not spelled out by the customer. The other is what the result should be, and it may apply to in-process stages or to finished products (sometimes referred to as *accept/reject criteria*).

Responsibility for Standards

The creation or adjustment of a standard involves a fundamental principle in quality control: Changes in the nature of the standard, or a new standard to replace the previous one, must come from the personnel responsible for the initial design of the process or product characteristic involved. Quality control may provide motivation and considerable assistance in instituting and coordinating these changes, but changes must primarily be the result of this type of cooperation, rather than an arbitrary input by the quality organization. If the supervisor of the activity involved is the usual source of technical directions at this point, the standard must be his or her basic responsibility.

The quality control organization's basic responsibility is to provide controls, but controls are not substitutes for supervision or for technical design responsibilities.

Determining the Necessity for a Standard

There are hundreds of individual performance criteria that must be met before a final product or a completed service is provided to the user or customer of an organization, but formal specifications or standards apply only to a minority of these criteria. If there were formal standards for every item of performance, the organization might be suffocated by observing and checking every detail of conformance. Specifications and standards, therefore, apply to a few highly sensitive operations rather than to the majority of such operations. Their purpose is to prevent changes or variations in conformance from entering the system at sensitive points, to reduce acceptance ambiguities, and to minimize disputes and conflicts.

Performance of a multitude of items is controlled by training, standard practice, the tools and facilities available, and supervisory attention. Standards cost time, money, and human resources to design and initiate in any organization, and they are very expensive to maintain if subjected to frequent changes occasioned by product design alterations. The best practice, therefore, is to keep them to an economic minimum. The same principle applies to controls, because a control cannot exist without a standard.

With this principle in mind, quality operations in resolving a defect source should first deal with the question of whether current standards are scrapped or revised. In some instances, a one-time investigation will suffice to reveal that the standards are not being effectively respected. This may occur because of a lack of an operator's familiarity with all details or to some change that he or she may have individually adopted in satisfying them.

Temporary or Fact-Finding Controls

If a preliminary investigation leaves some doubt as to how consistently the standard is being met by performance, a control requiring periodic sampling may have to be instituted on a temporary basis. As evidence accumulates and is interpreted either informally or with the formal techniques used in quality control, the pattern of results may indicate what action needs to be taken. Wide departures from the standard should be investigated to determine their cause. Whatever the result of the sampling, a decision must be made on whether the standard is now effective or whether performance variations need investigation to determine their cause.

If the standard is satisfactory but the observation of operations involving that standard shows that there are serious performance deviations "upstream" before the operations reaches the point covered by the standard, then we must look for the source of these extreme variations. Suppose, for example, that a point is found where serious departures or variations in performance occurred in an assembly operation. This makes it necessary to decide whether proper supervision can adjust the situation without imposing a formal standard. If possible and practical means exist to avoid a new formal standard, they should be employed and followed up to assure their effectiveness. The item in question, for example, might be the sequence in which certain bolts are tightened or a case in which subassemblies are formed into a final assembly. Operations to be standardized may also include the torque reading required on torque wrenches, allowable ranges of readings on test or inspection instruments for an individual item or operation, or the selection of a crucial tool. In fact, any limits of acceptable conditions or activities that could cause the result of an operation to be acceptable or unacceptable are subject to standardization. If "on-time" corrections cannot be applied, a standard may have to be devised.

Characteristics of Standards

A variety of possible standards are available. The characteristics of a useful standard are that it is readily understood and evaluated, that it has a proven relation to operations/performance, and, most important, that it is either provided by or is completely acceptable to the personnel responsible for the design or technical supervision of the operation to which it applies. Quality control is vitally concerned with a standard's capability of being evaluated on a sampling or audit basis.

Visual Standards. In some cases, troublesome operations require a visual judgment. These cases involve qualitative adjustments, which are often based on signs of wear or corrosion, the degree of surface roughness, the degree of disarrangement or distortion of a surface or structure, evidence of metal-to-metal impact or wear, scratches or gouges, discoloration, and a host of other variables that are not easily transferred into standardized or numerical data. Sensitive areas such as these call for the devising of a visual standard.

Visual standards may be photographs, diagrams, or a series of actual pieces of hardware to illustrate the varying degrees of acceptability or unacceptability resulting from the particular effect in question (see Figure 4-5). If from three to seven degrees or "steps" can be displayed from one end of the scale to the other, a choice of the limits of acceptability can be made by personnel who have experience in that particular operation. The standard may apply to the condition of the material as it enters the work station, or to its condition after the operations have been performed and before it travels on to the next point in the process.

The usefulness of the standards chosen must be proven by relating their observance to the results obtained at either the next step or as a final condition. The great value of newly established visual standards is the new visibility they usually afford of the sources of quality problems in the areas with which they deal. Their effect, after the organization has learned to observe them, will be to decrease the variation to conformance of requirements and to reduce the problems caused further along the line by undue variability. In some instances, either the customer or personnel who have been in contact with the customer should as-

Damage to Component Wires: Component wires should be free from nicks, cracks and other mechanical damage which causes a reduction in the cross sectional area or the current carrying capacity of the wire.

If, when viewed from any angle, a component wire is nicked or otherwise damaged so that its diameter is reduced by up to 20% this is a Class C Defect. If the diameter of the wire is reduced by more than 20% this is a Class B Defect.

If the wire is almost completely severed it is liable to failure and is unsuitable for use. This is a Class A Defect.

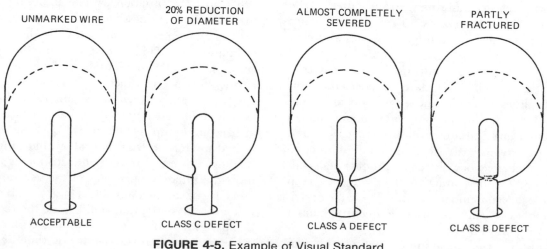

FIGURE 4-5. Example of Visual Standard
Courtesy of Canadian Marconi Company.

sist in making judgments as to the acceptability of various degrees and types of defect variations.

Adjustment of Standards

When a standard is first placed in use it should be considered tentative. Quality control can assist in making certain that the standard is appropriate and correct. The work performed should be sampled frequently and the results closely followed to the appropriate point where they may be evaluated for their effectiveness and relevancy. Quality control may have to document the relationship between results and the operations that produce them. If it is a quantitative standard, the technical tools of quality control will judge whether the limits of performance have been adequate in controlling the results. Evaluation may call for the standard to be adjusted either by changing the target or nominal value or by changing the limiting values of the operation. Evaluation also reveals whether operations may be expected to yield satisfactory results at their present level of performance.

Management of Follow-up Activities

After negotiating and establishing details of a standard for an activity or a condition that has been judged a troubled area, management must have a thorough understanding with supervisors regarding the directives that will be needed by operating personnel to consistently attain this standard. Operating personnel must be informed about what is wanted; they must be properly equipped and trained to meet the standard; and they must be informed whether or not their efforts result in a product that conforms to the standard. Emphasize repeatedly to supervisors the fact that control does not take the place of supervision. Operations must be carried on to meet standards whether or not a control sampling or auditing is anticipated.

Pitfalls to Avoid: Most production/QC conflict arises because of a lack of mutual acceptance of standards. To overcome this, certain actions must be taken:

- Ensure that quality standards are appropriate. Don't paint everything with the same brush, such as mixing government defense work with industrial production and applying the same quality standard. Gear standards to fitness for use.

- Use existing standards wherever possible—don't reinvent the wheel. Specialized firms, trade associations, and the government (especially the Defense Department) prepare a wide array of standards that can be used intact or with little modification.

- Keep idealists, academics, and theoreticians away from standards generation activity.

- Use the loosest possible standard consistent with market requirements.

- Write standards as clearly as possible; supplement with photos, sketches, and samples. Avoid ambiguities.

- Make sure that all affected departments comprehend the rationale behind the standard and accept the standard.

- Provide training in the application of the standard.

- As a matter of policy, enforce standards or change standards but don't continue to "accept as is" and ignore standards.

USE WORK AUTHORIZATIONS FOR COMMUNICATIONS AND CONTROL

Quality control management must ensure that only required and authorized work is performed if the cost of quality control is to be optimized. A system of work authorization can help prevent the following types of problems and productivity drains:

- Work on wrong tasks.

- Commencement of work before adequate quality planning takes place.

- Proceeding with special tests based on verbal go-ahead from a customer source inspector before receiving contractual coverage.

- Start of quality effort when valid job/charge numbers have not been established.

- Costly special-test jigs designed for a low-cost one-of-a-kind custom product.

A good work authorization system also provides a vehicle for communicating management, customer and/or government quality requirements. Typically, the following information is provided:

- QC cost budgets for major tasks

- product delivery schedule (that is, dates for final test)

4. *Business Outlook.* New programs, proposals, sales activities, and other noteworthy items.

5. *Cost Reduction Activities.* Implementation progress and results of QC cost reduction activity.

6. *General Operations.* General administrative subjects including significant accomplishments.

7. *News Memo Items.* Appropriate information that could be included in the quarterly Quality and Reliability Assurance News Memo sent to other departments or the company newspaper. If there is nothing to report under any of the seven headings of the report, the heading should be listed and the wording "nothing significant to report" written under the heading.

Conduct Efficient Meetings

A meeting is a golden opportunity for improving interdepartmental communications and mutual understanding and resolving quality problems. It

TABLE 4-1. Quality Topics for Monthly Report

- Preventive action activity
- Major corrective action activity
- High failure rate part numbers
- Significant engineering/design problems
- Significant piece part problems
- Configuration control, paperwork errors
- Prime workmanship discrepancies
- Personnel motivation/morale
- Burn-in findings, results of environmental tests
- Failure analysis, special investigations
- Use of sampling and other statistical techniques
- Analysis of field failures
- Rework, retest, scrap information
- Test equipment certification, calibration problems
- Component selection
- Organizational difficulties, communication problems
- Job environment: housekeeping, benches, space, lighting
- Adequacy of quality control operating procedures
- Materials and special progress problems
- Parts protection, material handling
- Outgoing quality level
- Follow-up/resolution of reported problems

is a vital communication element of a sound quality program. A meeting adds the human touch to

written quality policies, procedures, and standards.

Quality control people spend a lot of time in meetings discussing such things as inspection plans, nonconforming material, vendor problems, new government standards, and reliability program status. It is vital that this time be well spent and that active employee participation is achieved. Here are some ground rules for making your meetings more productive, inspiring, and efficient:

- Don't call a meeting unless there is a definite need for it and a decision can result from it.
- Don't invite anyone who does not have a say in the issue.
- Invite people who have the details, such as shop floor inspectors, when required.
- Circulate an agenda in advance so that people can be adequately prepared.
- Insist on punctuality.
- Stick to the topic(s) under discussion.
- Let everyone have his or her fair share of floor time.
- Don't insult, embarrass, or back anyone into a corner.
- Use a firm, mature chairperson to keep the meeting focused on the agenda.
- Send out minutes the same day—include action items for follow-up, designate responsible persons, and set due dates.

Pitfall to Avoid: Improperly conducted meetings may not only be inefficient, they can lead to demotivation, loss of direction, and confusion. Under no circumstances should a meeting become a win-lose confrontation (between production and QC, for example).

IF ALL ELSE FAILS—TRY DIRECT COMMUNICATIONS

As in all aspects of management practice, communication during the planning phase is crucial. Face-to-face communication is very important, but don't forget about visual communication—by use of the sample prototype—when words and drawings are inadequate.

Case in Point: A medium-sized manufacturing company was required to make a quantum-like jump in technology in order to get into the videotape recorder business. Since it required eighteen to twenty-four months to design and debug a videotape set of its own, there was considerable time to prepare the production units for their part in the implementation. The design group took the following communications measures. They are presented in the order of timing.

- Started a training program for the design team by meeting as a group and making a list of contributive seminars.
- Informed the sales unit by letter of the expected cost and the proposed sales features.
- By telephone, arranged a meeting for key engineers, industrial designers, quality engineers, and sales planners in order to work out objectives for the design unit. These were formalized in a form used for new products and sent to the general manager for approval.
- Advised inspection and styling groups verbally, then by letter, of the critical dimensions for the inside of the cabinet and of the special ventilation required.
- Sent a letter to the production and QC departments advising them of the need for new facilities, recommending that a separate production line be established for videotape units, including automatic test, and offering to run courses for technical personnel.
- Held a meeting with co-managers to develop a

final overall schedule for all major activities. Copies were made and sent to all managers and supervisors who would be concerned in any way with the upcoming change.

- The field servicing unit was shown a prototype and invited to make comments, which were recorded in a maintainability report.
- A general meeting was held for all supervisors concerned, explaining the expected impact of the new technology. They were encouraged to make preparations on their own initiative.
- A training session was held for the nontechnical managers and supervisors in order to communicate the basics of the innovation being planned.
- Advance release of drawings was made whenever possible, followed by a final release on specific data of all drawings needed to communicate the technical specifications of the design and to enhance planning activity.

Gradual introduction of the innovation was achieved by making maximum use of the available time to inform QC and production units many months in advance of the time they would actually be affected. This was done without any lengthening of the overall time required. There also appears to have been considerable involvement of the people who would be affected by the change, and this may have motivated them to help carry it out.

REFERENCES

Berkwitt, G. J. "Is the Policy Manual Obsolete?" *Dun's Review,* June 1969.

Carlsen, R. D., J. Gerber, and J. F. McHugh. *Manual of Quality Assurance Procedures and Forms.* Englewood Cliffs, N.J.: Prentice-Hall, 1981.

Crosby, P. B. *Quality Is Free.* New York: McGraw-Hill, 1979.

Erhardt, C. C. "How to Prepare a Quality Control Manual." *Industrial Quality Control,* Jan. 1965.

Harris, D., and F. B. Chaney. "Human Factors in Quality Assurance." *Autonetics Division Pub. No. P7-2787/501,* 1966.

Holmes, J. "Quality Manuals." *Quality,* n.d., 1968.

Topp, J. P. "Effective Communication—Its Relationship to Employee Performance and to Corrective Action," December 1967.

Turnbull, D. "The Manual—Why?" *Quality,* March 1980.

5

Planning a Dynamic Quality Program

Forecasting the future and determining how to take advantage of what it has to offer has long been one of the important functions of management. This function is called *planning*.

According to one definition, planning is "thinking about the consequences of your actions before you make them." Planning has also been defined as "thought in advance of action, resulting in a proposed method or scheme of action that includes classification of objectives, visualization of needs, and determination of the most advantageous course in terms of policies, programs, resources, and goals."

> For a quality product:
>
> D
> P L A N   A H E A

The technology explosion, resulting in an exponential increase in manufacturing techniques, processes, and methods, has made planning necessary at the operations level as well as at the corporate level. Today's quality manager lives and works in a complex environment. International competition, inflation, consumerism, and government regulation are powerful external forces. Bringing together the skills required in this setting, orienting them properly, and ensuring that plant goals and corporate objectives are met within the applicable financial and time parameters requires a meaningful plan of action that can be evaluated, approved, used for communication and control, and revised as necessary.

Planning offers the following benefits:

- *Direction.* A plan gives direction to the manufacturing/quality organization's efforts.
- *Standards.* Planning provides standards against which to measure project progress.
- *Cost reduction.* An integrated, well-conceived quality plan optimizes quality costs and avoids duplication of effort.
- *Unity.* The planning activity itself, as well as the resulting plans, result in a unified effort to achieve goals.
- *Time.* Well-prepared plans save time in making policy decisions. Any proposed course of action is evaluated in terms of its relevance to the overall plan.
- *Morale and productivity.* Employees and management react favorably to an increased sense of direction. Employees are more productive because they feel their efforts have a purpose, and management effectiveness increases.
- *Customer satisfaction.* A quality plan considers customer needs and requirements at the earliest possible phase of contract performance.

In Chapter 5, we explore the major technical tools involved in quality planning along with a rather large sprinkling of Cautions and Pitfalls to Avoid.

STRATEGIC PLANNING PROVIDES THE FOUNDATION

Long-range plans (five years or more) are prepared to guide the company in achieving ultimate or long-term objectives such as a reputation for

TABLE 5-1. Some Principles of Good Product Quality Planning

- Clearly identify your assumptions.
- Cover risky areas such as product qualification by contingency plans.
- Break the quality control job into subtasks such as procurement quality control.
- Express a plan in quantitative terms such as milestones, budgets, AQLs.
- Make sure suppliers are aware of expected quality levels.
- Give due attention to inspector and test technician training.
- Be aware that while every plan indicates an intent to attain a future objective, it must be based on, and can be no better than, present understanding.
- Be realistic; don't prepare pie-in-the-sky quality plans that can't be achieved.
- Coordinate quality planning with other organizational units.
- Extend plans as far into the future as you can predict reasonably and control effectively.
- Allow adequate time for management approval of capital equipment.
- Do not assume an ability to control events in the future that you do not control today.
- Provide for customer interfaces and special requirements such as source inspection, design review, or test procedure approval.
- Have product quality plans approved by those functions affected.
- Be prepared to change plans when required.

quality products, increased return on investment, or greater market share. Long-range plans set strategic goals rather than prescribe operational means for the achievement of these goals. Strategic quality program planning is vital to the continuing profitability of the firm. For instance, the pressures for safer, cleaner, and more reliable products are becoming stronger each year. Ways must be found to meet these increasing demands and still remain competitive.

To improve quality and reduce quality costs, there has to be a trigger for making changes to the status quo. Use the firm's strategic plan to force changes; include strategic quality and quality cost improvement plans (Figure 5-1). This gives product quality and quality costs the required management visibility, often lacking in many organizations. Because quality and quality cost improvements are set forth as business objectives (along with the more conventional business objectives) against which management performance is evaluated, there is effective motivation for action.

The quality manager must develop strategic quality plans that will assure continuous improvement of quality costs. This program must be integrated into the total company planning activities. Strategic quality planning is a continuous process of evaluations, decisions, and actions. All activities, customer demands, competitors' activities, the history of the quality role, and the future quality role must be considered in this planning. Strategic planning involves analysis to determine a strategy and actions to implement the strategy. Some of the advantages of strategic quality planning activities are:

- It forces quality management to look five or more years into the future.
- It will reduce planning time once it has been started because it is a continuous cycle.
- It is realistic because it attempts to consider all variables.
- It will result in a stronger quality program because it encourages involvement by other departments and vice versa.
- It will improve quality decisions because of the necessary evaluation of many alternatives.

Case in Point: A manufacturer of a complex electronics equipment used in air traffic control forecast a 37 percent sales growth rate over a five-year period. Armed with this strategic information, the director of quality initiated a soldering training school for both operators and inspectors. Setting up the school was not expensive, and its timely availability greatly enhanced the firm's ability to meet production delivery schedules at acceptable quality costs.

The quality costs on this project were, in fact, 11 percent below traditional costs.

Caution: Not all firms prepare strategic plans. In this case, it is folly for the quality manager to make a five-year plan solely for the QC department. She must plan in the same manner as all other departments. In the long run she might try to get the firm to consider strategic planning as a management tool.

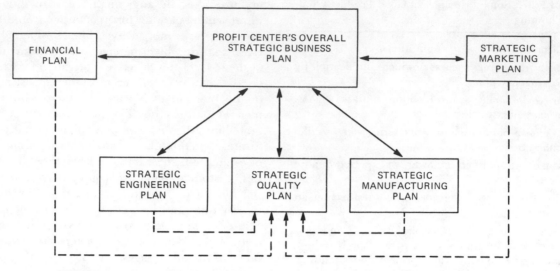

FIGURE 5-1. Relation of Strategic Quality Plan to Long-Range Plans
Courtesy of ASQC from the publication *Guide for Reducing Quality Costs,* 1977.

THE STRATEGIC PLANNING PROCESS

The basic steps in strategic planning are:

- Review past performance and present position.
- Appraise the environment.
- Set objectives.
- Select a strategy.
- Implement the strategic program.
- Report and evaluate the plan.
- Modify the plan as required.

The final step in the cycle provides needed inputs for the first step so planning becomes a continuous process. Following are general considerations for accomplishing each step in the cycle.

Review Past Performance and Present Position

A thorough review provides a realistic assessment of past performance, current conditions, and future potential. Typical indicators of the actual situation that should be reviewed are customer complaints, quality costs, reject rates, scrap rates, and test results. One good tool for making the review is the quality audit, which points out weaknesses in quality of manufacture, product design, or other aspects of the overall quality program. Ask:

√ What kind of quality program do we have?
√ Why this quality program?

√ What explains success or lack of it?
√ How do quality functions respond to changing product demands, shifting markets, and diversification?
√ How are the activities of QC integrated with other departments to ensure that quality standards are met?

Answering these questions will raise other revealing questions, point out performance against past objectives, and provide the necessary framework for effective planning.

The degree of research that goes into the review varies with each situation, but it is critical that the review be undertaken. You have to know where you have been and where you are now in order to decide where you should be in the future. Computers now make it much easier to obtain information on past performance.

Appraise the Environment

There are numerous environmental factors that may interact significantly with the quality programs. Typical examples are:

- the activities of other departments
- the quality performance of vendors
- changes in customer demands
- business and economic trends
- availability of capital funds
- new safety and liability regulations

- availability of skilled manpower
- actions of competitors

By distinguishing the controllable factors from the uncontrollable ones, evaluating the potential implications of each and continually monitoring the environment, the quality planning function can better understand and include their effect in the total planning program.

Set Objectives

From the status review and environmental information, the strengths and weaknesses of the quality program should be known. Specific objectives for improvement (with target completion dates) can now be established.

The objectives should include means of maintaining the strengths and improving the weak areas. Typical quality objectives relate to:

- quality performance of vendors
- yield rates for processes
- quality levels for products
- quality costs
- quality levels for customers

Give attention to both short- and long-range objectives including priorities for action. Review objectives frequently so they can be altered if environmental or other factors change.

Select a Strategy

Once clear objectives have been established, a definite strategy should be formulated and clearly stated.

- Consider all possible ways of accomplishing the objectives and develop a group of alternative strategies. Use pertinent records, reports, experience, and other company strategies.
- Evaluate all the alternatives that appear to have practical application. Be realistic and consider the effect on other departments.
- Select the final strategy and prepare the strategy statement. Review:
  1. consistency with other company strategies
  2. communicable aspects of the strategy
  3. assumptions behind the strategy
  4. most difficult part to implement
  5. most significant aspects of the strategy that differ from previous efforts
  6. economics of the strategy

Thorough consideration of the steps for selecting a strategy will maximize the probability of attaining the goals.

Implement the Strategic Program

Planning for the implementation of the strategy is the most important step of the planning process. Do the following to implement programs effectively:

√ Assign project action teams that make best utilization of the available human resource abilities.

√ Make team members aware of the importance of the project and their respective responsibilities.

√ Clearly define and describe the project, including publishing of schedules, responsibilities, and milestones.

√ Hold reviews to determine project schedule.

√ Remain flexible in the project to maintain direction toward the established objective.

√ Report and feed back the actions and results of the program.

Continuous measurement of the overall action program is essential to maintaining its effectiveness and sustaining it as a long-range management tool.

Report and Evaluate the Plan

The final step in the planning cycle is integrating the strategic quality plan into the total strategic plan and evaluating the costs and benefits of the plan. The reporting of the plan should include three documented features:

1. Summary report of all strategies, including descriptions, cost/benefits, due dates, and approval signatures.
2. Individual report of each strategy identifying justification, total costs, required resources, schedules, and approval signatures.
3. Regular status report of all strategies. Any necessary changes or adjustments should be reported.

Analysis and measurement of the effectiveness of the program provides guidance in managing the present program and direction for future strategic planning.

INTERMEDIATE-RANGE PLANNING BRIDGES THE GAP

The *intermediate-range plan,* or *business plan,* as it is sometimes called, serves some of the purposes of the long-range plan and some of those generally reserved for the annual plan. In planning long-range strategy, some goals difficult to set for a five-year period may be possible over a three-year term. Such goals are included in the intermediate plan. As an example, suppose a company intends to upgrade its facilities but cannot predict the type of equipment available at the end of five years. Instead, the company may set an intermediate goal of replacing its milling machines within three years.

Conversely, certain aspects of annual or immediate objective planning may be feasible over a period as long as three years. Wages serve as an example. Suppose that a company signs a three-year labor agreement. With this knowledge of their labor costs, management can establish certain immediate objectives, such as greater use of overtime to reduce the fringe benefit costs connected with hiring new employees.

Case in Point: An appliance manufacturer located in the Midwest made a conscious decision to buy rather than make piece parts and components. The decision was based on expected growth rates, cash and inventory factors, plant space constraints, and in-plant costs. The changeover was to be phased over three years. The implications for QC involved the following:

- QC would need to beef up incoming inspection capability.
- Several source inspectors would have to be acquired and trained.
- New purchase order QC provisions would need to be prepared.
- Additional quality controls regarding vendor tooling, first-article inspection, and certifications needed development and implementation.
- Existing shop inspectors would have to be transferred to other departments and retrained.

The use of intermediate plans varies from one company to the next. Some companies stress long-range goals in their intermediate planning, while others emphasize immediate objectives. This difference in practice should not be confused with the occasional employment of a three-year period for long-range planning.

Case in Point: A large international manufacturer of home appliances wanted to increase its return on invested capital (assets) over a three-year period. For competitive reasons, prices could rise only at the rate of inflation so that the improvement could be brought about either in improved profit margins or turnover or a combination of both.

$$\text{Rate of return on invested capital} = \frac{\text{profit}}{\text{sales}} \text{ (margin)} \times \frac{\text{sales}}{\text{assets}} \text{ (turnover)}$$

The planning sequence would be as is shown in Figure 5-2.

In this example, sales increase by 25 percent, but permissible assets remain the same. Thus, the asset turnover ratio must be improved. This can be accomplished by reducing fixed assets (capital equipment), which is unlikely, or by improving control over receivables and inventories. In the case of inventories, QC can help by introducing a parts standardization program, reducing inspection/test queue times in the factory, and improving purchased part quality. General and administrative (G & A) expense, as usual, does not decrease, nor do fixed costs. The QC budget has been left untouched, but, clearly, QC will have to assist in reducing production costs by emphasizing defect prevention. Manufacturing makes its contribution by economies of scale (25 percent sales increase helps learning curve), automation, and make/buy decisions. Quality control's greatest input here is to improve yields and reduce scrap, repair, and rework. This can be quantified and compared against targets.

Figure 5-2 illustrates the basic philosophy of *establishing the goal first,* and then programming the action necessary to attain that goal, rather than building the programs and action first and allowing the objective to become whatever is left at the end. Obviously, working in this sequence may produce unrealistic cost and expense reduction goals. This necessitates backtracking to previous steps to discover feasible combinations of actions. Planning is an iterative process.

ANNUAL PLANNING

Annual or immediate objective plans are developed to set the immediate operational goals neces-

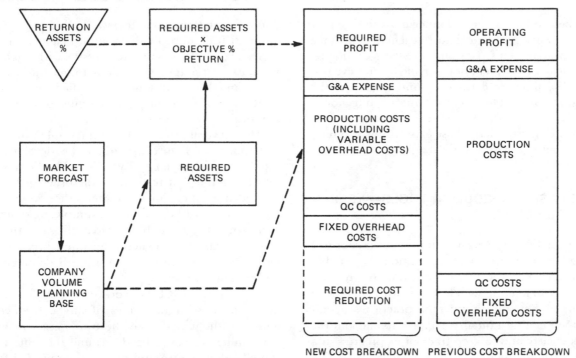

FIGURE 5-2. Costs and Return on Investment

sary to reach intermediate and long-range objectives. Most companies use a one-year accounting cycle, which coincides with the annual planning period. The annual plan commits company funds and other resources to the attainment of short-term goals. Funds are allocated directly to the departments responsible for taking action, and operating personnel are given planned courses of action to which to commit their efforts. The annual plan (budget) is covered in detail in Chapter 3.

On the operational side, the annual plan includes:

- product-design planning
- manufacturing planning
- procurement planning
- process control planning
- major facilities planning
- measuring and equipment planning
- manpower planning
- sales and service planning

MURPHY'S LAW AND QUALITY PLANNING

There are many reasons why the best-made quality plans can go awry. Unexpected failures, engineering changes, hold orders, inspector absenteeism, test facility breakdowns, and personnel training are typical examples. Of course, all those associated with quality control know the truth inherent in Murphy's Law: "If something can go wrong, it will." The following should be indelibly inscribed in the quality planner's notebook:

1. Tolerances will accumulate unidirectionally toward maximum difficulty of assembly.

2. Any arithmetic error that can creep in, will. It will be in the direction that will do the most damage to the calculation.

3. Suggestions made by the Value Analysis group will increase costs and reduce capabilities.

4. After spending months convincing engineering to perform a high temperature test, the chamber control system will go out of control.

5. A dropped tool will land where it can do the most damage. (Also known as the law of selective gravitation.)

6. The probability of a dimension being omitted from a drawing is directly proportional to its importance.

7. Interchangeable parts won't.

8. After extensive failure analysis, it will be found that the test jig was the primary cause of failure.

The product quality planner must foresee possible quality problems and bottlenecks and take preventative steps. Certain problems cannot be specifically identified, but provide for this eventuality by allowing extra time and money in the program plan. The extent of the contingency is determined by past experience with similar programs. If no experience base exists, think carefully about being too optimistic.

USE BASIC SCHEDULING TOOLS—KEEP THINGS SIMPLE

Some quality planners maintain that the course of design, test, and expenditure cannot be reliably predicted. Yet, the success of a quality program depends on making such forecasts with reasonable accuracy. Experience and a few practical scheduling tools enable a quality engineer to map out the work clearly and to keep track of its progress in a systematic manner.

PERT Charts

Consider a project made up of, say, eight tasks: specification review, functional test jig design, software test programming, vibration fixture design, packaging design, jig and fixture construction, debug and testing, and test procedure writing. How can the best picture be made of the relationships between these tasks and of the order in which they must be done?

One solution to this problem is a PERT (Program Evaluation and Review Technique) diagram. PERT can be made as sophisticated as necessary. You don't have to wrestle with highly technical computerized versions to get the benefits from this technique. Simplified forms of PERT are of great help in planning projects of any size.

After several trials, a diagram similar to the one shown in Figure 5-3 might be developed. Each task is represented by a line. The lines are joined together left-to-right in the order of their dependence upon one another—the order in which they must be done. For example, jig design and fixture design can be started at the same time. But the writing of the acceptance test procedure generally cannot be undertaken until debugging and testing is finished.

The rough PERT network of Figure 5-3 has been drawn with task lines of any convenient length, without regard to the time necessary for performing the task. To determine the time required for the entire project, the time needed for each task must be estimated. These times, in months, are noted on the diagram. The overall time for completion can now be found by tracing through the network from start to finish, using all possible direct routes and adding up the total time for each route. The path that requires the longest time is called the *critical path*, and this path determines the project duration.

What is the critical path here? The longest is the one through review, programming, and debug. This path, requiring five months, is the critical path. If the assumptions on which the net-

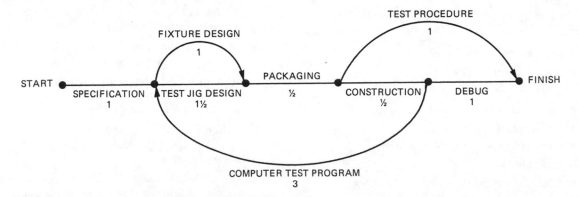

FIGURE 5-3. An elementary PERT diagram is all that is needed to picture the flow of tasks in a project and to determine a rough estimate of project duration. The various tasks are positioned in the diagram according to when they must be done in relation to other tasks. The numbers are estimates of the time (months) needed to complete each task.

Owen, R. P. "Charting a Course to Project Success," *Machine Design*, Nov. 23, 1978.

work is based are correct, there is no way to complete the project in less time than this.

Roughing out a basic PERT diagram not only gives a clearer view of the project as a whole, but forces one to think it through in enough detail to feel confident that no additional tasks have been overlooked.

If the quality manager prefers to stay with PERT, the original diagram can be time-scaled by redrawing it on a time field, as shown in Figure 5-4. Now the horizontal lengths of the task lines are time-significant. To show the interdependence of tasks falling in nonadjacent areas of the time schedule, dashed lines can be introduced. These lines indicate slack time—periods between the completion of one task and the start of a dependent task.

The heavy free-hand lines in Figure 5-4 are a useful means for depicting the status of a project at any given time. Drawn downward from the desired date, these lines are swung to the left as they cross a task line if that task is behind schedule; or they are swung to the right if the task is ahead of schedule. The amount of displacement should be roughly indicative of the degree to which the job is late or early. This display technique is equally useful on Gantt charts.

If more precision in project scheduling is necessary, the PERT technique can be made more sophisticated. Instead of assigning a single time for completion to each task, it is assumed that there will be uncertainty in estimating a job duration;

hence, there is only a certain probability that an estimate will be valid. The duration of an activity takes the form of a random variable following the beta distribution (Figure 5-5).

In order to account for statistical variance, the quality planner will make three estimates: the optimistic, "a"; the pessimistic, "b"; and the most probable, "m." These three estimates define a beta distribution curve from which a mean estimate,

$$t_e = \frac{a + 4m + b}{6}$$

is defined as having a 50 percent chance of completion. Thus, a and b are three standard deviations from t_e. Then,

$$\sigma t_e = \frac{b - a}{6}$$

where σt_e is the standard deviation of the beta curve. Calculating the t_e for each job is tedious, but is far more meaningful than the simple time estimate when the project is of a more uncertain nature, as in product development or preproduction.

Note: Although the PERT technique can be made as sophisticated as necessary, few projects will benefit from anything more elaborate than the basics outlined here. Avoid going overboard by trying to impress higher-ups or other department heads.

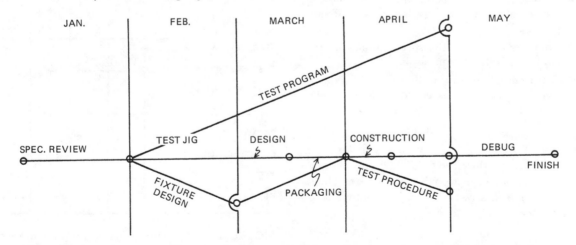

FIGURE 5-4. A more sophisticated version of the PERT diagram plots the various tasks against a time scale. The heavy vertical lines indicate the status of the project at any given time. Leftward loops indicate tasks that are behind schedule, straight lines indicate tasks that are on schedule, and rightward loops indicate tasks that are ahead of schedule.

Owen, R. P. "Charting a Course to Project Success," *Machine Design*, Nov. 23, 1978.

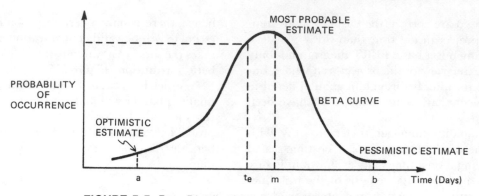

FIGURE 5-5. Beta Distribution of an Activity Duration

TRY THE GANTT CHART: IT'S EASY

The usefulness of a simple PERT diagram ends with the start of the project. Something more comprehensive is required to aid in picturing the progress of a project. Without a doubt the Gantt chart principles are the most extensively used scheduling techniques. They may be used with a simple chart drawn on graph paper or with one dressed up in some of the commercial display panels. There are distinct advantages to be found in Gantt charts:

- A plan has to be made. Often this is the most important advantage of any scheduling technique.
- They show the work that is planned and when it is to start and end.
- Gantt charts are easy to understand and work.
- Gantt charts are dynamic and show a moving picture of what is being planned and accomplished.
- They require very little space considering the amount of information displayed.
- Gantt charts are easy to draw and lend themselves to graphic variations for handling special problems.

A Gantt representation of this example project is shown in Figure 5-6. Each task appears as a horizontal bar on the time field. The position and length of the bar indicate when the task is scheduled to begin and how much time is allotted to its performance.

FLOW CHARTING POINTS THE WAY

A *process flow chart* is a symbolic or pictorial representation of the flow of data, production, authority, or controls (Figure 5-7). It may also show

the disposition of documents such as failure reports within a system and any other information considered desirable for analysis. Flow charts are used for such purposes as:

- Providing an overall picture of a present or proposed system, showing what goes on where.
- Spotting of bottlenecks, duplications, unnecessary operations, and missing quality operations.
- Providing a basis for analysis and evaluation through comparison of both present and proposed flows, so that efficiency, timeliness, cost, or other factors may be improved.
- Isolating problems of distribution, assignments of authority, and the interrelationships of operations.
- Grouping and visualizing the details of a written procedure, such as a corrective action system.

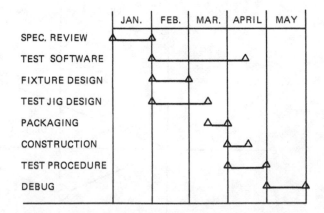

FIGURE 5-6. The Gantt chart is probably the most frequently used project-scheduling technique. It shows the time period allotted for the accomplishment of each task.
Owen, R. P. "Charting a Course to Project Success," *Machine Design*, Nov. 23, 1978.

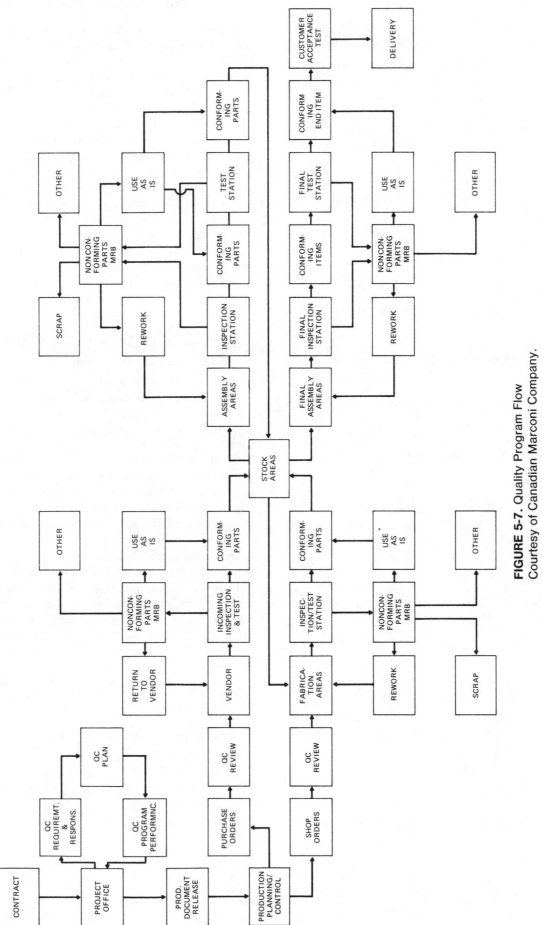

FIGURE 5-7. Quality Program Flow
Courtesy of Canadian Marconi Company.

● Acting as a systems "sales" device for the succinct presentation of proposals to management.

Charts, with their representative symbols (Figure 5-8), can eliminate pages of written description and therefore become one of the most effective means of communication.

Charts are a basic tool for the quality planner, and you must master the techniques associated

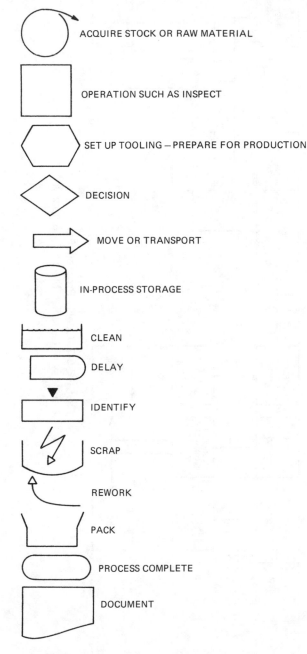

ACQUIRE STOCK OR RAW MATERIAL

OPERATION SUCH AS INSPECT

SET UP TOOLING — PREPARE FOR PRODUCTION

DECISION

MOVE OR TRANSPORT

IN-PROCESS STORAGE

CLEAN

DELAY

IDENTIFY

SCRAP

REWORK

PACK

PROCESS COMPLETE

DOCUMENT

FIGURE 5-8. Process Planning Symbols

with them. However, charts should be simple and cogent enough for utilization at all organizational levels.

Before a process flow chart is constructed, the sequence of operations should be carefully analyzed. Each major step in the process requires separate examination and representation. Much of the information needed for the construction of a process flow chart will usually exist within the organization. For example, the work of the industrial engineering department in (1) evaluating materials handling factors, (2) studying various time and motion aspects of work, (3) developing standards of various kinds, and (4) establishing cost data will generally provide a wealth of material pertinent to the analysis of process flows in addition to the engineering drawings. At each operation the quality engineer should investigate:

√ What is the output of this step in the process?
√ What materials are required?
√ What operations are involved?
√ What is the consequence of an inspection escape?
√ What quality controls are called for?

Caution: Checks should be made with departments and persons concerned to assure that information and evaluations are correct and up to date. All important operations must be portrayed in their proper location in the overall network. Finally, of course, even though a flow chart should be as simple as possible, it must also be complete.

In general, do not attempt to show more detail than is needed for quality control and other purposes. By avoiding needless clutter, the important highlights of materials, parts, and product flows are brought out. Here are some ground rules:

√ Show operations having a major bearing on quality distinctly, in separate boxes. Typically, these are:

● operations affecting quality
● simple processes, such as casting or molding
● operations that change the nature of product, such as annealing, painting, or plating
● in-process testing, inspection, or sorting
● points at which parts are added

- last-point inspections (points beyond which inspection is not possible)
- final acceptance

√ Combine operations having little or no impact on quality, such as a means of transportation, with a major operation. Operations of a sequential nature such as three sequential solderings may also be combined.

√ Combine several sequential operations, similar in nature and in their potential effect on quality, into one box. Such combining does not hamper the viewer's ability to search for and identify specific processing trouble spots when they occur.

√ Use separate charts when parts are produced for inventory or for otherwise multiple subsequent usage. Subsequently, one major chart may show how various individual parts are assembled into a final product.

√ Utilize several simple charts rather than one combined, complex chart. Subassemblies are best shown separately. As a result, several simple charts may show how subassemblies are processed to yield the assembly.

√ Show no more detail than is needed by (1) the manager of production, (2) the departmental managers concerned, and (3) the quality control personnel involved.

√ Trace the source of parts added at any step to its origin of entry into the plant. This applies to parts used early as well as those used late in the assembly process. Note the steps applied to purchased materials prior to assembly (such as the bending of rolls of material into various shapes).

√ Cross-refer inspection/test operations to appropriate documents. The code numbers serve as guides to inspection work instructions, test procedures, or other information sheets, where other important production, quality, and inspection information is contained.

√ Consider rework or sorting-plus-rework, which routinely occurs as a result of consistent and unavoidably high proportions of defectives, as a regular operation.

√ Beginning with the last operation, analyze each procedure step by step until the first operation is reached. The first step may represent the receipt of purchased parts or materials, followed by the inspection process.

√ Show external requirements such as customer source inspection or deliverable data as operations.

√ Continue the flow right through product delivery, including packaging and shipping.

THE PRODUCT QUALITY PLAN: WHERE IT ALL BEGINS

Perhaps the most significant and crucial quality control planning occurs when a new product is being introduced to production. The five phases in product quality control planning are broadly defined as:

1. Proposal phase
2. Planning after contract award
3. Process development
4. Preproduction
5. Production

In most cases, these phases will overlap in time in various areas of the organization. Sufficient lead time is usually the most vital problem in every phase. Various formal planning techniques, such as PERT, are effective devices for determining the most efficient application of the total available effort needed to keep production in step with schedule requirements.

Proposal Phase

For the purposes of this discussion the term *proposal* will be used in the broadest sense. A proposal is an offer to a customer in a build-to-order plant. Here, proposal includes proposals to senior management for the firm that manufactures to market and sales forecasts.

During the proposal phase, the most important consideration is normally cost. Each activity—such as production, engineering, and quality control—must calculate all the expected costs of producing the new item. The ruling criterion is that the calculated expected costs must be accurate. If costs are computed too high, the contract or sales may be lost to a competitor. If they are too low, profits will be less than expected or a loss could be incurred.

The quality control manager must compute the quality costs for the proposed contract. Appraisal, scrap, and rework costs are estimated from historical records of similar items produced by the company. Quality control analysts must also review the concept of the contract—including blueprints, specifications, and quality standards—for three specific areas that apply both to QC costs and to controls planning. These areas are:

1. extraordinary requirements for control
2. special equipment, facilities, operator training, and certification
3. QC inputs to make-or-buy planning

If extraordinary requirements for control include more tests than traditionally required, the capability for such performance may have to be intensively reviewed before a bid is entered, since a major modification or new measuring equipment may be indicated.

> *Case in Point:* A contract manufacturer of TV sets for department stores is asked to quote on 250,000 units with a twenty-four-hour burn-in cycle at 25°C. Besides requiring additional racks and working space, a test and test-record operation must be costed. All of this takes some effort and may involve special assurance records and customer approval of the proposed manner of satisfying the specifications. This must be budgeted as well as technically planned. The burn-in requirement in this case amounted to just under $1,000,000.

Special equipment for evaluation may require adjustment or negotiations with the customer to clear up side issues, which always arise. Special standards, training, and recruitment costs for training appropriate personnel to be operators are all budgeted in the bid phase.

Quality control should be a useful source of information during production and engineering joint planning on make-or-buy decisions. The capabilities of current processes and equipment should be known by quality control, since this information will influence the decision on whether to purchase an item from an outside source specializing in the field. Quality control must also budget for vendor control in many cases.

The remainder of QC activity in the proposal phase of contract planning is devoted to double-checking the budget for normal operations to make sure that the special adjustments to a QC budget for the contract are the only ones to be made.

Planning After Contract Award

The formal award of the contract (or internal work authorization) initiates the major planning operations of quality control. The first step here is to review the requirements for special and standard test equipment, since a long lead time is often necessary to fabricate or purchase this type of equipment.

Gauges and testing equipment are very necessary to a quality program, and newly developed types are often needed to determine if a new process is yielding a product that meets all required specifications. Final decisions on processing may be delayed, pending availability of this special equipment. The quality manager must plan to prevent these potential problems by ordering the equipment as quickly as possible and by determining substitute methods and equipment to accomplish the measurement or test—on an interim basis—if problems occur in obtaining the required equipment.

Detailed production work instructions are developed by the planners in the manufacturing group. These instructions provide the detailed step-by-step sequence necessary to manufacture the end item; they must be audited for clarity and completeness by quality control planners, since they provide a framework around which the inspection plan is developed.

The major management considerations that should be included in quality planning are as follows:

a. The product quality plan must include specific time-phased measurable events planned and scheduled concurrently with other functions. If detailed schedule information is not available, guidelines and priorities should be established.

b. Establish desired quality levels for each area of production. These are important because they determine the number of items that will be inspected and the frequency of measurement.

c. Include special inspections or tests, including environmental tests, in the plan whenever necessary. Requirements for these special inspections or tests may be included in the contract, regulatory codes, or product specifications. A careful review of all applicable specifications must, therefore, be made to meet contractual and company goals.

d. Whenever a new product is introduced to production, review the quality control and standards manual to assure continued adequacy.

For example, changes may be required because of changes in the production process.

e. Additional test equipment and facilities may be required for technical or capacity reasons. Raise capital appropriations in order to ensure the timely availability of this equipment.

f. Review calibration requirements for gauges and test equipment to determine the adequacy and the capability of the laboratory to perform the necessary calibration.

g. Classification of defects is an important consideration throughout the entire planning period. It is the responsibility of the quality control department to assure that this classification-of-defects list is complete and accurate. A well-conceived classification of defects, agreed to by quality control and production personnel, will avoid many difficulties and arguments later in the production stage.

h. Assign inspection stations or checkpoints where inspection operations will be performed throughout the process. Select these stations in such a manner as to ensure that quality defect errors in processing will be determined at the earliest possible time so as to optimize quality costs. Each checkpoint should relate to an inspection instruction, test procedure, or process control document along with the appropriate quality standards.

i. Quality control has a responsibility to review contracts or purchase orders with suppliers to assure that quality specifications are accurate and complete. Determine whether the item should be inspected in the vendor's plant or after it is received. Establish liaison with the quality control activity of the vendor to assure that effective control will be established over purchased items. Appropriate quality clauses should be clearly stated on purchase orders.

j. A standards review is necessary to coordinate new or changed standards both in plant and with the customer (also vendor, if involved). This is often the most troublesome item in the program since many standards cannot be specifically defined in absolute terms. When a new item is introduced, an actual standard may require direct negotiation with the customer. The customer occasionally doesn't know exactly what he needs or wants until he sees his item as hardware rather than as a series of drawings. Determine standards as quickly as possible since this will alleviate problems in the production phase.

New inspection instructions, tests, and sampling plans may require retraining of personnel.

Training programs must be carefully established to ensure that all required personnel receive this training prior to the actual production phase.

Process Development Planning

The next major phase in quality control planning is *process development*. During this phase, pilot operations are sometimes conducted. These operations may consist of building a complete end item, or they may be limited to subelements of the end items. The purpose of this phase is to check out the feasibility of new production processes or possibly new testing requirements. This activity provides only a limited amount of experimental material; however, it initiates the following quality control operations:

- The first test of inspection and test plans to determine their adequacy. This includes the actual inspection of the product for characteristics that can be inspected and tested at this time.
- The first opportunity to evaluate the controllability of processes within prescribed parameters.
- The first evaluation by inspection or testing— either nondestructive or destructive—of the first pieces of hardware made by the process.
- The first clarification of standards. This may require joint review by quality control, engineering, and the customer.
- The first feedback of operational information to all concerned activities.

Document and analyze all information obtained in the process development phase very carefully. All items produced are manufactured individually and are actually handcrafted in many cases. It cannot, therefore, be stated in absolute terms that the production process, involving volume production, will yield the same quality of material as that produced in the process development stage. Information obtained, however, is vital in determining potential quality problems in the future.

PREPRODUCTION QUALITY PLANNING

Delays in development often occur because the engineers find that they had previously erred in some conclusion. More often than not, the error occurred because a nonconforming or unevaluated substitute item was used to build a prototype; the test technique used was invalid; or the test equipment was either incapable of performing the intended test or was out of calibration. The savings in time and money potentially available from avoiding such errors are typically large.

The planning for appraisal activities associated with preproduction material and product will inevitably be different from that for production. Nonetheless, the two programs should be compatible with each other and preproduction quality planning may well provide the basis for the activities and equipment to be incorporated into the manufacturing quality plan. The extent of the production plan should provide a model for the preproduction plan. Sophisticated planners often seize the opportunity to test new products in the preproduction environment before introducing them into the production-related operations.

The preproduction phase is the first opportunity for quality control to check its plans using actual production information. Test items produced during the preproduction phase utilize the actual equipment components, and processes that will be used during the production phase. These test items are, therefore, very similar to the items that will be produced in the production phase.

Information obtained from inspections and tests during this period are used to validate the information obtained on the special items produced during the process development stage. More and better information is obtained during preproduction because actual operations are being performed. All quality characteristics and tests can be measured and performed during this period. Modifications to the inspection plan must be made wherever the plan fails to provide the necessary coverage. The entire operation must be closely controlled during this phase since any deviations to quality permitted at this time are likely to be continued at the start of full production.

If all is well and the prototype is ready to release for production, a formal procedure can be used to ensure coordination. A typical prototype-release-and-acceptance form reads as follows:

> The development of this product is now complete. It meets all the specifications and market requirements, including unit cost set forth by Marketing. From all of the tests performed, we conclude that it will give satisfactory performance when properly applied. Therefore, as of this date, the above is released from the prototype phase and accepted for production.

Senior representatives of engineering, marketing, manufacturing, and quality control sign this formal declaration. This step is formal because it is the final step before a company's resources are committed for production and sales. Effective coordination is more likely if everyone knows they are going to have to agree and support moving into sales and production, and their agreement is backed up in writing.

THE PRODUCTION PLAN: THE PAYOFF

The production phase requires the greatest expenditure of quality control effort because of the large human resource requirements necessary to accomplish the inspections, monitor the tests, and analyze the data in this phase. The production phase, however, must be considered an anticlimax to all of the planning and refining effort that has previously gone into the quality control plan.

Production processes must be standardized so that each operation is conducted the same way on each item. This standardization must also include inspection. Inspection personnel must inspect each item according to the plan. If left to their own resources, each inspector will accomplish the inspections in a manner that he or she deems most effective. This always leads to problems, because no one person in the inspection flow can anticipate all the future inspection operations.

Nonstandardized inspections result in overinspection of some characteristics and no inspection of others. The effect is that quality problems are not discovered until late in the production process. This is in direct opposition to the quality control mission, which is the earliest detection and correction of defects. Furthermore, inspection methods must be evaluated for ease of application, sequence of inspection, and mechanization.

Pitfall to Avoid: Give the inspector some latitude for initiative. If management tells a person exactly how to do something and prohibits him or her from deviating from the plan, management assumes all responsibilities for the results. An inspector who is forced to rigidly adhere to her plan has only one responsibility—compliance. She has no personal feeling toward her work, the product, or the obvious discrepancies that occur outside her area of responsibility. She may notice a discrepancy in the product, process, or system but ignore it by rationalizing to herself, "They will tell me if they want me to look at it."

Quality control engineers perform an important function in the production phase. These personnel are selected because of their engineering background, knowledge of the production process, experience in measurement and inspection, and ability to sell ideas. It is their responsibility to live with the product during this phase, to analyze the direct and indirect factors bearing on problems, and to come up with workable solutions.

If all quality control planning were perfect, we would have no quality problems. Remember, however, that plans affect people and people affect plans. The quality control system must provide continuous monitoring of the production activity to determine when quality levels have changed. This is primarily accomplished through the accumulation and analysis of quality data, failure analysis, and complaint investigations.

The quality control manager must continually review his or her plan to determine if it is still valid. When conditions dictate, he or she must revise the plan to provide the necessary control to assure a quality end product.

PLAN FOR ECONOMIC YIELD

One critical planning parameter that requires attention is *yield*. When there is a recognition by all levels of management that the tendency to variability in each production process is similar to that of engineering tolerances; and when it has been recognized that the profit projection, to be reliable, must be based on a predicted percent yield of good parts, and that this depends on the known degree of compatibility between process capabilities (natural spread) and engineering tolerances; then, and only then, can the production plan be said to be rational. Unforeseen events that reduce the yield below the predicted level disturb production schedules, inventories, and budgets.

Case in Point: A West German firm that exported its line of cameras to world markets was particularly sensitive to the timely availability of its new line of sophisticated cameras. Compliance with the production schedule was of strategic importance, and yield was a major factor. The manufacturer was successful because the "homework" had been done. Specifically:

- The quality engineers had been required to determine the natural *spread* of each production process by statistical analysis. This information had been disseminated through all levels of engineering and management.

- A production policy that required that no job be assigned to a production process unless that engineering tolerance limits were equal to, or in excess of, the natural spread of the process had been imposed.

- When circumstances made this impossible, the quality engineers were called upon to predict the yield, and the predicted yield was noted on the work order as an attainable target.

- Each production process was controlled by a control chart prepared by the quality engineer, posted by the operator, frequently checked by the supervisor, and monitored by the inspector.

- Production management, quality engineers, production engineers, operators, and inspectors cooperated to maintain the yield at the predicted levels.

- Indications of abnormal variation appearing on the process control charts triggered prompt corrective action.

- All production control records contained actual percent yield, compared with the predicted yield.

Product yield has an immense impact on the income statement. Consider the case of a five-person toy factory working forty hours per week, fifty weeks per year. Their net output of 90 percent yield (the planned value) is 100,000 board games. (111,111 units released to the shop floor). At $10.00 per hour loaded rate, the total factory cost, ignoring material, is

$$40 \ \frac{hrs}{week} \times 50 \ \frac{weeks}{employee} \times 5 \ employees \times \frac{\$10.00}{hour} =$$

$100,000 per annum

or $1.00 per unit. Using a 1.5 mark-up, this results in sales of $150,000 per annum with $20,000 pre-tax profit (assuming $30,000 G & A expense). If, however, the yield falls to 80 percent, the saleable output will be only 88,888 × $1.00 × 1.5 = $133,-332. The total factory costs are still $100,000 and general and administrative costs (administration, accounting, marketing) are still $30,000. Hence the firm will obtain a profit of $133,332 − 130,000 = $3332. Thus a 10 percentage point drop in yield causes the firm's profit to be reduced by $16,668 or 83 percent! This occurs because, in addition to the direct yield loss of $11,112, the G & A expense is not recovered and the potential profit on the scrapped units is foregone.

FORMAT OF THE PRODUCT QUALITY PLAN

It is important to streamline the plan by defining only those activities unique to the product. Existing procedures, standards, and forms should be used as much as possible. The basic elements of a product quality plan are as follows:

1. *Cover page* contains title, date, document number and originator, and approval signatures.
2. *Revision page* lists page(s) and date(s) changed.
3. *Scope* identifies breadth of coverage of the plan.
4. *Applicable documents* and *reference list* gives name and revision (or date) of all relevant customer, government, or company documents referred to in the text.
5. *Background* provides supporting background information to all users of the plan. This includes, where applicable, such items as: identification of the customer, type of program, description of deliverable hardware or service to be rendered, reference documents, security requirements, delivery schedules and controlling work orders.
6. *The Program Management* section identifies:
   (a) Tasks and milestones required to be accomplished for control of quality (e.g., first article inspection qualification test).
   (b) Scheduling quality tasks to be time-phased with other management functions to assure proper interface.
   (c) Assignment of quality responsibilities for inspection, test, and compliance to specific quality activities.
   (d) Requirements for feedback of quality data; it summarizes reports for analysis and corrective action and quality costs analyses.
7. *The Organization* section covers:
   (a) Necessary charts or narrative data that depict the position and organizational relationship of the quality functions to other managerial and operational elements of the organizational structure.
   (b) Lines of authority for management and operation of the quality program and identification of key personnel.
   (c) Flow charts reflecting lines of communication for exchange of system quality information as related to data collection, analysis, feedback, and corrective action.
   (d) Relationship and control over vendors, subcontractors, and suppliers with respect to quality.
8. *The Quality Program* section includes the procedures and methods that indicate how and to what degree quality will collaborate with other activities in order to establish acceptable levels of quality for conformance purposes. More specifically, it tells how quality control will:
   (a) Review technical documents, such as specifications, drawings, engineering changes, etc. for clarity and adequacy of quality requirements and instructions.
   (b) Review design, components, inspection, test, performance, and safety requirements to assure inclusion of measurable quality criteria in drawings, purchase orders, inspection plans, and test procedures.
   (c) Participate in design reviews, environmental tests, and reliability tests for control and validation purposes.
   (d) Assure that measuring, inspection, and test equipment are certified, calibrated, and controlled.
   (e) Assure control of special processes, material, fabrication, workmanship, packaging, handling, storage, transportation, installation; and checkout of equipment, spares, modification kits, and services.
   (f) Control data collection and failure analysis, test data recording sheets, feed back deficiency data, implement corrective action, and maintain follow-up until problems are resolved.
   (g) Determine that work instructions and assembly procedures assure compliance with drawings, process specification requirements, and quality standards.
   (h) Assure vendor's compliance with requirements of purchase orders. (Include a list of engineering critical components.)
   (i) Provide adequate incoming inspection (AQLs, critical characteristics, etc.) of purchased items.
   (j) Control nonconforming material and take corrective action.
   (k) Coordinate with or supply data preparation activities with correct and current information, including service bulletins, technical manuals, and maintenance instructions.
   (l) Implement configuration control including serial numbers, lot numbers, date codes, and nameplates as appropriate.
9. *Appendices* normally include applicable forms, organization charts, product flow charts, and a list of acronyms.

LEARNING CURVES AND QC MANPOWER PLANNING

Decreasing unit labor cost with increasing production quantities is a known fact. Some companies experience it as a by-product of their production methods. Other companies have had an even greater realization by forecasting a desirable and attainable rate of progress and controlling production activities to the predetermined goal. The practical application of this phenomenon is accomplished in the form of *learning curves*.

Learning curves are a powerful personnel forecasting tool. They allow basic standard time data to be used for estimating all production quantities and all complexities of product. Standard time data set the *minimum* time in which a unit can be made, and the learning curve projects the *actual* time of these units produced during the build-up to peak efficiency.

Concept

The learning curve principle states that when the production of a product doubles, the new cumulative average cost (usually expressed in hours) declines by a fixed percent of the previous cumulative average. This fixed percentage represents the learning achieved. The principle is more easily understood by examining the three columns below.

human resource requirements, space requirements, and jig requirements; estimating total costs, budgeting, scheduling, purchasing, and pricing; determining cash requirements; and many others.

Pitfalls to Avoid:

- Labor reduction per the learning concept does not just "happen." It is *made* to happen. Many companies have bid quantity production jobs on the learning curve theory and then have sat back waiting for the labor reductions to take place. A shop that is left to devise its own methods and tooling and set its own standards of output will show little or no improvement throughout the entire production run. On the other hand, the shop with definite controls in the areas of QC methods, tooling, work measurement, and manufacturing cost systems can keep itself within the projected requirements.

- A learning curve has to be recognized for what it is: a valuable tool, but one that must be used with a great deal of care and professional judgment. For example, the total hours for 1000 units is 11 percent greater with a 75 percent curve than with a 74 percent curve. Those persons who attempt to substitute mathematical

Cumulative Production	Cumulative Average Hours per Unit	Ratio to Previous Cumulative Average
1	100 hours	—
2	90	90%
4	81	90%
8	72.9	90%
16	65.6	90%

If the curve is plotted on arithmetic coordinate graph paper (Figure 5-9) an exponential curve results. A log-log plot (Figure 5-10) results in a straight line, which is easier to interpret and project.

First used in the aircraft industry, the concept of the learning curve has received increasing acceptance, and the technique is now applied to a number of products that require repetitive operations, including electronics and electromechanical items, engines, machined parts, and various other components. At first, learning curves were used only to calculate the effect of learning on the number of labor hours required to produce a given number of units. It is now used for a number of other purposes, including forecasting

formulas for informed judgment are doing themselves and their organizations a profound disservice.

- The reduction of direct labor cost at the expense of engineering or special test equipment funds is another area of false economy. The learning curve projects only direct labor hours and is not concerned with tooling or engineering cost. It would be foolish to spend $100,-000 on measuring equipment to save $15,000 in direct labor.

Cautions: There are a number of factors relevant to the application of learning curves that must be considered:

(a) union opposition to productivity improvement

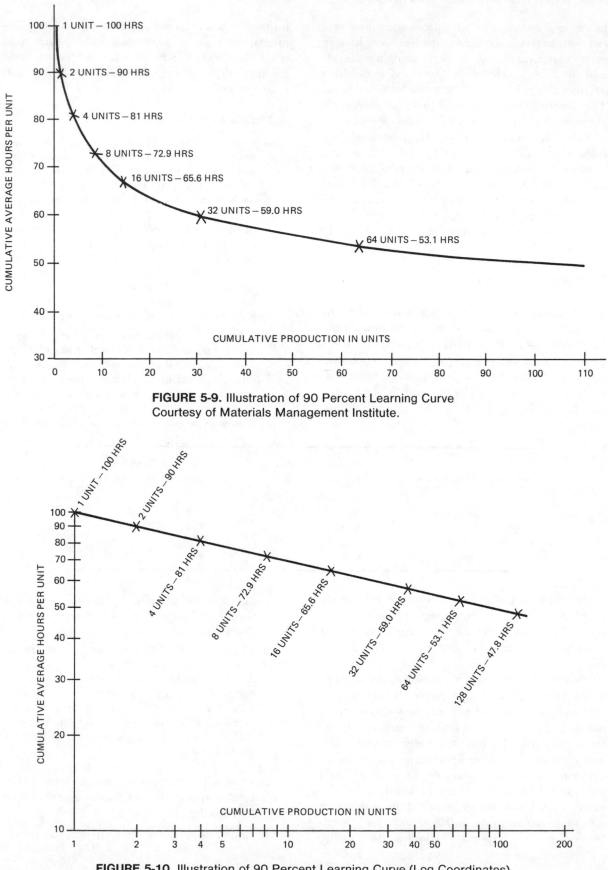

FIGURE 5-9. Illustration of 90 Percent Learning Curve
Courtesy of Materials Management Institute.

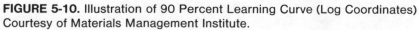

FIGURE 5-10. Illustration of 90 Percent Learning Curve (Log Coordinates)
Courtesy of Materials Management Institute.

(b) effects of prior learning (eg., limited model changes)

(c) lack of production continuity

(d) unplanned workmanship, material, or part problems

(e) unstable design(s) resulting in engineering changes

(f) unbalanced scheduling

(g) introduction of automatic test equipment

(h) poor employee morale or training

Theory

The mathematics of the learning curve are relatively straightforward. Figure 5-11 indicates that the learning curve is a hyperbola of the form.

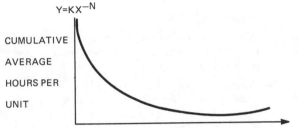

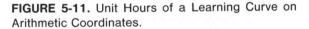

FIGURE 5-11. Unit Hours of a Learning Curve on Arithmetic Coordinates.

Where Y is the cumulative average value of X units, K is the value of the first unit. N is the value of the slope, which is a measure of the rate of reduction. On log-log paper, the curve is represented by the equation:

$$\log Y = \log K - N \log X$$

which of course plots as a straight line. To solve for the percent of learning (L) we take two points X_1, X_2 on the learning curve. Thus,

$$Y_1 = KX_1^{-N} \text{ and } Y_2 = KX_2^{-N}$$

If $X_2 = 2X_1$ then $L = \dfrac{Y_2}{Y_1} = 2^{-N}$

Stated another way,

$$N = -\log L / \log 2$$

The slope N of a 90 percent learning curve is then equal to

$$-\log 90/\log 2 = \frac{0.04576}{0.30103} = 0.15201$$

The relationship between the unit cost and the cumulative cost (Y) can be readily established. Clearly,

$$Y = KX^{-N} = U/X$$

where U is the cumulative cost for X units.

Hence,

$$U = KX^{-N+1} \text{ and } u = \frac{dU}{dX} (-N+1)KX^{-N} = (-N+1)Y$$

where u is equal to the unit cost. For example, if L = 0.90, K = 100 hours, and X equals 10, then,

$$Y = 100(10)^{-.152} = \frac{100}{1.419} = 70.5 \text{ hours}$$

The corresponding unit cost (u) at this point would be $(-N+1)Y = (-.152+1)(70.5) = .848(70.5) = 59.8$ hours. A scientific calculator is ideal for solving learning curve problems.

The rate of learning is determined by many factors. These include:

- personnel turnover
- design stability
- capital investment policy
- quality controls
- organization of work
- quality of supervision
- rate of production
- quality of tooling and measuring equipment
- manufacturing control systems
- previous experience
- effectiveness of corrective action systems
- extent of preproduction planning
- size and complexity of item

Contrary to the widely held belief, direct labor is responsible for only 25 percent of learning. Logistics—paperwork contribution, such as order writing, blueprint issuing, etc.—is responsible for 35 percent of learning. The remaining 40 percent is a function of management. It includes supervision, engineering, planning, and tooling. Management, together with all indirect labor, is thus responsible for 75 percent of learning! While the above percentage figures are to be considered nominal, experience has shown them to be relatively proportional for complex manufactured units where assembly forms a considerable portion of the work.

Generally speaking, machined or detail parts are likely to show a learning curve of approximately 95 percent. Subassemblies, in which details are assembled together in groups of two or more, could show a learning curve of approximately 87 percent. Minor assemblies might show a curve of 84 percent, major assemblies 80 percent, and final or unit assemblies could show as much learning as 70 percent. These different and subcomponent curves, weighted, might produce a final manufactured or constructed unit with an overall composite curve of 80 percent to 84 percent. Least squares analysis can be applied to historical actuals to determine the line of best fit for a particular product and organization.

Example

A manufacturing company determines that the demand for its new diesel calls for a production schedule like that in the first two columns of Table 5-2. If the first unit takes 100,000 hours and an 80 percent (L) learning curve is assumed, future personnel requirements can be determined.

In this example, $L = 2^{-N}$ or $0.8 = 2^{-N}$. Clearly $N = 0.322$. Using $Y = KX^{-N}$ for the first 9 units we have

$$Y = 100,000 (9)^{-.322} = 49,500$$

For the cumulative quantity of 25 units

$$Y = 100,000 (25)^{-.322} = 35,000$$

Column 6 (total hours per month) is obtained by subtracting $9 \times 49,500$ from $25 \times 35,000$ ($875,000 - 445,500 = 429,500$). The balance of the table can be similarly completed. If the latter figures are divided by the number of hours worked per month (in this case 200), the needed number of direct employees can be obtained. Thus, it can be seen from Table 5-2 (right-hand column) that about 2,228 employees are required in the first

month and about double that number in the last month, whereas the number of units produced per month increases almost nine times.

By proper projecting of personnel requirements, recruitment, load balancing, and overtime plans can be initiated.

CHECKLIST FOR QUALITY PLANNING

Because of the complexities of quality planning, even experienced quality practitioners require a checklist. Proper use of a checklist assures that all factors have been addressed. The questions can be used to establish quality plans for use in proposals, as part of a product planning meeting or design review, or as a basis for the preparation of a product quality plan.

Marketing

- What is the anticipated market life of the product? What growth does it possess? Will it have a model change each year?
- What quantity is expected to be built the first year? Second? Third? Or is it a one-shot product?
- Is a list of required capital equipment purchases available?
- Why should a customer buy the unit from your company and not from the competition? What are the good points of the competitive unit? Have you a competitor's sample?
- Does the growth cycle for the product include meaningful new features? Will the price remain constant for these improvements?
- Is the design compatible with available test and user equipment?

TABLE 5-2. Calculation of Personnel Requirements

	PRODUCTION SCHEDULE		PERSONNEL CALCULATIONS			
Month	Units per Month	Cumulative Number of Units	Cumulative Average (From Exhibit VII)	Cumulative Total Hours	Total Hours per Month	Total Direct Employees per Month
1	9	9	49,500	445,500	445,500	2,228
2	16	25	35,000	875,000	429,500	2,148
3	22	47	28,000	1,316,000	441,000	2,205
4	30	77	24,500	1,886,500	570,500	2,853
5	40	117	21,500	2,515,500	629,000	3,145
6	52	169	19,000	3,211,000	695,500	3,478
7	65	234	17,000	3,978,000	767,000	3,835
8	80	314	15,500	4,867,000	889,000	4,445

- Who is the buyer? Who is the ultimate customer?
- Will the customer likely develop a second or third source?
- Will additional or modified equipment be required for special tests?
- What effect does the geographical location of the plant have on manufacturing costs, suppliers, schedules, travel, and shipping costs?

Schedule

- Has a time-phased schedule of research, development, prototype, preproduction, and production phases been prepared?
- What contingency dollars and time are provided in the plan?
- Is the due date of new capital measuring/test equipment consistent with project schedule? Can rental units fill the gap?

Budget

- How many years will it take to repay the capital investment in this product?
- How much will special-to-type test and inspection equipment cost?
- Has a cost budget been set for QC activities?
- Have the adverse effects of engineering changes been provided for?
- Have sampling plans been considered for each area of production?
- Are quality requirements or tolerances too stringent?

Contractual

- Do acceptance test procedures require customer approval?
- What is the point of inspection and acceptance?
- Where is the f.o.b. point?
- Are there any unusual quality-records retention requirements?
- Will use of customer furnished parts be involved?
- Is customer source inspection required?
- Will the developmental program be burdened with complex reports to customer or government?
- Does customer require recording of measurement and test data, or will go/no-go testing be acceptable?

Engineering

- Have any new parts, materials, or processes utilized in the product been evaluated?

- Has tolerance accumulation analysis been accomplished?
- What derating (safety factor policy) has been employed?
- Are all parts ratings consistent with worst-case environmental conditions?
- Has a Failure Modes and Effects Analysis (FMEA) or fault tree analysis been performed?
- What design controls are needed? When?
- How many new developments or modifications does design and tooling involve?
- What development testing was done? Environmental testing? Destructive testing? Safety testing?
- If the design was used before, what was its cost breakdown, yield, and failure history?
- Have assemblies been broken down into discernible functional blocks?
- Has previous test, service, and failure analysis experience been considered in the new design?
- Have major changes been made to adapt it to the present requirements?
- Will maximum use be made of standard parts and proven designs?
- Have all operating environments and parameters been considered?
- Have drawings been reviewed for clarity and completeness? If not, will they be?
- Has a classification of characteristics program been applied to drawings?

Purchasing

- Who are the major subcontractors or vendors?
- Have long-lead-time items been identified?
- Has purchasing obtained and/or approved the prices and sources used in estimating the product cost?
- Are all sources approved by QC? Any sole sources?
- Will vendors own the special tooling, or does your purchase order state that such tooling belongs to the buyer?
- Which components will be tested at incoming?
- Do any items require source inspection to maintain adequate control?

Production

- Will some items require a destructive evaluation (always costly) to avoid expensive rejects or time-consuming reviews of borderline products at a later stage? (Without a thoroughly planned approach, a hasty method of sectioning or dissecting an item may waste valuable opportunities for a more complete evaluation.)

- What percent of parts, modules, and components, will be made in house?
- Are manufactured items consistent with in-house capabilities?
- Are process capability studies complete?
- What ground rules determine the "make vs. buy" decisions?
- Is the product easy to troubleshoot and repair?
- Are assemblies and subassemblies inspectable?
- Have any required special handling procedures been identified?
- Have any modifications or additions to inspection work instructions been prepared?
- Have appropriate quality levels and standards been defined?
- Will the redesign reduce in-plant rejects? Or increase them?
- Have engineering critical parts been identified for special controls?
- Is the approval of a regulatory agency required for this product?
- Do existing procedures comply with special government requirements?

- Are any special codes involved—building codes, military, industry, or government standards?
- Has automatic testing been considered?

Field Support

- What are the warranty and guarantee plans? Will your service department be the sole repair source?
- Are any limited-life components used?
- Have maintenance manuals been prepared?
- Have controls been established to limit unfair service and repair practices by distributors and repair centers?
- What will be the stock plan for maintaining spare parts in the plant? At the distributors? What spares does customer require to be available? For how many years?
- Will spare parts or components be readily interchangeable?
- Have storage effects and packing requirements been evaluated?
- Will self-test features be incorporated where practical?
- Will service life be dependent upon hours or cycles of operation?
- Does the product require any preventative maintenance or periodic inspection?

REFERENCES

Archibald, R. D. "PERT/CPM Management Systems for the Small Subcontractor." *Small Business Administration (SBA) Administration Practices Bulletin,* No. 86, n.d.

Barker, E. M. "Why Plan Your Inspection?" *Quality Progress,* July 1975.

Birnbrauer, H. "Project Planning Made Simple." *Machine Design,* May 12, 1977.

Gage, W. G. "The Product Quality Plan." *1976 ASQC Technical Conference Transactions.*

"Guide for Reducing Quality Costs." *ASQC,* 1977.

Jordan, R. "How to Use the Learning Curve." Materials Management Institute, 1965.

Kivenko, K. "Predict Your Production Costs with Learning Curves." *Production Engineering,* Aug. 1977.

Owen, R. P. "Charting a Course to Project Success." *Machine Design,* November 23, 1978.

6

How to Keep Customers Satisfied

Knowing how to appeal to customers through their particular wants is the secret of successful selling. People buy things not for the things themselves, but for the service those things perform.

Case in Point: A manufacturer of abrasive cloth was losing his market share and couldn't understand why. His laboratory tests showed good compliance with specification. When he checked with key customers, he found that they exhibited little interest in the specification. What concerned them was something called "cost per hundred pieces polished," and his cloth had the highest cost, as seen by the user.

Customers appreciate it when you show a genuine, friendly interest in helping them get the best goods for their purpose. There is a bonus value involved if the customer ends up with a lively anticipation of enjoying what he has purchased. The customer has not bought a suit, but her appearance in it; he has not bought a vehicle, but a car of prestige; she has not bought professional service, but freedom from trouble.

All the deep-seated elements of human nature are involved in the effort to locate prospects and to win customers. A particularly strong one is the desire for value. People today are price-and-value conscious. They will not insist upon lower-priced or lower-quality goods if they can be shown that higher-priced goods will give them better value in use.

This means that a salesman must know his products, be able to discuss their construction and performance in an intelligent way, be confident when he emphasizes the special product qualities. A good salesman is a goldmine of information and help. He has studied the merchandise he sells until he is an expert judge of quality, fit, good taste, and appropriateness. He has absorbed ideas from the experience of customers. His function, as he sees it, is to help the buyer get the best for his money. He has respect for what he is selling, and that respect is contagious.

Many people will not want to know the horsepower of a snow-blower, but they do want to know if it will start in cold weather and move the snow off their driveways. A can opener must open tins easily and safely; a conveyor belt must run smoothly and bear the weight (without undue sagging) that will be carried on it. Garments, besides having the desired good appearance, must clean without shrinking and face the sun without fading. If the salesman cannot tell the facts about qualities like these, he should say so, and then find out.

Finally, before approaching prospects with the idea of turning them into customers, we need to set ethical standards. As many articles are bought because of our faith in people as because of our faith in merchandise. This is the secret selling power of a sound quality program.

UNDERSTAND YOUR CUSTOMER

It is instructive to consider the customer or the user of services which are to be provided by the organization. Many or all of the following statements may be true, concerning his situation:

- He does not know exactly what he wants a desired product or service to do for him.
- He does not know the manufacturing aspects of the hardware or services he requires.
- He does not have the facilities for servicing the product.
- He does not know the nature of the processing required to give him the product he has asked for.
- He is unaware of the nature of many standards involved in producing what he has required. He may have his own ideas of standards, which may have an unknown relationship to similar standards in the producer's organization.
- He does not know whether certain deviations from conformance will be critical or not for certain characteristics he has required in his product.
- He does not know whether some questions of possible defects can be settled without certain field tests or tests performed, in turn, by his ultimate customer.

Most of these statements deal directly with standards. The implication here is that the customer usually does not know the exact characteristics of the product he or she wants. Often the customer is unsure about the product until he or she receives it and puts it to work in a real operating environment.

Many questions, certainly those about standards, should be raised in the planning stage before actual operations commence. On the other hand, many standards that were not contemplated at the start of the activity will be involved by the end of a production operation because of a series of unforeseen problems and situations.

Some of the problems just mentioned are less difficult to solve after the customer is completely informed as to what he or she needs and after the fine points on the design of the product have been worked out. In that case, the customer (indirectly) and the manufacturer must still face the problems of unforeseen changes caused by the impact of outside forces on the manufacturing process. There is much interchange of information at all times between the customer and the producing organization, some of it technical. Although the typical manufacturing organization prefers to contact customers through its sales and marketing

people, it is evident that the high traffic of technical details rapidly outgrows the abilities of a sales organization to handle them adequately and in the required time. As a result, much communication will flow directly from internal departments of the organization to appropriate locations within the customer's organization. This is an additional control problem: Without management control of customer contact, misunderstandings can occur and unwarranted decisions may be made that will not be uncovered until their correction becomes expensive.

Note: The customer is sometimes part of a complex business with many functions, disciplines, and specialists. Each will have his or her own views, which may blur objectives.

> Customers may not always be right but they are never wrong.

THE QUALITY OF REPAIRS

An effective QC program for a product can be totally nullified if inadequate follow-up service is provided. We might, for instance, have a component failure in our TV set. We would not be satisfied with the "design" of the service if the repair person took the set to the shop to replace the faulty tube, tested the set for an entire month, and finally returned it to us with a considerable charge for the service. In this case, the service would have been too elaborate, and we would be dissatisfied with it.

On the other hand, he might quickly detect and remove an offending part in our own house, replace it, and leave without testing the resulting performance of the set. This often results in an additional failure occurring within a very short time, since other marginally performing parts would then be likely to fail or reveal their condition detrimentally. Even though he charged very little for his work on the one visit, the quality of his service would be inadequate, and we would find ourselves paying for another service call. Quality of services as well as hard goods can either be overelaborate or inadequate.

Failure of the quality of the repair person's service to conform to requirements may occur in other ways. He might be pressed for time and replace a component which needed only minor adjustments. (A customer may never be aware of this type of failure to conform to ethical standards, and thus foot the bill for the extra cost involved.) The opposite situation might also occur. The serviceperson might effect a temporary repair and adjustment because she had forgotten to carry a proper supply of spare components with her, and as a result we would shortly be forced to make another service request. Furthermore, she could also be guilty of failing to check out a common symptom of approaching failure, because she lacked reasonably expected knowledge or training. We would normally be unaware of the technical content of the repairperson's service and thereby be exposed to considerable expense by failures of quality of conformance to the normal or expected technical standards for technical service.

Poor service causes abnormal downtime or loss of business that may be costly for customers, inconvenient, or simply aggravating. A customer having once experienced poor service quality may be a reluctant buyer next time.

Service quality can be improved in several ways:

√ Adequately staff your service department.

√ Ensure modular design to permit rapid failure identification and replacement.

√ Provide good accessibility so that items can be troubleshot and easily removed.

√ Provide sound technical training of servicepeople on your product.

√ Plan for adequate supplies of spare parts. If standard parts are used, this problem is significantly reduced.

√ Design proper field test equipment and inspection aids.

√ Supply technical and maintenance manuals.

√ Develop a good field-failure reporting system.

√ Select servicepeople with tact and diplomacy.

√ Promptly reply and act on customer complaints.

√ Check buyers installation (if applicable).

√ Validate modification kits and service bulletins.

Observation: Japanese firms encourage quality feedback from salespeople, repairpeople, distributors, retailers, and customers. Field service organizations often report directly to the manufacturing manager rather than to the sales manager, as in most U.S. companies.

INTERFACING QC WITH MARKETING

This book uses the broadest definition of marketing to include the functions of marketing, sales, pricing, contracts, and product service. One of the key roles of marketing is to be the major interface between the customer and the company's internal organization. Since companies exist to profitably provide products and services that satisfy customer needs, marketing inputs are essential in identifying and communicating these needs. Marketing's quality responsibilities include:

● Accurately determining the customer's quality requirements.

● Seeking QC evaluation of quality requirements during the bidding stage.

● Assuring that prices reflect unusual quality requirements or tasks so that these tasks are not poorly accomplished.

● Assuring that customer requirements are accurately reflected in internal work authorizations and design specifications in a timely manner.

● Establishing with others in the organization quality standards for products not completely specified by the customer, regulatory bodies, or trade associations.

● Participating in the product development and verification cycle to the extent necessary to assure that the required product characteristics are included in the product.

● Ensuring that care-and-use manuals, special test equipment, and other product support activities are accomplished.

● Honestly advertising and marketing the products to assure that the customer knows what he or she is purchasing.

● Obtaining information on product performance and failure from customers.

● Reporting product performance information to those responsible for solving problems and improving products.

● Actively participating in the corrective action programs on chronic field problems.

● Administering warranty claims honestly and fairly.

● Responding promptly to customer complaints.

● Providing periodic sales forecasts.

Observation: In the real world, the observed performance of marketing departments is rarely congruent with the list of quality tasks just given. Order bookings continue to be the major parameter by which a marketing department is measured. For this reason, QC involvement in customer interfaces is essential.

Case in Point: A leading manufacturer of consumer durables analyzed the reasons for customer returns over a six-month period. The breakdown was:

marketing/sales	35%
manufacturing	32% (17% production, 15% vendors)
design	15%
shipping	10%
customer error	5%
other	3%

Marketing errors were found to be due to three basic causes:

1. The company salesforce sold customers something special and failed to follow through to notify manufacturing and engineering of the changes involved (19%).
2. Incorrect order processing resulted in the wrong product being made and shipped (10%).
3. Customer complaints were not adequately attended to (6%).

USING PRODUCT QUALITY AS A SALES TOOL

In addition to lowering production costs by decreasing scrap, rework, and repair, a sound quality program can be used to promote sales and increase market share. Maytag, for instance, bases its entire TV advertising program for appliances on a repairman who sits around with nothing to do. The Zenith slogan, "The quality goes in before the name goes on," is known throughout the Western world. Tektronix, a leading manufacturer of test equipment, uses "Committed to excellence," DIT-MCO International Corp. uses "Quality testing quality," and Levi Strauss, a manufacturer of jeans, says "Quality never goes out of style."

Advertising approaches are not limited to slogans. Product quality is exploited in several ways by stressing operational benefits: low downtime, reduced maintenance costs, and long life. The quality control program itself is sometimes em-

phasized by citing the large number of tests and inspections imposed on a product before shipment. Photographs graphically portray no-nonsense inspectors examining the final product with critical eyes. Still other firms show films or slides of the rigorous engineering tests carried out during product development.

Some firms fill their front lobby with framed certificates of achievement, zero-defects awards or Government Quality System approval letters. Sometimes these are packaged together as a comprehensive selling document.

Case in Point: A machine shop in the U.S. Midwest specializing in precision work was aggressively trying to increase sales. The QC manager suggested that the firm's quality reputation could be a major selling point.

Various QC approvals (letters, testimonials, etc.) sent to the firm by its existing customers were bound together in brochure form and sent to prospective customers. The sales campaign was a whopping success.

Some large firms can attribute their growth to providing quality products and services. IBM, Xerox, McDonald's, and ITT come readily to mind. Japan has built its entire industrial growth plan on high-quality products, perceptively marketed.

A Harvard University study found that companies having high market share and superior quality have the highest return on investment (ROI), and that product quality and market share usually, but by no means always, go together. The study also found that when quality is relatively low, there is a strong negative relationship between marketing expenditures and ROI, confirming the old adage that, "It doesn't pay to promote a poor product" (see Figure 6-1).

Sometimes a firm may have so much confidence in its products that it may translate the benefits into concrete terms. This can take the form of money-back guarantees, low-priced annual maintenance contracts, or formal uptime guarantees.

Case in Point: A machine tool manufacturer faced a very competitive market situation. Because of a superior ruggedized design and stringent manufacturing quality controls, the firm was able to offer a six-month rather

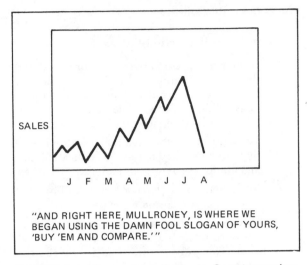

SALES

J F M A M J J A

"AND RIGHT HERE, MULLRONEY, IS WHERE WE
BEGAN USING THE DAMN FOOL SLOGAN OF YOURS,
'BUY 'EM AND COMPARE.' "

FIGURE 6-1. Some Advertising is Counterproductive.

than a ninety-day warranty. As a result, sales surpassed forecasts by 28 percent.

Caution: Despite the benefits of enhanced product quality, there are several instances where quality of design must take into account style, technological change, or utility. One particularly interesting example is the trend in useful life of consumer durables. The force of a healthy economy has resulted in a slightly decreased lifetime for classic items such as refrigerators and home laundry units. Among many possible contributors to this situation are two major considerations. The increased complexity of design has forced trade-offs in material and methods to avoid an undesirable increase in price. Equally important is the tendency of each owner to desire the newest and latest model in an era when design and manufacturing technology have made design changes available at an explosive rate. The assumption, justified by the consumer's purchasing habits, is that he no longer wants an appliance that will last fifteen or twenty years, and he will not tolerate the prices of long-lasting items that look out of style because they last a long time. But, intermediate-term reliability is still important. In these cases, new capabilities that make the product an innovation would be emphasized. A range of control features that extend its flexibility of use; style features in color, shape, texture, and material; lowered noise levels in operation; decreased energy use; and increased portability or storage convenience, where applicable, are all extolled. It is

wise for the quality manager to really understand the nature of the marketplace his or her firm is serving.

REVIEWING REQUESTS FOR QUOTATIONS

A Request For Quotation (RFQ) is a document supplied by a buyer (customer) as a means for a seller to prepare a quotation for products and/or services. The response to an RFQ forms the basis for a contract or purchase order award. Before a contract is issued and signed, there usually is preliminary communication between the seller and the buyer. At this stage, all the buyer's requirements are stated or referenced, and furnished to the seller. The buyer realizes that any changes made to the requirements after reaching agreement will cost more money. The seller agrees to conform to all requirements when signing the contract.

RFQs can be simple agreements with no references, or standard with clear terms and conditions, or complex with many references and/or supplemental documents. In these complex contracts lurk the revelations that must be found before progress on contract negotiation advances too far.

There are two aspects that QC must review. The first deals with contract terms and conditions, the second with nonroutine QC tasks.

The specific contractual provisions worthy of extra attention include:

- applicable part numbers and revision letters (for identification of product)
- change control procedures
- loose contractual verbiage
- customer approvals
- source inspection
- product liability
- material review delegation
- waiver/deviation reports
- warranty
- inspection
- personnel certification
- product identification and serialization
- care of customer-furnished property
- correction of deficiencies
- record retention requirements
- source selection approval

- control of tooling and special test equipment
- packaging, packing, and marking
- customer inspection and test plan evaluation

Loose Contractual Verbiage

Some of these provisions are examined in the following sections.

Contact your contracts department when you see phrases such as "workmanship shall be best commercial practice," "experts in the field," "state of the art product," "shall be of the highest quality," "a best efforts quality program," "specifications shall include but not be limited to" or "a full warranty including any and all latent defects."

Customer Approvals

For job-shop work, the final manufacturing drawings and specifications are transmitted via the sales department to the customer for his or her final approval. Only when the sales, engineering, manufacturing and QC departments have reached a complete understanding with the customer should full-scale production of the product be initiated.

Production without customer approval is usually done at the risk of the manufacturer. Yet waiting for this approval may cause delays involving major losses or other undesirable consequences. In such a case, it may be acceptable to promptly transmit to the customer a drawing on which the following precautionary note is stamped:

Customer Liability
Parts are being processed according to the attached drawing, specifications, and tolerances. If there is any disagreement, notify this office by phoning [area code and exchange number] not later than [date].

Modifications, revisions, and adjustments can then be agreed to by verbal communication. As soon as possible, however, new drawings, showing the agreed-upon changes, should be developed by the manufacturer and confirmed by the customer. Verbal agreements, of course, always carry some degree of risk; such agreements should be kept to an absolute minimum.

Customer Surveillance

Customer surveillance implies the following:

(a) Customer representative(s) are provided with the accommodation and facilities required for the proper accomplishment of the required tasks. This includes office space, telephone, and secretarial services.

(b) Technical and other assistance is provided to the extent required to permit verification, documentation, or release of material.

(c) Inspection and test records are readily available for on-site customer review.

(d) Gauges and other measuring and testing devices are available to customers on a shared basis. This must be provided for by the governing contractual provisions.

(e) Trained company personnel may operate inspection/test devices of a complex or specialized nature as required by the customer during his or her assurance/surveillance activities. (This activity must, of course, be funded by the applicable contract or purchase order because it involves double testing.)

(f) There is an ongoing audit of production, processes, and compliance with quality operating procedures. Any inspection or test performed by the customer must be on a planned, noninterference basis. Industrial and military security regulations may necessitate that the resident customer representative be escorted outside his or her office area. Remember also that resident representatives take up a lot of your people's time.

Case in Point: In one RFQ, the clause for customer surveillance was unnecessarily broad. It could have led to a source inspector sitting in the middle of the seller's assembly line. The QC reviewer added clarifying remarks stipulating noninterference surveillance and a requirement that the source evaluator be accompanied by a seller representative during quality surveys.

Source Inspection

Case in Point: One Quality Control manager in the nuclear power industry had been hit so badly by the direct and hidden costs of source inspection, he distributed fifty framed copies internally of the following:

Dear Customer:
We have three (3) ways of selling inspection hours.
(1) Regular rate $15.50/Hour
(2) If you *watch* $31.00/Hour
(3) If you *help* $62.00/Hour

Warranty

Case in Point: A warranty provision in a RFQ for a ground radar system asked that the warranty period commence after the buyer had turned over the radar to his ultimate customer. In this case, the QC reviewer stated a maximum retention period for the seller and costed the increased period of warranty coverage based on:

- inspection, acceptance, and rejection
- personnel certification
- product identification and serialization
- care of customer furnished property
- correction-of-deficiencies provisions
- quality record retention requirements
- traceability
- source selection, special processing, and subcontract approvals
- control of tooling and special test equipment
- packaging, packing, and marking requirements

The QC tasks are also reviewed for cost and schedule impact. Any unusual, extraordinary, or high-risk elements including probability of achievement and consequence should be flagged for management attention. This typically involves a review of the specification and related documents for compliance. The primary areas involve performance parameters, tolerances, AQLs, reliability, maintainability, safety, use of standard parts, environmental conditions, and use of high-reliability parts.

Deliverable data can also add significant costs. Included here are reliability predictions, quality plans, material review, personnel résumés, test procedures/reports, nonstandard-part data submittals, certificates of compliance, and test data.

Case in Point: One revelation lurking in a contract increased costs by $1600 because order processing overlooked the customer requirement for test data to be furnished in accordance with a customer-referenced specification. This requirement was omitted from the shop work order. Fifty units were shipped. The customer requested the data before rejecting the units received. Since there was no data taken as required, the fifty units were returned at the supplier's expense for completion of contract requirements. Shipping costs alone accounted for $600.

Other tasks requiring additional funds include classification-of-characteristics programs, operator certification (e.g., soldering, welding), special process approvals, qualification or demonstration tests, formal design reviews, and first article inspection.

QC review of RFQs provides the following benefits to the company:

- QC gets to see the big picture early on in the game.
- The QC section of the proposal is well researched and helps it become a selling document.
- QC provides valuable inputs by using specialized expertise.
- QC can prepare time-phased quality plans for other departments to use. This often identifies schedule conflicts.
- High-risk areas (such as reliability demonstrations) are identified and can be properly addressed in the proposal evaluation process.

Case in Point: A shrewd reliability engineer negotiated the following clauses into a contract calling for a reliability demonstration test:

Chargeable Reliability Failures

All failures will be considered chargeable reliability failures with the exceptions listed below. An equipment reliability failure is defined as the inability of a previously acceptable item to perform its required function within previously established limits.

a. A failure caused by another failure: At least one equipment failure shall be counted when a dependent failure is claimed.
b. A failure caused by an accident, mishandling, or abuse during the reliability test.

c. A failure caused by an installation error.

d. A failure that cannot be verified by test instrumentation, inspection, or analysis.

e. A failure caused by an item of equipment being subjected to environmental stresses beyond the designed specification requirement.

f. Failure caused by an identified problem area, including workmanship for which corrective action has been previously established but not necessarily implemented on the failed equipment provided that:

   (1) Prior to completion of testing on the designated reliability test lot, the corrective action is proven by test or analysis to be effective in eliminating the failure source to the satisfaction of the procuring activity.

   (2) A production-contract configuration-effectivity point for the corrective action has been agreed to.

Note: If multiple failure(s) of the same type occur(s) in one or more items of equipment before corrective action is defined, only one failure will be counted, provided that prompt corrective action satisfactory to the procuring activity is taken to eliminate the failure source and provided that the conditions (1) and (2) above are met.

g. A failure that would be deleted by a correction to either the equipment specification or test specification that the buyer agrees should be changed.

h. Component failures that have no effect on the ability of the system to perform its required function within previously established limits.

i. A failure occurring during burn-in or post-repair burn-in tests.

j. Failures that occur during postreliability testing (e.g., acceptance testing).

While one may question the validity of these exceptions, the fact is that the reliability engineer helped protect the interests of his employer by clarifying a potentially controversial area of contract performance.

- Unusual cost items can be estimated and included in the bid price.
- Extra measuring equipment needs can be identified.
- Additional manpower requirements are identified.

- Exceptions or counterproposals can be logically developed.
- Needs for approvals by regulatory bodies, (eg., UL, FAA, FDA, etc.) are determined.

Figure 6-2 provides a summary sheet for management review.

Caution: Reviewing the RFQ and sending in a well-prepared proposal is fine, but the ultimate purchase order from the customer may not reflect all the additions, deletions, or changes. Make sure that purchase orders or contracts are compared to RFQs and proposals in order to close the loop.

CUSTOMER INSPECTION AND TEST PLAN EVALUATION

Customers and some regulatory bodies sometimes require a copy of a manufacturer's inspection and test plan. The purpose of the inspection and test plan review is to assure that it is adequate according to the following criteria:

- Inspection and testing is preplanned.
- Personnel, facilities, and inspection equipment are planned for.
- The inspection is adequate with respect to method, frequency, and coverage.
- It is understandable and adequate for all who have to use it.
- All quality personnel have detailed, documented instructions.
- The customer can verify in advance that the contractor has done all these things.
- The customer's surveyor has a basis for carrying out surveillance.
- There is a record of the inspection and test planning.

Note: The applicable subcontract or purchase order should call out this requirement. The delivery date should be specified, usually well ahead of first delivery.

Some manufacturers have a number of pat excuses for not supplying plans or procedures. Here are some of them and some possible responses from customers.

1. *"You can see them in our shop."*
   (a) We have a policy of reviewing them at our own place in the quiet of the office where there is less chance of confusion.
   (b) We cannot afford the expense of doing it away from the office.

RFQ QUALITY REQUIREMENTS ANALYSIS

CUSTOMER NAME	RFQ NO.	CONTRACT TYPE

PRODUCT DESCRIPTION

START DATE	END DATE	QUANTITY	MAXIMUM RATE/MO.

IDENTICAL TO OR SIMILAR TO PREVIOUS CONTRACT(S)?   ☐ IDENT.   ☐ SIMILAR   ☐ NO

IF NO, EXPLAIN

ARE QUALITY STANDARDS CLEAR? ☐   DIFFICULT TO INTERPRET? ☐   UNCLEAR? ☐

IDENTIFY SPECIAL OR UNUSUAL QUALITY-RELATED REQUIREMENTS
(USE EXTRA SHEETS IF NECESSARY)

SUMMARY STATEMENT

ADVANCED METROLOGY TECHNIQUES

SPECIAL INSTRUCTION EQUIPMENT/FIXTURES/GAUGES

SPECIAL TEST EQUIPMENT

SPECIAL OR UNUSUAL SKILLS

WORKLOAD/MANPOWER

OTHER

ANALYSIS MADE BY	DATE	REVIEWED BY	DATE

FIGURE 6-2. RFQ Quality Summary Sheet
Courtesy Canadian Marconi Company.

    (c) We require copies for distribution to the engineer, end customer, legal, etc.

    (d) The subcontract calls for them to be submitted.

2. *"They are proprietary procedures."*

    (a) What is proprietary about them?

    (b) Proprietary to whom?

    (c) Everybody does it that way.

    (d) That is a fairly standard method and we do not consider it proprietary.

    (e) Delete the proprietory aspects and then submit.

    (f) We have means of protecting proprietary information if necessary.

3. *"Our people are experts—they don't need procedures."*

    (a) Good, then let them write the procedures before you lose them.

    (b) They may be experts, but they still need to be advised on which method and frequency is required.

    (c) Procedures satisfy us that you have planned the job, considered the need for ordering special gauges, and ensured everyone knows the requirements; and they provide a record of what was done.

    (d) Procedures are required so that our surveyor knows what is planned and what the QC engineer agreed to was adequate.

    (e) Procedures maintain continuity regardless of sickness, holidays, new employees, etc.

    (f) Detailed procedures for inspecting *every* characteristic are a requirement of the program standard, but we are only asking for the less straightforward ones.

    (g) Hiring experts to do a simple job is expensive.

    (h) Procedures prevent unnecessary duplication of work.

    (i) Would you not prefer our people to survey the work against your procedures, rather than against their own ideas?

4. *"That's standard shop practice."*

    (a) Good, then here is a good place for a standard shop practice procedure. It will not have to be detailed within the plan; just reference it by number and send us a copy to look at.

    (b) We want to check your standard practices against those in applicable codes and contract requirements.

5. *"It will cost extra."*

    (a) Fine, send us a copy of the bill.

    (b) Give us a cost estimate with full back-up details.

    (c) Your competitors don't charge for this.

    (d) You agreed to submit them in your sales proposal and cost quotation.

For a growing number of products and industries, customers want to involve themselves in a supplier's test and inspection planning. It is a trend that the more progressive firm ought to accept rather than resist—it just might result in a better, safer product.

A WORD ABOUT LICENSING

Licensing agreements are in many ways a "product" that is "sold." Such an arrangement requires special QC considerations.

Case in Point: An American firm noted for its innovative high-technology products licensed to a Japanese organization the Far Eastern rights to its new line of robots. The Tokyo-based corporation sent over a team of production experts including a senior quality engineer to discuss the quality control aspects of manufacture. Among the tasks performed during the three-week stay:

1. Reviewed design documentation, safety tests results, and reliability predictions. Major observation: drawing tolerances appeared too severe.

2. Secured copies of all inspection instructions, test procedures, process control documents, and QC procedures; queried rationale for certain measurements and controls or lack thereof.

3. Thoroughly discussed workmanship and other quality standards, including talks with shop floor people.

4. Reviewed rejection reports, failure analyses, and yield summaries in detail, so as to assist in quality planning.

5. Followed product flow from incoming inspection through shipping, making note of all test/measuring equipment, machinery, tooling, and "tricks of the trade." Hundreds of questions were asked during this five-day activity.

6. Visited three most critical suppliers to discuss acceptance criteria and expected quality levels. Side benefit: personal relationship established.

7. Set up dates for critical milestones:

    • date for joint review of proposed assembly line in Tokyo

- date for joint review of first robot built
- dates for qualification start/completion
- date for next visit to U.S.

8. Established communication channels for handling problems, failures, engineering changes, and general questions.

When the visitors left, the U.S. manufacturer's quality control manager commented, "These past three weeks have been strenuous, intensive, and probing. As a result, I think I've learned a few things about our own product and ways of doing things that I didn't consider before. A few of these will have to be changed. It has been an illuminating experience."

IMPROVING THE COMMUNICATION OF QUALITY REQUIREMENTS

The timely and accurate communication of customer or market quality requirements is not easy. It is probably one of the weakest communication loops in the industry. There are, however, some general approaches that have proven relatively successful over the years.

√ *Design review* keeps the design effort sharply focused. Unnecessary, costly frills, unsafe conditions, or missing functions/features will usually be uncovered.

√ *Product planning committees* allow QC, engineering, and manufacturing to better understand product concept, market needs, and expected sales volume.

√ *Statements of work,* initiated by marketing, try to provide the work demands and milestones required to generate a new product.

√ *Cost and price targets* usually limit engineering design options and save time otherwise wasted by evaluating expensive design solutions or costly high-reliability parts.

√ *Specifications* attempt to provide quantitative and qualitative design goals.

Caution: Marketing should describe *what* is required, not *how* it is to be accomplished.

√ *Prototype evaluation,* a detailed critique of a prototype model, can usually detect if engineering, manufacturing, or QC has gone astray.

√ *Supporting data*—market surveys, competitive data, product applications, market size—pro-

vide valuable insight to the required design and QC activities.

√ *Preliminary product support plan* allows the designer and QC to evaluate Mean Time To Repair (MTTR), accessibility, self-test features, and physical packaging approach.

THE NATURE OF CUSTOMER COMPLAINTS

Even when both the buyer and the seller are competent, careful, and well-intentioned, some purchases are bound to go wrong. There will be returns to accept and adjustments to arrange. The seller must be tactful and patient with those who are difficult to handle. Get complaints out into the open. Apologize promptly and without reservation when the mistake is yours. Never allow a customer to lose face, even when he or she is wrong.

Firms differ in the extent to which they classify and evaluate complaints from their customers. Except in extreme cases, complaints are an unreliable measure of customer service effectiveness. It is estimated that less than 25 percent of all causes of customer dissatisfaction are ever verbalized into complaints. In addition, complaints rarely are representative of the firm's customer mix. A cross-section of complaints is certainly not a cross-section of the market; it's only a cross-section of the more vocal people in the market. Furthermore, only a small percentage of complaints are placed directly with the manufacturer. The number that filters back from distributors and retailers is understandably quite a bit less.

This doesn't mean that complaints aren't useful in identifying specific weaknesses in your QC system or outright customer service failures. Indeed, when a customer does register a complaint, you are getting an unparalleled opportunity to sell him more solidly than he's ever been sold before: Effective complaint-handling is high on most customers' lists of priorities in selecting potential sources of supply.

It must also be recognized that customer complaints are not always product-quality based. Here are a few examples:

- The product was not delivered on time (sometimes occurs because of faulty order processing).
- The units were shipped to wrong address.
- Invoice payment due date does not agree with terms of contract.
- Replies to queries were slow.

- The wrong product was selected by sales for the particular customer application.
- The shipping container was inadequate.
- The shipment was incomplete.

Such discrepancies have a strong bearing on customer satisfaction. Several companies have implemented a shipping-paperwork quality control approach sometimes referred to as *invoice inspection*. Where applicable, such a control point can drastically cut down customer complaints.

Case in Point: One month after invoice inspection was introduced in a large N/C machinery firm, nonhardware customer complaints were reduced by 50 percent. Among the items discovered:

- The invoice (and hardware) part number revision level did not agree with the customer purchase order (PO).
- The requirement for a certificate of compliance had not been included in internal work authorizations.
- Technical manuals did not accompany the equipment as was required.
- The release note form used was not the one required by the customer.
- The shipping order was incorrect and contained several omissions.
- Invoices contained numerous typographical errors and transpositions.
- A serial number had been duplicated.
- Some computer peripherals not on the PO were listed on the invoice.
- A customer source inspection stamp was not evident on the paperwork as required by the PO.

USING FIELD PRODUCT FAILURE INFORMATION

Operation failure/discrepancy data is recognized as an extremely valuable information source. Failures not always detectable in-plant provide a basis for corrective action and/or product improvement. For this reason a high degree of emphasis should be placed on an organized and disciplined approach to complaint investigations.

Action on a customer complaint should entail:

- correction of the condition in the product which caused the complaint—that is, restoration of service—and
- correction of the basic cause of recurring problems.

The first action, which almost automatically occurs, is often the only action taken on the complaint. A good quality program should require that more be done. Necessary actions beyond restoration of service are:

- Investigation to determine if the incident is isolated or a general problem.
- Analysis of the problem for cause.
- Elimination of the cause.
- Regular attention to chronic problems by reporting them and the status of correction to responsible management.

Warranty claims, product audits, and formal field service failure forms provide a steady source of fairly reliable data, although field servicepeople sometimes ignore some aspects of this paperwork routine. These reports usually contain all information pertinent to the failure, such as:

- customer
- location
- customer complaint
- description of problem
- part number and serial number
- repairs necessary
- estimated repair cost

When properly completed, they can be used to pinpoint the products or components of products that are failing and the reasons for failure.

Customer complaints sometimes appear on Corrective Action Request (CAR) forms routed to the contracts, marketing, or sales department. Government agencies have their own specialized systems. Telexes, letters, and irate phone calls are other sources of information. Regardless of the medium, the data should be collected because it is a very important indicator of customer dissatisfaction. Some ground rules:

√ Inform all departments of the need for timely feedback of this information.

√ Centralize the failure data bank, whether it be under marketing, sales, contracts, customer service, or QC.

√ Organize failure data by customer name, failed part number, geographic region, or other appropriate sort.

√ Designate responsibility for determination of failure cause and corrective action recommendations.

√ Set a target response date and issue interim reports to the customer, if necessary.

√ Cover field product failure data collection by an operating procedure, and periodically audit.

√ Encourage distributors and dealers to feed back customer complaints.

Quality is a marketable commodity for which money will be paid. If it can be determined that customer satisfaction is lacking, market efforts will have to be increased in order to overcome the buildup of sales resistance. If, on the other hand, customer satisfaction is very high and performance is outstanding, this is an indication that market effort may be directed toward emphasizing this fact. Customers may be willing to pay for higher quality and reliability. The lower the demands and downtime costs experienced, the greater the likelihood that the customer will be willing to pay higher initial prices or perhaps utilize the next lower-priced item available from the same supplier. It is, therefore, extremely important from a dollar and cents standpoint to find out what field performance is.

Observation: A satisfied customer can lead to other side benefits. The best compliment a QC manager can receive is to have a customer remove its resident surveillance inspection because the QC manager has shown that his or her team can do the job, even when the going gets rough. Remember, QC has to press hard to conquer the elusive, underlying problems that perpetuate repetitive failures. No one else is going to spearhead the effort for you.

HANDLING DEVIATION AND WAIVER REQUESTS

The handling of deviations and waivers is an important customer interface. For our purposes, a *deviation* is defined as a specific written authorization, granted before the manufacture of an item, to depart from a particular performance or design requirement of a specification, drawing, or other document for a specific number of units or specific period of time. A deviation for a temporary time period might, for example, be requested relating to an alternative material because the delivery schedule cannot be met unless the deviation is granted. An engineering change might not be appropriate because the documented design is regarded as superior to the alternative. Unless unusual circumstances exist, deviations affecting safety are not submitted. Suggested deviations that would affect service operation or mainte-

nance are best covered by appropriate revisions in drawings and technical manuals via formal engineering changes.

A *waiver* is defined as a written authorization to accept an item that, during production or after having been submitted for inspection (including tests), is found to depart from specified requirements; but it nevertheless is considered suitable for use "as is" or after rework by an approved method. If the discrepancy does not affect contract end-item performance, safety, size, weight, reliability, or serviceability, it may, in general, be handled by a Material Review Board (MRB).

When a justifiable reason for not following a customer requirement exists, a formal mechanism is needed for orderly review and approval. Deviations or waivers should be documented to allow ready identification of its nature. Also, management and quality control approvals should be provided. (See Figure 6-3.)

A loose set of standards for authorizing deviations can lead to many variations from standard practices. These variations can create confusion among the staff and inevitably lead to more work and destruction of existing systems. Therefore, quality management must ensure that deviations do not become an escape route from the manufacture of compliant products and services.

When requesting a deviation or waiver from a customer, the following points should be highlighted:

√ Describe in detail the nature of the proposed departure from the technical requirements of the affected engineering drawings and specifications.

√ Explain the reasons that make it impossible or unreasonable to comply with the engineering drawings or specifications within the specified delivery schedule and tell why the request is proposed in lieu of a permanent engineering change.

√ Define any side effects on test procedures, test equipment, or inspection instructions.

√ If a similar request was previously approved, evaluate why the problem has recurred.

√ Describe any corrective action that has or will be taken to prevent a recurrence.

√ Indicate and describe in detail any effect on logistic support material including publications.

There are some problems with the handling of waivers that should be avoided; these are illustrated in the following Cases in Point.

SELLER'S REQUEST FOR DEVIATION/WAIVER
(SRDW)

1. SELLER'S NAME & ADDRESS	2. SELLER'S MFG CODE	3. SRDW NO.
	4. PURCHASE ORDER NO.	5. DATE
	4. PURCHASE ORDER LINE NO.	6. DEVIATION ☐ WAIVER ☐

7. SPECIFICATIONS AND ENGINEERING DRAWINGS AFFECTED

SPECIFICATION OR DRAWING NO.	REV	MFG CODE	SPECIFICATION OR DRAWING NO.	REV	MFG CODE

8. SELLER'S PART NO. AND NAME

9. TITLE OF DEVIATION OR WAIVER

10. DESCRIPTION OF DEVIATION OR WAIVER

11. NEED FOR DEVIATION OR WAIVER (REASON)

12. EFFECT ON DELIVERY SCHEDULE	13. PRODUCTION EFFECTIVITY
14. EFFECT ON P.O. PRICE	15. QUANTITY OF ITEMS INVOLVED
16. RECURRING DEVIATION/WAIVER ☐ YES ☐ NO	17. CORRECTIVE ACTION

18. EFFECT ON LOGISTIC SUPPORT MATERIAL INCLUDING PUBLICATIONS

FIGURE 6-3. Typical Deviation/Waiver Request
Courtesy Canadian Marconi Company.

Case in Point: The sales manager informed the chief inspector that the customer had authorized a certain waiver. Acting on this information, the discrepant material was shipped. It was rejected upon receipt. Apparently, the buyer, who was nontechnical, had not understood the nature of the discrepancy and had "not really accepted the waiver." *Moral: Get waivers approved in writing.*

Case in Point: A case of interpretation of workmanship standards prevented the shipment of a large number of motor generator sets. The customer QC representative was formally contacted for an official interpretation. Put on the spot, she opted for the more severe interpretation even though it was subsequently discovered that another source had been supplying sets for years with the looser interpretation. *Moral: Sometimes a formal waiver request is not the best way to determine product acceptability.*

DESIGN AND ADMINISTRATION OF PRODUCT WARRANTY

A contemporary warranty for a complex or consumer product might be:

> Except for a warranty of title and the warranty set forth herein for repair or replacement of the articles supplied hereunder, no other warranty, express or implied, including, but not limited to, those of merchantability and fitness for any particular purpose, shall apply to the articles supplied hereunder; and seller shall have no other obligation or liability to purchaser or any other person for any loss, damage, or injury whatsoever that may be sustained by anyone as a consequence of any defect in or failure of the articles supplied hereunder and whether attributable to a defect in design, material, or workmanship or any other cause whatsoever. Furthermore, purchaser agrees and undertakes to indemnify and save harmless seller, its officers, employees, agents, or representatives, from any such claims for any loss, damage or injury.

Warranties can be a very positive sales tool; if poorly administered, they can drive customers to the competition. Warranties must be reasonable,

properly costed, based on product characteristics, and well managed. Here are some considerations in the design and administration of a warranty program:

- Is the warranty policy useful to customers?
- Has the warranty statement been reviewed by legal counsel?
- Have consumable items such as lamps and fuses been excluded?
- Are all exclusions clear?
- Is the method of measuring the warranty period adequately defined? This can be stated in terms of elapsed time from date of purchase, "on" time, a specified "on" time, or elapsed time, whichever comes first. Degree of wear, such as in tires, can be used to define prorated warranties.
- Is there control over unauthorized maintenance, such as tamper-proof seals?
- How long will the item be stored prior to sale, and will this storage impact reliability and, hence, warranty?
- Is the use environment known?
- Is the unit marked, labeled, or otherwise identified so as to signify existence of warranty coverage?
- What controls exist to prevent nonallowable or duplicated charges being assigned to a warranty account?
- Are customer warranty claims promptly attended to?
- How are high-cost purchased items included in the product handled from a warranty point of view?
- Does warranty apply to design deficiencies?
- Who pays shipping charges?
- Are the personnel assigned to warranty administration tactful, diplomatic, and sufficiently flexible?
- How are out-of-maintenance (e.g., lubrication schedule not followed) or customer-induced failures handled?
- Are warranty failure information and costs collected and distributed to applicable operating departments?
- Who determines whether a warranty claim is valid? How are controversial cases handled?
- Is enough time and effort spent analyzing the nature of warranty returns?

Caution: Some firms deliberately "doctor" warranty costs in order to look good. Be on the lookout for mischarged accounts and delayed charges.

Observation: The accounting distinction between a warranty claim and a debit claim is significant. In a warranty claim the cost impact is limited to the cost of effecting the repair. A debit note results in a reversal of the shipment revenue, thus decreasing net sales, increasing inventory, and decreasing operating profits in the current period. The starting point of a warranty is a crucial aspect that requires careful attention.

Treat the Customer Right

Customer representatives come to visit your plant for QC surveys, design reviews, source inspection, witnessing of tests, and progress review. Whatever their reason, they must be made to feel comfortable. Consider these points:

- Meet out-of-towners at the airport and deliver them safely to their hotel.
- Pick them up at the hotel in the morning if your plant is difficult to reach from the hotel.
- Help them make return travel arrangements.
- Take your visitors for lunch and/or dinner if circumstances are appropriate.
- Allow source inspectors reasonable use of your measuring equipment.
- Give visiting customer representatives a private room for preparing notes, holding meetings, or telephoning back to their plant.
- Take them shopping or sight-seeing when the day's work is done.

Pitfall to Avoid: Don't be excessive or insincere in your hosting; this can backfire and cause you real trouble.

Caution: Good manners cannot substitute for a quality product. Treating a customer well has the following benefits:

a. You will establish good working relationships.
b. The customer will feel comfortable and will be less likely to complain.
c. The customer may call you before sending a Corrective Action Request (CAR).
d. You will have a competitive edge on future bids.
e. Buyer/seller communications will be more informal.

PACKING AND SHIPPING: THE FINAL STEP

A significant number of customer complaints involve product shipment. Quality control does not stop at the end of the production line. Handling, transport, and storage introduce many perils to the product. Some of these are fully predictable: temperature, humidity, vibration, and shock. Others are the result of ignorance, carelessness, and blunder. In some cases the product is in greater danger from handling and transport than from actual usage. The following seven-step program for protecting a product during transportation is recommended:

1. Define the packaging objectives.
2. Determine the method of shipment including routing.
3. Determine the ability of the product to withstand the transportation hazards. Tests can be run that simulate shock, vibration, and other transport damage. The stresses are measured in terms of frequency (cycles per second), g levels of deceleration, pulse shapes, and other quantifiable measures. The experience gained is subsequently included into specifications for packaging and vehicle loading.
4. Interpret the test data to compare the product's resistance to the simulated environment with the predicted environmental hazard level.
5. Decide on a course of action based on the test data (e.g., modifying the product, changing the distribution method) or
6. Select a packaging material.
7. Combine the package with the product and together subject them to final testing. This can be done by trial shipment or simulated laboratory testing.

Once you've got the correct packaging, the shipping department will need to have:

1. Standard packaging instructions that cover all items to be shipped and a training program to assure employee understanding.
2. A procedure requiring loose or "spare" items to be packaged and identified as carefully as the major product.
3. A policy of continually evaluating carriers and updating packaging methods and material storage. (Several companies include "g" shock indicators with their shipments; results are checked upon receipt at the other end.)
4. An organized method of reporting any shipping damage complaints to the shipping department.

5. An area for packaging and shipping preparation that is clean, orderly, properly equipped, and well laid out.

Case in Point: A computer manufacturer tests its read-only storage units on a vibration table to simulate transportation. This test has resulted in a 25 percent savings over former methods and has virtually eliminated costly field servicing from transportation shock and jolts.

Some products, such as drugs, may be made in batches that may be released only after tests are completed on a sample. When the batches are being held, special inventory procedures are needed to assure that unreleased product is not inadvertently sent to the customer. The shipping department must, in fact, work to a requirement that only articles bearing evidence of QC acceptance can be shipped. This control is easily integrated into an invoice inspection system, discussed elsewhere in this chapter.

Even if the end article survives shipping, product storage can cause problems. Large quantities of raw materials, components, and finished products are constantly in storage, awaiting further processing, sale, or use. To minimize deterioration and degradation, various acts can be taken:

1. Establish the shelf life of the product based on laboratory and field data.
2. Establish standards to place limits on time in storage.
3. Date the product conspicuously to make it easy to identify the age of the product in stock.
4. Design the package and control the environment to minimize expected and unexpected degradation.

A common weakness in these programs is the failure to *date* the product conspicuously. Sometimes this failure is just due to poor technique. For example, iron in open storage rusts away if the rust preservative is not changed annually. However, some failure to date conspicuously is the result of deliberate marketing decisions: The dates can be put on the back of the product or on the front in tiny print because the advertising has priority, or because there is a fear of dating the product in a way that enables the customer to know if he is getting out-of-date product. These reasons, if ever valid, now have become obsolete. Conspicuous dating on outer cartons as well as on the unit package aids in traceability and stock rotation, and in establishing age of inventories.

The return on investment on quality cost improvement projects in the physical distribution area usually leaps over the corporate return threshold easily. The amazing thing is that they are so often overlooked.

KEEP IN CONTACT WITH THE FIRING LINE

The alert QC manager should make it a point to keep in contact with the action of the factory, distributors, customers, and users. Get out of your office and visit the combat area. Quality management should take every opportunity to see products in operation and to personally investigate major or chronic problems. There is no substitute for seeing a problem firsthand. The following benefits may be expected:

- Positive customer reaction to your interest.
- Detection of user problems that have not flowed through normal communication channels.
- Improved ability to relate design and manufacturing standards to field performance.
- Identification of actual conditions of use; often these are significantly different from those used as the basis for design.
- Determination of need for improved field test equipment or maintenance procedures.

Case in Point: A quality engineer visited the repair shop of a major airline to see how her firm's equipment was being maintained. She noticed that the airline had failed to purchase a relatively inexpensive special test unit sold by her firm and as a consequence inadequate tests were performed at great cost. After purchase of the $1700 unit, repair times decreased and product integrity improved.

- Identification of installation problems, which are often neglected sources of product quality information. Troubles in this phase are frequently not recorded or reported in a formal way. Each person visiting a customer location should be alert to the need for feedback of product performance data to responsible management. Consideration should be given to preparation of a form or guide for this purpose for use by marketing, design engineering, quality control, or other functions who have occasion to make such visits. It is important that these reports be collected and analyzed along with other feedback data to discover real-world performance problems.

QUALITY ASSURANCE OF INSTRUCTION MANUALS

Achieving customer satisfaction is a fundamental goal for any manufacturer. This is done, in part, through the communications channels that are established between seller and buyer. There are many channels: advertisements, sales literature, salespeople's contracts, instructions manuals, and, if the product breaks down, the repairperson. Of these, instruction manuals are perhaps the most important.

More than any other single document, the instruction manual, properly prepared, gives the complete picture of the product. It can be the chief instrument for ensuring proper performance, reliability, and safety of that product. In case of litigation, instruction manuals serve as documented, *prima facie* evidence of warnings and instructions concerning the avoidance of danger or injury.

Two types of manuals are common: the owner's manual and the service manual.

The *owner's manual* instructs the buyer in the proper use and care of the product. It may also convey a sales message to enhance acceptability. The text is usually very readable, the illustrations simplified and informative, and printing may utilize more than one color. Any instructions for maintenance and repair are made as simple as possible. The owner's manual must contain adequate precautionary statements against foreseeable misuse or mishandling that could result in injury to the owner or others.

The *service manual* is designed for the person who will maintain and repair the product. Its objective is to convey a message that will help ensure the performance, reliability, and safety of the product. It carries a more detailed message than the owner's manual, relating these six major facts about the product:

- What it is.
- How it is installed.
- How it is operated.
- How it works.
- What is in it and where to find it.
- How to maintain and repair it.

The service manual also identifies potential hazards to the repairperson, who, in the course of maintenance and repair, may come into contact with high voltage, dangerous hydraulic or pneumatic pressures, radiation, or toxic or fragmenting materials.

Both definitions are generalizations, of course, because the manuals will reflect the product. A complex device such as a computer will be accompanied by both basic types plus many others of special purpose. A simple product may need only the simplest of manuals—perhaps only a single page.

Most faults in manuals can be summed up in one word: *invalid.* The manuals simply do not represent the product. Here are the main reasons and proposed solutions:

Undocumented Changes. There are two primary sources of such changes. The first is that design and production are dynamic processes in which change is a key factor—change in design, in components and materials, in layout. This results in changes that may not appear in the manuals, causing such glitches as wrong designations for controls, components pictured but not present (and vice versa), and disassembly procedures that make little sense because parts were added or removed without notifying the writer.

The second kind of undocumented changes are those that result from field experience. Too often, instruction manuals continue to exist without being updated to reflect changes in the product.

Whatever the cause of inaccuracies, the result can be a costly, time-consuming, and often impossible activity that does not engender good customer manufacturer relations. Worse, the product may be damaged in the process of use or repair, or it may cause injury.

Solution: Set up an effective system of notification of engineering and production changes, with all editions of the manuals firmly in the loop.

Wrong Slant. Instruction manuals must be adapted to the capabilities of the users. Owner's manuals, for example, should not be so simplified that they fail to tell how to make the product perform properly; nor should they be so detailed that the owner is confused. A service manual must not compel a highly qualified repairperson to wade through a series of detailed procedures for an elementary test, although a less qualified person should be given such information if he or she needs it.

Of all the problems with manuals, establishing the proper slant is probably the most troublesome because of the wide range of experience, education, and motivation of the users.

Solution: Carefully analyze the needs of the intended users, with the objective of achieving a level of detail that will satisfy the broadest cross-section.

Omissions. Through oversight by the writer, manuals may fail to cover essential topics. Consequently, the user must fill in the gaps, if he or she can.

Solution: Careful planning of content by one who knows the needs of the user. A detailed outline that serves as a firm foundation for text and illustrations is essential.

Unnecessary Complexity. To be effective, a manual must tell exactly what the user needs to know—no more and no less—and in words that can be easily understood with one reading.

Solution: Although instruction manuals are often prepared by technical writers, the ultimate responsibility for their validity and clarity falls upon the engineering staff. This is appropriate because the designer knows more about the product than anyone else: its strengths, weaknesses, and potential hazards. The designer thus knows what makes a manual effective or ineffective.

Inaccuracies, omissions, wrong slant, and unnecessary complexity can be avoided and reduced by a two-step process called *validation and verification.* It should be made an integral part of the quality assurance system.

Validation deals primarily with inaccuracies and omissions. Members of the engineering staff who know most about the product check every procedure, every part location, every reference. In short, they check every detail to ensure as nearly perfect a match between product and manual as possible.

Verification helps detect major faults such as wrong slant and unnecessary complexity. It is equivalent to field testing in which the actual user does the testing. For example, people may be asked to comment on the owner's manual that accompanies a household product. Actual repairpeople are assigned to make repairs on equipment gimmicked with typical breakdowns. They are expected to make those repairs using only the instructions provided in the service manual.

Such verification is being increasingly recognized as the only sure way of finding out what customers think of the whole package—the product as well as its instruction manual. It must be an aggressive assurance process backed by an equally effective control procedure for dealing with any problems that are uncovered.

MODIFICATION KIT PROOFING (KEEPING CUSTOMERS SANE)

When it is necessary for equipment in the field to be modified for performance or safety reasons, or simply to bring the equipment up to the latest configuration, appropriate quality planning is necessary. Usually a modification kit is sent out to the field in order to effect the required physical changes. The Engineering Change Committee will usually indicate if proofing of the mod kit and associated instruction is required, where it is to be accomplished, and by whom. *Kit proofing* means that the installation instruction and kit must be validated before shipment. Typical QC controls include:

1. Examination of the modification kit instruction for clarity, completeness, and appropriate safety cautions.

2. Physical checking that the kit when installed per the modification instruction actually can be practically accomplished in a workmanlike manner with available tools.

3. Functional test, if applicable, to ensure that the modification performs its required objective and does not degrade previously acceptable functions or safety features.

4. Test and inspection of parts kit for compliance to drawings.

5. Documentation that kit proofing has successfully been accomplished by quality control.

6. Ensurance that appropriate technical or maintenance manual revisions are sent with the kit.

Kit proofing cannot be left to chance. It should be covered by a quality control operating procedure so that engineering, material control, field service, and technical publications groups are aware of the requirement. An ineffective control over this element of change can lead to downed equipment and very unhappy customers.

CUSTOMERS, SAFETY, AND PRODUCT LIABILITY

With product liability claims mounting to the millions of dollars and the judgments in many cases doing the same, insurance premiums for many companies are becoming prohibitively large. Some companies have even been forced out of business as a result of these two factors. The prudent enterprise must control many areas to forestall such litigation.

Obviously, the closer any company comes to designing and manufacturing a product that cannot fail and cannot injure anyone under all conditions of use or reasonable abuse, the safer the company is. Of course, at the same time it must be making a product that will sell. Although perfect success in such an endeavor is unlikely, the careful examination and improvement of product and process designs and the thorough application of established QC control elements throughout the operation will materially reduce the risks to which the enterprise would otherwise be exposed.

The product may be a very good one in every technical respect, but it is only as good as the customer perceives it to be. Customer perception may be significantly influenced by sales personnel, by public and private statements, by management, and by advertising. It is therefore imperative that these sources of potential misrepresentation be properly controlled. Sales personnel should be made thoroughly aware of the actual capabilities of the product and of the exact limits of what they may promise the customer in product performance and service. They should also know the legal implications of any unauthorized quality, performance, service, or application guarantees they may give the customer. Such guarantees are inducements to purchase. Any samples or models shown or given to customers must be entirely representative of the product being sold.

Advertising must be carefully constructed and reviewed so that it tells or implies no more than the truth about the product's capabilities. To give the potential customer the impression that a product will last for ten years, when the design life is five, or that it may be used by anyone, when only professionals can use it safely, is to expose the manufacturer to large and unnecessary risks. Only advertising that tells the truth should be used.

Proper marketing includes three basic duties:

(1) the duty to give appropriate instructions for safe and proper use of the product; (2) the duty to warn of dangers inherent in the product when used in a proper manner and for its intended purpose; and (3) the duty to provide adequate warnings of the dangers and hazards inherent in a reasonably foreseeable but unintended use of the product. The duty to warn generally arises when the danger presented by a product exceeds that contemplated by the ordinary consumer. A cause of action predicated on strict tort liability is comprised of four essential elements: (a) a product that is defective; (b) a product that reaches the consumer with substantial change in its condition from the time it was originally sold; (c) a defect that renders the product unreasonably dangerous and (d) an unreasonably dangerous defect that causes injury to the ultimate user.

Contract law is involved in the case of warranty breach; negligence and strict liability are covered by the law of torts. A *tort* is a breach of a duty, other than a contractual duty, which gives rise to an action for damages. Since legal action under warranty must derive liability from contract, there must be privity of contract (direct contact) for the action to proceed. Because of warranty limitations under contract law, U.S. courts, in the case of the consumer, apply the concept of strict liability in tort (that is, a manufacturer can be liable without fault).

The theoretical underpinning for a strict tort liability action against a product supplier is threefold: manufacturing defects or flaws, design defects, and marketing defects, the subject of this section. Marketing defects involve (1) the failure to provide *any* warning of the risks or hazards involved in the use of a product, (2) the failure to provide an *adequate* warning of the risks or hazards involved in the use of a product, and (3) the failure to provide appropriate and adequate instructions and directions for the safe use of a product.

There are four essential elements that comprise an actionable marketing defect:

1. The product supplier must actually know or reasonably foresee the risk of harm inherent in the product or that may be involved in the intended or reasonably anticipated use of the product.

2. The product must possess a marketing defect.

3. The absence of the warning and/or instruction must render the product unreasonably danger-

ous to the ultimate user or consumer of the product.

4. The failure to warn and/or instruct must represent a causative factor in the product user's injury.

Bulk supply presents a particularly difficult problem. For example, chemicals sold by truck transport or rail transport are normally expected to be placed in smaller containers for ultimate sale to the public. It is realistically impossible to affix any type of label or provide any type of accompanying document that would follow the product to its ultimate destination and the ultimate user. Consequently, the intermediate distributor occupies a particularly important position in the distributive chain of bulk products that, because of dangerous conditions or hazards, require warnings and directions for safe use to the ultimate user.

Prescriptive drugs, and apparati such as intra-uterine devices, constitute an exception to the general principle that the product supplier must warn the ultimate user of a product. The duty to warn is discharged when the manufacturer adequately warns the physician of dangers associated with the drug of the medical device. The duty to warn, of course, must be reasonable under the circumstances. The rationale for this exception contemplates that the physician is a learned intermediary who knows the patient and is the party best qualified to make an informed choice after weighing the utility and benefits of the drug or medical device against the risk of harm inherent in its use.

Product liability laws in the U.S., Canada, and elsewhere are in process of change, but at the time of this writing there is no uniform statute of limitations that operates to limit the manufacturer's eventual risk. For this reason, the business should be prepared to defend itself against failure of any product it has ever produced and to react rapidly and effectively when such a failure occurs. This translates into retaining indefinitely the records that demonstrate concern for and control of the safety and reliability of the product, both through preventive efforts and corrective action. Such records might include those of design and development, purchased material, internal processing, packing, shipping, warehousing, installation, service, field performance, failure, and customer complaint. (See checklist on this page.)

Of course, not every piece of data, record, or item of correspondence must be retained. The retention/disposal decision should be based on a realistic evaluation of the classes of documents involved. Certainly, those that any prudent person would keep to support a position should be retained; their unavailability might raise suspicion in the minds of the courts.

Caution: Selective disposal of records from within a class can be extremely damaging in court.

The producer must also be prepared to undertake a product recall in the event of a safety or performance problem developing in the field. To do this effectively requires specific knowledge of which items are suspect, of where they are in the distribution cycle and with customers, of what is to be done with them, and of the personnel needed to deal with them. Also necessary is documentation of the effort and its results, including selected publication to capitalize on the organization's response for future commercial benefit.

Records retention and product recall are directed toward minimizing the extent of and conducting a successful defense against a product liability claim and are, therefore, of vital concern. Our main interests, however, must be toward preventing a valid claim in the first place. Causing grief to customers is not the way to achieve orderly and profitable growth.

CHECKLIST OF RECORDS RETENTION FOR PRODUCT LIABILITY

Maintenance of clear and adequate records is a primary responsibility of the quality manager. However, recordkeeping is an important element required not only of the quality control manager but of all departments within the company if the product liability threat is to be reduced. Compare your records with the list shown below:

√ Organizations and societies to which the company's professional employees and any consulting firms belong.

√ List of all drawings and plans pertaining to the product including changes.

√ List of all foreseeable uses of the product.

√ List of all patents and patent applications pertaining to the product.

√ List of all approved sources of raw material and components used in the product.

√ Manufacturing process sheets that detail the sequence and methods of product manufacture, including control points.

√ List of all safety devices and features included in the product.

√ Engineering data on all the safety factors and analyses used in the design of the product.

√ Complete list of all advertising materials, brochures, and representations made about the product.

√ List of all test procedures, reports/data, and controls for quality control of the product. The retention time for quality records is of prime importance. Regulatory standards, legal codes, and other documents should be scrutinized to determine the minimum retention period.

√ Personnel records showing education and training of all professional personnel.

√ List of information given to purchasers and ultimate users of the product (decals, plates, instruction books, maintenance books, etc.).

√ List of all purchasers of the product by date.

√ Serial numbers or lot control procedures.

√ Copy of quality control manual.

A WORD ABOUT LIFE CYCLE COSTING

Life cycle costing looks at the total costs of securing service from long-life products (see Figure 6-4). In many instances these costs, over the useful life span, are several times the original purchase price. Life cycle costing is a technique for optimizing the user's costs rather than those of the manufacturer.

Case in Point: A new, complex electronic system is to be developed. The user decides that all repairs must be performed in the field with highly skilled engineering technicians. The maintenance manual can then be reduced to a set of schematics. The training program can be held to a minimum, and the test equipment can be standard. On the other hand, the logistic spares must be distributed as wide as the equipment is deployed with a full range of parts at each location. Conversely, if only regular maintenance personnel are employed, manuals will have to be detailed, and simplified special test equipment must be designed. In some cases, it may be impossible to repair in the field and a service depot capability will be required. This impact will change maintenance support cost estimates drastically.

The largest item in the support cost bill is for the repair and maintenance of systems. The sum of labor and material outweighs all other support costs. Two prime variables are identified with the

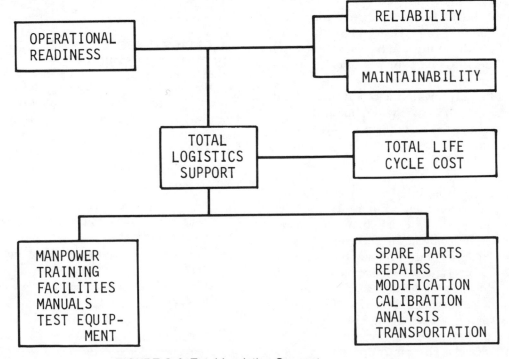

FIGURE 6-4. Total Logistics Support

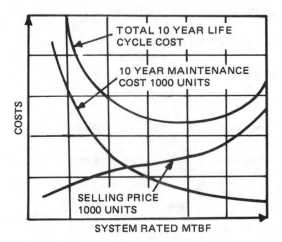

FIGURE 6-5. Total ten-year cost, ten-year maintenance cost, and procurement cost, against MTBF. Courtesy of Canadian Marconi Company

cost of technical services. The first is systems reliability. The second is maintainability, which is the characteristic of the design that determines the ease of maintenance and the repair of the equipment after a failure. The mean time for a maintenance action includes time for troubleshooting, repairing, testing, and so on, all of which are closely related to the cost of the services.

Higher reliability contributes to much greater systems effectiveness and to a reduction in life cycle costs. The current practice is to define reliability requirements in terms of MTBF based on systems effectiveness or mission requirements. In many cases, the MTBF specified is that level attainable, using standard parts and processes. This practice does not always result in optimum life cycle costs.

Very large savings can accrue through establishment of higher reliability levels within the latest state-of-the-art-attainable MTBF in spite of increased initial procurement costs. The total selling price of the system at the standard reliability level is a relatively small proportion of the total program cost. Though this proportion increases as the reliability goes up, the total cost curve decreases at a much more rapid rate. Thus, by procuring high-reliability and maintainable systems, large total program cost savings will accrue over time (see Figure 6-5).

Maintainability is related to life cycle cost in the same manner as reliability. The influence of Mean Time To Repair (MTTR) on cost is significant. The MTTR of equipment may run from a few minutes to several days. This includes, of course, all maintenance tasks accomplished in the field and repair depots. Careful equipment design can greatly increase product maintainability.

All this sounds great. One may therefore ask why life cycle costing is still in its infancy after all these years. The primary reasons are:

1. The planning horizon of most users is usually one year, so that purchase decisions are optimized for the short run.

2. The preparation of suitable documentation incorporating life cycle costing is hampered by a lack of competent personnel. Extensive education is required in this area of logistic support, which includes the costs incurred by the manufacturer, the purchaser, and the user.

3. The predicted values for MTBF, MTTR, and system effectiveness are not credible because of deficiencies in current techniques.

4. The maintenance budget usually comes out of a separate cost pool so that organizational difficulties hamper the decision process.

5. Extended warranties, legal remedies, and other approaches are available to force manufacturers to make good on their claims and commitments.

Users are gradually pushing to force manufacturers to consider these life cycle costs. In the printing industry it is now not uncommon for paper mills to compensate users for downtime of presses in the event of paper breaks. The same practice is emerging in the case of synthetic yarn breaks in the textile industry. The airlines buy engines under a contract that guarantees the cost of maintenance; the excess is charged to the manufacturer. Telex exchanges, telephone systems, and nuclear reactors are covered by availability guarantees. A continuing expansion of this trend can be expected. Such provisions make the users' costs a direct factor in the manufacturers' thinking, which is as it should be.

REFERENCES

Balaban, H. S. "Reliability Improvement by Profit Incentive." *Quality,* Nov. 1978.

Bickford, J. J. "How to Fit in with the Product Planning Committee." *Machine Design,* Nov. 1972.

Burns, V. P. "Warranty Prediction: Putting a $ on Poor Quality." *Quality Progress,* Dec. 1970.

Cattell, G. R. "What to Do When Warranty Costs Zoom." *Production Engineering,* July 1980.

"Finding and Keeping Customers." *The Royal Bank of Canada Monthly Letter,* July 1976.

Judelson, P. J. "Estimating Quality Control Engineering Costs for Proposals." *Industrial Quality Control,* Nov. 1967.

Kirchhof, E. H. "Oh! What Revelations Lurk in Contract Review." *Quality Progress,* May 1976.

Kivenko, K. "12 Key Elements to Consider in a Product Safety Program." *Evaluation Engineering,* June 1976.

Mertz, O. R. "Quality's Role in ROI." *Quality Progress,* Oct. 1977.

Robertson, J. A. "Analyzing Field Failure." *Quality Progress,* Jan. 1969.

Schoffler, S. "Impact of Strategic Planning on Profit Performance." *Harvard Business Review,* March/April 1974.

Stewart, R. L. "Product Liability and Quality Management." *Quality Progress,* Feb. 1969.

7

Managing Human Resources for Optimum Productivity

Good people are the foundation of effective quality programs. No amount of fancy procedures, automatic test equipment, or computerized information systems can compensate for a lack of competent personnel. Inspectors, test technicians, reliability analysts, statisticians, and quality engineers must be capable of doing their jobs efficiently and creating the right professional image for the quality control department. The proper management of human resources is one of the most critical jobs of the quality control manager. A Canadian steel company sums it up neatly: "Our product is steel—our strength is people." The chairman of the board of a highly successful multinational put it in another way: "You can always judge a manager by whom he surrounds himself."

This chapter discusses proven ways of recruiting, developing, and motivating quality control personnel.

COMPENSATE QC PERSONNEL EQUITABLY

Despite the steady growth of the quality control movement over the past few decades many personnel departments continue to downplay the importance of QC personnel. Salaries, increases and general growth of QC personnel are adversely affected by these attitudes. The battle to convert these attitudes must be considered a strategic goal, because without good people the quality program will falter. Here are some approaches to raising job grades (and salary ranges) to fair and appropriate levels within your company:

√ Use data from other companies in your industry preferably in your geographic locale.

√ Demonstrate your lack of success in attracting acceptable applicants to open personnel requisitions because of lower salaries.

√ Educate and indoctrinate the personnel department in the benefits to be found in a sound quality program.

√ Point to the success of the Japanese in using quality control as a basis for international sales.

√ Acquire salary statistics from professional societies.

√ Make sure job descriptions reflect educational and/or certification requirements, customer/government interfaces, legal implications, and consequences of error.

√ Provide visibility on technological advances in quality control including new computer-based measuring equipment, advanced statistical methods, and failure analysis techniques.

√ Show turnover statistics from your department.

√ Obtain support from allies in other departments, such as engineering, procurement, contracts, or whomever personnel seeks advice from.

√ Periodically send copies of newspaper or magazine articles dealing with product liability settlements to key personnel department managers.

√ Point out the cost and possible consequences in time, money, and reputation if manufactured products reach the market in a defective state.

Pitfall to Avoid: Avoid direct comparison of QC personnel salaries to other departments. Such comparisons are often taken as an attack on the reasonability of their salary levels.

RECRUITMENT METHODS FOR QC PEOPLE

Skilled quality people are in high demand but short supply. Yet, the acquisition of good people is essential to the successful implementation of a sound quality program. There are several methods of acquiring these hard-to-find people, and all should be considered.

√ *Promote from within.* Inspectors, test technicians, and lab personnel are all candidates for promotion. Look carefully at other departments. Don't restrict your search to the QC department. Always post the job internally before looking outside the company.

√ *Advertise.* A well-written ad can attract a wide range of candidates. Highlight job challenges, growth potential, and company benefits. Prepare advertising that is most likely to be read by the kind of applicant you are looking for.

Case in Point: A tire manufacturer was looking for a seasoned reliability and safety manager. Because of the importance of this position, the ad was run in the Careers section rather than in the general Help Wanted section. Wednesday, Friday, and Saturday were chosen as the run days. Over thirty replies were received, and a manager was hired within three weeks.

√ *Use local newsletters.* One firm routinely advertises in the regional newsletter of ASQC. The price is right (free) and usually evokes a high response from a select audience.

√ *Attend trade shows and conventions.* Besides providing knowledge, trade shows are an excellent vehicle for identifying potential candidates. It has been estimated that one person out of every six attending a convention or trade show is there primarily to recruit employees.

√ *Use your contacts.* ASQC or trade association members are often a ripe source of candidates.

Caution: Don't make job offers to source inspectors visiting your plant. This practice breeds ill will and can be misinterpreted as a means of neutralizing an effective inspector.

√ *Use unconventional approaches.* Creativity and imagination can go a long way toward improving the recruitment process.

Case in Point: The calibration laboratory manager of a British steel maker became involved in the quality certificate program of a local university. As a lecturer, she was exposed to many up-and-coming quality practitioners. Over the years, she regularly recruited former students she had identified as capable workers.

√ *Try the bounty system.* This system involves using your employees as recruitment officers. A bounty, say $300, is offered to any employee who recommends a friend or associate in another firm who is ultimately hired. This system must, of course, be a company policy before it can be used.

√ *Look at hard-hit industries.* In 1980, the U.S. auto industry suffered severe personnel cutbacks. An astute producer of jet engines capitalized on this situation by sending an interview team to Detroit and Windsor. Six out of eight open requisitions for mechanical inspectors were filled the first day.

√ *Broaden your search.* Look and search more actively among groups that have not traditionally been part of the mainstream QC management group: women, minority groups, and so on.

Managers have to recognize that it is becoming increasingly difficult to hire someone who is already qualified and experienced in the job they want performed. You may do better to decide what basic skills you want and be prepared to train *in-house* and *long-term*. Although this is expensive initially, these apprentice training programs can have many important payoffs for the company.

HIRING: DETERMINE JOB REQUIREMENTS FIRST

No QC manager would think of attacking a problem without first establishing goals. Yet, many managers neglect to determine job requirements first when it comes to hiring new staff members.

They do not explicitly identify the technical skills and personality traits a prospective candidate should have to fill the position effectively. As a result, managers go into the job interview with only a vague idea of what they are looking for. They end up assessing the candidate on the basis of factual information they already possessed or on general impression.

A specific list of job requirements is needed before the interview begins. Once the criteria are known, the interview can be structured to ascertain whether or not a particular applicant possesses these essential traits. When a job description already exists, the job is made that much easier.

All too often a graduate engineer is hired to perform a QC engineer's job simply because he or she is a graduate engineer. A professional engineer may or may not be the best choice. The individual must have the overall qualifications, communications skills, and *motivation* to perform the quality engineering task satisfactorily.

Pitfall to Avoid: In some companies, job requirements are artificially inflated so as to increase job grades and salaries. In the long run, of course, the company's competitive position is eroded. The QC manager should try to avoid this practice and set an example for the plant. If, however, company management does not correct the situation, quality management will have to protect its interests by taking its cue from management.

SELECTION CRITERIA FOR ASSURANCE SCIENCE PERSONNEL

It should be stressed that appropriate criteria can be established only in relation to a specific job. Essential criteria for one position may be only remotely desirable for another.

√ What level of education must the candidate have to be considered? In what field of science, mathematics, or engineering? Would graduate work be beneficial? What kind of education is absolutely necessary, regardless of work experience, and what would be acceptable in lieu of experience? For example, educational criteria may be relatively more important for the young, inexperienced quality engineer than for the one who has ten years' experience.

√ Are there any special skills, abilities, or certifications that the ideal candidate should possess? These may have been picked up, for instance, during military training, Peace Corps experience, or extracurricular training courses.

√ What skills must the applicant have used on prior jobs? What types of projects must he have worked on? What types of measuring equipment must he be familiar with? To what extent, if any, must he have displayed leadership or managerial ability?

√ Does the job require that the person work more than a forty-hour week? Are long days or weekend work often necessary?

√ How important is the ability to cope with stress and manage conflict?

√ How significant is motivation, persistence, and drive?

√ Is the position closely supervised, or must the applicant have the self-motivation to meet schedules and objectives on her own?

√ Must the new recruit be able to relate well to other departments, customers, or clients, or will he work in relative seclusion? Quality personnel usually have high visibility and a wide range of interfaces.

√ Are sensitivity, maturity, and tact essential for this particular job? Maturity, especially, will be a critical qualification for the job if the applicant will have supervisory responsibilities, either now or in the future. Sensitivity, or awareness of others, is an essential characteristic for all QC people.

If every desirable trait is given equal weight, the manager will be looking for a nonexistent perfect candidate. It is a good idea to rank priorities according to their importance. When the time comes to evaluate the candidate, the manager will have an idea of which qualifications the candidate must meet and which can be viewed as options to trade against other qualifications or characteristics she may lack.

HOW TO CONDUCT THE SELECTION INTERVIEW

The prime purpose of an interview is to obtain information. This can be achieved by planning and controlling the interview and by breaking the interview into several well-constructed phases.

I. Preinterview Requirements

1. Familiarize yourself with the candidate's application or résumé.

TABLE 7-1. Select Questions for QC Job Applicants

Work History

1. Tell me something of your past work history.
2. What areas of your work have you found particularly rewarding?
3. What did you dislike most about these jobs?
4. What measuring and test equipment are you familiar with?
5. Are you a member of ASQC or other professional society? If not, why not?
6. Are you technically or management oriented? Explain.
7. How important do you think QC is to company profits?
8. What role do you think ethics should play in a competitive business environment?
9. Are you an ASQC-certified quality engineer or technologist?

Profile of Applicant

1. What are your three greatest strengths? What areas are you trying to improve?
2. What five things or projects have you done that you are most proud of?
3. How important is salary compared to other aspects of the job?
4. What does the word *success* mean to you?

5. What would be the ideal job for you?
6. Where do you want to be in five years? Where do you think you'll be?

People Skills

1. How do you get along with people?
2. What type of people annoy or upset you?
3. How well are you able to accept direction from others?
4. What kind of leader are you? Elaborate.

Job Change

1. Why are you interested in changing your present job *now?*
2. Why are you interested in our company?
3. What types of jobs are you looking for?
4. What aspect of QC is of most interest to you?
5. What do you think you would find most rewarding about this job?
6. What contribution do you think you can make to our organization?

Administrative

1. Does your company know you are looking for a job?
2. If hired, how soon would you be able to start work here?

2. Select a quiet, private area where you will not be interrupted when conducting the interview.
3. Clarify for yourself the areas that you wish to discuss with the applicant.
4. Know the salary range for the job opening.

II. Introductory Phase (time limit: five minutes)

In the introductory phase, structure the interview so that your expectations and time frame are clear to the applicant. In this phase the interviewer gets to know the applicant and makes him or her feel at ease so that communication can begin to flow freely. Once the candidate appears to be calm, comfortable, and willing to talk, the manager or supervisor can move on to the assessment phase.

III. Assessment Phase (time limit: twenty minutes)

Ask open-end questions. This allows the applicant to answer more fully than close-end questions,

which limit the interviewee's response to a yes or no. An *open-end* example question is, "What did you find satisfying about your past jobs?" A *close-end* question might be, "Do you work well with older people?"

Table 7-1 lists some questions to ask the prospective QC employee. Remember, the more you talk, the less the applicant will talk. This is the phase where the interviewer determines whether or not the candidate meets the job criteria.

At the close of the assessment phase, ample time should be left for the *influence-and-sell* portion of the interview. Just as the assessment phase is designed to meet the needs of the interviewer, the influence-and-sell portion is designed to meet the needs of the candidate. During this stage, the interviewer answers any questions the candidate may have about the company or the job and, if she feels that she will offer the candidate the position, attempts to convince him that it is right for him.

It should be recognized from the beginning that the intelligent candidate is interviewing the interviewer. Would I want to work for this person? Is this a progressive, innovative company as reflected in the style of management? What emphasis do they place on quality and safety?

IV. Final Phase (not more than five minutes)

The final phase is devoted to bringing the interview to a satisfactory close by letting the candidate know what will happen next, when he can expect to hear of the company's decision, and other such details.

It is vital to use and interpret the information that you get back from the candidate. The idea of finding a good fit between the organization and the person is central. It is not simply a question of "Will this person do the job well?" but "How well will this individual be able to become part of the organization?" Does her working style work well with Manager X to whom she will be reporting? Is this an authoritarian organization? Can this individual work in that type of an organization?

INTERVIEW BACK-UP TECHNIQUES

Although the interview is the primary source of information on evaluating a candidate, there are many other tools that can be used to provide additional information. However, since the application of some of these techniques is limited somewhat by legal constraints, they must be used with care.

Written testing of any kind has become increasingly suspect in recent years. It is looked upon more as a means of discriminating against certain people than as a way of gaining knowledge. If used, testing should be done with the aid of a professional consultant or testing service, and with full knowledge of the governmental or legal restraints on its use as an employment technique.

Specialized tests for inspection, blueprint reading, and psychological evaluation are commercially available. These include:

- Gilford Zimmerman Spatial Visualization Test (blueprint reading)
- King Factor Aptitude Test of Dimensions (ability to deal with sizes and shapes)
- Minnesota Clerical Test (clerical aptitude and recordkeeping)
- Gilford Zimmerman General Reasoning Test (arithmetic reasoning)

You must also design special tests tailored to your industry or company. These tests typically relate to the use of specialized measuring equipment; knowledge of applicable codes and standards; technical skills such as biology, metallurgy, chemistry, or electronics; and general reasoning.

Reference checks of various kinds are still widely used as screening tools. Personal reference checks and previous employment checks are most popular. The latter are becoming increasingly difficult to handle, since many organizations are adopting strict rules about releasing information on former employees. Leave the job of checking references to a professional.

College transcripts or *military records* are difficult or impossible to obtain these days. The U.S. Defense Department has recently adopted a new procedure that prohibits release of a DD-214 service record without the individual's permission, and most colleges and universities are following suit.

Background checks can be run through professional organizations that specialize in such investigations. Take care that the investigators are discreet, are proceeding in a manner unlikely to cause embarrassment to the firm, and are not violating any of the statutes of the states in which they are operating.

Physical examinations including visual acuity (critical for inspectors) are required by many companies. They are not illegal as long as the exam is structured and implemented in such a way that it is not discriminatory in regard to age, sex, or other sensitive factors.

Although all these selection tools and techniques can be valuable in the candidate evaluation process, none is a satisfactory substitute for a well-planned, well-conducted interview. They should be considered only as supplementary selection tools.

EVALUATING INTERVIEW RESULTS

The QC manager or supervisor who has carefully established his criteria and has programmed his objectives should have little trouble in evaluating candidates. The easiest way to perform the evaluation process is to use a specially developed rating matrix chart. First, each candidate is rated in terms of the specific job-related criteria involved, then the ratings are compared in the light of the criteria priorities that were determined before interviewing was begun. The selection should be such that the job will maximize the strengths and minimize the weaknesses of the person who is eventually hired. Some companies make it a practice to have prospective senior employees interviewed by several managers from different departments with whom the applicant is likely to come into contact. This brings about a broader perspective and cross-check that is crucial to the selection of competent quality practitioners.

Pitfall to Avoid: Sometimes the right person is not easy to find. It's generally wise for the long term to go for quality people even if it means leaving a position open a little longer. If the quality program is to succeed, it must have competent professionals. If an experienced person is just not available, then at least hire a talented junior person who has growth potential and train him or her on the job. Don't settle for drop-outs, discards, or second choices.

PQC PEOPLE: A SPECIAL CASE

Procurement Quality Control (PQC) people are truly a special case. All personnel in PQC careers meet vendors. Remember, a PQC person at a vendor's plant represents your company and his or her actions are a direct reflection on your company's reputation. Therefore, you must select personnel who will represent your company in a truly professional manner. You must also create an atmosphere of professionalism to guide these people.

The days of hiring the outdated inspection foreperson who has not kept up with modern quality control have long since passed. Procurement quality control requires competent, mature, enthusiastic, and professional people. The person must know the product and be able to monitor the quality system to assure compliance with requirements.

The manager must see that his people are properly informed on the requirements before going out on a job. This is very important to the product's quality and your professional image. It is also important that he knows the company's goals and history of relationships between the supplier and your company.

Maturity is not a function of age but rather a measure of judgment and ability to assume responsibility. Procurement quality control requires people who can forcefully, but calmly, enforce requirements. She must be able to identify problem areas and solve these without engaging in personality clashes. Tact, discreetness, and diplomacy are key job requirements.

The person on the road gives up a great deal of his or her personal life. To the uninitiated, travel has a certain glamor. Visiting three cities in three days, putting in an eight-hour-or-more day and then traveling four more hours, spending ten hours on stand-by at an airport and arriving home at midnight—all these tend to tarnish the glamor. A less dedicated individual would quickly want out. Marital problems are not uncommon because of the inconvenience and stress that traveling can cause on the home front. It is well to ascertain that the spouse is in full concurrence before a person's accepting a job that requires extensive traveling.

It is up to the QC manager to create the proper atmosphere and guidelines. Copies of the "Ethics and Human Relations of Vendor-Vendee Relationships," published by the Vendor-Vendee Technical Committee of ASQC, or something similar could be adopted as a company standard.

Another management responsibility is to have clear ground rules with regard to traveling, expense accounts, car rentals, overtime, and so on. The manager must then make sure that she and the employee abide by the ground rules.

Management from a distance is difficult at best. How do you measure if your employee is doing the job and is doing it properly? Some tips that have been used are:

√ Check rejection rates for source inspected items.

√ Periodically rotate source inspectors among different plants.

√ When a person is supposed to be at a vendor's plant—particularly overtime—call him or her. Consistent nonattendance tells the manager a lot about the person's dedication.

√ Visit vendors personally. A vendor's lack of comment on your representative indicates a mediocre or unsatisfactory performance. Questioning can usually reveal the truth.

√ Listen to the vendor's gripes. Buried in these may be an indication of lack of performance by your representative.

√ Compare the expense accounts of one person to another on similar trips. The high flyer will show up.

√ Travel with PQC people and observe their performance.

√ Measure the time it takes to accomplish specific tasks. Wide variations against your estimated time may indicate a problem.

√ If you're good at reading between the lines, trip reports will tell you a lot.

√ Check with purchasing for an evaluation of your PQC people. They often have interesting views about their effectiveness.

CONSIDER NEW EMPLOYEE INDUCTION

The first few hours and days on a job have a lasting impression on new employees and affect quality attitudes and quality consciousness. It is, therefore, extremely important that this phase be handled properly. Here is a brief set of ground-rules:

1. Put new employee at ease: "Welcome to XYZ Company."

2. Provide brochures on the company and its products as well as details on benefits plans, vacations, and pension.

3. Try to emphasize the quality image and philosophy of the company.

4. If hourly paid, show location of time clock and instruct in card punching: who, how, when.

5. Show location of washroom facilities, cafeteria, medical area, and clothes rack.

6. Advise time of lunch period and coffee breaks.

7. Introduce to immediate associates.

8. Explain and/or stress any special departmental rules such as safety precautions, quality procedures, necessity for punctuality, etc.

9. If possible, let employee *see* his or her assignment being done by another person. In any case, explain previous operation, outline of the operation, succeeding operation, end use or result. Stress importance of his or her operation to the success of the team (what happens if job is not well done).

10. Explain, in detail, the employee's operation or responsibilities. Explain what is expected in terms of quality, quantity, degree of initiative to be taken.

11. Provide a plant tour pointing out work flows, housekeeping, workmanship standards, test facilities, and nature of product.

12. Initiate on-the-job training.

13. Invite questions whenever information is required and advise whom to ask in your absence.

14. Have a congenial associate accompany the new employee to lunch.

15. Follow up later to see how things are going. Timing depends on job cycle, but first check-up should not be later than two days even in long-learning-time jobs. Another follow-up in two weeks is also called for.

Observation: Most of these items will be applicable, with or without modification, when an "old" employee first joins your department or section. Some are important whenever a new assignment is given.

MINIMIZE OFFICE POLITICS

Excessive office politics weaken a quality organization, injures many innocent victims, and destroys motivation. Here are some ideas on how to keep office politics to an absolute minimum:

- Set favorable examples for subordinates.
- Avoid favoritism among employees.
- Have clearly defined areas of responsibility for everybody.

Case in Point: The reliability and safety engineering departments in a large diesel engine plant were constantly trying to outfox each other. The wasted effort was noticed by other departments and even customers. The primary cause of the bickering was that management didn't divide job responsibilities between the two departments.

- Establish feedback mechanism.
- Concentrate corrective action on problems, not witch-hunting.
- Be honest in your dealing with others.

When in doubt, tell the truth.

Mark Twain

- Break up cliques and empires.
- Expose dirty tricks and backstabbing; stop such activities dead in their tracks.
- Keep people busy—idle people gossip.
- Create a team spirit.
- Eliminate incorrigible politicians.

- Base promotions on achievements and contributions to organizational goals.
- Discourage finger pointing, "political" memos, and nasty confrontations.

Case in Point: Receiving inspection cannot prevent all defective purchased material from hitting assembly lines. In one large manufacturer of electrostatic precipitators, the record was, however, enviable. Nevertheless, whenever an inspection escape (undetected nonconformance) did occur, the production manager unduly ranted and raved. The existing general manager failed to intervene, so QC always took the blame. When a new general manager entered the scene, he immediately got the two departments together, and monthly shipments were regularly met with a minimum of fanfare.

ENCOURAGE CREATIVITY AND INNOVATION

The potential for creativity in the typical company control department is much greater than is generally realized or utilized. The reason is that the typical department is structured to facilitate the execution of assigned tasks. This fosters a regimentation that suppresses the creative talent so vital to developing original approaches to quality improvement and cost reduction.

Here are some specific suggestions for restructuring the work environment to encourage creativity and innovation:

√ Welcome and encourage a diversity of ideas and opinions from QC engineers, inspectors, and test technicians.

√ Allow creative people to take as large a part as possible in decision making and in the formulation of departmental planning.

√ Encourage your people to visit other plants, both vendors and customers. Many innovations and tricks of the trade can be learned.

√ Support investigations into new capital equipment for better quality control.

Case in Point: As shown in Figure 7-1, a spot-weld controller uses high-frequency acoustic emission to produce consistently good welds without overwelding. In this case, signals are out of the range of human hearing and re-

quire sophisticated monitoring equipment to discriminate between noise and signals. Although overwelding produces acceptable joints, it also causes rapid electrode deterioration and promotes excessive expulsion of liquified metal from the weld nugget. Expulsion, which begins at the completion of a good weld, emits a characteristic sound that is easily distinguishable from other acoustic emissions associated with the formulation of the nugget. The transducer feeds these emissions to the controller, which detects the expulsion signal and stops the weld current.

√ Subscribe to quality control-oriented magazines, trade publications, and foreign journals. The seed of many a good idea has come from reading about the experiences of others.

√ Make sure that promising people are not bogged down with specific tasks every moment of the day. Innovative people need some time to think, without having their thought tied to a particular activity or project.

√ Occasionally, allow individuals to try out their pet ideas without premature criticism. Provide a reasonable margin for error. Punitive action for every mistake or failure leads to excessive dependence on safe ways of doing things.

√ Use brainstorming to solicit ideas. A short meeting of six to ten people can result in dozens of ideas. Use the blackboard to jot down the ideas as they occur. Five or six of these will be worth evaluating further.

√ Fund attendance for ASQC or other appropriate professional society annual conventions. The papers, tutorials, and particularly the informal get-togethers can provide a wealth of new quality control ideas and approaches.

√ Provide personal recognition for accomplishment and deliver adequate, concrete rewards for each achievement.

√ Look into new technology and techniques. For example, holography has definite applications in product inspection; the scanning electron microscope can be used in the materials lab, not just in R&D; and new statistical techniques, coupled with computer power, can provide insight into chronic QC problems.

√ Encourage exchanges of information and opinions between individuals, groups, and departments, but with a reasonable amount of freedom for individuals to follow leads that are contrary to group ideas.

A mind is like a parachute—to be any good it must be open.

ENCOURAGE AUTHORSHIP

The ability to communicate written material effectively is a powerful attribute of a QC manager, quality engineer, failure analyst, or inspector. Several companies actively encourage employees to publish in technical journals and magazines; there are numerous benefits:

1. The exposure can be motivational to the employee.
2. The research work done for the article may be useful to the company.
3. The experience gained from researching, writing, and editing embodies professional development at its best.
4. Seeing the article in print provides a measure of fulfillment and satisfaction.
5. The writing skills obtained during the publishing process will help quality people write more concise, better-organized reports and clearer letters and memos.
6. Publishing enhances the growth potential of the author.
7. The company position is enhanced because it becomes better known.
8. Some magazines pay a modest amount for articles. (Most companies permit employees to retain this compensation; it is taxable, however, as earned income.)

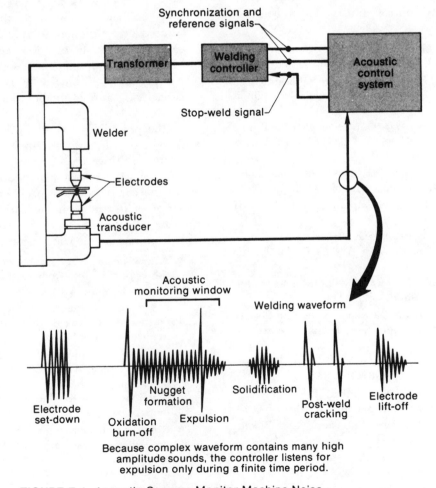

Because complex waveform contains many high amplitude sounds, the controller listens for expulsion only during a finite time period.

FIGURE 7-1. Acoustic Sensors Monitor Machine Noise
From Curry, D. T. "Scientific Manufacturing," *Machine Design*, May 22, 1980. Used with permission.

Cautions: If your company is supportive of employee publication of learned papers, it must be careful of certain business aspects.

1. Require employees to obtain company approval, before publishing job-related material. Ensure that no company trade secret, proprietary information, or competition—sensitive material is published.
2. Make sure the author publishes under his or her own name and not the company's (unless otherwise agreed).
3. Don't let employees become full-time authors—one paper a year is more than enough.
4. Advise employees of copyright restrictions.

Here are a few periodicals to get you started. This list is by no means complete. You should consult professional and trade associations and library reference sources for those journals and magazines of direct concern to his or her engineering, quality control, and related responsibilities.

1. *Assembly Engineering.* Hitchcock Publishing Co., Hitchcock Bldg., Wheaton, Illinois 60187.
2. *Chemical Processing.* Putnam Publishing Co., 111 E. Delaware Place, Chicago, Illinois 60611.
3. *Control Engineering.* Dun Donnelley Publishing Co., 222 S. Riverside Plaza, Chicago, Illinois 60035.
4. *Evaluation Engineering.* BPA, 1282 Old Skokie Rd., Highland Park, Illinois 60035.
5. *Factory.* Morgan-Grampian Inc., 16 West 61 St., New York, 10023.
6. *Hydraulics and Pneumatics.* Industrial Publishing Co., 614 Superior Ave., West, Cleveland, Ohio 44113.
7. *Infosystems.* Penton/IPC Publishing, Penton Plaza, Cleveland, Ohio 44114.
8. *Journal of Quality Technology.* American Society for Quality Control, Milwaukee, Wisconsin 53203.
9. *Machine Design.* Penton/IPC Publishing, Penton Plaza, Cleveland, Ohio 44114.
10. *Plant Engineering.* Technical Publishing Co., 13015 Grove Ave., Barrington, Illinois 60010.
11. *Production.* Bramson Publishing Co., Bloomfield Hills, Michigan 48013.
12. *Quality.* Hitchcock Publishing Co. (address under *Assembly Engineering*).
13. *Quality Progress.* American Society for Quality Control, 230 W. Wells St., Milwaukee, Wisconsin 53203.

USE JOB ROTATION

Job rotation involves reassigning people to different positions after they have mastered the work they are doing. Although this technique has certain problems, it offers the company significant improvements in staff versatility and improved productivity and morale. Of course, not all people like to be reassigned to a new job periodically. Some prefer a stable routine and the security of doing work in which they have a proven ability. However, a certain percentage of people do require frequent challenges and changes in the nature of their work to keep their interest and motivation high.

Case in Point: At one company on the East Coast, a quality auditor strongly objected to her supervisor about her doing virtually the same kind of work for six years. She was bored and unchallenged by the work and wanted a reassignment to a different technical area so that she could expand her capabilities. She confided to an associate that she was probably working at 50 percent of her capacity because of the boredom of the job.

In the preceding example, the employee's efforts to be transferred from audit work to quality planning was thwarted by the supervisor because he did not want to lose his experienced auditor. While this can be a serious problem, a wider view in terms of its value to the entire organization must be taken into account.

Below are some benefits of job rotation:

- A new person may see better ways of doing things because of a fresh view of the operation.
- Morale is improved because the bored expert has a new challenge—that of being a good teacher and having the opportunity of exercising leadership skills.
- Versatility is improved. Under special situations, experienced people will be available from other groups to be temporarily assigned to one function that is behind schedule and needs more people power.
- Rotation can help train people in various aspects of the organization so that they can be promoted into jobs that require an understanding of its overall activities.
- It can motivate people into added effort because of the desire to show that they can learn quickly and do good work in this new area.

(Special pay scales tied to multiple skills can help encourage people into widening their capabilities.)

- The experienced person training someone from another discipline or group will be motivated to use his or her time more effectively so that normal assignments are completed in addition to performing the training activity.
- It can promote a better understanding among organizational groups.

Caution: Job rotation must be used with care—if used too much or uncoordinated, it can adversely affect general efficiency. Labor agreements must also be considered.

Here are some rotation combinations that seem to work:

1. quality engineer and reliability engineer
2. inspection foreman and assembly foreman
3. quality auditor and quality planner
4. quality engineer and industrial engineer
5. test supervisor and incoming inspection supervisor
6. quality administration and product costing
7. statistical practitioners and engineering computer programmers
8. procurement QC and buyer
9. reliability engineer and maintainability engineer
10. failure analyst and process engineer
11. inspection and test personnel (assuming compatible technical knowledge)

12. environmental lab operator and calibration lab technician

TRAINING QUALITY PEOPLE

One of the most persistent quality management problems has been staffing the QC organization with qualified personnel. To promote technical competency and keep up with the state of the art, training is of the utmost importance. The best QC woman or man today will no longer be satisfactory in five years, if he or she does not keep abreast of technological change. Well-thought-out and efficiently executed employee training programs can make significant contributions to effectiveness. In-house seminars, on-the-job training, university extension courses, correspondence courses, and society conferences provide benefits that include better product quality, fewer customer complaints and lower manufacturing costs.

Case in Point: An inspection supervisor for a small foundry attended the annual ASQC Technical Conference, which happened to be in his city. After two days, he had discovered (1) a new technique for casting process control, (2) a unique low-cost NDT measuring device, and (3) a little-known U.K. handbook reference on aluminum castings.

Keeping up with advancing technology, new quality control techniques, improved measurement methods, and new approaches to human re-

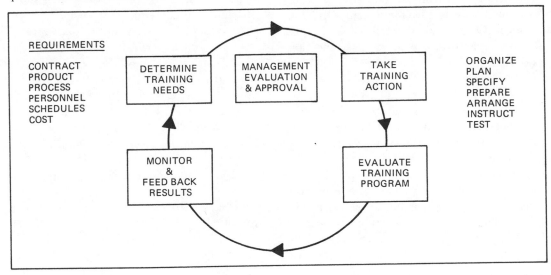

FIGURE 7-2. Training Process Cycle
Courtesy of Canadian Marconi Company.

lations can pay large dividends. *Not* knowing can be very costly, especially if the competition, local or international, implements them first. Organizations like the American Productivity Center, the American Society for Quality Control, the European Organization for Quality Control, and the American Institute of Industrial Engineers are excellent sources for innovations. Trade associations, professional societies and shows, training films, videotapes, technical publications, and books and intercompany information exchanges are a few sources that can produce valuable information. Trained employees have more confidence and motivation in their work, which results in improved productivity, successful systems implementation, and innovation.

> If you think training is expensive, try ignorance.

KEEP INSPECTION EYEBALLS CALIBRATED

Major quality errors are usually caused by some engineer, supervisor, or executive rather than an inspector. However, the collective errors of the inspectors may influence many managerial decisions and affect the quality reputation of the company. Inaccurate inspection can bring down the best quality program. It is therefore important to test inspection personnel periodically for accuracy. First, it is wise to provide a demonstration kit for use by QC management in their defense against production attacks when costly inspection escapes occur.

Printed below is a story that can be used to demonstrate the ineffectiveness of 100 percent inspection. Assume that the letter "G" is defective product caused by the Gremlin. Give the test to the production manager. Allow him or her about three minutes to count all the Gs.

Not unexpectedly, production will not come up with the required number of Gs, which is eighty-three. Inspection accuracy is in fact rarely better than 85 percent, and even this figure degrades rapidly with increasing part complexity. Production should back off for at least a month after this test.

Now that we have demonstrated that 100 percent inspection is not 100 percent effective, we

> WHILE STROLLING THROUGH A GLEN, A GIDDY ENGLISH GIRL TRIPPED ON A RATHER LARGE, ALMOST GIGANTIC FROG. THE GIRL STAGGERED BUT REGAINED HER FOOTING AND WAS ABOUT TO GO ON WHEN THE FROG BEGAN TO SPEAK AND GESTICULATE TO GAIN THE GIRL'S ATTENTION. "I HAVE NOT ALWAYS BEEN A FROG," HE CROAKED. THE FROG'S GREEN COLORING SEEMED TO GLOW BRIGHTLY AS HE CONTINUED, "I WAS ONCE A GRACIOUS KNIGHT, A GENTLEMAN CALLED GALLANT GEORGE GRENVILLE, BUT WAS CHANGED INTO THIS GHASTLY FROG YOU NOW SEE BY AN UNGODLY, MAGICAL GENIE. THE SPELL CAN ONLY BE BROKEN IF I GAIN A GIRL'S GOOD GRACES AND SPEND A NIGHT IN HER GARDEN." THE AGOG GIRL WAS SKEPTICAL, OF COURSE. SHE GAZED AT THE FROG'S PLEADING EYES AND SOON HER GIDDY NATURE GAVE WAY TO HER DOUBTS. GIGGLING, SHE DECIDED TO GRANT THE FROG'S WISH AND TOOK HIM HOME STRAIGHTWAY, PUTTING HIM BY HER GARDEN GATE. THAT NIGHT THE GIRL SLEPT GRANDLY AND SURE ENOUGH, WHEN SHE AWOKE THE FOLLOWING MORNING, THERE ALONGSIDE HER GARDEN GATE WAS THE GRACIOUS KNIGHT, GEORGE GRENVILLE. WELL, STRANGELY ENOUGH, FOR A LONG, LONG TIME THE GIRL'S MOTHER DID NOT BELIEVE THAT STORY.

must face the fact that even achieving 85 percent accuracy requires training, inspection planning, vision testing, and periodic accuracy testing.

Testing for the visual ability of the inspector should be considered one of the most important factors in the management of a quality control system. This one factor alone can cause the inspector to unknowingly fail in most of his or her tests and will most certainly account for a low rating by the supervisor.

Fully 85 percent of the people who seek eye care do so because of discomfort—headaches, eye strain, or seeing difficulties. Few go to find out if they can see as well as they should for the work they do. Additionally, a person may have excellent vision for one job, poor vision for another. A truck driver must be able to see far ahead on the road; an inspector must read a micrometer only inches away.

The Snellen test, given employees when they are hired, consists of reading a chart on the wall. The ability of each eye to perceive small details at a distance may be important, but it is only one of the many factors that go into seeing performance. Coordination of both eyes—their ability to focus on an object without effort and with instantaneous precision—is another important factor. To determine this we must measure the eyes by means of a binocular instrument such as the Ortho-Rater, developed by Bausch & Lomb, Inc. There are several other such instruments on the market, all of which do a remarkably good job. Using these instruments, a visual acuity score can be obtained. Since the visual skills required for any job can be reduced to numerical values, they can be made a part of the skill requirements for the inspection job. Some companies include an annual vision test in the job requirements.

Once acceptable visual acuity is achieved, inspection accuracy can be measured. Inspector accuracy is the degree to which the inspector correctly makes decisions on product quality—that is, accepts product that meets specifications and rejects product that does not. The inaccuracy is not only that bad product is accepted, but also that good product is rejected.

Inspection deficiencies are due to several types of causes:

- criminal acts such as fraud or collusion
- falsification for the personal convenience of the inspector
- intermediate errors because of bias, rounding off, overzealousness
- involuntary or inadvertent errors because of blunder, fatigue, and other human imperfection

A variety of plans have been developed to evaluate the accuracy of inspectors. These plans recheck the product before and/or after the inspector has finished inspection. A disadvantage of most plans is that the inspector's accuracy depends on the quality of work submitted to the inspector—a factor that cannot be controlled. The Juran-Melsheimer plan, however, is independent of incoming quality and is expressed by the formula:

Accuracy = percent of defects correctly identified =
$$\frac{d - k}{d - k + b}$$

where d = number of defects reported by the inspector
k = number of good units rejected by the inspector
$d - k$ = true defects found by the inspector
b = defects missed by the inspector
$d - k + b$ = true defects originally in the product

If d is the number of cases reported by the inspector as defective (45, for example) and k is the number of cases reported by the inspector as defective but actually not defective (say, 5), then $d - k$ will be the number of true defects identified by the inspector (40, in this case). Now suppose b is the number of defects missed by the inspector but found by the quality auditor in a check of the former's activity (10, in this example). Then $d - k + b$ will be the number of defects originally present, or the sum of those found by the inspector and those missed by him (50, in this case). Hence,

$$\text{Percentage of accuracy} = \frac{d - k}{d - k + b}$$
$$= \frac{45 - 5}{45 - 5 + 10} \times 100\% = 80\%$$

In application of the plan, periodic check inspection is made of the inspector's work. Data on d, k, and b are accumulated over a period of months to summarize the inspector's accuracy, which avoids undue emphasis on any one lot checked.

Special situations sometimes occur. For example, the various inspection jobs may vary greatly in the inspection time required, or an occasional lot may be extremely defective for one characteristic and the inspector may miss it on every piece. Such situations can readily be handled by simple adaptations of the basic formula.

IMPROVE INSPECTOR ACCURACY

There are several established ways of improving inspector accuracy depending on the nature of the problem.

√ Provide clear inspection standards and supplement by photographs, stereophotographs, visual aids, or physical samples.

√ Utilize an accept/reject matrix.

An untold number of otherwise acceptable products are reworked or scrapped to improve their cosmetic appearance. Surface finish is a classic case in which many unnecessary dollars can be spent. Solution: Try an accept/reject matrix.

√ Use job rotation to reduce boredom.

√ Consider job enlargement to reduce monotony of highly specialized, short-time-span inspection tasks.

√ Try job enrichment techniques. A job may be enriched by an individual undertaking greater responsibility or by being involved in decisions about planning and organizing the work.

√ Use magnification where appropriate.

Surface

Class A	A	R	R	R
Class B	A	A	R	R
Class C	A	A	A	R
Defect				
1. Very light scratches no dings or scuffs				
2. Light scratches very light dings or scuffs				
3. Moderate scratches light dings or scuffs				
4. Heavy scratches moderate dings or scuffs				

A = Accept   R = Reject

Surface Class

A: Directly viewed smooth and opaque surface.
B: Directly viewed textured surfaced, directly viewed smooth and transparent surface, and obliquely viewed smooth and opaque surface.
C: All others

Definitions

Very Light: Can be seen but not felt.

Light: Can be felt with fingernail but not fingertip.

Moderate: Can be felt with fingertip but not measurable.

Heavy: Deep enough or wide enough to be measured.

Scratch: One, two, or three thin lines.

Dings: Dents or nicks.

Scuffs: Many tightly grouped scratches.

√ Employ special measuring equipment where human sensory skills are too variable or inadequate, not cost effective, or susceptible to fatigue.

√ Provide suitable well-lit and comfortable work space.

√ Employ inspection work instructions to control nature, scope, and sequence of inspection.

Caution: These instructions are often regarded as unnecessary paperwork, and the resistance to a system of formal inspection instructions can be strong. A recent development is the use of audiovisual systems (tape recordings combined with slides) to provide instructions to operators and inspectors.

√ Ensure valid calibration policy on measuring equipment.

√ Support your inspection staff against witchhunts, reprisals, and undue interruptions.

√ Develop practical, human-engineered inspection procedures. If the procedures are inconvenient, tedious, archaic, or inefficient they probably will not be followed or will be error-prone.

√ Provide adequate product training so that inspector knows the function and end use of the product.

√ Provide feedback from customer complaints, audit reports, and accuracy tests to stimulate corrective measures.

√ Hire adequate staff so as to minimize overtime, constant harassment from expediters, and general stress buildups.

It is important to know whether problems of inspector accuracy are mainly management controllable or operator controllable, because the road to improvement differs markedly. Management-controllable errors require improvements in inspection plans, equipment, and methods. Operator-controllable errors require the tools of the behavioral sciences.

CONTROL OVERTIME

Final inspection and test are end-of-the-line functions and, accordingly, subject to heavy overtime demands. Excessive chronic overtime is undesirable for several reasons:

(a) Payroll is higher because of premium payments.

(b) There can be adverse effects on day shift productivity, attendance and inspection accuracy.

(c) Inspector fatigue and increased absenteeism can occur.

(d) Overtime may proliferate as a way of life.

(e) Overtime has a long-term effect on health and marital status.

(f) It is poor example for QC to set.

The most productive use of overtime is the ten-hour day, split into five-hour segments, for not more than eight days in a row. Then a four-day rest before returning to the overtime schedule should be allowed. This involves returning to an eight-hour day on Thursday and Friday with the weekend off.

Note: Half a day of overtime on Saturday is usually very nonproductive. Targets should be set in terms of individual maximum overtime hours per period and maximum percentage of basic hours worked for a group or cost center.

INSPECTOR CERTIFICATION: IT'S WORTH LOOKING INTO

Inspector certification is a technique by which each inspector is "qualified" before he or she is allowed to perform a specific (usually critical) inspection task. With this program, only certified inspectors perform the inspection task. Ideally, each inspector would be qualified to perform more than one inspection task. Therefore, the problem becomes one of determining how to certify each inspector.

A typical approach to inspection certification is outlined below:

1. Select the most critical inspections.
2. Train inspectors to perform these specific inspection tasks.
3. Evaluate and test the inspector's capability to assure that his or her results are within normal test error (or similar to a standard). The test and evaluation can be either a written test or a physical performance of the inspection.
4. Submit a certification certificate to the inspector upon passing the examination.
5. Monitor the inspector's progress through an inspection effectiveness record. If the effectiveness results show a degrading performance of any inspector, then a recertification of the inspector is required.
6. All inspectors should be recertified each year by having their test and inspection evaluated once again.

Some applications of inspector certification are:

1. soldering inspector
2. chemical technician
3. x-ray inspector
4. rubber inspector—visual inspection
5. zyglo inspector (NDT)

These are some applications, but the concept of certification can be applied to nearly all aspects of inspection that are considered critical.

RECOGNITION: TODAY'S UNFILLED NEED

The performance of a quality practitioner depends on two factors: ability to perform the required tasks and desire to execute those tasks to the best of one's ability. Very often, a person with less ability but greater desire than another will turn in a better performance—which gives some indication why managers have a preoccupation with motivation.

A person's desire to improve performance depends on the perception of how one's efforts will help to satisfy personal needs and goals. By understanding a subordinate's distinctive attitudes and expectations, a manager can create a work environment that will encourage higher performance and better quality.

Before one can initiate a motivational climate, certain *demotivators* must be eliminated. According to Frederick Herzberg, removal of these demotivators are a necessary but not sufficient condition for full employee motivation. The typical demotivating factors in a quality department include:

- Lack of top management support for commitment to the quality program.
- Inadequate measuring and test equipment.
- Unreasonable or unsafe working conditions.
- Inequitable salary scales for QC personnel.
- Lack of recognition for QC department achievements in cost reduction, yield improvement, or corrective action.
- Perception, real or imagined, that the quality budget is singled out for cuts.
- Constant yielding of quality factors to cost or schedule considerations.
- Inadequate training on new products or new technologies.

The following ten points form the foundation of industrial motivation:

1.. *Make people know they are important.* Most people desire to be accepted on a par with others. People like to be asked for opinions, to give advice, and to be looked upon as outstanding in his or her group. This is particularly true of shop floor inspectors and test technicians. Give recognition of accomplishments (Figure 7-3).

2. *Recognize individual differences.* There are psychological differences among people. Too frequently, it is erroneously assumed that the same desires, goals, and interests will appeal equally to all members of a group. Likewise, a manager may feel very strongly about a subject, but may discover that it has a much different degree of intensity for a subordinate. It is vital to understand the makeup of the individual.

Case in Point: A usually efficient and pleasant inspector for a defense contractor producing a fire control radar became slow, nasty, and error-prone. His supervisor tactfully lectured him on the need for high quality and accurate inspection. No change in behavior was observed until it was learned that the inspector's personal allegiances did not coincide with the ultimate customer of the equipment—a certain Middle Eastern country. After reassignment to another contract, the inspector returned to his normal state.

3. *Give adequate guidance.* The typical employee wants some orientation but resents explanations and requests carried to excessive details. Yet, extreme permissiveness is as frustrating as too rigid instructions, orders, or supervision. QC supervisors, in fact, set a plant-wide example reflecting such supervisory attributes as planning, attention to detail, professionalism, responsiveness, accuracy, integrity, and diligence.

4. *Practice participative management.* Employees like to be consulted about changes that might affect them. They want to be a part of and know what is going on. It would be extremely unwise, for example, not to have appraisal personnel involved in the planned acquisition of a new automatic tester or CNC coordinate-measuring machine.

- Hold weekly meetings with the staff, specifically to elicit their opinions and suggestions on the department's work.
- Set up a suggestion box.
- When you point out a mistake an employee made, ask him or her to suggest a remedy for it.
- Listen to your employees' suggestions, complaints, requests, and statements and try to act upon them.

5. *Treat people fairly and equitably.* Humans believe in getting what they can get within the limits of what constitutes a square deal. When difficulty arises in understanding a situation thoroughly, take time to explain, to answer questions, and to show that the action is justified based on the facts and circumstances in the case.

6. *Be a good listener.* By listening you will gain greater understanding and more information, and you may impress others with your interest and fairness.

7. *Avoid arguments.* Many people dislike arguments because they do not settle differences. Very seldom is the loser of an argument converted to the viewpoint or cause of the winner; usually the breach in the original differences is broadened.

Case in Point: The director of reliability of a leading chain-hoist firm insisted on the use of a certain material in one of the parts of a new design of hoist. The project engineer argued against the need for the more expensive material. Because the reliability director was skilled in negotiation and at performing well at meetings, she "won" the argument. Subsequent relations between the two departments were never the same, and design defect prevention activities were compromised.

8. *Maintain contact with firing-line people.* Too often the busy quality executive stays in his or her

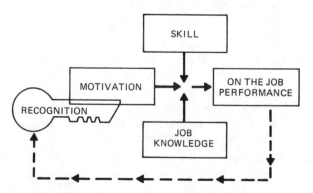

FIGURE 7-3. Recognition Is the Key to Performance.

office, goes on trips, or attends meetings and has no time to visit the production area or engineering offices. As a result, he or she loses vital contact points for firsthand information on how things are going and what's bothering people. When the quality manager visits people at the working level, they feel more important because they think what they are doing is important and thus take more pride in their work.

Case in Point: Salaried employees and supervisors took over production during a strike of hourly employees. The manager of a department reported that he found many machines out of order, some badly in need of maintenance, one a candidate for immediate replacement. Production doubled when he tuned up the machines. Were it not for the strike, he would never have known about the sad state of the machines, and production would have continued at half the capability of the process. "Well Bill," said the plant manager, "you know whose fault it was, don't you?" Yes, he knows. From now on, there will be a system by which employees may report trouble with machines or with materials and that these reports will receive prompt management attention.

9. *Avoid constant nit-picking.* Nit-picking is the criticism of minor details that do not materially contribute to the effectiveness, quality, or use of a system, product, or operation. Nit-picking has a number of harmful physical and psychological effects, such as demotivation of the person being nit-picked, wasting of people's time, and diverting energy from the purpose of the work being examined. The avoidance of nit-picking is crucial to interdepartmental relations, as any mature quality control person has learned through bitter experience.

10. *Create opportunities for growth.* The best form of motivation is the chance for advancement in both position and salary. If an employee is reminded how well he or she can do within a company, that person will do the best job possible to achieve this goal. A related management policy would be to promote from within to the greatest extent practicable. If there is no goal to shoot for, it is extremely difficult to stimulate and motivate employees. This is one reason why product quality usually deteriorates during a layoff.

> Man is only motivated by unfilled needs.
>
> A. H. Maslow

Support Your People

Quality people don't have P & L (profit and loss) responsibility. The benefits of controlled product quality are not as apparent as meeting monthly shipment targets. Quality cost savings are generally more elusive than those in purchasing, for example. Because of these characteristics, the job of the quality practitioner is often frustrating and lonely. Quality control management must, therefore, fully support their people when disagreements or conflicts arise.

Case in Point: A project engineer accused a reliability analyst of playing a numbers game and formally complained to the director of reliability. The director responded by showing how failure rate data was collected, and introduced the project engineer to the basics of reliability mathematics. It was also pointed out that the analysis was exactly in accordance with contractual requirements. Had the director not provided the necessary backup, the analyst would have been rendered totally ineffective.

Be on the lookout for the following areas where management support is crucial:

- rejection of nonconforming material
- corrective action effectivity points
- decision not to ship discrepant goods
- performance of preventive tasks such as prototype testing, reliability analysis, or drawing review
- failure analysis of customer-rejected material
- approval of cost center budget(s)
- appropriation of measuring and test equipment
- adoption of new quality standards
- interpretation of drawings and specifications

There will be times when your people will be technically wrong (relatively easy to handle) or simply make a bad judgment call (difficult to handle). Under no circumstances should the quality manager openly criticize or contradict the staff—this must be done in private. Mutual agreement should be reached on how to best extricate the quality function from the painted corner so that the employee at least knows the boss was behind him. Without management support, QC people quickly lose their usefulness, influence, motivation, and assertiveness. They will degenerate into ineffective, risk-avoiding nice guys.

Periodic formal expressions of recognition—positive performance reviews, salary increases—are not enough to keep employees' spirits and performance high. It is a manager's daily task to support employees and show them by words, tone of voice, facial expressions, and degree of attentiveness that they are worth every bit of the time he or she is spending with them.

EMPLOYEE PERFORMANCE REVIEWS: GATEWAY TO GROWTH

Any quality manager soon discovers that personal success or failure depends on the performance of his or her staff. To help achieve top performance, you must assess the strengths and weaknesses of staff members and determine how to maintain or increase their effectiveness. Periodic reviews of each employee's work progress are crucial to making and communicating these judgments.

Many otherwise quite capable QC managers analyze, rationalize, and agonize until their office walls are covered with paper before committing to a piece of test equipment requiring an investment of $400,000 and, therefore, an annual depreciation charge of $40,000. Yet the process of evaluating and making recommendations regarding the training, compensation, and career path of a $40,000-a-year quality engineer typically requires one half of a piece of paper, reluctantly prepared in one half-hour once a year.

Purpose of the Review

The challenge is to conduct the review in a systematic, thorough, and people-oriented manner. Each review should be conducted with the following objectives in mind:

Clarify work objectives. The progress review is an opportunity for the manager and subordinate to reach an understanding about the quality, time, and cost parameters of the employee's performance.

Realize potential. Few employees stand still; they improve or get worse. With mutually determined goals, the employee can set up a structured program of self-improvement.

Defuse potential problems. Even in the best environment, employees have gripes, misunderstandings, and ambitions that do not always come to the manager's attention unless he or she makes a special effort to get at them.

Case in Point: A test supervisor was frustrated by the frequent breakdown and unreliability of his aging and obsolete voltmeters. The cost for replacement was not high, but management took no action because the problem was not clearly identified. Good two-way communications can prevent such information gaps. Teamwork requires that tensions within the group be defused before they get out of hand.

Exchange business information. Does the employee know all she should about her job, opportunities within the company, services offered by the company, the organization of the company, test equipment acquisition plans, and the company's prospects for the future?

Before the Review

The progress review cannot be reduced to a pat formula because all managers are not alike any more than all subordinates are alike. But regardless of your style as a manager, the following suggestions will help make the review a success:

Develop a Good Attitude

- How can I place the emphasis on being helpful?
- Can I keep quiet long enough to let him develop his ideas?
- How can I encourage her to say what is on her mind?
- Do I have the courage and humility to admit that I may be wrong; am I willing to change my mind if proven wrong?
- Am I more concerned with my feelings than with those of the person I am reviewing?
- If we disagree, can I keep from arguing?

Do Your Homework: Have the file of the person to be reviewed on hand during the review, but fix the main facts about his or her work history in your mind beforehand. Review his or her previous evaluation. What has changed since the last review? What did you talk about in previous reviews?

Know Your Objectives.

Pick the Right Place and Time: Do not attempt the review except in an office or some other room where both of you can be seated with no one else in hearing distance. Don't start a review unless you sincerely believe you will have enough time to finish it. Pick the right time. Avoid conducting a performance review just after a disciplinary action.

Conducting the Review

Although the details of each progress review will vary, the basic structure and objectives will remain the same for all interviews.

Provide a Casual Opening: Here is a sample opening to illustrate how a progress review might start: "We see each other every day, but we don't have much chance to talk. So I am planning to take time out every so often and sit down with you and each of the others in the department for a personal talk. I'd like you to tell me how you feel about your job. I want to give you a chance to talk over any problems and ideas you have. At the same time, I want to talk with you about the work you have been doing. Through such a talk, I think we can help each other."

Focus on Good Points First: Pick examples from achievements in quality cost reduction, defect investigation, or vendor corrective action. The idea is to put the employee at ease and get him or her to open up.

Suggest Improvements in a Positive Way: Usually it is best to avoid critical words such as "faults," "mistakes," "shortcomings," and "weaknesses." Be constructive. Talk about how improvement can be made, not about what has been done wrong. Experience has shown that this often may be handled most tactfully by asking first for the other person's views. Where does he feel he might show improvement? In what respect does he think he can do a better job? If he is overly agreeable, get him to state his plan for self-improvement.

Managers who try this method for the first time are surprised at the capacity for self-appraisal possessed by most people. Frequently, employees are more critical of themselves than the manager is.

Avoid Arguments: Don't push too hard for agreement, but make a note of disagreements for future talks. Remember that the good effect of this talk is limited by the extent to which it is accepted. Argument is likely to silence without convincing. Don't hesitate to share or take the blame. And by all means avoid comparisons with other people.

Discuss Future Goals: Not everybody wants to be promoted. Yet everyone wants to have a hopeful view of the future. To understand a subordinate, you should try to get the person to talk about his or her hopes and expectations. Does she want a promotion? Does she think she is ready for it? Does she want a transfer to a different department or line of work? (If you would prefer not to bring up this subject ask yourself, "If a person wants a transfer, would I rather know about it or not?") Does she want to remain on this job, growing in status through increasing skill and seniority or is she just working in the present job temporarily until something better comes along? Is she planning early retirement?

As a manager, you will be in a position to counsel subordinates. What should he do to achieve his aspirations? What can he do on the present job to increase his chances of promotion? Would additional product knowledge or statistical training help?

Cautions: 1. You are taking a tremendous risk if you try to predict the future. Don't make promises unless you are sure of your position. Circumstances may change so that you cannot make good. If this happens, the effect on the person may be disastrous and you will probably never be able to explain it satisfactorily. Also, be careful that you don't imply more than you state. Keep statements simple and direct. The other person may be inclined to read into your words much more than you intended.

2. Be cautious about telling a subordinate that his goals are impossible. Don't discourage any sincere effort to improve. If his goals seem to be unrealistic, point out the difficulties tactfully, but allow him to draw his own conclusion.

Permit Free Discussion: You cannot anticipate people's thoughts completely. Be careful not to crowd out the other person's ideas by falling into a routine. Make sure that you give him an opportunity to comment on anything that is on his mind. Does he have any problems or questions? Can you be more helpful in any way? Does he have suggestions of any kind to offer? How does he feel about this type of review?

One increasingly popular approach is for the supervisor and his subordinate (or the QC manager and the director of production) to leave the plant and lunch together. The relaxed and less-structured atmosphere of a restaurant can sometimes break down barriers and stimulate communications. For obvious reasons, this technique must be used very selectively.

End with Encouragement

Assure the person of your willingness to talk further if there are any questions or suggestions at a later date. Success should be gauged not by how much you or he have said, but by performance.

> Work is accomplished by those employees who have not yet reached their level of incompetence.
>
> Reflection on the Peter Principle

REFERENCES

Birnbrauer, H. "Taking the Sting Out of Performance Reviews." *Machine Design,* September 8, 1977.

"Establishing Educational Programs in Quality and Reliability." Education and Training Institute, ASQC, 3rd ed., 1975.

Gaubatz, C. "Quality Control—A Career." *Quality Progress,* September 1979.

Harris, D. H. and F. B. Chaney. *Human Factors in Quality Assurance.* New York: John Wiley & Sons, 1969.

Holman, J. L. "An Analysis of Employee Motivation." AIEE Transactions, June 1969.

Kidwell, J. L. "The Inspector—A Critical Factor in the Reliability Equation." *Industrial Quality Control,* September 1965.

Myers M. S. *Every Employee a Manager.* New York: McGraw-Hill, 1981.

Petrolino, B. "Do-It-Yourself Editing." *Machine Design,* March 2, 1972.

Pollack, T. "Bringing Out the Best in Your People." *Production,* November 1972.

Quality Motivation Workbook. ASQC, Quality Motivation Technical Committee, 1967.

Reynolds, E. A. "Training QC Engineers and Managers." *Quality Progress,* April 1970.

"Strategy in Working with People." *Royal Bank of Canada,* Monthly Newsletter. February 1977.

Woodland, R. A. "Some Thoughts on Employee Relations." *The Industrial Manager,* May/June 1970.

8

The Role of Practical Management in Quality Control

Virtually everyone can benefit from a practical management orientation. The need for practical management is especially important for quality control. The degree of need for this management orientation varies, depending on the experience and training of the managers involved. But even an experienced and successful manager can have voids in his or her background, may have forgotten old rules that were learned the hard way, has failed to put good rules or techniques into practice, or is not aware of some of the more recent management tools. The need for continual professional growth and the application of proven management practices are essential in today's complex and dynamic industrial environment.

Practical management involves focusing the manager's attention on a relatively small number of critical functions that can be effectively tackled to successfully achieve work needs. The following checklist pertains:

√ Keep in touch with overall company objectives, plans, and needs and communicate them to your people.

√ Focus attention on tasks, ideas, and products that will provide the company and customer with the greatest quality payoff.

√ Help your people get work done efficiently by providing needed facilities, measuring equipment, and people, and by removing roadblocks when they occur.

√ Provide leadership by choosing or helping your people select the right things to work on and the optimum methods to accomplish this work.

√ Provide discipline; even highly motivated people need to have some framework, rules, or system to work within.

√ Be a catalyst for fruitful innovations in cost reduction, yield improvement, and measurement techniques.

√ Solve people problems effectively and quickly.

√ Prevent your people from accepting unrealistic budgets and schedules that are bound to lead to failure and demoralization.

√ Build solid relationships with functions interfacing with quality control.

In this chapter, numerous tips, techniques, approaches, shortcuts, and tactics are explained to help you get on with the job with the greatest efficiency and effectiveness.

BE RESULTS ORIENTED

Being in quality control today is one of the toughest, most demanding jobs going. Not only are you challenged on all sides in traditional style by production, engineering, and sales, but now you're also subject to the increasingly strident demands of consumer groups and a sophisticated public. On top of this, a proliferation of regulatory bodies

141

is forcing you to absorb and implement a multitude of complex and sometimes contradictory laws and regulations. And, if that isn't enough, someone's already whispering in your ear about the forthcoming change to metric measurement.

Survival in this kind of atmosphere isn't easy. Many quality control practitioners tend to drift to the more sophisticated, higher-technology techniques and pay little attention to the basic, commonsense methodologies that have suported them for years and made them successful on the job. The new technology sometimes can be used in the organization beneficially, but recent advances in technology have drawn us further and further away from the realities of getting a job done. Management by objectives is the road to a successful and economical quality program. Aim high; set high standards of achievement. Remember:

If you aim low enough, you'll never be disappointed.

Don't look at things narrowly. Broaden your outlook and focus on results. Before embarking on any major change, first ask yourself, "How will this change affect sales or profits? How will this change contribute to company goals?"

Be a businessperson, not just a technical specialist. Define the role of quality control in terms of overall company objectives. Don't allow the dazzle of technical expertise to blind you to the realities of business life. Evaluate your function in terms of dollars and cents and contribution to sales. Remember that statistics and other technical tools are strictly a means to an end; their only function is to help get the job done. The fanciest, most sophisticated analytical method is only as good as its ability to achieve results in the most economical and efficient manner. If a simpler established technique will do a better job, then use it. Abandon the exotic method and focus on the shortest path to task accomplishment.

ATTEND TRADE SHOWS

Trade shows, exhibitions, and trade fairs provide an excellent opportunity to see what the competition is doing. Traditionally, marketing and sales people attend these shows to discover performance, new features, and prices of competing products. It's a good idea to send a QC person to these shows periodically. Experienced eyes can usually spot some valuable cost-saving pointers, not readily apparent to marketeers. At the same time the person's horizons will be expanded and motivation will be increased, especially if the person will staff your booth.

Case in Point: A QC manager for a U.S. medical equipment firm attended a European trade fair. Equipments from Japan, France, the U.K., and West Germany as well as the U.S. were on display. As a direct result of the trip the manager learned the following:

- Many equipments contained QC tamper-proof seals. These were useful in controlling warranty claims and potential product liability actions, but were not used by his company.

- Without exception the components used were of a far lesser quality than he had suggested be used in his firm's design.

- The accompanying sales brochures of the Japanese firms stressed reliability and quality in addition to price. His company, although superior in this area, failed to seize the opportunity.

- A potential British second source was found for a dial indicator that had presented a severe quality problem.

- European performance standards and measurement techniques were slightly different from those in North America. Changes in test procedures would be required for export sales.

- Customers, at least in this market area, were really sensitive to appearance and "cosmetics." This reassured him that his inspection criteria were a true measure of customer needs.

Management by Emphasis

Management by emphasis has more to do with effectiveness than efficiency. You can spend your time very efficiently doing many trivial things, or effectively doing the few important jobs that need doing even if not too efficiently. Effectiveness, then, is a measure of your total impact on the growth and survival of your company. Efficiency is doing things right. Effectiveness is doing the right thing by concentrating your resources and efforts.

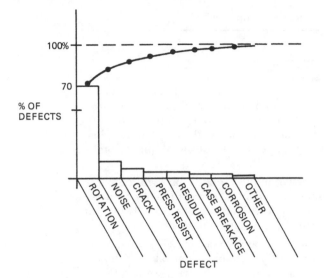

FIGURE 8-1. Pareto analysis, using four months' data, showing that switch rotation accounts for 70 percent of defects.

Management by emphasis means simply addressing oneself to the task of identifying and performing well those few vital activities that have the greatest impact on the job at hand, and relegating to second place the less essential activities. Pareto's Law provides the basis for applying management by emphasis:

> In any series of elements to be controlled, a certain small fraction, in terms of numbers of elements, always accounts for the major portion in terms of effect.
>
> Wilfredo Pareto

A few percent of the quality characteristics of your product account for the bulk of scrap and rework (Figure 8-1). A few percent of the various piece parts entering the final product account for the bulk of the scheduling and delivery date failures. A few percent of your purchase orders account for the bulk of your dollar purchases. A few percent of all the reasons for failure account for the majority of your equipment downtime. A few percent of the decisions you make account for the bulk of the total effect of all your decisions. It is always true that the first few percent of customer complaints will account for about three-quarters of all your warranty dollars. The last 80 percent of the items in the line will account for only a small percent of the total dollar sales. In the same way,

a few percent of the total employees on your payroll account for the bulk of the personnel headaches, accidents, suggestions, and so on.

Table 8-1 provides some practical applications of Pareto's Law as it applies to quality control. For any organization, the implication of management by emphasis is enormous. It involves assigning the most capable people and the greatest resources to those activities that will have the greatest impact on the success and growth of the enterprise, and relegating the routine and the humdrum to those resources and personnel as can be spared from the mainstream of activity. Better and more economical product quality will be a direct consequence.

MANAGE YOUR TIME CAREFULLY

Time is the most basic and vital human resource. Unlike other resources, it cannot be accumulated or stored. Once spent, it cannot be retrieved. Thoreau once wrote, "It is not enough to be busy . . . the question is: what are we busy about?" You must plan and budget your time and energy effectively.

- Is your time constantly being wasted by other people?
- Have you become the victim of paperwork or red tape, with increasingly less time to devote to primary quality control responsibilities?
- Do you attend too many unnecessary or unproductive meetings?
- Are you always under the gun tending to last-minute tasks, making it difficult for you to meet deadlines that seem to sneak up on you without warning?
- Do you have too many interruptions by unexpected visitors or telephone calls?

Here are some time-saving ideas:

√ Don't read everything. Delegate reading assignments to subordinates and ask them to note interesting articles and ideas. When the publication returns to you it will have been pre-screened. (You'll also get insight on what your managers think is important.)

√ Only send typed memos when you must confirm, remind, clarify, or communicate with several people. Otherwise, use the phone. Extra benefit: immediate reaction.

√ Always keep a pocket or desk diary at hand for jotting down ideas that come to mind. This

TABLE 8-1. Practical Application of Management by Emphasis

IF	THEN
You spend much time in procurement quality control	Perform an ABC analysis of your inventory. Devote the bulk of your quality control and paperwork efforts to the vital 15 percent of your purchased parts that represent 85 percent of your failures. Apply little control to the trivial many, those 85 percent that represent only 15 percent of your total quality problems.
There are many causes of failure of your product	About 15 percent of the various causes will be bound to produce about 80 percent of your failures. Identify these vital few causes and devote 80 percent of your quality control efforts to them.
You have production delays because of measuring equipment breakdowns	You will find that about 20 percent of your equipment represent 80 percent of your breakdown hours. Increase your inspections and preventive maintenance drastically on these vital few equipments. Decrease your other activities accordingly.
There are significant quality losses due to engineering changes	Rank changed items according to criticality and adjust control efforts accordingly.
You are constructing an addition, installing a test facility, or repairing the floor	Identify the items that are part of the critical sequence of events, and concentrate on keeping these on schedule.
You want to improve materials handling or shipping procedures	Identify those vital few products, containers, or procedures that represent the bulk of the job. Design a new procedure to handle these vital few. Ignore the many trivial considerations until your major plan has been implemented.

saves sifting through dozens of scraps of paper. Some of the best quality cost-reduction ideas have been achieved in this manner.

√ Use a tape recorder. Very small units are available for $100 or less. Design reviews, conference minutes, and note-taking can be recorded, reviewed, and erased. A recorder is a particularly useful aid to memory and understanding—you need to listen to information about two or three times to assimilate it well. Thus, the device can reward you greatly in multiplying your use of time.

√ Establish a uniform filing system. Make sure you have a written guide to what's filed where. Purge files regularly. Desk organizing and tickler files may be useful. Desk organizer categories include: "urgent," "dictate," "to do," "review," "file," and "discard." Tickler files are for items needing future attention, filed by the date you expect to begin them.

√ Eliminate clutter—stacked desks are time wasters. Piles of papers are distracting, and retrieval is slow and inefficient. Restrict work on your desk to the priority projects. Stick with them until they're completed.

√ Use the telephone—millions of people are as close to you as your telephone. The cost, as compared to the overwhelming advantage, is inconsequential. Long-distance direct dialing makes it possible to have contacts at minimum cost throughout the continental United States. Wide Area Telephone Service (WATS) is employed by many business, industry, and government institutions. There is no excuse not to get into action and contact the persons who can help you accomplish your quality objectives.

√ Use travel time on trains and airplanes for reading QC and reliability journals and writing business letters.

√ Don't kill time. We all have times when we are waiting for some reason. This type of time should be employed in some useful activity. You can read books, periodicals, memos, or test reports during these periods. Rescuing these fragments of time can result in an accumulation of many hours of useful knowledge over a year.

√ Avoid paper wars—don't fall into the trap of trying to solve quality problems by letter or memo. Contact the other party and solve the problem on a face-to-face basis.

√ Use a daily planner—don't let trivia get on your schedule. Stick to tasks that optimize quality costs.

√ Speed up your reading. One way to improve your knowledge, your usefulness, and your fitness for more responsibilities is to read as much as possible about the assurance sciences, your company, and the industry. Experiment to find the speed-reading technique that best suits you.

BE ANALYTICAL AND OBJECTIVE

Quality control generally has a tough time making its case. To the extent that QC is objective and quantitative, each person can more effectively do the job. Corrective action, nonconforming material dispositions, design improvements, and the acceptance of standards will all come easier if people understand the basis for your position. There are five basic ways of objectively making your case:

1. *Mathematical Analysis.* This is perhaps the weakest method, since your mathematical models can be challenged. If, however, the analysis involves natural laws of physics, chemistry, biology, or electronics, you should easily be able to make your case. It requires that your quality engineers be capable of making such analyses and not be limited to statistical methods. Reliability and operating life are two of the toughest parameters to credibly analyze.

2. *Test.* Actual test data is generally accepted as indisputable fact provided that proper test procedures and equipment have been adhered to. Accordingly, actual test results should be used whenever possible. Advancements in NDT technology have greatly helped in making formerly elusive test data readily available.

3. *Inspection.* Physical inspection, supported by cross-sections, microphotographs, magnified results, or blow-ups are usually effective. If, however, fundamental quality standards are themselves controversial, this approach may have limited value (unless defects are obvious ones—cracks, open circuits, wrong polarity). Usually inspection may have to be combined with test, experience, and/or logic in order to make your

case. Cosmetic items such as color, scratches, appearance, and luster can best be controlled by mutually agreed-upon standards, production samples, and color chips.

4. *Demonstration.* Long arguments can be avoided by the use of demonstration methods.

Case in Point: A maintainability engineer performed an analysis on a piece of equipment and stated that the specified MTTR (Mean Time To Repair) criterion could not be met because of poor accessibility. The designer vehemently disagreed. The quality manager suggested that the dispute be resolved by physical demonstration. When the designer could not remove the eighteen screws (with three different heads) in the required 2.4 minutes, she conceded the point and agreed to redesign the unit.

5. *Experience.* History repeats itself, particularly where failures are concerned. Prior records, failure analysis reports, or customer complaints can be brought forward in order to prove that the defect under review has in the past been the cause of customer dissatisfaction.

There are other approaches that have proven useful, primarily as supplementary tools:

- Logic and reasoning.
- Computer simulation (see Chapter 11).
- Accelerated tests (see Chapter 9).
- Simulated environmental testing (the biggest problem is that people can challenge the simulated environment).
- Similarity to previous problems.
- Statistical analysis (probabilistic analyses are difficult to explain and defend, particularly to nontechnical personnel) (see Chapter 10).
- Reference to learned papers and articles.
- Physics of failure techniques (very sophisticated, often costly approach).
- Opinion polls wherein several functional, unbiased "experts" from different disciplines give their view on relevant quality matters.
- Cost-benefit analysis (see Chapter 14).

Subjective, opinionated, and emotional approaches to quality control are neither justified nor effective. Hard, quantitative, well-researched facts will enable QC to do a professional, cost-effective job.

Once you've unequivocally proved that there is a failure or problem worthy of attention, the next step is to deal with management's key motivator—money.

Calculating the true cost of a failure at various points in the product stream can help you get high-level support for your quality improvement efforts. Typically, the cost rises exponentially from incoming inspection to a field service call. Consider the basic costs with a failure in assembly:

- time lost due to disruption of a failure
- time to fill in reject tickets
- troubleshooting costs to isolate failed part(s)
- time to acquire replacement part(s) including storeperson's time and paperwork
- cost of replacement part(s)
- time to remove failed part(s) and replace with good part(s)
- time to reinspect assembly
- cost for retest

Depending on your operation, you may also incur material review costs, additional set-up costs, and failure analysis costs, not to mention the possibility of damaging the assembly during repair or extra handling. A field failure will typically be an order of magnitude more expensive than a final acceptance failure.

The total figures will usually stem the opponents of corrective action and put them in a more favorable mood. Make sure someone in accounting checks your cost figures though. Be very conservative in your cost estimates.

PROVIDE PLAUSIBLE QUALITY REPORTS

The quality manager might, for example, prepare a monthly summary for management that would present the quality performance in a given area, or for the plant as a whole.

It is important that such reports for management be checked for plausibility by the quality manager before release. The person with the maximum authority in quality assurance, the person who will have to answer if the report is challenged, is best qualified to recognize implausibility. The quality manager should prepare the summary. It's the best possible way of keeping in touch with what's going on. Overall measures of quality performance are the chief subjects of communication between the quality manager and top management.

Consider, for example, a work area like a machine shop. You have decided that, while some pieces are small and many, and some are large and few, the percent defective at first inspection is the true measure of quality.

It is true that some pieces that are rejected at the first inspection may be accepted by the disposition "use as is," but these should not be used to amend the reading at the first inspection. Even if the engineers change the drawing to match the review-accepted parts, the first score should not be changed. The task was to make pieces in conformance with the drawing as it was; the quality of conformance must be measured by the degree of success against that standard.

When you prepare such reports, you might consider writing in as a footnote what is counted in the numerator and the denominator of the quality measure. It could remain a part of the permanent format so that, as the report circulates, everybody will be informed as to exactly what is being measured.

A new report has been prepared and presented for your signature. It reads:

Percent defective

Last month	This month
4.8%	1.2%

Before you rush the glad news into circulation, ask yourself, "Is it plausible? It is true that the people in the machine shop are conscientious and responsive to requests for corrective action, but an improvement from 4.8 percent last month to 1.2 percent this month sounds too good to be true."

There is a bit of a problem in putting a percentage on the magnitude of the improvement. It looks like an improvement of 300 percent; but when one is counting improvement from high numbers to lower numbers, can one achieve more than 100 percent? This would be the complete elimination of all defects.

We must then count it as an improvement of 75 percent. Do not hesitate to explain how you arrived at this figure. Indeed, statistics should always be accompanied by explanatory notes; one of top management's many aggravations is statistical reports without comments.

Now you have to check for plausibility. The

first step might be to check the totals of rejected pieces and of pieces submitted for first inspection for this month and last month. The error might be right there; it's easy to make an error when one's fingers are flying over the computer keys.

If that doesn't do it, call in the inspection supervisors and quality engineers for a diagnostic session and brainstorm it.

- Had there been an accelerated use of statistical process-capability information with a consequent substantial increase in the yield of acceptable parts?
- Was new production equipment put into service?
- Had there been a notable decrease in the number of engineering changes?
- Had certain part numbers with traditionally high rejection rates simply not been scheduled this month?

One way or another, the figures will be confirmed or found in error. If the latter, correct the report; if the former, be sure to comment on the causes for the improvement; be lavish with congratulations.

Observation: Moving averages can be more representative of quality trend by filtering out the month-to-month transients.

Another area of cost reporting that causes confusion is scrap. *Unplanned scrap* refers to defective material that cannot be reworked to the requirement and therefore must be discarded. *Planned scrap* is what you have left over after punching round holes in a rectangular sheet. Normally, the major part of the scrap cost is the added value invested in material prior to scrapping it. For this reason the calculation of scrap cost should be reviewed very carefully to make sure that everything appropriate is being included.

√ Is there a distinction between the scrap resulting from shop errors and the scrap resulting from an engineering change?

√ Does the salvage value of scrap enter into your quality cost statistics?

√ Is there a requirement that all scrap must be turned in, or do you have a sudden increase before annual vacation shutdown or the end of the fiscal year?

√ Does your scrap cost contain total expenditure, including burden?

Watch Your Interfaces with Top Management

In addition to technical expertise, the quality manager needs a business orientation. Keep these pointers in mind:

√ Top management is very busy. Keep quality reports short, preferably one 8½″ × 11″ sheet. Attach appendices if absolutely necessary.

√ Always try to relate quality performance to financial parameters such as inventory investment, return on capital employed, costs and profits.

√ Don't be an alarmist or sensationalist.

√ Make sure your memos or reports are well organized, logically structured, neat, and free of typographical errors.

√ Be prepared and armed with facts. There is nothing worse than to approach top management with missing or incorrect data.

√ Show concern for such items as order bookings, schedule compliance, warranty costs, and monthly shipments.

√ Avoid QC jargon such as AOQL, MTTR, and Steady State Availability, unless you are sure your boss is comfortable with them.

√ Don't be a nuisance. See top management only when you have something concrete to say or ask.

√ Send senior management copies of favorable customer surveys, letters, or reports. Annotations should give credit to all functions who contributed, not just QC. Try to relate to increased sales.

IMPACT STATEMENTS IMPROVE EFFICIENCY

The quality control function is a function whose policies, procedures, and practices have a direct effect on nearly every organizational unit within the company. More often than not, a change in QC policy or practice is not thought through for its impact on the entire company, thus adding costs, decreasing efficiency, and/or building resentment.

Case in Point: In 1979 the U.S. Food and Drug Administration (FDA), under pressure from consumer groups, decided to remedy patient ignorance. It proposed that nearly 400 prescription medications be accompanied by simply written instructional leaflets about the drugs. These Patient Package Inserts (PPIs), would explain, among other things, what the drug was used for, how it should be taken and for how long, possible side effects, even how to store it.

The idea seemed innocent enough; nonprescription, over-the-counter drugs, which are generally less powerful, have long come with printed consumer information. But the FDA's proposal quickly brought a storm of controversy. Drug manufacturers were worried about legal repercussions should a drug user develop a rare side effect unmentioned in a PPI. Though the FDA figured that the cost of preparing, storing, and distributing leaflets would add only an average of 6¼¢ to each prescription, professional groups assessed the extra tab at 22¢ to 35¢. In addition, pharmacists, who would hand out the brochure with the filled prescription, were afraid that the leaflets would provoke a rash of time-consuming questions from customers. Some said that they would be forced to charge a fee for such consultations. Also, they feared being put in the uncomfortable position of seeming to second-guess the doctors.

Many physicians contended that the leaflets would interfere with the doctor-patient relationship. Some stated that some patients—for instance, those suffering from schizophrenia or cancer—would be better off not knowing the precise nature of their ailments; yet they would probably be able to deduce the diagnosis from the insert. Still other doctors feared that PPIs could be seen as quasi-legal documents defining minimal standards of care, and thus expose them to more malpractice suits.

Perhaps the most serious concern (shared by doctors, drug manufacturers, and the FDA) was that a laundry list of possible adverse effects could scare off patients from needed medication.

The FDA has since modified its requirement but only after a lot of cost, controversy, and conflict. Quality control management would be wise to learn from this example. Changes in statistical sampling practice can wreak havoc with production costs; alterations in material review procedures can slow down production; and additions to data recording requirements can slow down production flow. An impact statement for every major addition, deletion, or change in quality control procedure is, like those used for assessing the environmental impact of new construction projects, a necessity of modern industrial life.

DON'T SHOOT FROM THE HIP

Some managers have found that they can be fairly accurate decision makers by making snap decisions without time-consuming research, meetings, or thought. However, this approach can be dangerous when overconfidence leads the manager into a quick decision that has many ramifications to the organization and company. Thus, the habit of shooting from the hip without careful aim can miss a major target and really hurt the manager. Quality control management especially must portray an image of logic and fairness.

Experience has shown that a manager can get into trouble even in apparently minor hip-shot decisions. Therefore, while an extensive investigation into each problem is not needed, the ramifications should be systematically considered before making most decisions. Although the decision-making process may take ten to sixty minutes of private thought or investigation, it is well worth the investment because an error on even a minor area can result in dozens of wasted hours by others.

Case in Point: A QC supervisor was going to a meeting with the director of quality of his division when the director spied a statistics clerk talking to someone. He turned to the manager and said: "I saw her talking to that quality engineer two days in a row. Fire her."

When the supervisor talked to the clerk, he found that she was on her coffee break on both days and was, in fact, talking shop.

As a result of this snap decision, about two hours were wasted and people were upset.

EASE THE PAIN OF REJECTION

We are reminded that when in ancient times a messenger, spattered with blood and sweat, arrived from a distant battlefield to report defeat, his account was received with rising anger, and then he was beheaded as the bearer of bad tidings!

In the machine shop, on the assembly lines, or in final test, the potential for such incidents is ever present. But whether they are solved in a manner conducive to continued working harmony between the operating departments depends on the quality manager. Once he or she has acknowledged that the quality control act having the most impact on colleagues is the rejection of material, and that this is never going to make them happy, and that they shouldn't expect it to, then steps can be taken to mitigate their distress.

In anticipation of such incidents, the QC manager should establish good communications with his or her colleagues. Avoid being known to them only as the person in charge of the people who reject their purchased supplies, their machined parts, and their assemblies. Then, when a schedule-disturbing rejection must be made, there will be some possibility of an unheated dialogue.

The quality manager should instruct line supervisors to be alert at all times to the presence of urgently needed parts in their sections, and to see that they get prompt attention. He or she should see that information about a rejection of urgently needed material does not reach the victim by a routine rejection report. The person's supervisor, or the QC manager, in an exceptional case, should phone in the information, having already confirmed that the rejection is a true report, having already set up a review with the engineer, or being prepared to offer the services of an inspector if production will work overtime on the rework.

By such actions, the quality manager will temper the violence of psychological reaction. He or she will, moreover, create a managerial atmosphere in which colleagues will be more inclined to listen to the recommendations for the introduction of process control, for the more careful selection of suppliers, or for corrective action.

Case in Point: A batch of vitally needed components arrived at receiving inspection only to be rejected after sampling inspection. Fifty shop people would be idled by the lack of this component, and important customer delivery dates would not be met. The quick-acting QC supervisor authorized 100 percent sorting and informed purchasing and production control. The vendor immedi-

ately corrected his process and air freighted a replacement batch. Production control used the components made available through sorting and directed the balance of workers to other jobs. The fast response from QC saved $5000 in idle time in addition to satisfying customer delivery requirements. Added bonus: The prompt feedback of defect information allowed the vendor to correct his process quickly.

AVOID "TUNNEL VISION"

Employees are not forbidden to visit a specific activity (security is not a consideration in this discussion), but over the years they gain a strong impression that their supervisors frown on trips away from the immediate work area. The point is that they are not encouraged to visit other departments where related activities take place.

Case in Point: A metrology engineer who for years had calibrated accelerometers for environmental test inadvertently visited the test lab. For the first time she saw how accelerometers were being used. She had never made such a visit before, even though the environmental test area was literally only a stone's throw away. The environmental test people had never visited the calibration lab, either. This is a striking but by no means rare example of "tunnel vision."

Quality control management should encourage informal but planned visits to other departments. The potential benefits include:

- *Assistance during emergencies because of cross-training.*
- *Better utilization of personnel.* Sometimes managers must cope with a temporary personnel surplus. For instance, work in the calibration lab might be caught up, providing an excellent opportunity for metrologists to be assigned temporarily to learn about environmental testing. (Don't forget to consult the union first.)
- *Better utilization of existing equipment.* When people from one activity visit another activity and see their test equipment (in use and/or in storage), they sometimes recognize that they could share an item, rather than duplicate it.
- *Greater justification for new equipment.* Discussion might reveal a need for new equipment, and to-

gether you could be able to justify its purchase, if neither department alone could justify it.

- *Job enrichment.* Managers are being exposed to new concepts about work that is unnecessarily dull and routine. They are being encouraged to vary such work with added responsibility. What better way to enrich the work of, say, a quality engineer, than by asking him to conduct a series of informal briefings? In preparing for those briefings and in answering questions from those attending, he will probably discover valuable new aspects of his work. And from the visitors he may gain new appreciation of how his work (and his activity's work) are important to other activities. He will feel more integrated and become better motivated.

- *Cross-fertilization of ideas.* Typical questions might include "Why do you . . . ?" or "Why don't you. . . ?" or possibly, "How about . . . ?" Most such questions are answered easily. But occasionally they will lead to consideration of new techniques that might work better than existing methods, saving time and money and even eliminating outmoded or unnecessary steps, reports, and forms.

The time away from the job may cause overhead costs and work backlogs to rise modestly. A manager must balance these relatively small costs against the potential benefits. Ideas brought back might increase efficiency or eliminate a present task. (Management has always coped with medical leave, vacation, and other mandated time away from the workplace.)

Pitfall to Avoid: Don't block such visits because of the fear that your people may find other work more interesting or rewarding and request transfers. Perhaps you already know that your peoples' work is boring and unrewarding. Your people aren't permanently attached to QC. There are many attractive jobs not just in other departments but everywhere. In the worst case at least a valuable employee stays within the company and the transfer can be accomplished in an organized manner.

PLAY THE DEVIL'S ADVOCATE

This is one of the most difficult yet necessary roles of quality control. When new products and processes are introduced, someone must ask "What can go wrong?" and must thoroughly investigate every detail with that thought in mind. The job is not to say what can go right, but rather to determine what can go wrong and then do whatever needs to be done to prevent it.

Because the role of devil's advocate has a negative connotation, most people will shy away from playing the role and asking the necessary questions. Of course, when nobody in the organization scrutinizes the details, there is bound to be trouble later on down the road. Either somebody forgot some important detail or somebody did something wrong, or both.

Unfortunately, and this happens too many times, the quality control person who conscientiously asks those embarrassing questions is ridiculed and accused of not being positive. The questioning of detail is many times abhorrent, for example, to the marketing person who wants to push ahead with the new product at all costs—and skip the details.

The rather imposing job of the quality control practitioner, under these circumstances, is to persevere in as positive a fashion as possible, explaining his or her role as one that will contribute substantially to advancement of the total project. It might be readily apparent, for example, that some supposedly minor detail could hold up the project indefinitely unless it was soon resolved. But it never can be resolved unless it is first brought to the surface—and that is customarily the job of quality control.

You can close your eyes to an unpleasant fact and avoid an unpleasant confrontation during the product planning and implementation phases. But when the product reaches the field and fails in the customer's hands, then it's your baby—not the design engineer's who goofed a critical tolerance nor the chemist's who made a terrible mistake in the original formulation. *You* will be the one management asks that embarrassing question, "How did you let this get into the field?" Regardless of what happens inside the factory, once you have bought off the product, it is yours, 100 percent yours.

Typical ploys for getting attention:

- Cite examples of previous "disasters."
- Point out current regulations in liability law.
- Quote chapter and verse from the customer's contract.
- Refer to company policy and procedures.
- Demonstrate that failure is inevitable if current plan of action is implemented.
- Calculate reliability, expected yield, and potential scrap in order to make your case.

- Compare planned action to those of toughest competitors.
- Refer to previous failure or defect analysis reports.
- Have cost estimators take a crack at the new design.
- Acquire support from purchasing, production, field service.
- Perform abbreviated but legitimate tests and present failures, side effects, and observations.

LOOK INTO QUALITY CIRCLES

In the early 1950s, the Japanese competitive threat still seemed minimal. Cheap prices, low quality, and poor service were the primary characteristics. As time passed, Japanese quality improved. With competitive prices, Japan overtook the U.S. and Europe in a well-planned sequence —portable radios, home radios, stereos, cameras, steel, bicycles, motorbikes, motorcycles, automobiles. The factors (or excuses) often cited for this success are indicated in Table 8-2.

Lest one conclude that the economic challenge has been totally lost, consider American industries that have retained world leadership—weapon systems, aircraft, computers, and semiconductor production. These industries have performed well internationally because of:

- strong emphasis on product quality and reliability
- strong direct and indirect government support
- relatively high R & D investment
- challenging jobs for employees
- constant technological challenge
- productivity increases in excess of labor wage increases
- heavy investment in automation
- aggressive worldwide marketing

Competitors of the Japanese will have to address each of these factors, and quality is certainly at the top of the list.

Following World War II, the Japanese undertook to revolutionize their product quality in order to make their goods saleable in the world market. The central feature of that revolution was a massive training program for directors, managers, supervisors, and technological specialists. As this program permeated through the company hierarchies, from top to bottom, this question arose—should we also give training programs to

TABLE 8-2. Factors Behind the Japanese Miracle

- Active government support for exports, coupled with close industrial liaison.
- Tough trade barriers (duties, tariffs, certifications, bureaucracy) to protect local market.
- Until recently, significantly lower wages and lower standard of living than U.S.
- National training on product quality based on adaptations of Western QC concepts and statistical techniques.
- High investment in research and development, including extensive work in production machinery, material handling, and measuring equipment.
- Long-term approach to product development, capital equipment, and market penetration.
- Heavy investment in modern production facilities after World War II.
- Minimal expenditure for military personnel or hardware.
- An instilled attitude of craftsmanship, zero defects, and conformance to requirements.
- Employment-for-life concepts that have enabled quality circle and other productivity-enhancing techniques to flourish.
- A certain national desire to "win the peace" to make up for the disgrace of losing World War II.
- Until recently, an artificially low value for the yen with respect to the U.S. dollar.

the workforce on how to attain and improve quality? The conclusion was to carry out such training but on a voluntary basis; the companies would offer the training courses, but the workers would decide whether they wished to accept the training or not. The response of the Japanese workers was extensive. Since 1962 about 7 million workers have undergone this training. The training form features interdepartmental groups of ten or so workers seated around a table; hence the name *quality circle*.

Quality circles provide an instrument through which management can close the communication loop through participative management (Figure 8-2).

Management must recognize that worker involvement means a sharing of power. It means further that by sharing power there will be a dilution of management's traditional power and a new concentration of power in the worker. This is

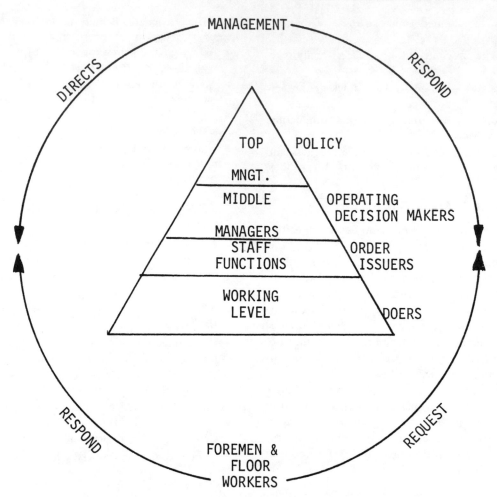

FIGURE 8-2. Communications Links of Quality Circle within Traditional Organization
Based on the artwork of Dr. J. R. Fisher, Honeywell.

a revolutionary concept and difficult for many managers to understand.

A quality circle is a relatively autonomous unit, composed of a small group of workers (ideally about ten), usually led by a senior worker and organized in each work unit. Participants are taught elementary techniques of problem solving including statistical methods. It is, in principle, a voluntary study group that concentrates on solving job-related quality problems. These problems are broadly conceived as improving methods of production as part of company-wide efforts. Some typical efforts include reducing defects, scrap, rework, and downtime. These activities, in turn, are expected to lead to cost reduction and increased productivity. At the same time, the circles focus on improving working conditions and the self-development of workers. The latter includes development of leadership abilities of forepeople and

workers, skill development among workers, improvement of worker morale and motivation, the stimulation of teamwork within work groups, and recognition of worker achievements. Above all, the circles involve recognition that hourly workers have an important contribution to make to the organization.

There are some observations about quality circles that should be highlighted.

- The quality circle is not limited to solving problems in product quality.
- The quality circle concept involves a significant extent of worker participation in decision making on matters previously regarded as solely the responsibility of the supervision. Senior and middle managers must be willing to accept such participation.
- The training of managers and supervisors must precede that of the workers. This training is not

only in the techniques but in the entire idea of how to work with quality circles.

- Adoption of the quality circle concept outside Japan does not require copying the Japanese practice on details of application. For example, should training be done during working hours, or after hours? What extent of payment should be made for time spent working on projects? The need is to establish practices that are compatible with the culture. The Japanese practice evolved in response to the nature of their unique culture.

- The contribution of quality circles can be significant but not major. Most of the company's quality problems must be solved by the managers, supervisors, and professional specialists.

- The quality circle is a management philosophy and a way of life. It is not another zero-defects program aimed solely at workers.

Pitfalls to Avoid:

1. Don't try to copy the Japanese version—tailor it to your plant, management style, and culture. Quality circles are only a part of total management commitment to product quality.

2. Proceed slowly—allow three or four years for the concept to take hold from top management down to the shop floor.

3. Provide adequate training to middle managers, supervisors, and forepeople, then to shop floor personnel.

4. Don't go it alone—union involvement is mandatory.

5. Layoffs, demotions, and bumping lead to a direct cancellation of the beneficial aspects of quality circles. Use automation, temporary employees, subcontracting, and overtime to deal with overloads rather than building a large staff that must be let go after the peak is over. Try to approximate the Japanese approach to lifetime employment.

6. Don't put all the emphasis on higher productivity, more output, and cost reduction. Employees want to know what is in it for them. Highlight such parameters as employment stability, personal growth, and job satisfaction.

SET UP A REALISTIC QUALITY COST SYSTEM

The ultimate objective of a quality cost system is to produce acceptable product at minimum total cost and on schedule. A quality cost system is a separate product-oriented system of cost control

that cuts across departmental organizational lines. Costs included in the prevention, appraisal, and failure categories are not limited to those of the quality department but include such efforts by all departments involved. A quality task is a quality task no matter who performs it, and a quality cost is a quality cost no matter who incurs it. One big advantage of a quality cost system is that it puts together in one place bits and pieces of information that otherwise may be reported in various places and in various units without any common denominator. Because the activities of implementing a quality cost system are distinct from usual quality control activities, special consideration should be given to assuring a successful and profitable program. Following are a dozen key steps in implementing the system.

1. *Secure top management support.* Quality costs can be a sensitive area, and management must be completely behind the system to ensure adequate teamwork among the various plant departments. Many other departments, particularly accounting, may ask what business it is of the quality department to be concerned with costs and accounting. If management does not fully understand and wholeheartedly support the quality cost system, its implementation should not be pursued. The impact of quality decisions/costs must be carefully explained to top management because ultimately it is their money you spend.

2. *Use the experience of others.* Read available literature, attend quality cost courses and visit firms that have already established a system. Plan the system in detail. Ensure that the costs for all the elements add up to the total and that no major costs are omitted or duplicated.

3. *Don't try to make quality cost system all encompassing at the outset.* Let the system develop and mature.

4. *Define cost accounts carefully.* Determine the cost elements or tasks to be included and those to be excluded (e.g., pollution control, maintenance services for other departments, safety test equipment).

Three basic categories of costs are included in an operational quality cost system:

Category	Effort to	Concerns
1. Prevention	Prevent bad product	Resources
2. Appraisal	Measure the product	Product
3. Failure	Correct bad product	Bad product

Although this phase of setting up the system is important, one precaution is needed. Much valuable time can be lost in quibbling over details or splitting hairs. To get a handle on failure costs is important; to draw fine lines between prevention and appraisal is not as important. Once categorized, however, the rules should be followed consistently; and if changes in categorization rules are made, past data may require adjustment or correction.

5. *Orient, educate, and train those involved with the system before implementation.*

6. *Use existing cost accounts as much as possible.* Don't set up too many new work elements or your key initial supporter (accounting) may lose interest. After the system has been working and has proved to be of benefit, the accounting system can be modified and refined.

7. *Never let QC generate cost reports.* This is the domain of the accounting department. Besides, report veracity will be more readily accepted if it is prepared by accounting.

8. *Keep reports simple.* Prepare concise, to-the-point reports for management. There might be a need for great detail at the working level, but reports to management should follow the BROAD principle: Bosses Require Only Analyzed Data.

9. *Generate timely reports.* The usefulness of a quality costs system is important both to short-term and long-term effects. Certainly long-term trends—that is, over a period of months—can stand some delay. However, the system's short-term advantages must be achieved by timely accounting and reporting. Day-to-day or week-to-week decisions cannot be made with quarterly cost summaries.

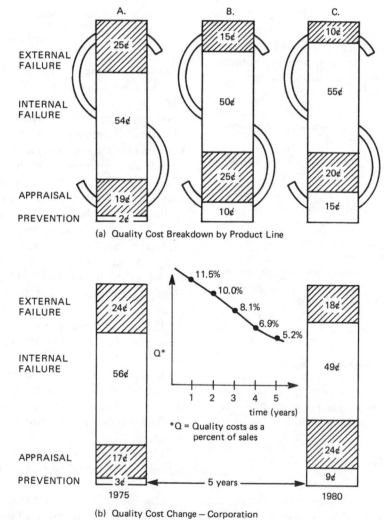

(a) Quality Cost Breakdown by Product Line

(b) Quality Cost Change — Corporation

FIGURE 8-3. Two Possible Formats for Presenting Quality Costs

10. *Ensure reports are used.* The report to management, which in most cases should be monthly, should have a sufficiently distinctive cover to identify it readily from other reports. Use charts rather than a tabulation of many numbers (Figure 8-3). Draw attention to areas requiring action.

11. *Keep the report distribution in check.* Only people who can really use the reports should get copies. Remember also that the report contains competition-sensitive data.

12. *Establish a mechanism for action.* All of the planning, data accumulation, and reporting will be of little value (actually an expense) without a mechanism for action. Such a mechanism can be established at all levels of supervision and management, but to be really effective it should involve top management.

Case in Point: One large company requires that divisional managers submit quarterly quality cost reports through their financial managers to corporate headquarters. These reports include the past history of quality costs and a prediction by quarter for one year ahead as evidence of future planning for improvement.

Remember: The whole idea is to optimize total quality costs (see Figure 8-4).

BUILD YOUR IMAGE

There are some things a quality manager must do to ensure acceptance among management ranks. No book on quality management would be complete without at least mentioning the importance of projecting a successful image. Here are a few parameters:

- Look successful—your clothing, your desk and/or office, your speech, and your attitude toward money should project the image of a successful, but not necessarily flamboyant, person.
- Use QC data effectively.
- As a minimum, have working status charts (singularly or combined) in your office that show:

a. Receiving inspection rejects—number of items received per week and inspected per week.

b. In-process rejects—number of each item submitted and rejected (lot or sample basis) per week, per department. Special charts in problem areas to show rejections per unit, rejections by category, and responsibility.

c. Final test/inspection rejects—same as item b above.

d. Warranty claims and/or warranty rejects—number of items shipped and rejected by category and by customer (or area as applicable), by month, and cumulative for a year. Ratio of warranty claims to actual warranty repairs (showing unjustified or incorrect claims). Direct cost of warranty repairs.

e. Quality cost—total applied hours and overtime hours per week.

f. List of agreed-upon open corrective actions, by department or vendor, with responsible individual names and due dates.

g. List of open customer/government inspection complaints, by category, date for completion and responsibility.

Pitfall to Avoid: It is all too easy for QC to be a constant source of bad news, low yields, customer complaints, and high scrap. An astute quality manager will always salt his or her reports and oral presentations with an ample sprinkling of favorable data.

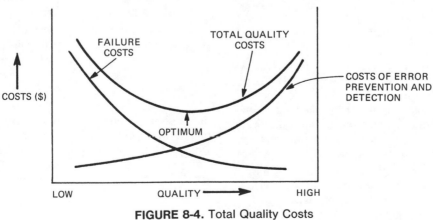

FIGURE 8-4. Total Quality Costs

● Collect and use industrial IOUs.

Case in Point: The purchasing manager selected a source that had been disapproved by a QC survey team. Serious problems ultimately arose and were detected at incoming inspection. The QC manager discreetly ignored the problem. Purchasing fell into debt.

● Teach your boss a new technique, buzz-word, or acronym (Pareto analysis, quality circle, LTPD). It lets him know you're up to date.
● Give credit to peers and subordinates.

Caution: The credit must be earned, and the extent of publicity must match the scope of the achievement. If exaggerated or insincere this tactic can backfire.

● Work on high-visibility problems.

> If you are not part of the solution, you are part of the problem.

● Be constructive and diplomatic (see Table 8-3).
● Display the right reading material (e.g., *Business Week, Harvard Business Review, Fortune,* and *Forbes,* in addition to *Quality Progress* and *Quality and Evaluation Engineering*).
● Answer memos and letters promptly. It generally requires only a little more time to give a quick answer to a memo than to earmark it for later action. A modern technique is to handwrite a quick response on the bottom of a typewritten memo. A photocopy is then made for your files and the original is sent back to the sender.
● Return phone calls promptly.
● Avoid keeping people waiting outside your office. If you have earned the right to an office, it does not automatically grant you the privilege of keeping people waiting to see you. The person who waits until 2:15 P.M. for a 1:30 P.M. appointment may be inwardly seething with anger and humiliation. If he or she is the production manager, expect production/quality interface problems next month.
● Be thick-skinned. Quality control is a functional "hot spot," so you better get used to criticism, hostility, and being challenged. The modern quality manager must be resilient,

TABLE 8–3. A Contrast in Style

Combative Style	Diplomatic Approach
"Rejected."	"Unable to accept because . . . ."
"You are totally nonresponsive."	"You appear unwilling or unable to . . . ."
"This is a bunch of junk."	"This is not your usual high standard of quality."
"Fix it or I'll go see the V.P."	"Without prompt corrective action we are inviting higher management attention."
"You can't ship this."	"Shipping this is in violation of company policy."
"Your people are stupid and incompetent."	"Additional workmanship training is warranted."
"This is the third time this has happened."	"There is strong evidence to suggest that corrective action now appears in order."
"Why . . . . ?"	"Why not. . . . ?"
"I want your answer by . . . ."	"Can we get together on this tomorrow?"
"The process is out of control."	"The process is not working smoothly."
"The rejection rate is 20 percent."	"The yield is 80 percent and improving, but . . . ."
"Use your brains."	"Maybe you should take another look at the problem."
"This item does not meet the specification/drawing and should be scrapped."	The following discrepancies have been noted and require disposition."
"This process must be stopped immediately."	"We advise you look into your process because inspection has noticed a very high rejection rate."
"We need five more days to inspect those items and the customer will just have to wait."	"Can we look into the possibility of using a sampling plan in order to meet delivery requirements?"

calm, and collected under pressure and be able to play hardball in the big league.

- Avoid painting yourself in a corner. Always allow for the fact that you may be in error. Even the laws of physics have changed over the years. Leave yourself an escape path through which you can depart with grace.

> Wouldn't it be nice to be as sure of anything as some people are of everything?

- Solve quality problems at the lowest possible organizational level. The QC manager who frequently appeals to the boss or who constantly goes over other people's heads is courting disaster. Even sending information copies of memos to senior officials is a form of industrial combat that quality people should use very selectively and infrequently.

- Build an outside reputation. Becoming director of an ASQC technical committee can help you (and the QC department) get treated with the respect usually afforded a powerful individual. It won't hurt your salary either.

- Offer an explanation for your actions. Few people willingly comply with orders if not given a logical explanation of why the order is given. The person who develops a reputation of giving orders without any justification may wind up with more enemies than allies. By giving *reasons* you involve people in your objectives and these become their own.

PERFORM WELL AT MEETINGS

Business meetings, justifiably, are sometimes referred to as dog-and-pony shows—people use meetings to display themselves to advantage. Usually at least one person present will be a higher-up. When you are trying to impress a higher-up at a meeting, keep in mind that you are not trying to dominate or win control of the meeting. You should be trying to impress your boss and higher-ups with your good judgment and management potential. Keep the following tactics in mind if you want to shine at meetings:

- Don't be the first presenter.
- Ask set-up questions.
- Listen carefully to comments on preceding ideas for clues to a negative response to something in your presentation.
- Allow others to talk. People who dominate

meetings often do so because they are tense or trying too hard to create a good impression. Unless you have called the meeting and its primary purpose is for you to dispense information to others, avoid overtalking in meetings.

- Never present your *best* idea first. The energy level is too high at the beginning of the meeting, so you are apt to get clobbered.

- Never be overly enthusiastic about an idea. Presenting it modestly disarms hostile forces.

- Be courteous to the ideas of others and you may get the same treatment.

- Don't present your ideas too slickly. If you do, your opponents will get suspicious and seek even its slightest faults. Use a flip chart, view graph, or slide presentation format. This provides a structured approach with associated time economy and clarity benefits. It is also possible to run through dress rehearsals with your staff before making the presentation.

- Don't spring "surprises" at meetings.

Case in Point: An overly aggressive QC manager surprisingly announced some very disappointing scrap cost figures at a meeting attended by the divisional vice-president. The production manager was embarrassed and caught off guard. She had neither been appraised of the data nor had she been advised that such data would be brought up at the meeting. The resentment brought on by this poor example of industrial etiquette was to be deep and long lasting. Two years later, during an economic downturn, the QC manager was let go. Any manager who doesn't know what "winning the battle and losing the war" means should try another occupation.

> Success consists of getting up just one more time than you fall.

SHARPEN YOUR NEGOTIATING SKILLS

Negotiation takes place when two parties with different objectives seek to reach a mutually satisfying agreement. Knowing when and how to negotiate is vital to the success of the quality program. The importance of negotiation cannot be overestimated. It is a key element toward successful quality improvement and corrective action. It is the principal means by which QC and other organizational units achieve their objectives. Negotiation is a difficult art that requires a knowledge of the psychology of individuals, small groups, and large organizations, and the exercise of judgment, tact, and common sense. It is a special skill, different from, and often more difficult to acquire than, technical or administrative skills.

The following are typical of the kind of statements that invite negotiation:

- "The night shift did it."
- "These must go by the end of the month."
- "We're not paid to inspect it."
- "It has always been like that."
- "This is good enough."
- "Only a small percentage is defective."
- "The customer will never know."
- "We've never had complaints for that."
- "We have made thousands like that."
- "You can't expect everything to be on the drawing."

A number of tactics and techniques have been developed for use in negotiation. The experienced negotiator should be familiar with all of them and may even find it desirable or necessary to use them in a given situation. However, techniques must be used carefully; they should not be used indiscriminately, particularly those involving pressure, just to show expertise as a negotiator. Negotiation cannot be conducted in a highly charged atmosphere. The best negotiation technique is the use of logic and persuasion.

It is impossible to apply the same strategies and techniques to each negotiation. A negotiation is affected by:

1. the nature of the issue—material, review, corrective action, application of quality standards
2. the differences between the two parties
3. relative bargaining strength of the two parties
4. the personalities involved

The more experience two negotiators have in negotiating with each other, the more difficult it will be for either to use the same techniques. Like other game players, they will become familiar with each other's strategies, and this will reduce the number of techniques available to each.

Following are a number of techniques used in negotiation. All are, of course, intended to be used in the best interests of the company.

- *Clear, Simple Language.* One of the best negotiation techniques combines logic and persuasion with clear, simple language. Many disagreements arise from semantics, not real differences of opinions. To reach agreement it is necessary that each side understands the other.
- *Make the Other Party Appear Unreasonable.* This can be done by making concessions on minor points and then asking for concessions on major issues in return.
- *Place the Other Side on the Defensive.*
- *Blame a Third Party.* QC can explain its reluctance to compromise on a certain position by stating that it contradicts company quality policy, it is not in accordance with contractual requirements, or it violates national safety codes.
- *Good Guy–Bad Guy Technique.* A lower-level inspection supervisor is normally the bad guy. This technique obviously cannot be used too frequently.
- *Appeal to the Emotions.*
- *Raise Straw Issues.* A common technique used by QC is to raise straw issues such as minor nonconformances and then concede them after lengthy discussion. The ultimate aim is to be able to trade concessions on a straw issue for compromises on a real issue.
- *Pretended Misunderstanding.* This technique involves pretending that you do not quite understand the statement made by the other side. This device is particularly useful when you feel that the statement is not clear or feel that the other negotiator's thinking lacks organization. Your pretended lack of understanding will force the person to clarify both his or her statement and thinking and give you time to organize yours.
- *Pro and Con Analysis.* This approach is particularly useful in MRBs and design reviews. It is a device in which one party lists the points favoring a proposition under one heading and those opposing it under another. The complete list forms a clear, concise analysis of the problem. In certain situations, it may be helpful to encourage the other side to get all the facts and consider both sides before arriving at a conclusion. Of course, this technique should end up proving that the position that the analyzer advocates is the logical answer to the problem. It is particularly useful for summarizing the other side's arguments and using them to your own advantage. It can be used to correct faulty

thinking, to force an impartial consideration of the problem, and to put the negotiation on a professional level. It can also be used to correct an obvious mistake or misunderstanding on the other side of the table without coming out with a flat statement that they are wrong.

- *Agreement and Rebuttal.* The technique of agreement and rebuttal, the "yes—but" technique, is often a valuable approach to negotiations. In using it the negotiator seems more reasonable and conciliatory than he may in fact be, since he is couching his disagreement with the other side in terms of agreement. Most important it helps the negotiator to develop arguments that use the opponent's own words and examples.

- *Ignorance and Obstinacy.* One of the best negotiation techniques may be genuine ignorance or obstinacy. Someone once said, "You can negotiate with a liar, but you cannot negotiate with a fool." One effective technique to bolster up a weak case is to put a half-informed person (every QC department has one) opposite a skilled, informed negotiator. One of the most painful things is to watch a professional negotiator, accustomed to dealing with other professionals, attempt to negotiate with an uninformed, unprepared negotiator who complicates his or her ignorance with obstinacy. Of course, the more informed party may simply call off the negotiation if his or her bargaining position permits.

- *Threats (with Style).* Such tactics as threatening to increase the frequency of audits in a certain "soft" work center or suggesting that very unfavorable yield performance will be disclosed can often speed up a negotiation. Any threat made in negotiation must be carried out or it will reflect on the common sense of the person making it. Every good threat has a history of action to back it up. The ultimate effect of a policy of threat is to so cow the opponent that he or she anticipates the threatener's desires and behaves accordingly. A threat should not be made unless the party making it has made a careful analysis of its effect on both parties.

- *Specialized Jargon and Mathematical Tools.* QC can choose from a variety of specialized assurance science terms, statistical techniques, and mathematical gymnastics to convince an unsophisticated foe.

Caution: Negotiating skills should be used to enhance the profit position of the company, not the ego of the quality manager. Unethical tactics such as outright lies, deliberate misinterpretation of standards, falsification or distortion of test data, references to untraceable sources, clandestine use of government regulatory and inspection agencies, bluffing, and the like have no place in a well-oiled quality program.

THE FINE ART OF WHISTLE-BLOWING

The contemporary quality manager comes across many controversial situations regarding product safety, reliability, or compliance with regulatory codes. Reconciling a manager's right to dissent with his or her employer's demand for loyalty is not easy. Corporations are not democratic institutions, so they are under no compulsion to tolerate what they may consider to be deviant behavior. For their part, quality people tacitly agree to forego complete independence of action where their employers are concerned in return for a certain amount of security. But if an employer demands that its quality people agree with illegal, dangerous, or fraudulent practices, many otherwise faithful employees may decide that the price for keeping silent is too high.

Keeping silent versus speaking out is usually a no-win situation. Speaking out may result in reprisal; keeping silent may be irresponsible and/or illegal. Of course, there is always the option to quit, but finding an equally beneficial job may not be easy. And it may be impossible once you are established as a whistle blower.

Caution: Be sure of your allegation. The legal definitions of what constitutes unlawful behavior, an unsafe product, or danger to health are often far from clear or certain. Is it negligent to design an aerosol can without a safe means of failure? Only a jury knows for sure.

Blowing the whistle on an employer is not a step to be taken casually. In fact, it is not a step to be taken at all, in most cases. But if you feel compelled to speak out, first try to answer the following questions:

- Is my knowledge of the matter complete and accurate?
- What are the objectionable practices and which public or other interest do they harm?
- Is my protest based on a clear illegality, a potential illegality, a danger, or an improper business policy?
- How far can I go inside the organization with my concern or objection?

- Have I exhausted all internal mechanisms for correcting the situation?
- Will I be violating any rules by contacting outside parties, and if so, is whistle-blowing nevertheless justified?
- Will I be violating any laws or ethical responsibilities by not contacting external parties?
- Has each step through company channels been properly documented?
- Once I decide to act, what is the best way to blow the whistle—anonymously (leaks), overtly, by resignation before speaking out, or in some other way?
- What will be the likely short- and long-term responses from various sources—inside and outside the organization—to my whistle-blowing action?
- What should be achieved by whistle-blowing in this particular situation?
- Is there another way?

Elbert Hubbard, an old-fashioned philosopher, said it best:

> If you work for a man, for heaven's sake work for him. Speak well of him and stand by the institution he represents. Remember, an ounce of loyalty is worth a pound of cleverness. If you must condemn and eternally find fault, resign your position, and when you are on the outside, damn to your heart's content. But so long as you are part of the company, do not condemn it. If you do, the first high wind that comes along will blow you away, and you will never know why.

Observation: The U.S. Department of Labor has developed procedures to protect employees in private industry who blow the whistle on their employers for violating certain federal laws. For example, there are special employee-protection provisions in the Safe Drinking Water Act, Water Pollution Control Act, Toxic Substances Control Act, Solid Waste Disposal Act, Clean Air Act, and Energy Reorganization Act. These laws stipulate that no employer may discharge or discriminate against an employee with respect to pay, working conditions, or job privileges because the employee reported company noncompliance with the laws. The protection covers all employees.

Case in Point: The quality manager and project engineer of a farm machinery company rejected a quantity of product. The marketing manager appealed to the president. After listening to both sides, she accepted responsibility by signing the rejection notice release. This would appear to be in accordance with the ASQC Code of Ethics under "Relations with Employers and Clients."

> Each Society member will act in professional matters as a faithful agent or trustee for each employer or client. . . . He will indicate to his employer or client the adverse consequences to be expected if his professional judgment is overruled.

However, times are changing, and the above case and ASQC's Code of Ethics may be an inadequate response to a plaintiff's legal counsel. Before discovery procedures, liability-under-tort law provided no way for the plaintiff to make a case against individual quality people or engineers who were to blame for a malfunction. When the plaintiff turns up sufficiently damning evidence, criminal charges can be brought against an individual, if the obvious result of his or her actions could be personally harmful to someone.

Examples of such cases:

- Covering up a product failure of some type.
- Knowingly selecting and applying an unsafe device to the product.

Negligence is usually easier to prove, and it includes such acts as:

- Erroneous labeling of one item as another.
- Failure to review or respond to a subordinate's report showing a defect.
- Making a calculation error during test.
- Jumpering of safety devices for final testing and failing to remove the jumpers after completion of testing.

Look into the possibility of including a "hold harmless" clause in your employment agreement. A lesser protection is a covenant against suit by the employer for negligence related to product liability claims.

The following "unorthodox" strategies may help in resolving a situation without quite having to blow the whistle:

1. Use internal politics to get two powerful managers to battle each other on the issue.

2. Anonymously send copies of the reported situation to the company's legal counsel. Lawyers can always be counted upon in this type of situation.

3. Distribute copies of recent product liability judgments. It just might scare someone into action.

4. Ask that appropriate caution notes be included in technical manuals and/or on product. It's a half measure but better than nothing.

5. Get the union, employee association, or an important board of directors member involved. Don't use your name unless you plan on leaving the company soon.

REFERENCES

Birnbrauer, H. "Managing Time: The Priceless Art." *Machine Design,* October 26, 1978.

Curry, T. D. "Scientific Manufacturing." *Machine Design,* May 22, 1980.

Drucker, P. F. *Managing in Turbulent Times.* Toronto: Fitzhenry and Whiteside Ltd., 1980.

DuBrin, A. "Winning at Office Politics." Van Nostrand Reinhold Co., 1978.

Gabriel, B. L. "SEM in Materials Science." *Quality,* June 1980.

Hayes, G. E. "QA: Management and Technology." Charger Productions, Inc., 1974.

Holmes, J. "It's All Been Said Before." *Quality Progress,* January 1970.

Pollock, T. "Looking Backward for Progress." *Production,* February 1974.

Raudsepp, E. "Encouraging Creative Nonconformity." *Machine Design,* June 12, 1980.

Reoch, J. M. "Holography—A New Dimension." *Quality Progress,* May 1972.

Tustin, W. "Laboratory Managers: Avoid 'Tunnel Vision,' " *Test,* June/July 1980.

Wilkinson, R. "What Makes a Manager Successful?" *Assembly Engineering,* December 1978.

9
Preventing Defects and Increasing Profits

Too many quality control organizations today have capable manufacturing controls, good customer-problem feedback, and effective vendor liaison, but they fail miserably when it comes to exercising control over new product design. Yet the very nature of the activity demands quality control participation. There are many reasons for this need, perhaps the most important one is the need to control product design to assure customer satisfaction.

It has been estimated that for every dollar spent by QC during product development, in excess of $100 will be saved in repairing and correcting defects or failures during the product life cycle. Quality control has a unique capability to assist engineering in providing cost-effective, reliable designs because of their production and field failure data banks. No quality control system can be considered complete and economical unless it actively participates in preventing design-originated defects. QC people must constantly battle the management dictum:

> Sufficient moneys to do the job correctly the first time are usually not available; however, ample funds are much more easily obtained for repeated major redesigns.

Figure 9-1 provides an overview of typical quality and reliability tasks associated with the development of a new product. This chapter shows you how to go about preventing defects, developing safer products, and designing producible, competitive products.

WHY QUALITY OF DESIGN IS DEFICIENT

Some of the problems encountered in manufacturing firms are found among the following:

1. Most designers are not given an overall picture of design requirements and the maturity of the equipments suffer as a result.

2. Many designers lose interest after getting the new product to perform satisfactorily once. Production problems and associated paperwork are considered pesky diversions.

3. Some designers are not familiar with the inherent weaknesses of parts and tend to believe all parts advertisements or form biases based on incorrect or limited performance observations.

4. Many companies do not require that part tests be designed properly and that test results be published for use by all other company personnel.

5. A designer's work seldom is reviewed by anyone besides the designer's supervisor, who may be too busy to examine it carefully.

6. Engineering frequently does not stipulate to quality control and manufacturing which parts and devices are critical and how to handle them.

7. Designers often do not know how to calculate the "time-to-failure" of the design they have created.

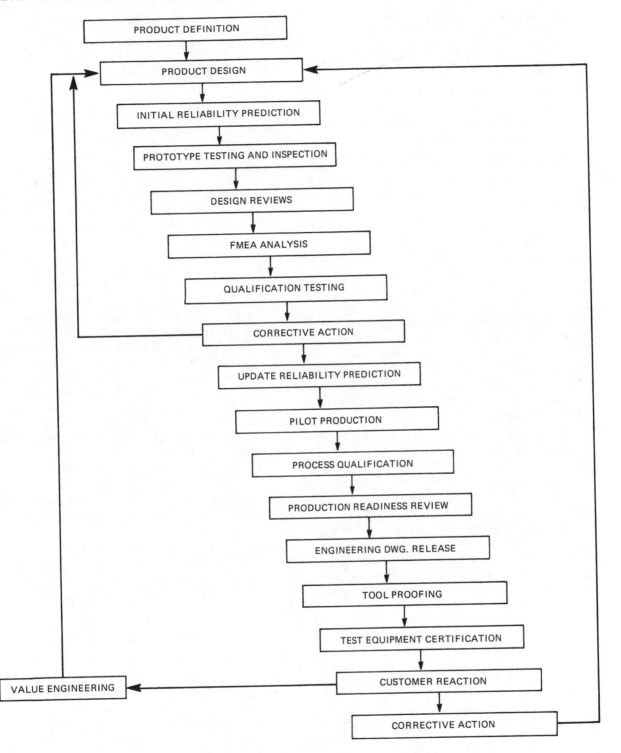

FIGURE 9-1. Defect Prevention Activities on New Products

8. Many companies do not have an organized approach to malfunction investigations.

9. Designers select manufacturing processes that are not congruent with selected tolerances (Figure 9-2).

10. Up-to-date standards or preferred-parts-and-vendor lists do not exist in most cases.

11. Often there are no environmental tests on samples of the product.

These are the common situations that lead to product unreliability. The resolution of these will go a long way toward making a manufacturing firm mature.

It is instructive to view the design project through the eyes of the project engineer before attempting to offer help. He or she is often faced with a tight, unrealistic schedule, limited funds, and enormous technological problems. The new product must work to increasingly tighter tolerances and environmental conditions, and must meet stringent product safety, energy conservation, and pollution abatement requirements. Simultaneously, the engineer must cope with standards programs, corporate bureaucracy, and skilled personnel shortages, and keep up-to-date with technological changes.

Given these conditions, a quality manager wanting to initiate design reviews, reliability testing, stress analysis, and a maintainability demonstration will meet a brick wall. The winning strategy is to provide cost-effective, timely services that will help the individual designer meet his or her primary job goals. Once the benefits of simple assurance tasks are seen, he or she will become addicted and approachable on the more sophisti-

cated (and costly) design defect-prevention activities.

DEVELOP QUALITY DESIGNERS

The best way to bring about quality designs is to apply quality designers to the task. Engineering management can make this happen by using these dozen practices:

- Hold your project engineers responsible for their jobs from conception to completion. Custom building a few units that pass "qualification tests" does not relieve the project engineer of the responsibility to have the drawings and specifications represent a producible, reliable, and value-engineered design. This includes full responsibility for a quantity of early production units, albeit with direct assistance and full cooperation from the production team.

- Ensure that design engineers glean new information continuously—from trade journals, test equipment engineers, vendors, and production personnel. Send your engineers to other companies to see, ask, and listen. Insist on a detailed trip report and/or debriefing soon after their return.

- Force a marriage of R & D knowledge and production experience in all phases of development work.

- Make sure that designers do not jeopardize costly downstream actions by slippages of decisions, inadequate or late releases of drawings, and inadequate or late definition in specifications.

- Assure an adequate engineering job with a good design review.

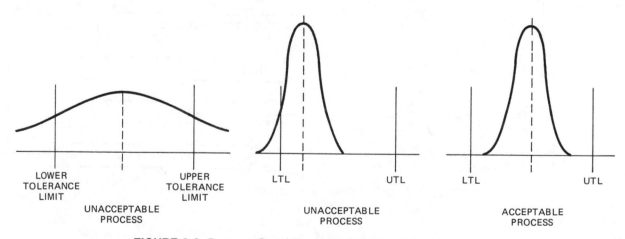

FIGURE 9-2. Process Capability Versus Design Tolerance Limits
Courtesy of Canadian Marconi Company.

- Make sure that drawings are accurate and complete. Be sure that development drawings have adequate material and process callouts. Have a review and sign-off by an independent checker, using established standards wherever possible. Insist your engineers speak a specification language. When an engineer procrastinates about putting details on a part drawing that would enable another supplier to make it, watch out.

- Require that engineering demonstrate that the product is producible by the methods available. To do this, the project engineer must assemble and adjust the unit and be present when manufacturing personnel try to do the same. Every development engineer should try (not just watch) key manufacturing assembly/test processes, and should review each drawing while touching the actual part or parts. This is the best control to assure that engineers do not build a few developmental units with great care—then produce units whose final requirements are unrealistic, unnecessarily costly, or result in a low yield in production.

Pitfall to Avoid: Never allow designers to operate in isolation, away from problems or production.

- Require design engineers to draw the expected distribution of selected parameters (including the error band representing test equipment accuracy and repeatability) in relation to specification requirements before testing.

- Test early, test thoroughly, and perform selected overstress tests. Push engineers to overtest until a damaging overstress condition or failure is approached. You'll be surprised how much more knowledge they'll gain about the product. Usually the cost and time to repair are minor.

- Make sure that design debugging occurs during the development stage—not on the production floor. Do not release production drawings and test procedures until engineering can show test data on representative samples that meet all performance requirements, including those under extreme conditions and with well-established and controllable output parameters.

- Involve designers with material review boards, defect investigations, and customer complaints.

GOOD ENGINEERING CONTROLS HOLD THE KEY

As many seasoned QC veterans will testify, the lack of engineering controls, discipline, and design review can raise havoc in the factory. The list that follows has been used by manufacturing managers to explain away nonaccomplishment of monthly shipment revenue targets, cost overruns, excessive inventory, and poor quality.

1. Last minute engineering changes.
2. Special processes cannot be held in tolerance economically.
3. Drawings are ambiguous, confusing, and incomplete.
4. Technical manuals not available (and must accompany shipment per contract).
5. Yield is 30 percent or less.
6. Product is uninspectable and/or difficult to troubleshoot.
7. Engineering issued hold order in third week of month.
8. Late drawing releases.

These problems can be minimized and prevented if the engineering function is effectively managed. This includes such actions as:

- Ensuring that development engineers know what to shoot for in terms of performance.
- Preparing and updating project milestone charts.
- Tracking schedule progress on weekly or monthly basis as required.
- Providing adequate funds for quality, reliability, maintainability, manufacturing, test, and other important functional inputs into the design process.
- Holding weekly progress reviews.
- Generating status reports and "get well" plans.
- Providing adequate coordination of development tasks.
- Supervising, coaching, and assisting engineers when they face tough design problems.
- Ensuring that tradeoff areas are clearly identified and approved by management.
- Bringing in specialist consultants when required.
- Encouraging the use of proven designs, processes, and parts in new designs.
- Actively supporting design reviews, testing, and configuration management disciplines.
- Providing engineering with the proper tools, supporting functions, and environment to do the job properly and efficiently.

Engineering tasks, by nature, typically involve greater time variability. This, however, should be the reason rather than the excuse for effective planning and management. The result will be the timely availability of producible, safe, reliable, and competitive designs.

> There must be the will to produce a quality article.

CONFIGURATION MANAGEMENT PROVIDES SIGNPOSTS

Management of change has been an essential ingredient of any program involving the development, production, delivery, and use of complex products. The discipline that deals with a system for managing technical and hardware change is termed *configuration management*. It allows you to build the same item again and to support the product in the field.

Configuration management (CM), which applies technical and administrative surveillance, frequently is defined in terms of its three major functions: (a) identify and document the functional and physical characteristics of an item; (b) control changes to these characteristics; and (c) record and report change processing and implementation. Ineffective configuration management wastes time and money and erodes confidence in the product and company.

Case in Point: A proposed design improvement was not submitted for evaluation to other groups that might have been affected by the change. After spending $3500 revis-

ing the design and drawings, the engineer accidentally discovered that the new design would require revision of another major component that interfaced with it. Since this change would have required an investment of an additional $18,000, management canceled the original change and the drawings had to be returned to their original configuration.

Essential to configuration management philosophy is the resolution to establish specifications for each program requirement, including specifications for determining that the requirements have been met—certainly not a new idea to quality control personnel.

The specifications establish base lines, and major problems typically include three of them:

1. The *functional base line* is defined by a system specification. It must be established before the program enters the initial user-contractor relationship. Together with the formally approved changes later incorporated into it, it will govern system (or item) requirements for the rest of the program.

2. The *allocated base line* is fixed by a series of development specifications, among which the total system requirements are allocated. It must be established before the program can enter the full-scale development phase.

3. The *product base line* is based upon detailed specifications and drawings that functionally and physically define the production item eventually put into use. It may be established when production is initiated, or concurrently with delivery of

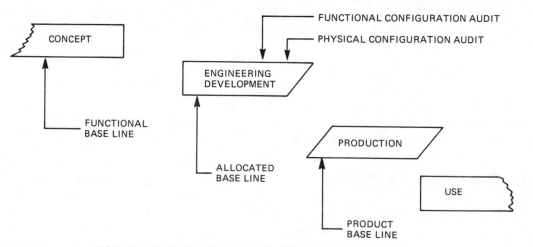

FIGURE 9-3. Relationship of Base Lines to Program Phases

the first production unit. Which point is chosen depends on such factors as whether or not the developer is preselected to be the producer and how much control at the repair parts level is needed by the user during initial production activities. These three formally established base lines constitute the configuration identification aspect of configuration management. Figure 9-3 shows their relationship to the program phases.

It should be emphasized that base lines can do five things for higher management when it really wants to manage internal product development:

1. Provide management with an opportunity to formally assess project progress in discrete steps.
2. Help ensure the product is on the right course before it has gone too far off track.
3. Establish a mutually and explicitly agreed-upon design status with management knowledge and agreement.
4. Allow management to cut off a project that is floundering with little chance of success. Thus, funds can be conserved or transferred to a more promising product.
5. Allow management to stop work temporarily on a project because of funding problems or a higher-priority task. The base line provides a hard reference point from which to reinstate the project in the future without returning to ground zero.

A special type of quality assurance operation is used to ensure that the newly developed system is ready for release to production: Two audits provide the assurance that the big step can be taken with confidence. The functional configuration audit is used to determine that development requirements have been met. The physical configuration audit checks the production technical data package (the documentation that will establish the product base line) to ensure that it accurately and adequately reflects the development item chosen to represent production configuration. Between them the two audits ensure an unbroken link between the functional base line established by the system specification and the item that finally goes from the production lines into the users' hands.

Case in Point: At one company a configuration audit team found a 10 percent discrepancy between a newly developed digital voltmeter and its drawings. This discrepancy was found in spite of the fact that the voltmeter had been inspected by QC.

Before the product base line, QC has two major functions: verification of developmental hardware against development specifications and other technical requirements, and proofing of acceptance inspection equipment designs and procedures. No product base line should be considered complete until these functions have been performed.

Control at the production line depends largely on the diligence with which quality control:

1. Verifies that the engineering drawings used for manufacturing purposes are officially released documents.
2. Verifies that manufacturing planning instructions and manufacturing order packages contain the applicable configuration identification numbers of the applicable drawings and standards.
3. Verifies, at selected inspection points, that the hardware configuration confirms to released engineering drawings and documents any differences.
4. Verifies that items procured from subcontractors comply with the applicable configuration documentation.

Configuration control involves systematic evaluation, coordination, approval or disapproval, and release of changes or waivers to an established base line. Its objective is consideration of all relevant information, including complete cost data, to ensure that a good change decision can be made. A major function of configuration control is the elimination of unnecessary changes by being able to promptly determine the full impact of a proposed change.

Configuration accounting involves keeping accurate records of the product's configuration as defined by drawings, specifications, and other documents. It also involves keeping records of proposed changes, approved changes, and changes incorporated into hardware. A key element is the confirmation that "as engineered" changes are correctly reflected in the "as-built" hardware. It is quality control's responsibility to provide this data by verifying, on the production line, that all approved engineering changes are incorporated into hardware at the specified times, and by ensuring that this information is documented and fed into the configuration status files.

Pitfalls to Avoid:

- Controls and requirements must be based on real need and be justifiable in terms of cost versus benefits. If the controls will not result in improved schedule compliance and considerable cost savings, they should be rejected (except when they are needed for safety or required by contract).

- Failure to enforce system requirements—if a requirement is set up, then it must be followed. Otherwise, get rid of it.

- Failure to periodically review system for missing elements or obsolete requirements or documents.

DESIGN REVIEWS SAVE TIME AND MONEY

Design reviews are control devices for assuring that the product design is on schedule and meets contract requirements, customer specifications, cost targets, and project technical objectives. These reviews may be held to evaluate specific subsystems within the product or the entire product. Review meetings should be held during various phases of the project (see Figure 9-4).

The key features of a design review are:

- Independent evaluation of the design by qualified personnel from design, marketing, purchasing, manufacturing, safety, and quality control.

- Careful comparison of the design with previously established base-line requirements.

- Identification and elimination of designs that are not responsive to customer requirements; are unreliable; or use parts that have been found too expensive, unsafe, or difficult to install, or that have high failure rates.

An effective design review provides management with the following benefits:

- Staff capabilities are improved.
- The design is really what is needed.
- The design is evolving on schedule and ready for the next phase.
- The design is documented according to project requirements.
- The staff, management, and customer are informed as to project design status.
- Design changes are avoided.
- Production costs are reduced.
- Customer satisfaction is enhanced.

Case in Point: This case involved a large, heavy cabinet casting to be mounted outdoors. This intermediate design review had the designer, manufacturing and reliability engineers, marketing representative, and the manufacturing and design engineering supervisor in attendance. The design review meeting lasted three hours, preparation time estimated at nine manhours, and investigations took thirty-five manhours—a total of sixty-two manhours (approximately $1000).

Cost estimates were available for each part. There were a total of sixteen items raised that required further analysis. Of these, ten resulted in recommendations for making modifications in the design. One of the simple questions raised regarded the number of bolts needed to hold the watertight door closed. After checking pressures, structural strength and gasket hardness, torque capability of bolts, and so on, the engineer reduced the number of bolts to eight from twelve.

One of the more complex questions, which resulted in a performance, reliability improvement, and a design change, con-

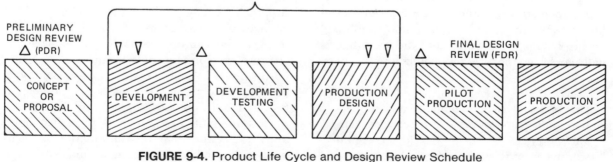

FIGURE 9-4. Product Life Cycle and Design Review Schedule

cerned moisture accumulation inside the cabinet.

Obviously moisture is not good, but the design review group wanted facts. An investigation revealed that moisture came from condensation within the unit as well as from connecting hardware. An automatic drain valve at the bottom was suggested; the connecting hardware could be fitted with traps to eliminate moisture from that source. As a result of drier conditions, the size of the unit could be reduced by a rearrangement of parts inside the cabinet. The removal of the majority of moisture now allowed the normal operating heat to keep the unit dry.

In this case, no formal estimate was made of the cost or savings contributed to by this design review. Since the moisture removal is now incorporated, customer complaints have been reduced. It should be noted, however, that it would take only a reduction of twenty-five service calls (average $40 each) to achieve a breakeven position, and that this would happen within two months at present incidence rates. The production release date was delayed by one week, but new units were ready for delivery one month earlier than scheduled. Other improvements reduced the net number of parts by nine.

Cautions: Management should be careful to avoid unneeded changes or to impose their personal preferences upon the designers. If the design meets originally defined requirements, then managers should restrain themselves.

- Don't assume design review will just happen. It requires management involvement.
- Make design review a company policy, otherwise its implementation and success will be endangered.

Case in Point: In addition to a documented policy, one Ottawa-based firm withholds development funds for the next phase until appropriate design review minutes have been formally issued.

- Don't let the review of the design become a review of the designer. Considerable tact is required by design review participants.
- Avoid preaching. Be objective and prepared to

make constructive suggestions based on facts and experience.

To achieve effective design reviews, take the following steps:

- Plan the review a few weeks in advance.
- Issue a memo defining the review requirements and scope. Be sure to guide the reviewer's focus on the major aims of the review so that unnecessary comments and changes are minimized.
- Send each reviewer a design package for review before the meeting.
- Assign one person to coordinate the meeting and to keep minutes.
- Keep an accurate record of what action items are required and who is responsible. Also specify the date the action should be completed.
- Review action items at end of the meeting and distribute to attendees.
- Follow up to make sure action items are implemented. This is usually done by the design review coordinator or project manager (Figure 9-5).

RELIABILITY ANALYSIS: SOME COMMON TECHNIQUES

Application and Environmental Analysis

The principal objective of application and environmental analysis is to establish a good understanding of how the system will be developed and utilized. This includes identification of the realistic limits as well as the average conditions that can be expected for different missions, operational uses, or portions thereof. This provides a valid basis for establishing the essential capability of parts and materials to be used in the equipment. In this regard, the analysis contributes to the fundamental criteria for achieving product reliability.

Prediction

Predictions are performed using a variety of techniques, such as parts counts or numbers of active elements, and similar function or equipment approaches. They can be made rather quickly and at low cost, but their only output is a reasonable estimate of how difficult it may be to achieve the requirement. Nevertheless, predictions of this type are the only means of making this determination

DIVISION IMPLEMENTATION OF DESIGN REVIEW

1. Product Selected is _____

   Approved by ⎰ General Manager   Date _____
              ⎨ Engineering Manager   Date _____
              ⎬ Reliability Manager   Date _____
              ⎱ Designer   Date _____

2. Chairman of Design Review is _____

3. Secretary of Design Review is _____

4. Participants (and Observers, if any) are:

   a. _____
   b. _____
   c. _____
   d. _____
   e. _____
   f. _____
   g. _____

5. Schedule:

	Goal Date	Actual Date
Orientation Meeting	_____	_____
Design Review	_____	_____
Design Review Minutes	_____	_____
Design Review Final Report	_____	_____

6. | Issuance of Orientation Notice | _____ | _____ |
Issuance of Design Review Notice—		
Agenda	_____	_____
Issuance of Minutes	_____	_____
Issuance of Final Report	_____	_____

7. Results of Design Review (for Management Reporting) are:

   a. Number of items questioned   _____
   b. Number of action items assigned _____
   c. Cost of preparation   _____
   d. Cost of review   _____
   e. Cost of investigation   _____
   f. Change in reliability   _____
   g. Change in performance   _____
   h. Change in manufacturing cost   _____
   i. Change in material cost   _____
   j. Change in schedule   _____

FIGURE 9–5. Form for Tracking Design Review Activity

at the concept and preliminary design stages, and they are needed for initial guidance on other tasks. Predictions of this sort are often called for in proposals with several updates during the program, usually involving more detailed methods on successive predictions. The effort expended is often considerably in excess of the value derived, particularly if performed other than early in the program when changes can be made without serious consequences. Ineffectiveness of predictions relates to their being based on broadly defined parameters and average experience pertaining thereto. Even those that are organized on the basis of detailed treatment of the multitude of parameters that affect reliability do not satisfactorily cope with the considerable variability that occurs within some of the key parameter areas.

TABLE 9–1. Design Review Group Responsibilities and Membership Schedule

GROUP MEMBER	RESPONSIBILITIES	TYPE OF DESIGN REVIEW		
		PDR	IDR	FDR
Chairperson	Calls, conducts meetings of group and issues interim and final reports.	X	X	X
Design Engineer (of product)	Prepares and presents design and substantiates decisions with data from tests or calculations.	X	X	X
Reliability Engineer	Evaluates design for optimum reliability consistent with goals.	X	X	X
Quality Control Manager or Engineer	Ensures that the functions of inspection, control, and test can be efficiently carried out.		X	X
Manufacturing Engineer	Ensures that the design is producible at minimum cost and schedule.		X	X
Field Engineer	Ensures that installation, maintenance, and operator considerations were included in the design.		X	X
Procurement Representative	Assures that acceptable parts and materials are available to meet cost and delivery schedules.		X	
Materials Engineer	Ensures that materials selected will perform as required.		X	
Tooling Engineer	Evaluates design in terms of the tooling costs required to satisfy tolerance, functional, and volume requirements.		X	
Packaging and Shipping Engineer	Assures that the product is capable of being transported and handled without damage.		X	X
Marketing Representative	Assures that requirements of customers are fully understood by all parties.	X		
Design Engineers (not associated with unit under review)	Constructively review adequacy of design to meet all requirements of customer.	X	X	X
Specialists on components, value, human factors (as required)	Evaluate design for compliance with goals of performance cost and schedule.	X	X	X
Customer Representative (optional)	Generally voices opinion as to acceptability of design approach and may request further investigation on specific items.			X

Pitfall to Avoid: Watch out for overly optimistic reliability predictions. Avoid obviously fictitious statements and "too easy" approaches to reliability problems. Yet try not to get the reputation of being negative. Don't spend half your time reporting what you don't know about the highest reject history. Are the failure rates you are using commensurate with in-house test results?

The technical merits of reliability prediction for mechanical, electrical, and electronic systems has been well covered in the literature. What is clear is that while the numerical figures may not be accurate in an absolute sense, they are accurate in a relative sense. It simply isn't worth the time and effort to argue about the failure rates of individual components. A more effective practice would be to use reliability predictions as a basis for identifying the relatively low-reliability functional blocks and concentrate defect prevention activity on them.

Case in Point: A leading manufacturer of car stereos routinely analyzed electronic circuits using the exponential distribution assumption. While all departments agreed that the assumption was tenuous in their application, the simplicity of calculation was traded off against gains in prediction accuracy. In order to service designers promptly, a minicomputer was used to crunch out the numbers. Circuits yielding a predicted mean time between failures (MTBF) of less than twice the design goal were singled out for redesign.

Stress Analysis

Stress analysis is a hybrid between parts application analysis and prediction. Once a detail design has been finished and a prototype is fabricated, the detail stresses (mechanical, electrical, thermal, etc.) can be determined for each part. This data can be used to calculate a detail stress-analysis type reliability prediction. This task relates part application against its capabilities. As a prediction, the principal limitations of other techniques also apply here and, although considerably more detail analysis is employed, areas of significant variability remain. Thus, the increase in prediction accuracy is nominal and normally not commensurate with the cost involved. Usually the point of time when this analysis is performed

occurs after the time for most effective utilization of reliability predictions. One way around this is to develop a set of derating guidelines for various classes of parts and distribute this to individual designers. This then puts the onus on the engineering department to design in reliability rather than on QC to analyze it after the fact.

Worst Case Analysis

Worst Case Analysis is the calculation or experimental determination of the capability of a functional block to perform satisfactorily with parts operating at their adverse tolerance limits or end-of-life values for critical parameters. It constitutes a bridge between the basic parts application task and effective design. When applied on a judicious and selective basis to new designs or critical applications that tend to show problems, this task usually provides reliability improvement for reasonable additional cost. Firms utilizing computer-aided design can readily introduce this type of analysis into the product development process through simulation or other techniques.

WATCH YOUR FAILURE MODES

Failure Mode and Effects Analysis (FMEA) is a design evaluation procedure that consists of listing all potential failures in a system and identifying those that are critical to operational success or safety. The method is a useful tool for reliability predictions, design reviews, test planning, inspections, and product certifications.

FMEA consists of four basic steps: (1) defining the basic functions of the system, (2) outlining the ground rules for the failure analysis, (3) describing system hardware, and (4) listing all possible hardware failures and their effects on system operation.

System functions are best defined with a block diagram showing signal interfaces between major functional blocks (Figure 9-6). Generating a functional diagram early during preliminary design identifies design weaknesses that can be corrected with a minimum impact on system cost and production schedule.

Ground rules for the analysis establish conditions under which the analysis is to be performed, such as the level of analysis (equipment level, functional-block level, or component level), a definition of primary and secondary objectives of the

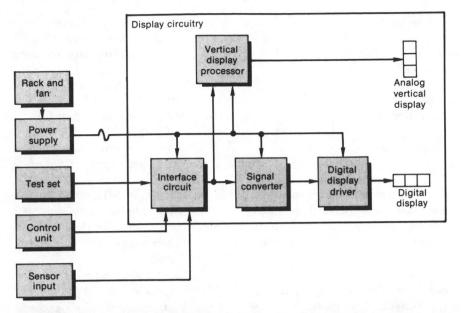

FIGURE 9-6. The first step in FMEA is to define the system to be analyzed with a block diagram showing basically how the system operates. This block diagram shows a commonly used instrument and test-equipment circuit that displays input signals in analog and digital form.
Courtesy of *Machine Design* magazine, from the article "Pinpointing Potential Electronic System Failures," by K. Kivenko, April 7, 1977, pp. 86–7.

analysis, and a definition of failure and system operating modes.

System hardware is described in as much detail as possible with component lists, specifications, and possibly equipment photographs and sketches. A description of the physical layout of the hardware should also be included because many potential layout-related failures are not obvious from functional or schematic diagrams. For example, close spacing of components and conductors on printed-circuit boards may cause overheating and/or electrical shorting. Also, circuits that are functionally independent but physically connected may be mutually affected by a single failure.

Failure of system hardware and its effects on system functions are listed and ranked according to severity and probability of occurrence (Figure 9-7). Thus, critical failures may be identified with particular attention given to failure-prone components such as electromechanical devices (trimpots, switches, pushbuttons, connectors, and motors) and limited-life items (batteries, fans, displays, and relays).

In listing potential failures, external influences to be considered include leaking fluids, excessive vibration, hermetic seal damage, temperature or pressure changes, electrical interference, fire damage, jamming of mechanical linkages by foreign bodies, high humidity, freezing water, lightning, and transportation damage.

The results of the analysis are reviewed, and corrective action is taken to remove unacceptable failure modes. The discipline associated with this technique ensures that a thorough study of equipment failure modes is made.

REVIEW PARTS LISTS EARLY

A component or reliability engineer reviews preliminary parts lists to identify parts with known poor quality histories, unproven parts, and misapplied parts.

Case in Point: A components engineer reviewed seven parts lists on a certain project. Of the 450 parts involved, the components engineer found 44* parts (nearly 10 percent!) that needed designer attention:

Sources not qualified   16
Sources disqualified   5

* Deficiencies sum to more than 44 because some parts had multiple deficiencies.

Misapplication of part	27
Sole sources	19
Cheaper alternates available	38
Poor quality history	11
Safety deficiencies	2
Excessively low life	1
Existing standard parts available	14
Part history and vendor unknown	2

Because costs and time consumed are relatively small in relation to the benefits derived, designers will normally be happy with this service. It must, however, be accomplished in a professional manner.

Pitfall to Avoid: Don't broadcast your findings and embarrass the individual engineers.

The informal route has many benefits particularly in the small firm or small project. For larger projects, a more formal approach to parts control may be in order.

Case in Point: In one Japanese automobile firm, every single part must be approved by production, quality control, reliability, and purchasing. Until the parts are given at least a tentative approval, no additional work (mechanical design) or costs may be incurred. Standard parts are assumed to be automatically approved.

Caution: If formal controls are paperwork jungles and are time-consuming, you may find design projects stretched out and technical innovation subdued. Formal controls may also be part of the contract. This is especially true in the nuclear, construction, and defense industries.

Case in Point: A junior designer for a defense industry firm submitted her parts list for a simple circuit to the program parts control board. The reply from the board provided a quick but effective education for the designer. All of her twenty-eight parts were rejected.

Basis for nonstandard parts used not established	4
Source from foreign countries not acceptable	1
Military part available—commercial not acceptable	7
High-reliability parts not used (see contract spec xx)	7
Jewel bearings not from mandatory domestic sources	1
Selected source not on QPL [Qualified Parts List]	2
Material is not fungus inert	1
Relay and capacitor not of "sealed" type	2
Parts from MIL standard not applicable to missile systems	2
No qualified vendors for part	1
Lower-weight alternative available	1
Battery selected violates safety specification	1
Part number "abc" exceeds cost target for entire assembly	1
Long-term parts availability not likely	2

Most companies have some sort of preferred parts list. These parts should be used as much as is practicable not only for reasons of established performance but for commonality and cost reduction. Design reviews can be very helpful in identifying the few "critical" (high cost, tight tolerances, state of the art, long lead time) parts or suppliers requiring evaluation, qualification testing, audit, or other special actions. This also ensures that the parts physically exist and are not just a published specification.

Case in Point: The specification sheet for a decoder/driver integrated circuit from a vendor not previously used raised some concerns in the mind of a components engineer participating in a routine review of parts list. A subsequent check of this part revealed that it had never been in volume production and that performance specs were not supported by test data. A plant survey further indicated that there were no other established customers for the part and QC procedures did not exist. The firm switched to an established part until the vendor could demonstrate the performance claims.

The use of development samples is liable to lead to undue confidence in a component, which

Device Name	Function	Failure Mode	Failure Effect	Failure Detection Method
Vertical display processor	Drives analog display to value proportional to input signal	No output	No analog display	Visual
Digital display driver	Drives digital display to value commanded by signal converter	No output	No digital display	Visual

FIGURE 9-7. The final step in FMEA is listing possible hardware failures and their effect on system operation. This listing shows only two of the many possible circuit failures. Courtesy of *Machine Design* magazine, from the article "Pinpointing Potential Electronic System Failures," by K. Kivenko, April 7, 1977, pp. 86–7.

is subsequently dispelled when the first production batch is received. *All samples, other than those drawn from normal production sources, should be treated with caution.* It is worth noting that the trend toward miniaturization has tended to increase component complexity. Perhaps the most significant aspect of complex components, from the point of view of evaluation and control, is the fact that they are increasingly the product of complex processes, so that processes are becoming almost more important than the component per se from a reliability point of view. Many of the potential failure modes can only be appreciated by those having some knowledge of the chemical and metallurgical aspects of the processes involved.

In any event, vendor component specifications should be read very carefully not only for what information they provide, but for the information they do not contain. Practically nothing favorable can be read "between the lines" of a specification since it would have been stated explicitly if known or favorable.

Case in Point: Engineering tests on a pushbutton switch for use on an airborne navigation system indicated multiple failures in an intermittent mode and a stuck mode. A subsequent visit to the vendor by PQC indicated that the switch had never been vibration or humidity tested, was not sealed, and was not the appropriate switch for the

application. The spec-sheet had never mentioned environmental factors, and for good reason—the part was intended for the home appliance market.

Purchased part problems are costly, cause huge delays, involve redesign, and can even jeopardize sales or qualification approval. Many of these problems can be prevented if a simple set of guidelines is adhered to during the selection phase:

√ Use proven, qualified standard parts as far as is practicable; try to obtain commonality with other existing projects.

√ Perform evaluation testing of newly available parts. Be wary of using the latest device available on the market.

√ Identify critical items and concentrate on them.

√ Use existing information sources such as GIDEP (Government Industry Data Exchange Program), other users, and other divisions.

√ Establish personal contact with components engineering, purchasing and incoming inspection as early as possible.

√ Prepare clear, concise specifications and discuss them with vendors before procurement.

√ Perform vendor surveys on new vendors or on existing vendors supplying critical items before incorporating them into the design. Try to avoid sole-source situations.

√ Assist incoming inspection in the development of test jigs and procedures for the more sophisticated parts. Identify key performance parameters and critical characteristics.

PARTS STANDARDIZATION CAN IMPROVE QUALITY

The proliferation of purchased component parts is a major cause of quality problems, loss of inventory control, and excess stocks. Parts standardization means choosing a multisourced part with established performance characteristics, and using it in as many applications and product lines as is technically feasible. This avoids many "specials" and nearly similar parts from entering the inventory system.

Component standardization has been the subject of many investigations. Literally dozens of studies and reports have been made in recent years concerning increased costs from the proliferation of component parts for new equipment. There are, however, some myths about standardization that should be understood:

- *Use of standard parts will yield a reliable and safe product.* Only proper application of the right part from competent vendor(s) will accomplish a reliable design.
- *Multiple sourcing is a logical fallout of a standards program.* On the contrary, there is some evidence to suggest that sole-sourcing is a result of too rigid standardization programs.
- *Standardization is easy to administer.* Volumes and volumes of data attest to the bureaucracy of a "mature" standards program.
- *A standard part allows for an efficient design.* Unfortunately, it is a documented fact that most standards programs are not responsive to technological change.

Item growth in the supply bins can be minimized when unnecessary new items are not designed into a piece of equipment. The major roadblock to this approach is the equipment designer—will he or she use standard parts? It does not seem unreasonable that the product designer will use standard parts provided he or she can:

1. Conveniently determine which available standard parts will meet his required application. The information must be as complete and accurate as possible.
2. Easily communicate his component needs to a knowledgeable parts specialist and receive a fast response.

3. Be assured that controls for component selection and use of standard parts will not stifle his freedom of choice and compromise his design.

If a standardization program can be established along these lines, the potential advantages of standardization are many and varied. Engineering advantages include such items as:

- reduced time in processing new product designs
- debugging of designs through established reliability
- common language

The quality control of incoming inspection is made easier by the use of standard parts through:

- explicit specifications
- better control of end product
- reduced and simplified inspection

Purchasing departments also gain advantages with the use of standard parts:

- increased purchasing power, larger amount of fewer items
- reduced lead times
- more suppliers bidding on a competitive basis
- more reliable delivery and hence fewer production delays and material substitutions

Inventories and production conditions are improved with the use of standard parts:

- reduced capital requirements and funds tied up in inventory
- control fewer inventory items
- more familiarity in assembly fabrication and less rework

For those readers who require a more analytical approach, consider the following example. The basic Economic Order Quantity (EOQ) formula yields the equation

$$C^* = \sqrt{2Auc}$$

where A is the set-up cost, u is usage per unit of time, c is carrying cost per unit of product per unit of time and C^* is the cost associated with the EOQ. If we compare the C^*'s, given A and c for a product, with total annual demand ku, in the case where (1) demand is ku for a single product against (2) where demand is u for k different types of product, the impact of standardization should be self-evident.

Clearly

$$\frac{C^*_2}{C^*_1} = \frac{k \sqrt{2Auc}}{\sqrt{2A(ku)c}} = \sqrt{k}.$$

Since this is greater than one, it pays to standardize.

Case in Point: In a \$1 billion computer manufacturer, the use of voluntary part selection (standardization with style) resulted in fewer than 4000 part types being purchased each year to build a full line of large and small computers and a full range of peripherals. This limitation on the total parts used occurred during a period of several years of rapid growth in the company, coupled with its technical leadership of its industry segment. A rough estimate of the savings accrued was in the \$1 million range.

DON'T TOLERATE ARTISTIC TOLERANCING

Tolerances, perhaps even more than quality standards, are a primary cause of undue costs. Shop people have concluded over the years that tolerances are based on random chance. In essence, tolerances have lost their credibility in many instances.

Case in Point: A leading manufacturer of air conditioning equipment continuously accepted out-of-tolerance parts because they would fit into a higher-level assembly. Over time both production and QC had developed their own set of perfectly acceptable tolerances. A new general manager became aware of the situation and investigated. The engineering manager stated that his tolerances were indeed very tight because "production always seemed to foul things up."

The costs of tighter-than-necessary tolerances can be summarized as follows:

- Better-than-necessary manufacturing equipment
- Tighter-than-necessary tool tolerances
- Better-than-necessary gauges and/or test equipment
- More-frequent-than-necessary calibration checking
- More-frequent-than-necessary process control checks

- Larger-than-necessary sample sizes for product acceptance
- 100 percent inspection where sampling might do
- More internal scrap, rework, repair, reprocessing than necessary
- More time consumed than necessary in material review
- More specification changes that need not have been made
- Increased inventories due to yield loss

Clearly, rigid enforcement of realistic tolerances is a wiser policy than loose enforcement of tight tolerances.

What can be done to improve the situation? Here are a few ideas:

√ Indoctrinate designers that excessive tolerances for weight, dimension, electrical performance, thickness, or any parameter dramatically impacts price competitiveness.

√ Make designers explain their selection of tolerances, especially tight ones.

√ Consider using statistical tolerancing techniques.

√ Provide cost-tolerance charts to designers so that designers are aware of the cost implications of unduly tight tolerances. (Here is where process capability data pays off.)

√ Train designers in the mathematics of error analysis and computer simulation.

√ Make tolerances a major factor in design reviews.

√ Ensure that engineers use calibrated measuring equipment when setting critical tolerances.

Pitfall to Avoid: Don't create an atmosphere whereby tight tolerances are automatically attacked. There may be many valid reasons for stringent tolerances, including such factors as regulatory requirements, environment (the tolerance under ambient conditions must be tighter than at environmental extremes), reliability, or field interchangeability. The main idea is to make designers sensitive to the adverse impact of *unduly* severe tolerances.

LOOK INTO STATISTICAL TOLERANCING

The tolerances that every design engineer assigns by the hundreds, while individually adding little to production costs, have a collective impact that is substantial. These costs tend to increase exponentially with tighter tolerances.

The design engineer tends to consider that the tolerance put on the drawing is also the manufacturing tolerance. Actually, this is not the case. The drawing tolerance is further reduced by 10 to 20 percent to allow for such manufacturing variables as tool wear, machine capability, elastic deformation, temperature differential, operator error, and measurement error.

Statistical methods applied to tolerancing provide significant production savings. The laws of statistics and probability can be used to predict how a group of independent variables (part tolerances) combine to form the assembly tolerance. As the quantity of tolerances in an assembly increases, the likelihood of obtaining the max-min condition becomes more and more remote, and the expected assembly tolerance appears to become more and more elusive. By the application of statistical methods, the expected tolerance is actually less elusive. Since a quantity of random variables will approach the normal distribution, the expected tolerance can be determined with a high degree of confidence.

To determine the expected tolerance range of an assembly, it is necessary to combine the frequency curves of the individual part tolerances into a single frequency curve covering the entire assembly. The individual frequency curves are combined by means of the standard deviation. The probability law which applies is:

The standard deviation, sigma (σ), of the sum of any number of independent variables (assembly tolerances) is the square root of the sum of the squares of the standard deviations of the independent variables (part tolerances).

For a given tolerance of $\pm a$, the normal distribution representing 99.73 percent of the cases is equal to $\pm 3\sigma$, or conversely, one standard deviation is a/3. If all tolerances are equal (that is, $\pm a$), the standard deviation of the sum of the variables is $\sqrt{n(a/3)^2}$ where n is the quantity of equal tolerances. Thus, for any given probability, the ratio of the assembly tolerance to the part tolerance is given by z/3 n, where z is the σ spread for a given probability as obtained from normal probability tables.

However, in the real world, equal part toler-

ances seldom occur. In this case, the statistical assembly tolerance (T_a) is computed from the formula

$$Ta = \sqrt{T_1{}^2 + T_2{}^2 + T_n}$$

where T_n represents the tolerance of the nth part. For fewer than four or five tolerances, it should be known that the distribution is normal. If the distribution is not known, drawing tolerances should be assigned between the max-min tolerance and the statistical tolerance. For more than four or five tolerances, normal distribution can be assumed, because of the normalizing effect.

The degree to which tolerances can be opened by statistical methods is so astounding that many engineers are reluctant to fully accept the statistical method; they prefer to assign tolerances intuitively between the max-min extremes and the statistical limits. For more details on the theory of statistical tolerancing see J. M. Juran's *Quality Control Handbook,* 2nd edition.

The normal distribution is the result of the manufacturing operation being set up to produce at the nominal dimension (midpoint of the tolerance range). The normal distribution also results from quantities of nonnormal distributions being combined. A nonnormal (usually rectangular distribution) represents the distribution that could be expected if:

- The process is not being controlled.
- The operator is allowed to produce parts anywhere within the tolerance limits.
- Various set-ups produce some parts to the upper tolerance limits and some to the lower tolerance limits.
- There is excessive tool wear.
- There is excessive rejection or scrap rates.

Regardless of the individual tolerance distributions, the pattern formed when distributions are stacked together will approach the normal shape with sufficient samples.

The more parts in the assembly, the more pronounced the normalizing effect. Thus, regardless of the shape of individual distributions, the stack-up distribution will approach the normal shape. The effect of additional cumulative distributions makes the normal curve taller and narrower. Thus the standard deviation representing the curve becomes smaller in proportion to the extreme spread.

Cautions: Statistical tolerancing methods are based upon a number of assumptions. The design engineer should be aware of the assumptions, evaluate them for possible sources of error, and make appropriate allowances. Error may be introduced from:

- Application of normal distribution practice to an insufficient quantity of nonnormal cumulative tolerances. Skewed distributions are inherent in some manufacturing processes.
- Operators working to the "safe" side of a tolerance to avoid scrap.
- Parts sorted or graded by the shop or vendors.
- Inspectors accepting parts that are marginally out of tolerance.
- The fact that any production run is finite whereas theory assumes a large (infinite) quantity. Small production runs are a particular problem.
- The theory assumption that the process is "under control."
- The fact that related dimensions that do not vary randomly or independently of each other cannot be treated by statistical principles.

Pitfall to Avoid: If the only use of individual mating parts is factory assembly, where numerous parts are available for selective fit, and there is no requirement for repair parts (interchangeability), a large selective fit allowance is suitable. Conversely, if the component is to be issued as a repair part, a high degree of interchangeability is required. Military items require an even higher degree of interchangeability because mission success and user safety may depend on component interchangeability. Such interchangeability provisions may form an inherent part of the sale and hence preclude the use of statistical tolerancing.

Another application of this rule provides some insight into the familiar $10\times$ rule for measurement tolerances. This rule can be expressed as:

$$\sigma_o = \sqrt{(\sigma_\rho)^2 + (\sigma_E)^2}$$

where

σ_o = standard deviation of observed data

σ_ρ = standard deviation of the product

σ_E = standard deviation of the measuring method

Simply speaking, this means that the observations from an instrument used to measure a series of dif-

ferent units of product can be viewed as a composite of (1) the variation due to the measuring method and (2) the variation in the product itself.

If σ_E is less than $\frac{1}{10}$ of σ_o then the effect upon σ_ρ will be less than 1 percent. The $10\times$ rule of thumb thus appears to be uneconomically conservative for many applications. For example, in evaluating a new indicator gauge, it was found that σ_o was 0.0011 inches. An experiment was conducted by using the gauge to check the same unit of product over several times. The σ_E of these repeated readings was 0.0002 inches. This included variations because of instrument and operator. Using the statistical tolerancing formula, σ_ρ equals

$$\sqrt{(0.0011)^2 - (0.0002)^2} = 0.00108$$

This was convincing proof that the errors in the indicator did not materially exaggerate the variation in the product.

QUALITY ASSURE YOUR ENGINEERING DOCUMENTATION

Engineering documentation is playing a greater role today than ever before. Every activity, from hardware concept through manufacturing to field maintenance, is dependent upon engineering documentation as its base.

Engineering documentation is every drawing or document that contains technical and other data that is released from engineering to procure, assemble, maintain, test, and inspect an item.

Quality assurance of engineering documentation means—and entails—a complete review of an engineering package, to *assure* that the item delineated is, in fact, sufficiently described—and can be manufactured and field-maintained at the lowest possible cost. This review should occur as soon as design documentation has been finalized and is ready for release.

Included in this assurance is the guarantee that the engineering documentation package contains sufficient controls for producibility, simplicity of operation, ease and accessibility of maintenance, and compatibility with the system in or with which it is to function. Included also is the guarantee that the technical data contained in the package can be easily understood and meets all design requirements and objectives.

The primary purpose of such a design checking group must be to inspect and assure that the de-

- timely discovery of areas of possible excessive wear, stress, or fatigue
- appraisal of need for changes or additions in protective finishes, coatings, or seals
- recommendations for cost reduction to avoid "gold plated" designs
- evaluation of design compliance with accepted workmanship and manufacturing practices

Case in Point: A farm equipment manufacturer had redesigned part of a new tractor. The subassembly was given to an inspector and a methods analyst, who between them had fifty years of industrial experience. They inspected the unit over a weekend to minimize the inconvenience to the design team. They found several discrepancies in the areas of inspectability, choice of materials and lubricants, and surface finish. The unit was returned on Monday, with an informal report. The resulting changes in product design led to easier inspection, lower production cost, and improved operating life. Estimated savings: $275 per tractor.

Caution: Don't damage the unit during inspection; it may be the only one around!

Don't aggravate the designer with minor or irrelevant points. Stick to major problems; offer suggestions for improvement wherever possible. Write the report objectively—avoid criticizing the designer. Differentiate between noncompliance with standards and subjective observations.

ENVIRONMENTAL SIMULATION TESTING

No amount of drawing review, reliability analysis, or computer simulation can surpass field testing. When field testing is not practical, too expensive, competition sensitive, or just too long, the next best thing is environmental simulation testing. A variety of tests that accelerate and simulate use conditions are normally run on early preproduction models to ascertain if design goals have been achieved.

Test early, test thoroughly, and perform selected overstress tests. Discovering weak design areas early will usually result in considerable dollar savings. It is much less expensive to change engineering drawings before starting final drawings. The savings could be enormous. More recently, the results of environmental testing have also pro-

vided the back-up data required in product liability disputes.

Typical of the tests that would be performed, depending on the product are:

high and low temperature
humidity
rain
sunshine
salt spray
product stability
vibration and shock
transportation and storage
sand and dust
explosion
fungus resistance
wear and fatigue
reliability/life

The size, organization, and capability of an in-house environmental test laboratory are dependent upon the degree to which a company wishes to become involved in conducting such tests. The determining factor is usually based on economic grounds and expected test loading. Even with a well-equipped in-house facility, this important testing is not always accomplished.

Case in Point: An international manufacturer of pumps had an up-to-date, extensive in-house environmental test laboratory run by QC. Hourly rates for each test environment were set. Engineers were reluctant to use the facility because of the costs involved. Company management changed the procedure of charging and included the costs in the engineering overhead cost pool, thus making the lab appear "free." Lab utilization increased 70 percent with corresponding improvements in product integrity.

Case in Point: A paper-oriented QC manager turned the administration of the test laboratory into a bureaucratic nightmare. Forms, approvals, and justifications were apparently more important than having important development tests performed. As a result, engineers and researchers avoided using the lab and gambled that good design practices would be sufficient.

One of the most important test programs is the product qualification test, which is normally done on preproduction samples. Regardless of the industry, such planning is crucial to meeting marketing objectives. Qualification testing is typically complex, requiring the coordination of many functions, test facilities, and resources. The following checklist pertains:

√ Is product configuration defined via drawings and/or other means?

√ Have test plan and specification been prepared and approved by relevant agencies and groups?

√ Are qualification test requirements and objectives clear and validated?

√ Has a contingency plan been established?

√ Have test resources (facilities, finance, personnel, technology) been forecast?

√ Have test budgets and schedules been determined?

√ Are data collection and QC policies established?

√ Has developmental prequality testing successfully been completed?

√ Are debugged test procedures available and customer concurrence obtained as required?

√ Are standard and special test equipment/fixtures available, calibrated, and certified?

√ Are test responsibility and management clearly defined?

√ Are test articles representative of production units?

√ Have QC acceptance test and final inspection been successfully completed on test article(s)?

√ Have arrangements for personnel accommodation and transportation been completed when tests are to be performed out of town?

√ Has final test report content, format, and approval authority been established?

√ Has the customer or applicable regulatory agency been adequately informed of test program?

Pitfall to Avoid: Watch out for the inherent high risk if only one unit is qualification tested. Test additional units at least in temperature, humidity, vibration, or other appropriate environment. Do not overlook the combinations of environments that the unit should survive.

DON'T FORGET HUMAN FACTORS IN DESIGN

With all the emphasis on product reliability, maintainability, and safety, it is quite easy to forget the human element. Products that foster effective procedures, work patterns, and personnel safety and that minimize discomfort, distraction, and any other factors that degrade human performance or increase error are the ultimate objective. New product designs must include consideration of human engineering, life support, and biomedical factors that affect human performance, including when applicable:

1. Fail-safe designs when failure can cause equipment damage, personnel injury, or inadvertent operation of critical equipment.

2. Proper labeling, color coding, and keying of items that can be misassembled or misused during production operation or maintenance.

3. Safe range of acoustic noise and vibration, and safeguards against uncontrolled variability beyond safe limits.

4. Protection from thermal, toxicological, radiological, x-ray, chemical, electromagnetic, visual, and other hazards.

5. Adequate space for person and equipment, and free volume for the movements he or she must perform during operation and maintenance tasks, under both normal and emergency conditions.

6. Adequate physical, visual, and auditory links between people and equipment under both normal and emergency conditions.

7. Efficient arrangement of indicators, labels, knobs, dials, controls, and displays.

8. Adequate natural or artificial illumination for the performance of operation, control, training, and maintenance.

9. Provisions for minimizing psychophysiological stress and fatigue.

10. Design features to assure rapidity, safety, and ease of maintenance in normal and emergency maintenance environments.

11. Satisfactory handling provisions and tools. (For example, don't expect someone to lift sixty pounds safely without a handle or grasp area.)

12. Consideration of workspace layout and maintenance access with personnel wearing operational clothing (a gloved hand, say, requires different design considerations from an ungloved hand).

Example: Some American cars provide examples of poor applications of human engineering principles. These do not include workmanship defects, lack of energy conservation, pollution deficiencies, or safety hazards such as rear gas tank explosions. The following list gives some examples of design deficiencies:

- Tinted windows to cut down direct sunlight are not inherent in the design of most models.
- Gauges and dials have been removed over the years and have been replaced with go/no go indicators.
- A driver's side control mirror is offered as an option, although a cigarette lighter, which supports an unhealthy, possibly lethal habit, is standard equipment.
- Ventilation systems have caused unnecessary asphyxiation deaths.
- Mechanical packaging is not supportive of good accessibility, component identification, and general ease of maintenance.
- Rear defogger is offered as option when it is necessary for safe operation in northern climates.
- Steering wheel obscures the odometer reading and/or fuel gauge indication.
- Inadequate guards, shields, and caution markings.

TRY A PRODUCTION READINESS REVIEW (PRR)

It is sometimes beneficial to perform a formal production readiness review on a new product. This is normally accomplished by personnel not associated with the project design. The objective is to independently assess the state of production readiness, when evaluated against the following or other specially developed criteria:

1. Milestones that demonstrate the achievement of a practical and producible engineering design have been met. This may also include regulatory body approvals and certifications.
2. Engineering problems encountered during development have been resolved with appropriate trade-offs against stated operating requirements so that production costs/schedules are optimized.
3. System configuration has been reviewed to determine the impact of any significant design changes on production. (Drawing release status is a key indicator.)
4. Adequate advanced production planning has been accomplished and required production controls established to ensure orderly production.

5. A systematic approach to standardization has been accomplished in the design process and parts selection to maximize the use of standard components parts and processes, consistent with product requirements.
6. Quality controls and tests to prevent manufacturing degradation of performance parameters have been established.
7. There is assurance of readiness of the manufacturing and production equipment, and status of accessory and ancillary items.
8. Planned production schedules reflect economy of operations and minimize financial commitments until all major development problems have been resolved.
9. A thorough assessment of the make-or-buy structure has been accomplished and procedures exist so control and visibility of the vendors and subcontractors can be effectively maintained.
10. Test program results and the status of qualification testing to determine production impact and risk have been evaluated.
11. Specifications and drawings have been reviewed to assure their adequacy for economical and efficient production.
12. Application of production tooling and test equipment to manufacturing during development has been assessed and the application of same to the production phase has been defined.
13. Material management system for determination of requirements, procurement, receiving, inspection, and materials handling, and storage, inventory control, control of finished goods, and shipment is adequate.
14. Production management systems used for providing management with timely production status information are effective.
15. The capabilities of major subcontractors and vendors have been evaluated and found adequate.
16. Constraints of laboratory or model shop capabilities versus quantity production requirements have been fully considered.
17. Quality controls and inspection procedures have been established for special or new processes to be used in production.
18. Availability of production labor skill requirements has been assessed and their acquisition adequately planned.
19. Planning has been made to assure timely release of manufacturing and inspection work instructions.

Since different companies may not be organized or function alike in their planning for, or manufacturing of, required supplies, it may not be necessary for each criteria to be reviewed and evaluated. There may be additional unidentified criteria that need to be included because of unique requirements. Therefore, the PRR evaluators must exercise discretion to ensure that appropriate production criteria are applied to determine production readiness posture.

ESTABLISH A PRODUCT SAFETY PROGRAM

Product quality cannot be evaluated without considering product safety. Unsafe equipment, besides leading to product liability claims, creates an unsatisfied customer. Product safety used to be taken as an inherent and implicit design goal. Possibly because it is so obvious, product safety has received inadequate attention. Product liability cases have risen exponentially over the years and so have settlement amounts. Liability insurance isn't the complete answer because of high premium costs, numerous exclusions, interpretation conflicts, high deductibles, and coverage dispute problems if the insurance carrier is changed. Thus, moral reasons aside, a good product safety program is a necessity in today's business environment.

The basic elements of a product safety program include:

- A written policy regarding product safety policies and organization.
- A technical data library containing relevant safety regulations, codes, and standards.
- Documented safety analyses such as fault tree analysis, failure modes, and effects analysis for each product.
- Design reviews that consider product safety.
- Engineering tests that evaluate products under severe and extreme conditions.
- A configuration control system that evaluates engineering changes.
- Clear recordkeeping practices such as those related to trade-off studies, safety tests and inspections, minutes of design reviews, raw material certifications, nonconforming material reports, and so on. See also Table 9-2.
- Product traceability systems such as customer lists, serial number, lot number, batch number, or date code.

TABLE 9-2. Product Safety Checklist

1. Do engineering drawings contain safety notes or highlight critical characteristics?
2. Does unit contain any hazardous or toxic materials?
3. Have appropriate safety factors and derating been employed?
4. Are rating and/or nameplates clear, concise, complete?
5. Does unit employ safety interlocks?
6. Have fail-safe principles been incorporated into design?
7. Does unit contain necessary override/disconnect capability and appropriate failure indicators?
8. Is equipment properly fused and protected?
9. Are external metal parts at ground potential?
10. Do switches/controls have protection against inadvertent operation?
11. Is it difficult to bypass safety features?
12. Has stress analysis been performed on structural parts?
13. Are sharp edges and burrs avoided?
14. Have necessary warning, caution, and danger signs been included?
15. Are all parts, wire, and materials flame-retardant?
16. Have safety-critical installation parameters been defined?
17. Has a worst case, fault-free, and/or hazard analysis been performed? (Don't forget computer software.)
18. Have redundancy or high reliability parts been considered in design?
19. Are compatible metals used or suitably coated to prevent corrosion?
20. Have safety-critical (e.g., fans, motors, batteries) parts been identified?
21. Is suitable drainage provided to prevent moisture accumulation?
22. Are all moving parts suitably guarded?
23. Are limit stops provided on pullout racks and drawers?
24. Have appropriate electromagnetic interference (EMI) precautions been taken?
25. Do technical manuals define all necessary safety precautions?

- Appropriate warning signs and labels where accident-proofing is not possible.
- Clear operating and maintenance manuals to ensure proper care and use of the product.
- Commercial advertising that avoids inferences or statements suggesting that misuse of a product is acceptable.

- A quality control system that routinely scrutinizes accident reports, customer complaints, and failure analysis results to ensure safe operation.

A product has to be safe to be used. It must meet an acceptable standard of safety for the utility it offers.

REFERENCES

Deger, E. and T. C. Jobe. "For the Real Cost of a Design Factor in Reliability." *Electronics,* August 30, 1973.

"Design for Producibility: The Golden Opportunity." Round Table Feature, *Production,* May 1976.

Engle, W. L. "Defect Free Drafting." *Graphic Science,* August 1968.

Jacobs, R. M. "Implementing Formal Design Review." *Industrial Quality Control,* February 1967.

Jakubowski, R. "Zero Defects—A Positive Approach to Quality Data." *Graphic Science,* August 1967.

Kivenko, K. "12 Key Elements to Consider in a Product Safety Program." *Evaluation Engineering,* May/June 1976.

Lowers, H. R. "The Role of Q.A. in Configuration Management." *Quality Progress,* June 1972.

"Reliability Reporting Guide," ASQC, 1977.

Software Quality Assurance Program Requirements. MIL-S-52779(AD), U.S. Department of Defense, April 15, 1974.

Spotts, M. F. "Dimensioning Stacked Assemblies." *Machine Design,* April 20, 1978.

Weiser, B. "Human Factor Effects on Reliability." *Industrial Quality Control,* December 1965.

10

Techniques for Improving Quality Management Decisions

The management of quality is essentially the management of uncertainty (risk). The risks can be associated with the accumulation of tolerances, choice of vendors, unexpected process failures, or product reliability. Quantitative methods and statistical approaches can help in the decision-making process, but sometimes even these valuable tools will not be useful. The lack of a suitable mathematical model may severely limit our choices. Yet decisions must be made.

> Some questions cannot be answered, but they can be decided.
>
> Harry S Truman

Constraints must be considered when making a decision. Typical business constraints affecting QC decisions include:

- limited funds available for capital investment, quality control budgets, or corrective action
- company economic position
- personalities of those affected by the decision
- management policies
- company politics
- organizational factors
- human factors
- legal, regulatory, or market considerations

There are several classes of decision making required of quality management. These are summarized in Table 10-1.

It is interesting to contrast the North American approach to decision making with the Japanese. In Japan, decisions are arrived at by concensus and take a relatively long time. In the U.S., decisions tend to be made by individual managers in a relatively short time. Implementation, however, is usually difficult and protracted compared with the Japanese approach (Figure 10-1).

Case in Point: An American auto executive remarked to the plant manager of a Japanese steel plant that the Japanese seemed to take forever to make a decision. The retort: "Maybe so, but you Americans seem to take forever to implement a decision."

The manager of the quality function is thus faced with a wide variety of long-term, intermediate-term, and day-to-day decisions. Each of these decision points involves risks with corresponding financial consequences. The cumulative effect of these decisions will determine if the quality program is economical and effective or costly and counterproductive. Chapter 10 provides some tools for easing the pressure.

THE DECISION PROCESS

The first step in the decision-making process is recognizing that a decision is required. All too often poor practices are implicitly tolerated or accepted because people don't realize that inaction is a form of decision making. It is generally taken

TABLE 10-1. QC Decision Areas

Nature of Decision	Application Areas	Decision Techniques & Tools
capital investment	purchase of automatic tester	decision theory, ROI, technical arguments
budgeting	cost center budgets, quality costs for proposals	forecasting, ratio analysis, experience
evaluation of test data	life tests, measures of improvement, identification of root causes	hypothesis testing, experimental design
lot quality	purchased material evaluation, special process controls, fabrication shops	control charts, acceptance sampling
QC operations	implementation of corrective action determination of cost-effective control points, selection of sampling plans	Pareto analysis, staff reports, operations research, breakeven analysis
Manloading	budgets, long-term projections, utilization of personnel	learning curves, forecasting, ratio analysis, queueing theory simulation, work sampling
quality status	job progress, problem areas	Pareto analysis, staff reports, failure analysis

for granted that a yes vote is cast when no effort to change the status quo is made.

Attack quality or personnel problems before they get out of control. Face problems squarely and make decisions when they are required. Procrastination, waffling, and shirking responsibility are not the hallmarks of a successful quality decision maker.

Once it is realized that a decision is required, you need the appropriate information. When the QC manager has accurate, relevant, and timely information he or she is in a strong position to select the optimum course of action. Subject information to the following tests:

√ Is the information accurate?

√ Is the information current?

√ Are the sources of the data reliable?

√ Does the information intuitively feel correct?

√ Is the information relevant?

√ Does the information correlate with other independent sources of information?

√ Will this information be valid in a week, a month, a year, five years?

√ Must the information be adjusted (e.g., for inflation, change in product mix, automation)?

√ Will the information source be accepted by higher management?

√ Is the information established fact or is it opinion, wishful thinking, theoretical, or a forecast?

√ Have assumptions (albeit logical) been segregated from basic information?

The next step is to enumerate the alternatives available to the decision maker. Each solution will have its constraints, some of which are noneconomic but nevertheless important. Company politics is one constraint. Next, the benefits to be

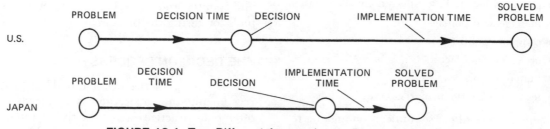

FIGURE 10-1. Two Different Approaches to Decision Making

obtained from each alternative are identified. Insofar as practical, benefits should be quantified in dollar or other acceptable units of measure. Likely side effects such as union opposition, people's feelings, or customer reaction should also be considered and weighed against the benefits *before* a decision is made. The costs, resources, and time required to implement each solution must also be determined. The final step is to evaluate the risks and possible consequences involved in each alternative solution. Often a summary matrix table plotted against the applicable decision parameters is useful.

Case in Point: A construction firm was responding to the terms and conditions of a customer RFP (Request for Proposal). The decision centered around the question of how best to respond to the stringent warranty provisions.

In this particular case, management offered alternative 3 in their bid. It turned out to be successful because the other bidders were either fully compliant but very expensive or totally noncompliant and deemed nonresponsive. In this example, the firm was willing to sacrifice immediate sales growth for stability. In every decision the objectives, attitudes, and strategies of the firm must be clearly understood.

AVOID THESE DECISION-MAKING TRAPS

A number of traps exist when the quality manager makes a decision. A list of the common causes for poor decisions follows:

- Being pressured into a snap decision.
- Incomplete or inaccurate information.
- Personal bias that causes distortion or ignoring of facts.
- False confidence in staff members who present a facade of absolute certainty or confidence without real experience or knowledge to back up their recommendations.
- Improper selection of people to research problem. They may have vested interests or closed minds that can affect their data-gathering ability. They may simply be incompetent in the area of investigation.
- Improper selection of information sources or data banks.
- Ignoring experience of other projects, companies, or industries.
- Failure to account for future changes in business, quality, or product mix.

Case in Point: A manager avoided purchasing sophisticated equipment that would have increased the productivity of her department because she had doubts about the demand for her staff's services in the next few

Alternative	Benefit	Estimated Cost	Possible Side Effects	Potential Decision Consequence	Business Risk	Constraints
1. take exception	lower risk of over-run and lower price	$ 30,000	removal from future bidders list	lose contract	very safe cost estimate	nil
2. accept provisions exactly as stated	win contract and corresponding profit	$150,000	nil	significant cost over-run if estimate is wrong	maximum could be $500,000	management policy
3. offer compromise alternative warranty clause	lower risk of over-run and lower price	$ 65,000	unknown, probably nil	lose contract	modest, about $10,000	nil

years. As a result, she did not spend the $100,000 budgeted for this action. Two years later, the department staff was reduced from 100 to 45 people and the nature of the work changed so that the new equipment would not have been able to be utilized more than 15 percent of the time, and its economic payoff with the 45-person staff would not have been achieved.

- Failure to consult those affected by the decision.

> A man convinced against his will is of the same opinion still

- Bad assumptions about the staff, product, or conditions. Sometimes assumptions are not even clearly identified and implicitly taken as fact.
- Generalizing an experience that may not be applicable to other situations.
- Unrealistic expectations. For example, a vice-president of corporate quality asked all division quality managers to prepare a new series of reports. He allowed thirty days for the first report. With fourteen divisions involved one would expect that some managers might be on vacation, away on business, deeply involved with another project, or on sick leave.
- Trying to make more than one major decision at a time. This breaks up concentration and can cause confusion.

Cautions:

1. Remember Mr. Pareto. Concentrate your decision-making efforts. Not all problems are exciting to work on. Routine or mundane problems require decisions too; more often than not, the less exotic the decision technique, the greater the consequence of the decision. Avoid spending disproportionate amounts of time on statistical or theoretical projects that are philosophically stimulating but won't do much for the bottom line or product quality. Don't get bogged down on trivia or marginal quality tasks. Connect with the real world of competitive business.

2. Don't overinvolve yourself in decisions that are someone else's responsibility. While cooperation is important, excessive involvement in other people's problems depletes energy and can compromise your decision-making ability. You can offer help, but don't stick your nose in where it doesn't belong.

3. Develop an alternate plan of action in case the decision turns out badly. Every decision has an element of risk in it. Therefore, the assumption that there is no chance of failure will prevent preparation of a contingency plan to correct a bad course of action.

Pitfalls to Avoid:

- Once the decision is made, it should be put into effect right away. Wavering or delays increase its chances for failure by weakening your resolve and your staff's confidence in its correctness or importance.
- Don't live with a bad decision—change it. While no one likes to admit a mistake, a strong leader can do it and gain respect at the same time.
- A half-hearted attempt in the implementation of a decision can undermine an excellent decision because the dedication and energy needed by the staff will not be mobilized toward its implementation.
- Consider constraints set by the environment and higher management. For example, if top management has set a hiring freeze and the decision involves hiring two quality engineers immediately, then it is not likely that the decision will be successful.

STAFF REPORTS HELP MAKE DECISIONS

In today's competitive and complex environment, most managers must depend on others for help in making decisions. It is often impossible for the QC manager to know every operational detail. Consultation with the quality staff will very likely be necessary before making a decision. The experience of others can thus lead the manager into failure or success based on the quality of this experience and its correct application to the present situation.

Staff reports are a common tool for decision making in industry. The procedure involves assigning a competent researcher to study and collect data in a particular area or problem so that the manager can have a documented source of information for decision making. For assessing the reliability of other people's experience ask yourself the following:

√ Is the individual's experience relevant?

√ Has previous information supplied been accurate?

√ Does the person have a personal reason for favoring a specific decision, e.g., an opportunity for promotion or a raise?

√ Is the individual's experience current or based on conditions that existed five, ten, or twenty years ago?

√ Is there corroborating information from other sources to support recommendations made?

√ Is the person's recommendation based on an understanding of the total picture or based on a narrow perspective?

√ Does the individual have the required knowledge of alternatives?

When the manager has considerable trust in the person preparing the report, the author's recommendations will be followed with only a cursory review of the report. In other cases, additional information may be required from other sources before making the decision.

The value of staff reports is that problem requirements are defined carefully, information is gathered systematically, and results are analyzed critically before a decision is made. The report also provides a permanent record for the basis of the decision. It can thus be referred to and reexamined at a future date by others or the manager to determine the effectiveness of this type of decision-making tool and its value for future decisions.

A *risk analysis report* is a special staff report that provides the manager with the staff's assessment of the risks involved in meeting a particular schedule, budget, or performance parameter. These reports are prepared in a highly systematic fashion and rely on the quantitative assessments of various task managers as to the percent probability of meeting a time, financial, or technical commitment.

This information is valuable to the quality manager who can then develop contingency plans and workarounds. For example, if the reliability engineer's inputs indicate that an equipment has only a 50 percent chance of passing a reliability demonstration test, then contingency funds for redesign will have to be employed and project schedules altered.

The QC manager can use this kind of information to keep higher management informed as to the risks involved, and this information can be helpful in establishing ground rules for negotiation with the customer or in how the project will be run and the priority rating it will be given.

BREAKEVEN ANALYSIS POINTS THE WAY

Breakeven analysis is used to determine the point where outlays (usually cost) are equal to benefits. Moving to either side of the breakeven point will favor one alternative or the other.

Consider the economic trade-off of sampling versus 100 percent inspection. If we assume, for simplicity, no inspection errors, then we can formulate a simple cost-balancing equation:

Cost of 100% inspection = cost of sampling + cost of an "escape."

In symbols this can be stated as:

$$NI = nI + (N - n) pA$$

or

$$P_b = \frac{(N - n) I}{(N - n) A} = \frac{I}{A}$$

where

N = number of units in lot

n = number of units in sample

p = fraction defective in lot

A = cost consequence of an inspection escape

I = unit inspection cost

P_b = breakeven fraction defective

If the fraction defective in the lot is less than P_b, the total cost will be lowest with sampling. If p is greater than P_b, then clearly 100 percent inspection will result in the lowest total cost.

Breakeven analysis can also be used to determine under which conditions special quality controls are warranted. A manufacturer has an order for 100,000 widgets. With his existing equipment they cost $.80 each with an average lot yield of 94 percent. If he installs a new piece of equipment, the variable cost per unit can be brought down to $.60, but yield may decrease. If the piece of equipment costs $18,000, the breakeven fraction defective (P_b) is determined by:

old cost = new cost

or

$$(.80) \frac{100,000}{.94} = 18,000 + (.60) \frac{100,000}{1 - P_b}$$

hence

$$P_b = 1 - .894 = .106 \text{ or } 10.6\%$$

The effectiveness of a quality control program can be studied by means of breakeven analysis. Assume a plant produces 35,000 units of product per annum. If fixed costs (F) are $10,000 and variable costs (V) are $3.333 per unit, and the selling price(s) is $6.666 per unit, then breakeven occurs when

$$F + V(N_b) = SN_b$$

$$\$10,000 + \$3.333(N_b) = 6.666N_b$$

or

N_b (the breakeven quantity) = 3000 units

If additional quality controls are added, the breakeven point will shift. Assume fixed costs increase to $11,000 but variable costs decrease to $2.266 per unit. The new breakeven point is

$$11,000 + 2.266(N_b) = 6.666N_b$$

or

$$N_b = 2500$$

This earlier breakpoint occurs because fixed QC costs generally increase more slowly than quality losses decline. If the price is competitive, sales volume will increase because of improved quality, thus further enhancing profits because the fixed costs will be spread over a greater number of units. In the worst case, prices could be cut without affecting previous profit margins.

INCREASE INSIGHT: USE HISTOGRAMS

A histogram is simply a plot of the number of occurrences (y-axis) versus the numerical parameter of interest (x-axis). Such a plot can be very informative about lot quality and assist in the visualization of mathematical calculations (Figure 10-2). The frequency distribution is useful in four important quality control jobs.

√ In new design control, it predicts the performance of a new product based on pilot-run data.

√ In incoming material control, it can provide insight into a supplier QC activity. Coupled with quantitative statistical analysis, a histogram is a very powerful tool.

√ In product control, it furnishes a technique for determining the amount of variation that may be expected from a given process or parameter.

√ In special process studies, its use as a pictorial aid may be very valuable.

Case in Point: The machine shop foreman claimed that the specified ± 0.001 drawing tolerance could not be economically held with existing drilling equipment; the designer claimed that it could. A representative production lot was plotted to resolve the issue. The resulting histogram conclusively proved that ± 0.0025 would be more appropriate. The designer then found she could actually live with ± 0.003 and the drawing was changed accordingly. Estimated annual savings: $7500.

Some typical applications of histograms include:

● Determining the process capabilities of machine tools and other processing equipments.

● Comparing inspection results between two factories or between two sections of the same plant.

● Examining the difference between the dimensional characteristics of similar parts produced in different molds.

● Indicating the variations among similar parts produced by each of two so-called duplicate sets of tools.

● Examining the accuracy of fit between mating parts.

● Analyzing the effect of tool wear during a long production run on a machine tool.

Pitfalls to Avoid:

● Don't use a technical term like histogram if your shop people are not comfortable with it. Try calling it a tally sheet or data log.

● Leave formulas and calculation aids off the tally form to maintain its simplicity. If, however, you have a shop floor computer or programmable calculator, analytical data may be obtained immediately.

● Ensure that readings are taken properly. This is especially important when very close readings are required. Inspectors definitely "like" some values better than others.

● Make sure that sample sizes are adequate and randomly selected.

● Use common sense and technical judgment. Recheck any data that doesn't feel right or jive with your experience.

CLARIFY YOUR THOUGHTS: USE DECISION TREES

Economic implications of many management decisions depend on some future state of affairs. Un-

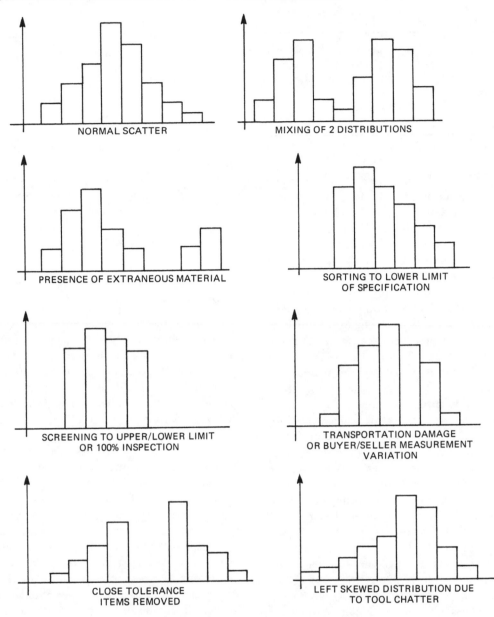

FIGURE 10-2. Types of Frequency Histogram

less this future condition can be accurately predicted, the decision is fallible. This problem becomes crucial when the quality manager turns his or her attention to the replacement of capital equipment or must make similar major decisions. The long-range outcome of the decision can spell economic success—or disaster—to the manufacturing operation.

Decision making is a process of selecting among possible courses of action. These alternatives must be evaluated and the best one selected. However, the best alternative—in terms of achieving long-range economic goals—depends on situations beyond the decision maker's control. Such uncon-

trollable situations are referred to as *states of nature.* A collection of mutually exclusive states of nature are considered in the decision. Together, alternatives and states of nature denote the outcome. If some consistent evaluation scheme is applied to the outcome in the form of a mathematical criterion, outcomes can be compared and the best alternative selected.

Each decision maker can reduce the risk and uncertainty of a decision to a minimum by collecting some data and making a few calculations. Statistical decision theory, which is well described in the literature, provides the basis for dealing with such uncertainties.

TABLE 10–2.

Projected Sales	Estimated Probability of Occurrence
10,000 units	0.4
20,000 units	0.2
100,000 units	0.4

Suppose that a manufacturer of an electronic assembly is considering the budget for the next fiscal year. Both manufacturing and quality assurance agree that the operator-controlled semi-automatic test equipment (ATE) currently in use is at its limit; it is in use three shifts a day, five and a half days a week. Manufacturing and quality have jointly requested the purchase of a sophisticated automatic test system at a cost of $200,000.

The controller, however, is reluctant to include the equipment in the budget because the results of the marketing forecast for the next year are not clear. While the company has been growing steadily, continued growth is not certain, and there may even be a downturn in sales.

Table 10-2 shows the possible sales events for the next year and their probabilities as forecast by marketing and sales. The sum of the probabilities for each mutually exclusive event must equal 1.0. Sales are currently 20,000 units per year.

The mutually exclusive acts under consideration are to buy the test equipment or to not buy the test equipment. The uncertainty (states of nature) is the volume of sales over the next year.

If the company purchases the automatic test equipment and sales increase, testing costs will be very low because the equipment is very efficient and will be effectively utilized. If sales remain the same or decrease, however, the equipment will be poorly utilized and total testing costs will go up.

If the company does not purchase the test equipment and sales increase, substantial overtime expenses will be incurred. It may even be necessary to build one or more semiautomatic testers. If sales stay the same or go down, the decision not to buy the test equipment would save the company $200,000.

Testing costs under the various events are shown in Table 10-3; Figure 10-3 shows the data in decision tree form.*

---

* Raymond J. Kimber, "The Decision Tree—An Aid to the Quality Professional," *Quality,* September 1979.

To simplify the decision tree concept, we assume that the $200,000 is the net cash flow and that it will be depreciated in the first year of operation.

Table 10-4 shows expected costs under both situations. The total cost is the sum of the investment in the automatic tester plus the recurring test costs.

Since, in this case, the goal is the smallest total expected testing cost, the optimum decision is to buy the test equipment. As with any decision made under conditions of uncertainty, a decision based on statistical decision theory is not always right; but it is always the best decision that can be made with the available information.

ARE YOU IN CONTROL? TRY CONTROL CHARTS

One of the most important tools used in process control is the control chart. A *process control chart* is a statistical device used for the study and control of repetitive production processes. It indicates the manner in which the process or system is operating and when to make corrections in order to maintain a conforming product service.

Variations in the quality of manufactured articles are inevitable. The sources of variations in manufactured products are materials, machines, people, and manufacturing conditions. By means of statistical quality control methods, these variations may be separated into two types of causes: (a) chance-causes—from random variations in the process, or (b) assignable causes—from nonchance variations. The separation of these two types of variations is the special province of the control chart. It is this separation power that makes control charts invaluable management tools.

Chance-causes of variations are (a) always present, (b) inherent in the nature of the process, (c) neither readily identifiable nor readily removable, and (d) not readily within our power to regulate.

If a stable system of chance-causes is alone operating in a process and causing the variations in quality, (a) the product cannot readily be improved except by basically changing or redesigning the process; (b) the process exhibits its "natural variability"; and (c) the magnitude of quality variations in the product can be predicted. Accurate predictions and sound decisions can be made only from data that comes from a stable system of chance-causes.

TABLE 10-3. Testing Cost Matrix

COST OF EQUIPMENT	BUY ATE		DON'T BUY ATE	
	$200,000		$0	
Cost of Testing		Total cost		Total cost
Decreasing sales	$100,000	$300,000	$ 100,000	$ 100,000
Constant sales	$200,000	$400,000	$ 200,000	$ 200,000
Increasing sales	$360,000	$560,000	$1,400,000	$1,400,000

A process is said to be *in a state of statistical control* when the observed quality variations are the same as would be expected when a stable system of chance-causes is operating. It is important to understand constant-cause systems because some such stable system of chance-causes is inherent in any particular scheme of production or service. The effects of such a constant-cause system are visible when no assignable causes of variation are present.

Assignable causes of variation arise from specific disorders in the process and (a) are potentially identifiable and removable, (b) are within our power to regulate, and (c) merit prompt in-

vestigation. If assignable causes are at work (in addition to the ever-present chance-causes), there is no way of predicting the variability of the product, and the product can usually be readily improved by detecting, identifying, and eliminating them.

The presence of assignable causes of variation can be detected by comparing the statistical pattern of variation we actually have with the pattern we would expect to have if chance-causes alone were operating. The control chart is the tool used for this purpose. The assignable cause of variation is identified and removed by an engineering investigation when it is considered eco-

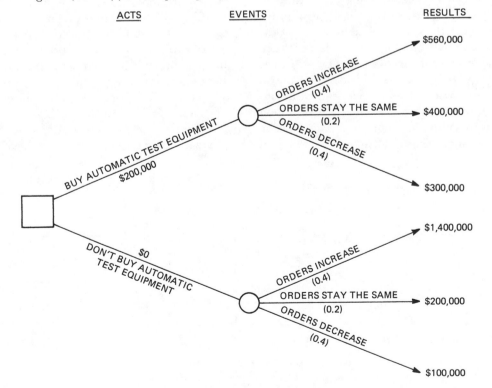

FIGURE 10-3. Decision Tree for ATE Example

TABLE 10-4. Expected Cost Table

ACT/event	Probability	Value	Expected Value
Buy test equipment			
Decreased sales	0.4	$ 300,000	$120,000
Constant sales	0.2	$ 400,000	$ 80,000
Increased sales	0.4	$ 560,000	$224,000
		Sum of expected values	$424,000
Don't buy test equipment			
Decreased sales	0.4	$ 100,000	$ 40,000
Constant sales	0.2	$ 200,000	$ 40,000
Increased sales	0.4	$1,400,000	$560,000
		Sum of expected values	$640,000

nomical to do so. It is frequently necessary to blend statistical and engineering skills in solving quality control problems.

The control chart is a graphical record of the quality of current production showing quality variations by a series of points plotted in time order of production. A control chart generally has the features indicated in Figure 10-4.

The central line indicates the average value of the appropriate characteristic. The control limits assist in judging the statistical significance of the quality variations from the central level. When only chance causes of variation are operating, the vast majority of points fall inside the control band, and the process is *in control*. Statistical control is established by the construction of action limits such that the occurrence of a point outside these limits suggests that assignable causes of

variation are very probably present and the process is out of control. Action should be taken to identify and eliminate such assignable causes. The actual identification and elimination of the assignable cause(s) still needs to be accomplished. The chart shows when you are in trouble, not what the trouble is. The fact that we know *when* assists in the determination of *what*. In addition, the control chart often gives a warning of impending difficulty. Steps can be taken to investigate the situation and prevent the trouble. Since the control chart gives a pictorial record of what is happening while it is happening, it aids in building quality into the product as it is produced.

Control chart theory supplies simple formulas and tables for computing the central and control limit lines. The control limits are set to strike a balance, based on experience, between looking for

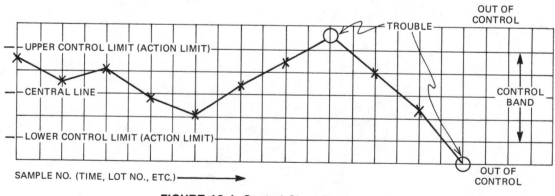

FIGURE 10-4. Control Chart Features
Courtesy of Canadian Marconi Company.

assignable causes when there are none present and not looking for assignable causes when they *are* present. The limits are usually ± 3 standard deviations. When a control chart is first applied to a manufacturing process, a state of control is not usually found. However, control must be established at a satisfactory level by the elimination of all assignable causes of variation from the process before maximum efficiency in the operation can be obtained.

> Quality must be built into the product—it can't be inspected into it.

Certain practical advantages may be realized when a control chart indicates that a process is operating in a state of control. The practical advantages are listed here:

- The variation between individual items is within an acceptable range.
- The quality of the product can be reliably judged by samples.
- The percent of product whose quality lies within any given limits can be accurately predicted.
- The amount of sampling inspection can be reduced.
- There is a basis for comparing the product with the specification because only chance variation is present and not assignable causes.

The control chart also gives useful production information such as (a) uniformity of product in terms of its basic variability, and (b) the average quality level of production.

It sometimes happens that the natural variation of a process is much less than the amount of variation permitted by the specification or tolerance limits. Under such circumstances, the process average may shift considerably within the tolerance limits without producing defective items. In such situations, it may not be worthwhile to take action to adjust for shifts in the process average. A special set of control limits may be computed to satisfy these conditions, and they are generally referred to as *modified control limits*. No attempt will be made here to discuss the theory and mechanics of this subject. However, a detailed discussion of the subject may be found in most statistical quality control texts.

There are two main types of control charts, depending on the two principal types of inspection:

1. Control charts for attributes (inspection by attributes)
2. Control charts for variables (inspection by variables)

Inspection is said to be by attributes when the unit of product is classified simply as *defective* or *nondefective* with respect to a given characteristic.

Inspection is said to be by variables when the quality characteristic to be inspected can be measured and is expressed quantitatively (pounds, feet, ohms, etc.).

The common control charts for attributes are:

1. Chart for fraction defective ... (chart for p)
2. Chart for number of defects per unit (or per hundred units) ... (chart for c)

The common control charts for variables are:

1. Chart for averages ... (chart for X)
2. Chart for ranges ... (chart for R)

The principal advantages of control charts for variables are that they provide more information about the process than does a p chart or a c chart, and trouble areas may be localized easier by their use. The chief disadvantages are that they are expensive to maintain, and a separate chart is required for each characteristic.

Example Using a C Chart

The opportunities for defects are numerous in many different kinds of articles, even though the chances of a defect occurring in any one spot are small. Whenever this is true, it is correct as a matter of statistical theory to base control limits on the assumption that the Poisson distribution is applicable.

It is normal in quality control work to define the upper and lower control limits at ± 3 standard deviations from the mean. In the case of the Poisson these are:

$$\text{UCL} = \bar{C} + 3 \sqrt{\bar{C}}; \; \text{LCL} = \bar{C} - 3 \sqrt{\bar{C}}$$

where $\bar{C}$ is the average number of defects per unit.

These equations can now be applied to develop control charts. The following data represent the number of defects found on each sewing machine cabinet inspected in a furniture plant.

Sample Number	Number of Defects	Sample Number	Number of Defects
1	8	14	6
2	10	15	4
3	7	16	7
4	7	17	5
5	8	18	8
6	6	19	6
7	9	20	4
8	8	21	5
9	4	22	7
10	7	23	4
11	9	24	5
12	6	25	5
13	5		

$$\bar{c} = \text{defects/unit} = \frac{160}{25} = 6.4 \text{ average}$$

$$\text{UCL} = \bar{c} - 3\sqrt{\bar{c}} = 6.4 + 3\sqrt{6.4} = 14.0$$

$$\text{LCL} = \bar{c} - 3\sqrt{\bar{c}} = 6.4 - 3\sqrt{6.4} \Rightarrow 0$$

All points are within control. There appears to be a trend toward a lower $\bar{c}$ in the second half of the chart. It is left to the reader as an exercise to plot the chart.

The application of control charts sometimes can be difficult because of short runs. Short runs are obviously troublesome because a certain preliminary amount of data is necessary to establish control limits. If the production run is fairly short, a new item may be due for processing by the time the controls for the present item being processed can be obtained. The obvious way to attempt to defeat the short-run problem is to control by type of work, by particular shop, by similar items successively processed, or by any other method that will "prolong" the run.

The only way to determine the method that can and should be employed to control a process is to examine all circumstances surrounding the specific problem and then make a decision. Whether control charts can be used successfully depends upon whether or not they fit the specific problem and actually work. There is no specific remedy to cure all problems; the available techniques must be tailored to cope with each problem individually.

Case in Point: As I was delivering a misdelivered envelope to a neighbor, I was met at the door by a man just on his way out with an envelope in his hand addressed to me. An even trade. My complaint to the regional postmaster brought the following reply:

> "Mistakes like the ones you point out are a source of irritation to us in the Canadian postal system, as they must be to you. This problem has been going on for years. We assure you that every mistake like the one that you mentioned is brought to the attention of the individual at fault."

"Going on for years" is a confession that the fundamental fault lies in the system. The trouble apparently is not localized by neighborhood, nor in time, nor is it specific to any one carrier. The most trivial control chart would make the true problem apparent: Unreliable delivery will continue until the system undergoes fundamental revision to reduce the possibility of mistakes. Meanwhile, the management unduly blames the carrier. Here we also encounter an important lesson in administration. This Postal Service has been sending a letter to a mail carrier at every mistake. It made no difference whether this was the one mistake of the year or the tenth: the letter was exactly the same. A letter sent to a reliable carrier is demoralizing: the carrier's interpretation thereof is that he is blamed for faults of the system. It is tempting to ask a question: What does the carrier who has already received ten warnings, all alike, think of the management?

EMPLOY DCF FOR CAPITAL EQUIPMENT INVESTMENT DECISIONS

Sound policies and methods are essential to management decisions in directing the limited funds available into those projects that indicate the highest profitability from among the many possible alternatives. An important criterion for such decisions is the financial evaluation of investment projects by the Discounted Cast Flow (DCF) method.

In the *discounted cash flow* method of evaluation, the future stream of net pretax cash receipts is discounted to present value by the discount rate that equates the present value of future receipts to the present value of the investment outlay. The discount rate so calculated is the percentage return on investment. From among the many alternative methods of evaluating investments, the DCF method offers several advantages:

- The analysis is made on the basis of cash flows and avoids any arbitrary assumptions in the accounting treatment of noncash items such as depreciation or in the amortization of initial expense.

- It properly recognizes the economic life and terminal value of a project, and the differences in economic life among alternative projects.

- It properly measures the time value of cash flows, giving more value to cash receipts in the near future and less value to receipts in the more distant future.

- It measures the return on investment in the same way that the values of investments are measured in the external financial markets from which company funds are ultimately obtained.

To grasp the concepts of the discounted cash flow method for calculating rates of return on investments, one must clearly understand the meaning of investment and investment return. A financial *investment* is an expenditure of money that is made with the expectation of recovery over a period of time that exceeds the expenditure. The future recovery in excess of the expenditure is the *return on investment*. The rate of recovery with respect to time is the *rate of return* on investment. The financial measurement of rate of return is the interest rate—the percentage ratio of excess return to investment per standard of time.

The element of time is inherent in all of these related definitions. The DCF method for measuring rates of return is based on the use of interest rates, which are compounded per standard period of time, in a way that recognizes the time value of money. It recognizes, for example, that one dollar received today is more valuable than one dollar received two years from now, and that one dollar received two years from now is worth more than one dollar received five years from now, because of the investment opportunities that are always available.

The concepts of the time value of money, and the DCF method for determining time values, can be most easily grasped by first looking at how invested money grows over time at an annually compounded rate of interest. If, for example, $1 is invested today for two years at a compounded annual interest rate of 10 percent, the return received at the end of two years will be $1.210.

$1.00 (1 + 0.10)^2 = \$1.210$

This relationship may be described symbolically. If D_o is the value of the initial deposit and i is the rate of interest per period, the dollar amount earned during the period is iD_o. The value of the deposit at the end of the year is given by the familiar formula:

$$D_n = D_o (1 + i)^n$$

When we speak about the future value of $1 invested today, we speak in terms of an interest rate. Inversely, if $1 is received at some point of time in the future, we speak of its value today being its *present value* at a particular *discount rate*. Discounting future income to present value is, therefore, simply the reverse mathematical process to determining the future value of an investment today at a compounding rate of interest. Discount rate equals interest rate. The difference in terminology is only due to the direction of the mathematical calculation in which a rate is being used.

In the types of compound interest calculations that most people are familiar with, the present investment rate of interest is usually given, and the problem is to find the value of the return received at some point of time in the future. In simple DCF calculations of return on investment, the mathematical input is the present investment and the return received in the future, and the problem is to find the rate of interest or discount rate that links the two inputs. The mathematical process is one of finding a rate that will discount the future receipts to a present value that will equal the value of the investment expenditure.

Note: The preceding examples and explanations deal with simple cases of a single investment expenditure being made now, and a single return being received at one point in the future. The evaluation of real life investment projects is somewhat complicated by the fact that the investment may not be just a single expenditure made now, and the return may be a number of cash receipts received at different points of time in the future throughout the economic life of the project. Nevertheless, the concepts and mathematical process are the same. By trial and error calculations, a discount rate is found that will discount all future cash receipts to a present value that equals the present value of the total investment expenditure.

To facilitate the process, standard discount tables are available that give the discount factors for various rates of return and points in the future. Alternatively, a calculator can readily provide the required answer. The trial calculations can be made at discount rates in 5 percent increments until a range is found that brackets the answer, and the answer can then be found by interpolation.

Case in Point: The following example of an investment project for a digital height gauge illustrates the use of discount factors to calculate the rate of return on investment. The calculation input is the estimate cash flow on the project, consisting of an investment expenditure of $3000 at the beginning of Year 1 and resulting cash receipts at the ends of Years 1 to 4.

	Investment Expenditure	Discount Factor 15%	Present Value
Start of Year 1	$3,000	1.000	3000
	Cash Receipt		
End of Year 1	$1200	.870	$1044
End of Year 2	1200	.756	906
End of Year 3	900	.658	591
End of Year 4	801	.572	459
Total	$4101		$3000

Since 15 percent is within management's tolerance band, the gauge would be purchased.

Pitfalls to Avoid:

- Use a realistic economic life for equipment. Normally one would use the shortest of (1) physical life, (2) technological life, or (3) market life of the product for which the equipment is being purchased.
- Don't forget to include expenses (noncapitalized) such as installation, periodic maintenance, and employee training in the analysis.
- The cost savings (cash receipts) must be conservative and should not imply any unrealistic precision.

The financial evaluation of project profitability will not necessarily be the only criterion for investment decisions. Other factors, such as degree of risk, strategic advantage, and indeterminant future alternatives, will all require managerial judgment, will influence a decision, and will in some cases outweigh the indications of financial evaluation. Nevertheless, financial evaluation will generally be an important criterion.

ACCEPTANCE SAMPLING

Inspection for the purpose of deciding on the acceptability of material is carried on at many points in the manufacturing cycle. For example:

- receiving inspection of incoming parts or materials
- process inspection at various points in manufacturing operations
- final inspection by the manufacturer
- inspection of the finished product by the purchaser

When material or parts are received from a vendor or from another department or plant, there are several methods of deciding whether to accept or reject the material or parts:

1. *No inspection at all.* This obviously involves a great risk of accepting material that is defective.

2. *One hundred percent inspection.* We can inspect every piece received. But, as is well known, 100 percent inspection is not 100 percent effective in removing defects. This is proven by manufacturing experience and by experiment.

In addition to the fact that 100 percent inspection is often less effective than sampling, it has other drawbacks:

- One hundred percent inspection is expensive.
- It obscures the actual risk involved, because the margin of error is not known.
- Because the margin of error is not known, the

information provided by one hundred percent inspection is relatively useless in improving the production process.

- One hundred percent inspection cannot be used for destructive testing, such as testing welds.
- Schedule delays.

3. *Spot-checking.* This is a compromise between no inspection and 100 percent inspection, but it means that many lots are accepted with no check on them.

4. *Acceptance sampling.* Acceptance sampling is the process of evaluating a portion of the product in a lot for the purpose of accepting or rejecting the entire lot as either conforming or not conforming to a quality specification. Acceptance sampling is scientific because it is based on the law of probability and can be proven through mathematics and through actual practice. Scientific sampling is a form of *statistical inference*—judging an entire lot on the basis of a certain number of pieces from the lot. The risks associated with sampling can be calculated.

The main advantage of sampling is economy. Despite some added costs to design and administer the sampling plans, the lower costs of inspecting only part of the lot result in an overall cost reduction. In addition to this major advantage there are others:

1. There is less damage to the product—handling incidental to inspection is itself a source of defects.
2. The lot is disposed of in shorter (calendar) time so that shop scheduling, inventory turns, and delivery are improved.
3. The problem of monotony and inspector error induced by 100 percent inspection is minimized.
4. Rejection (rather than sorting) of nonconforming lots tends to dramatize quality deficiencies and to urge the organization to look for preventive measures and keep vendors on their toes.
5. Proper design of the sampling plan commonly requires study of the actual level of quality required by the user. The resulting knowledge is a useful input to overall quality planning.
6. The smaller inspection staff is less complex to administer.

Sampling plans are usually selected from published tables designed for that purpose. The most widely used set of tables in American industry is the Military Standard Tables, commonly called MIL-STD. These tables have been approved by the Department of Defense. The MIL-STD-105D is applicable to inspection by attributes and MIL-STD-414 (ANSI Z 1.9) applies to sampling by variables.

Three kinds of sampling plans are in common use in industry:

- single sampling
- double sampling
- multiple (or sequential) sampling

It is possible to maintain the selected Acceptable Quality Level (AQL) with a plan of any of these types. Remember, though, that sampling inspection is an "after-the-fact" action—not a preventive action!

No sampling plan is perfect; there is always a chance that the sample may not contain the same proportion of defective pieces as the entire lot. On the basis of the sample, we may accept a bad lot or reject a good one.

Production supervisors must accept the fact that with any sampling plan they will receive some defectives. It may simply not be economical to try to cull out every defective piece reaching a department.

The risk of accepting a bad lot is known as the *consumer's risk*. The risk of rejecting a good lot is called the *producer's risk*. These risks are calculated and taken into account in designing specific sampling plans. For every sampling plan, the percentage of the lots of a given quality that will be accepted can be calculated. The relationship between the probability of acceptance and the lot quality for a given plan is called the Operating Characteristic (OC) curve. No quality manager should ever employ a sampling plan without first studying the OC curve.

The selection of an AQL is fundamental to the utilization of a sampling plan. The AQL is the maximum percent of defective pieces we can economically "live with." Ideally, the AQL is the most economical level of quality to maintain considering the cost of defective parts and the production and inspection costs of preventing them. (Some critics have referred to the AQL as "A Quick Look.")

Determining the AQL is an important and rather complex decision. Some of the factors that must be considered in establishing the AQL are:

- past experience with the quality of the particular item

- the critical nature of the part or material
- closeness of tolerances
- customer complaints
- the difficulty and expense of replacing the part later if it is found to be defective
- cost to attain the AQL

When the AQL has been determined, we have a measure of good quality. We want the sampling plan we select to accept nearly all (say, 90 percent) lots that are as good as or better than the AQL. We want to reject nearly all lots that have poorer quality than the AQL. We have to say "nearly all" because we know that any sampling plan has some risks and that we will occasionally make a wrong decision on the basis of the sample inspected.

Example: Suppose we have found that the breakeven percent defective is 3 percent and need to select an appropriate AQL using MIL-STD-105. The appropriate sampling plan should have a 50 percent probability of being sorted or sampled (that is, $P_a = .50$). Hence, we wish to find a sampling plan that has a $P_a = .50$ at 3 percent defective. For example, suppose resistors are received in 3000 piece lots. From Table I of MIL-STD-105D, the code letter is K. The following shows that the plan closest to having a $P_a = 0.50$ for a 3 percent defective level lies between .65 percent and 1 percent AQL (see Figure 10-5). In this particular example an AQL = 1 percent is most appropriate using the breakeven criterion.

The two main types of acceptance sampling plans in use today are (1) *attributes* and (2) *variables*. Attributes is the one most widely employed. The quality characteristic is classed as either acceptable or nonacceptable. It is usually the most economical method and with some quality characteristics the only method since no measurement can be made; the attribute is either present or absent.

In variables sampling the quality characteristic is measured and expressed as some quantity, such as length in inches for a mechanical part, or the capacitance in microfarads for an electrical capacitor. Variables plans have the primary advantage of offering equivalent protection with a smaller sample size compared to an attributes plan. In practice, however, these plans have had less application because:

- There is a strong dependence on the shape of the underlying distribution.

- Application is to only one characteristic at a time.
- Each measurement of a characteristic must be accurately made and recorded.
- A series of calculations are required after the measurements are made and tables must be consulted for constants.
- The result of the calculations is a figure of merit that is compared to a similar figure obtained by combining values extracted from the tables.
- Training and administration effort is more costly.

When production is slow or storage space is scarce it may be inconvenient or impossible to form products into very large lots. This consideration is very important because, as stated previously, the discriminatory power of a lot-by-lot sampling plan is primarily dependent on the sample size. Thus, if the lot is small, a large percentage of the lot may have to be inspected in order to obtain the necessary discrimination. The corresponding cost of inspection is high and the advantages of sampling are lost.

To solve this type of problem, plans have been developed for inspecting product produced by a continuous production process. These continuous sampling plans, in one form or another, are currently employed on such diverse items as aircraft engines, radio receivers, bearings, guided missile assemblies, ammunition of many types, and packing and packaging lines. A continuous plan adjusts the percentage of inspection to the quality of material being produced. If quality is good, little protection, hence little inspection, is required; if quality is bad, however, an acceptable product can be obtained only by sorting the good items from the bad.

Continuous plans, therefore, require the percentage of inspection to "oscillate" between 100 percent inspection and some preassigned sampling percentage. Hence, 100 percent inspection is utilized until evidence is present to indicate that good quality is being produced. When this evidence is present, 100 percent inspection is discontinued and sampling inspection installed. The sampling is then continued until evidence is present to indicate the desired level of quality is not being produced, at which time 100 percent inspection is reinstituted. For example, the simplest kind of continuous plan might require (a) 100 percent inspection until fifty-five consecutive nondefective items are found; (b) inspection of 10

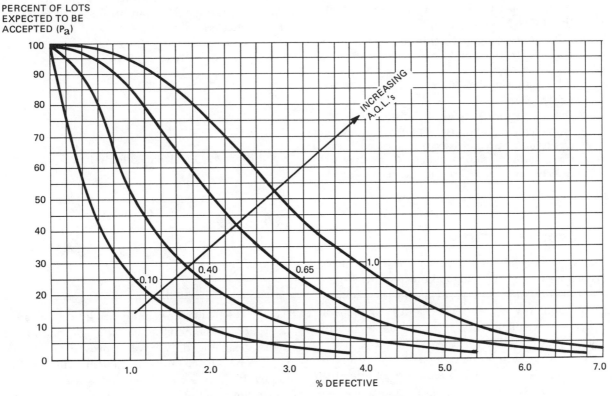

PERCENT OF LOTS
EXPECTED TO BE
ACCEPTED (P_a)

FIGURE 10-5. OC Curves from MIL-STD-105

Pa	AQL					
	0.10	0.40	0.65	1.0	1.5	2.5
	% defective					
50.0	0.55	1.34	2.14	2.94	4.54	6.14

percent of the items when requirement "a" is fulfilled; (c) return to level "a" when one of the sampled items is found to be defective.

This plan is a single-level plan because only one level of sampling is permitted. Single-level plans that do not immediately revert to 100 percent inspection upon discovery of a defect are also available. The occurrence of two defects within a sequence of a predetermined number of inspected items is necessary before 100 percent inspection is reinstituted in this type of plan.

Because continuous sampling does not require formation of lots, the concept of lot probability of acceptance does not exist. Hence, indexing the plans by means of the AQL is not practical. Each plan does have an associated Average Outgoing Quality Limit (AOQL) that is used for indexing the plan. For example, the plan discussed above has an AOQL of approximately 2 percent. The protection (AOQL) can be tightened by either increasing the required 100 percent of inspection number or by increasing the percentage of inspection when sampling. It should be noted that AOQL and AQL are not identical. In practice, the process average must usually be a maximum of only half as large as the AOQL in order to permit sampling to be exercised a reasonable portion of the time. Tables have been developed by H. F. Dodge and others for selecting continuous sampling plans to provide any desired AOQL.

Caution: The application of continuous sampling plans is relatively complex. If you feel the answer to your problem may lie in some sort of continuous plan, it will probably be best to consult a person who is thoroughly familiar with such plans.

Pitfalls to Avoid: Attempts to use acceptance sampling have run into trouble for the following reasons:

- Nonrandom selection of samples from the lot. This can be rectified by proper training and supervision.

- Faulty interpretation of the sampling plan. Again, proper inspector training can overcome this source of error.
- Taking of additional samples beyond those called for by the sampling plan in order to pass the lot. A common error is taking a second or third sample or discarding some of the rejected pieces.
- Refusal to accept "reject" decisions based on sampling. Although production will always go along with "accept" decisions, "reject" decisions are not condoned and usually result in 100 percent screening of the lot to keep assembly lines rolling.

TEST YOUR HYPOTHESES

Our knowledge about any process or lot advances accordingly as we form logical but tentative judgments about the lot or process and then subject such judgments to a test. The tentative judgment is frequently called a *hypothesis,* and the process of testing that hypothesis is a *test of hypothesis.*

These tests of hypotheses consist of making decisions relative to the truth or falsity of some beforehand judgment about a lot characteristic. The decision is based upon the results of a sample drawn at random from the lot.

In hypothesis testing, we tentatively assume the outcome will be negative (say, no significant difference in the output of the machine). This tentative negative assumption is called the *null hypothesis,* and is usually designated Ho. If Ho is proved wrong (statistically unreasonable), the result is clearly decisive. If it is not proved wrong, the result is said to be "not proven" under the conditions of the experiment. It is important to realize that a null hypothesis can never be absolutely proven or established by a finite sample experiment; it can only be disproved. If it is disproved, we accept the alternative hypothesis, Hi. A growing body of professional statisticians feel that two-sided tests should be used routinely because in all experiments there is some doubt about the direction of the outcome.

Example: A certain printing press is known to turn out an average of forty-five copies a minute. In an attempt to increase its output, a quality improvement is made to the machine, and then in three short test runs it turns out forty-six, forty-seven, and forty-eight copies a minute. Is this in-

crease statistically significant, or is it the result of chance variation? This can be answered by using the t distribution:

$$t = \frac{(\mu - \bar{X})}{s/\sqrt{N-1}}$$

N = 3 (given)

$$\bar{X} = \frac{46 + 47 + 48}{3} = 47$$

$s = \sqrt{2/3}$ (calculated from data)

$\mu = 45$ (given)

$$\text{Now } t_{observed} = \frac{\sqrt{3-1}\ (47\text{–}45) = \sqrt{3(2)} = 3.46}{\sqrt{2/3}}$$

Ho: $\mu = 45$ the null hypothesis

Hi: $\mu > 45$ the alternative hypothesis

Now at the 99 percent confidence level (*a one-sided test* is applicable here because we believe that the alteration could only have improved the press), $t_{0.99,2} = 6.96$ from tables of the t distribution (see Figure 10-6). Since $t_{observed}$ (3.46) is less than this, we cannot conclude that a significant difference in means has been proven and the machine alteration is not statistically significant.

If $t_{observed}$ had equalled, say, 9.5, then we would have to conclude that the machine really had made a significant output improvement. A value as high as 9.5 would have only a 1 percent chance of occurrence on the basis of chance variation alone. This is so unlikely that we assume that the machine alteration did really improve the output. We could be wrong, however, and if we accept Ho when it really should be rejected, we are making what is called a *type II error.* (The numerical value of the type II error depends on the true value of

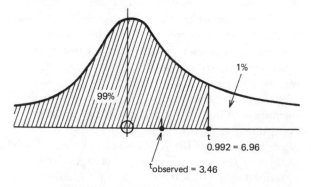

FIGURE 10-6. The "t" Distribution

the population mean.) If we reject a hypothesis that is really true, we are making what is called a *type I error*. Either type of error is undesirable, but the probability of occurrence can be assessed and minimized by judicious selection of sample sizes. (See Table 10-5 for a summary of formulas for the most frequently used tests.)

Observations: The fact that the sample does not give statistical evidence of change does not mean that there has been no change. It is proof only that there has been no change of such size that chance alone cannot explain it. If it is essential to detect small changes, the sample size must be increased. Even if the observed change is large enough to show up as statistically significant, a hypothesis test does not say how much change has actually occurred.

Nonparametric methods, in which only mild assumptions about underlying distributions are required, have also been developed. Such techniques include the Mann-Whitney test, the Wilcoxon test and the Wald runs test. These tests are covered in standard intermediate-level statistics texts. They should form an integral part of a QC person's statistical tool kit.

QUEUING THEORY

Production bottlenecks arise whenever too many items arrive at a machine or test station at the same time. These bottlenecks are called *queues* and generally occur because the arrival and servicing rate of material to be processed is not absolutely known or static. Queuing is a mathematical procedure for analyzing a waiting line.

TABLE 10–5. Summary of Formulas on Tests of Hypotheses

Hypotheses	*Test Statistic and Distribution*
1. H: $\mu = \mu_0$ (the mean of a normal population is equal to a specific value μ_0; σ is known)	$u = \dfrac{\bar{x} - \mu_0}{\sigma/\sqrt{n}}$ normal distribution
2. H: $\mu = \mu_0$ (the mean of a normal population is equal to a specific value μ_0; σ is estimated by s, the sample standard deviation)	$t = \dfrac{\bar{x} - \mu_0}{s/\sqrt{n}}$ t — distribution with n-1 degrees of freedom (DF)
3. H: $\mu_1 = \mu_2$ (the mean of population 1 is equal to the mean of population 2; assume that $\sigma_1 = \sigma_2$ and that both populations are normally distributed)	$t = \dfrac{\bar{x}_1 - \bar{x}_2}{\sqrt{\frac{1}{n_1} + \frac{1}{n_2}} \ \sqrt{[(n_1 - 1) s_1^2 + (n_2 - 1) s_2^2] / (n_1 + n_2 - 2)}}$ t distribution with DF = $n_1 + n_2 - 2$
4. H: $\sigma = \sigma_0$ (the standard deviation of a normal population is equal to a specified value σ_0)	$x^2 = (n-1) \dfrac{s^2}{\sigma^2}$ chi-square distribution with DF = n-1
5. H: $\sigma_1 = \sigma_2$ (the standard deviation of population 1 is equal to the standard deviation of population 2; assume that both populations are normally distributed)	$F = s_1^2/s_2^2$ F distribution with $DF_1 = n_1 - 1$ and $DF_2 = n_2 - 1$
6. H: $\rho = \rho_0$ (the fraction defective in population is equal to a specific value ρ_0; assume that $n\rho_0 \geq 5$)	$u = \rho - \rho_0/\sqrt{\rho_0 (1 - \rho_0)/n}$ Normal distribution
7. H: $\rho_1 = \rho_2$ (the fraction defective in population 1 is equal to the fraction defective in population 2; assume that $n_1 \rho_1$ and $n_2 \rho_2$ are each ≥ 5).	$u = \dfrac{x_1/n_1 - x_2/n_2}{\sqrt{\hat{\rho}(1 - \hat{\rho}) (\frac{1}{n_1} + \frac{1}{n_2})}}$; $\hat{\rho} = \dfrac{x_1 + x_2}{n_1 + n_2}$ Normal distribution

Three types of waiting lines often operate in business. One is that seen in a doctor's office, where arriving patients form one line and are served through only one station—the doctor. Another is seen in a barber shop where people form one line and are served through several stations—any of the barbers. A third type of queue is in a supermarket where customers form many lines and are served through many stations—the checkout counters.

Queuing theory is used to determine averages for: (1) queue length, (2) waiting time of an arrival, (3) arrivals who have to wait, and (4) idle time of a server. Such information can be used, among other things, to improve production flow. You might, for instance, assume that you can speed up service on an expensive machine by increasing the number of inexpensive production stations that precede it. You can test this assumption by using a queuing formula that would compare the average characteristics of your current waiting line with the new characteristics you think should improve the system.

Consider the simplest case of a single service station. In general, jobs (work orders) do not arrive at regular intervals, but tend to be clustered or scattered in some fashion. The Poisson assumption specifies the behavior of arrivals by postulating the existence of the average number arriving per unit time, a constant, such that the probability of an arrival occurring between time t and t + Δt is equal to Δt providing Δt is sufficiently small. An analogous statement applies to each servicing station (that is, probability a serviced unit is turned out during Δt is equal to $\mu\Delta$ where μ is the average number serviced per unit time if the work center is busy). If you bother to work out the mathematics, the average number of units in the system is

$$\bar{n} = \frac{\lambda}{\mu - \lambda} \text{ where}$$

n = number in system and P_n = probability of "n" in system.

P_o means there are no units in the system.

Other related formulas that may be derived or found in standard operations research textbooks are:

$$E(m) = \frac{\mu}{\mu - \lambda} \text{ average length of nonempty queues, and}$$

$$E(w) = \frac{\lambda}{\mu\ (\mu - \lambda)} \text{ average waiting time of an arrival}$$

If a work center with a mean service time of three minutes is faced with jobs arriving at intervals of ten minutes on average, we can make the following statements:

1. The probability (P) that a job will have to wait is

$$P = 1 - P_o = \frac{\lambda}{\mu} = \frac{0.1}{0.33} = 0.3$$

2. The average length of queues that form from time to time at the work center is

$$\frac{\mu}{\mu - \lambda} = \frac{0.33}{0.33 - 0.10} = 1.43 \text{ work orders}$$

3. The average waiting time of a work order is

$$\frac{\lambda}{\mu(\mu - \lambda)} = \frac{0.1}{0.33(0.33 - .10)} = 1.317 \text{ minutes}$$

These results frequently do not meet with initial intuition, but they do describe a very real situation. If the interval between arrivals were halved to five minutes ($\lambda = 0.20$) we would have the average waiting time of a work order rising to

$$\frac{0.2}{0.33\ (0.33 - 0.20)} = 4.66 \text{ minutes}$$

A heavily loaded work center is sensitive to small load variations because of queuing and other problems. For a work center subject to random arrival of work having random service times, as the load approaches 100 percent of capacity, the queue length $E(m)$ approaches infinity. In fact, if you think back to any experience you may have had in machine shops, incoming inspection facilities, computer rooms, supermarket checkouts, and so forth, you may recall that, as load passed about 70 percent of capacity, the problem of getting the load through the facilities became acute.

Case in Point: A manufacturer of naval direction-finding equipment received thirty lots of material per day. On the average, each inspector can inspect six lots per day. Using queuing theory we can determine the proper number of personnel to assign to this inspection station. Backlog (average number of lots in queue) can be taken as the decision criterion. This involves multiple servicing stations and a relatively complex model. From any Operations Research (OR) text the average queue length is found to be:

$$E(m) = \frac{\lambda\mu \, (\lambda/\mu)^k \, P_o}{(k-1)! \, (k\mu-\lambda)^2}$$

where

$$P_o = \cfrac{1}{\left[\sum \cfrac{1}{n!} \left(\cfrac{\lambda}{\mu} \right)^n \right] + \cfrac{1}{k!} \left(\cfrac{\lambda}{\mu} \right)^k \cfrac{k\mu}{k\mu-\lambda}}$$

k = the number of inspectors
λ = mean arrival rate (30 in this case)
μ = mean servicing rate (6 per day per inspector)
λ/μ = 5 (a constant for this problem)

Take a test trial at $k=6$.

Clearly,

$$P_o = \cfrac{1}{\cfrac{1}{0!}(5)^0 + \cfrac{1}{1!}(5)^1 + \cfrac{1}{2!}5^2 + \cfrac{5^3}{3!} + \cfrac{5^4}{4!} + \cfrac{5^5}{5!} + \cfrac{5^6}{6!} \cfrac{(6)(6)}{6(6)-30}}$$

$$= \cfrac{1}{1 + 5 + 12.5 + 20.83 + 26.04 + 26.04 + 156.24}$$

$$= \frac{1}{247.65} = .00404$$

Thus

$$E(m) = \frac{30(6)5^6}{5! \, (6 \times 6 - 30)^2} \times .00404$$

$$= \frac{180 \times 15625 \times .00404}{120 \times 6 \times 6}$$

$$= 2.63 = \text{average queue length}$$

If six inspectors are assigned, a small backlog of three lots will occur. If seven inspectors are assigned, the backlog will be reduced to just under one lot but idle time will increase. If five inspectors are used, the backlog will be so large that the howls will be heard from production control clear up to the general manager's office!

On a conceptual level, the use of queuing theory vocabulary and concepts may provide the executive with additional insight into many common business situations. And any manager who conceives of these situations in terms of arrival rates, service times, queue disciplines, and service channels has a head start over other executives in thinking of new alternatives to the existing ways of doing business. Queuing theory concepts should definitely form a part of the modern quality manager's options.

RESOURCE ALLOCATION

Allocation of resources can be tackled by quantitative methods. The general problem is to take n resources (say, inspectors) and assign them to n machines or jobs, knowing what the cost (or time) of each choice is. The task is to minimize the total cost of the assignment. This is a task that cannot conveniently be done by enumeration; for example, a mere four inspectors can be assigned to four machines in twenty-four ways. The Hungarian method quickly solves the problem. Take the relatively simple example of four inspectors to be assigned to four jobs, it being known that the time taken by each worker on each job would be as in Figure 10-7(a). Let us find an assignment that would minimize the sum of the times taken. We assume that all inspectors are paid at the same rate; if not, costs should be used instead.

The procedure is as follows:

1. First modify the time (cost) matrix, Figure 10-7(a). Deduct the smallest (nonzero) time in each column from all entries in that column, obtaining at least one zero in each column, Figure 10-7(b). For column A for instance, this is fifteen.

2. In each row of positive entries deduct the smallest time from all entries in that row. In Figure 10-7(b) this applies only to the second row because all the others already have zeros. The result is Figure 10-7(c) after subtracting 1 from row b. If step 1 had produced at least one zero in each row as well, this step would be omitted.

3. Now draw the minimum number of lines that will cover all the zeros. In Figure 10-7(c) three lines suffice. If there are as many such lines as there are rows or columns, an optimal assignment is possible. If not, the matrix must be changed. Here there are three lines instead of four, so the next step is necessary.

4. In Figure 10-7(c) subtract the smallest uncovered entry (which is three) from all uncovered entries. Enter the results in Figure 10-7(d). Then

JOBS

WORKERS

(a)

	A	B	C	D
a	15	18	21	24
b	19	23	22	18
c	26	17	16	19
d	19	21	23	17

(b)

	A	B	C	D
a	0	1	5	7
b	4	6	6	1
c	11	0	0	2
d	4	4	7	0

(c)

	A	B	C	D
a	0	1	5	7
b	3	5	5	0
c	11	0	0	2
d	4	4	7	0

(d)

	A	B	C	D
a	0	1	5	10
b	0	2	2	0
c	11	0	0	5
d	1	1	4	0

(e)

	A	B	C	D
a	0	0	4	10
b	0	1	1	0
c	12	0	0	6
d	1	0	3	0

FIGURE 10-7. Assignment matrices

add the same number to the elements at which the lines of Figure 10-7(c) cross [seven in line (a) and two in line (c)], obtaining ten and five, respectively. Enter these results in Figure 10-7(c) and complete the figure by entering the other covered elements without change.

5. Repeat step 3. In Figure 10-7(d) it is again possible to cover all zeros with only three lines. Therefore repeat step 4, obtaining Figure 10-7(e) in which four lines are necessary. Thus it is an optimal matrix.

6. Make the actual assignments, starting with the zero that is unique in its row or column. (If no such zero exists, start with any zero.) Here this is cC. Complete the assignment; as may sometimes happen, there are more than one. The two solutions are:

cC,aA,bD,dB; Time = 16 15 18 21 = 70 Ans.

cC,aA,bA,dD; Time = 16 18 19 17 = 70 Ans.

Typically, when this problem is given to quality planner trainees, the result is seventy-five hours or 7 percent less than optimum. More complex problems obviously require quantitative analysis rather than intuition to ensure optimality.

SIMULATE YOUR PROBLEMS

Situations frequently arise in which some method of sampling is indicated, but the actual taking of a physical sample is either impossible or too expensive. In such situations, useful information can often be obtained from some type of simulated sampling. Typically, simulated sampling involves replacing the actual population of items by its theoretical counterpart, a population described by some assumed probability distribution, and then sampling at random from this theoretical population by means of a random number table or computer-generated random number(s). The methods of taking such a sample, as well as the discussion of decision problems which rely heavily on such sampling methods, are often referred to by the general term *Monte Carlo methods.*

There are several advantages of the Monte Carlo approach over the just looking at the actual process and forming a history of statistical information. For one thing, simulated sampling, especially when done on a digital computer, can develop months or years of data in a matter of a few minutes. Another advantage is that manipulation can be made of those factors that are subject to control. For example, using Monte Carlo methods, we can readily assess the effect of adding one or more test facilities without actually having to go to the trouble and expense of installing them. Changes in queue discipline can be tried out experimentally on paper, without any disruption of the actual process itself. Simulation can also be used for statistically tolerancing stacked assemblies, evaluating functional units, or optimizing the location of QC stations along a production line.

To draw an item at random from a universe described by the probability density f(x), one proceeds as follows:

1. Plot the cumulative probability function*

$$y = F(x) = \int_{-\infty}^{x} f(u)du$$

2. Choose a random decimal between 0 and 1 (to as many places as desired) by means of a table of random digits.
3. Project horizontally the point on the y axis corresponding to this random decimal, until the projection line intersects the curve y = F(x) (see Figure 10-8).
4. Write down the value of x corresponding to the point of intersection. This value of x is taken as the sample value of x.

Example: The range of a sample is the difference between the largest and smallest values in the sample. Estimate the mean range in samples of five drawn from a Gaussian (normal) distribution.

We read off a sample of five from a random normal number table and obtain: 1.119, −0.792, 0.063, 0.484, 1.045. This sample has range 1.911.

Continuing in this way, we obtain ranges of 1.334, 2.633, 3.089, 3.844, 3.013, 3.825, 1.073, 2.488, 1.292, 2.390, 2.796, 2.841, 2.274, 2.827, 1,633, 1.112, 1.730, 3.353, 3.783, 1.433, 2.828, 3.883, 2.621, 2.250. These twenty-five separate observations of the range have a mean of 2.490.

Thus, our estimate of the mean range in samples of five from a normal distribution with standard deviation σ(and any μ) is 2.490σ. This compares with the exact theoretical value for the mean range in samples of five of 2.326σ.

Caution: Simulation is a widely used and extremely powerful tool. However, considerable knowledge of the process to be simulated is needed to use this technique effectively. Obtaining the knowledge in the required depth is expensive, and a balance must be reached between the cost of acquiring the knowledge and the potential benefits.

IMPLEMENT DECISIONS CAREFULLY

One of the greatest shortfalls of quality control managers is their inability to successfully implement even well-conceived decisions. All too often QC decisions are made without good business sense, are not coordinated with other affected departments, optimize the wrong variables, and are poorly sold and communicated and sometimes even forced on others. QC is one of the few departments whose mandate formally includes functional tasks (say, testing) and control tasks (for example, passing judgment on the work of others). For this reason, quality management must be cautious when making decisions.

Quality managers must learn to realize that a significant fraction of their decisions affect the orderly flow of work in other departments. Consequently, QC must coordinate many decisions with production, engineering, and procurement. The very act of soliciting comments from these departments on proposed quality decisions will help improve interdepartmental relationships; it will also probably lead to an improved decision. Table 10-6 lists some classic examples of how not to implement a decision.

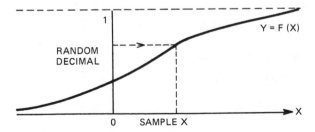

FIGURE 10-8. Monte Carlo Sampling: "Drawing an Item" from a Population with Cumulative Distribution Function F(x)

TABLE 10-6. Typical List of Quality Decision Failures

1. One of the four incoming inspectors was on sick leave for two months with a major illness. Rather than bring in temporary help or work overtime, the QC manager optimized his budget. The resulting parts shortages in assembly caused inventory buildups and missed deliveries.

2. All inspectors were granted vacation during a period when production was working 15 percent overtime.

3. A unilateral change in quality control operating procedures necessitated the hiring of two clerks in purchasing to provide the necessary data required by the changed procedure. This wiped out all the projected cost savings.

4. A new workmanship standard was introduced to the shop floor. Although it provided better control of product quality, it was not operationally effective because it had not been discussed with manufacturing, engineering, or supervision before release. The "not-invented-here" attitude is a powerful industrial force that QC must reckon with.

5. A batch of nonconforming material was physically scrapped and thrown in the scrap bin. Besides displaying gross industrial manners, QC had thrown out thousands of dollars of gold plated parts that could have been salvaged had the appropriate people been notified.

6. A QC auditor proposed costly revisions in material control practices to prevent recurrence of an unlikely event. These were successfully contested but only after eight memos and three meetings. Remember:

Advocates rest content that they argued well; deciders must live with their decisions.

---

7. Additional measuring equipment was purchased to deal with an increasing workload. Unfortunately, the product line using this equipment was to be phased out in six months and replaced by a new product requiring an altogether new approach to testing. This information was readily available from marketing, but no one had bothered to consult with them.

8. Company-funded educational assistance ($50) was denied to a quality engineer on the grounds that the course in finance had marginal relevance to her job. Besides being shortsighted, the manager should have given the benefit of the doubt to the engineer, especially considering the sum involved. At the end of the year the educational assistance fund was underspent and the QE requested a transfer to another department. This is a perfect example of being penny wise and pound foolish.

Pitfall to Avoid: Sometimes quality decisions are made based on an outburst of emotion. This can lead to the "bull in the china shop" syndrome, which gives QC a bad image. Stay cool, don't react to actual or perceived provocations before consolidating your thoughts.

REFERENCES

"Case Histories on Statistical Methods for Quality Control." ASQC, 1964.

Friedman, L., M Sasieni, and A. Yaspan. *Operations Research—Methods and Problems.* New York: John Wiley, 1959.

Kazmierski, A. S. "Work Sampling for QC Managers." *Quality Progress,* Jan. 1971.

Kimber, R. J. "The Decision Tree—An Aid to the Quality Professional." *Quality,* Sept. 1979.

Kivenko, K. "Better Decisions with Statistics." *Assembly Engineering,* March 1978.

Martin, W. I. "Economic Justification or How to Succeed in Applied Statistics." *Industrial Quality Control,* July 1967.

McCall, J. C. "Renewal Theory—Predicting Product Failure and Replacement." *Machine Design,* March 25, 1976.

Mundel, A. B. "Acceptance by Variables for Percent Defective." *Quality Progress,* Feb. 1977.

Schilling, E. G. "Variables Sampling and MIL-STD-414." *Quality Progress,* May 1974.

Shainin, D. "The Statistically Designed Experiment: A Tool for Process and Product Improvement." *Harvard Business Review,* July-Aug. 1957.

Shainin, D. "Unusual Practices for Defect Control." *Quality Management and Engineering,* Feb. 1972.

Sheffer, E. A. "Reduce Circuit Manufacturing Costs." *Electronic Design,* July 19, 1976.

Spotts, M. F. "Monte Carlo Simulation." *Machine Design,* Nov. 20, 1980.

White, L. S. "Shortest Route Models for the Allocation of Inspection Effort on a Production Line." *Management Science,* Jan. 1969.

- Increased utilization and more efficient use of machine tools and other capital equipment.
- Faster delivery time to the customer.

The CAD/CAM thrust in the manufacturing sector requires large amounts of user-oriented, mechanical, process, and systems engineering. With the advent of CAD/CAM, the design of the factory will be just as important as the design of the product. Development will lead increasingly to the marriage of both CAD and CAM into integrated design and production systems. The impact on product quality and the QC function will be enormous.

Quality control will have to change procedures and technical skills to cope with the integrated factory:

1. Emphasis will be placed on computer software quality assurance techniques.
2. Drawings will be replaced by magnetic tapes and other coded media, thus altering our concepts of configuration control and documentation.
3. Design specifications will have to be meticulously validated for fitness for use, safety, and completeness before commencement of engineering activity.
4. Early quality planning will become even more crucial to a product's commercial success.
5. Environmental, reliability, life, and usage tests will be a fundamental quality control activity.
6. Corrective action loops both in-house and with suppliers will have to be very fast.
7. Validation of machine and measuring equipment maintenance and calibration will be a major QC task.
8. Procurement quality control will become a larger portion of the total QC effort.
9. New sensors and measuring equipment will need to be developed and harnessed so as to be compatible with the real-time capabilities of computer-based manufacturing processes.

DO YOU NEED A COMPUTER?

One of the first decisions that a quality manager must make is to decide whether to use a manual or a computer-based system.

√ Can the planned application be handled practically without help from a computer?

√ Can manual systems update the data base rapidly enough to be useful?

√ Will a manual system provide the required information in every fashion in which the information may likely be required?

√ Is a manual system more economical to operate?

√ Can a manual approach cope with the expected rate of growth?

√ Can the computer do multiple tasks?

Case in Point: A small firm specializing in the manufacture of CB sets acquired an inexpensive microcomputer and line printer for quality data analysis. After debugging, the system provided weekly reports on the following Monday. Previously, with the manual system, the report had come out on Wednesday. Report accuracy was also greatly enhanced. The really big saving, however, came from an unexpected source —reliability engineering. A computer program was written to perform reliability predictions. Data-processing time was cut from eight hours to three minutes. The statistics clerk was no longer required and was transferred to an open position in accounting. The microcomputer system had literally paid for itself in two months.

√ Can the computer provide cost-effective reports not now currently feasible with a manual system?

√ Will the current organization, procedures, and people be able to use and maintain a computer-based information system?

Software costs are a large part of the cost of a computer system. You can often get a lot of "free" help, however. For instance, when creating a quality information system it is not necessary to reinvent the wheel. Many quality organizations have already created quality data systems, and they are willing to share their experiences with their colleagues in those instances in which proprietary information is not involved. Some government agencies, trade associations, or even your customers may loan you useful software packages. It is frequently not necessary to write special programs for computer or programmable calculators. The manufacturers of these machines make available many standard statistical and report-generating programs that require only that the data be submitted to them in correct form. *The Journal of Quality Technology* (an ASQC publication) also has a multitude of statistical programs available.

Caution: "Canned" programs don't always produce exactly what the individual quality control person needs; they usually require some modification which, in the end, may be more costly than writing the complete program to operate on a specific set of data.

A general purpose computer has many applications in the field of quality control. The following is a brief listing:

- quality information systems
- reliability prediction and worst-case analysis
- statistical analysis, control chart preparation
- quality cost analysis and reporting
- routine QC administration such as automated calibration recall and preventive maintenance schedules

EXAMPLE: AUTOMATED CALIBRATION RECALL

Even the smallest of job shops may have hundreds of measuring instruments for the production of parts for customers. In small shops, recalibration records may not exist or may exist only as cursory paperwork systems. At the other end of the scale, a larger company might have 100,000 measuring instruments with over 50,000 active at any one time. A great deal of scrap and rework can be avoided when the gauges used for set-up or acceptance are in calibration. They can be easily and economically tracked on an inexpensive microcomputer, thus reducing clerical costs, improving accuracy and timeliness, and increasing flexibility.

The typical instrument history software module consists of two subsystems: recalibration and usage. The first subsystem, recalibration, is usually a complete scheduling system in conformance with such specifications for calibration systems as MIL-C-45662A. Each time a gauge is recalibrated, a line of history is generated and is added to the existing history for the gauge. Recall reports are generated to provide advance notice of upcoming calibrations. Delinquency reports are generated for gauges that were not calibrated at the specified time. The recalibration subsystem also allows searches to be performed based on age, description, or physical location.

The usage subsystem maintains complete loan-and-return histories for each instrument or gauge. In addition, status reports are provided for active, inactive, lost, defective, and obsolete gauges.

Other quality control uses include:

- Simulation programs for use in statistical tolerancing, sampling plan evaluation, quality cost optimization.
- Computer-aided process planning and work sampling programs.
- Decision tree analysis.
- Feedback control, such as computerized trend analysis and signaling for corrective action.
- QC cost estimating, electronic spreadsheets.
- Machine sequencing logic, such as computer control on one or several inspection devices under programmed automatic operation.
- Electronic mail and facsimile communication with vendors and customers.

The opportunities are there, the technology is available, and prices are falling so rapidly that most inspection devices now have their own dedicated minicomputer or microprocessor. The challenge for QC is to intelligently apply this new technology to improve quality and increase productivity.

COMPUTERIZATION AND PEOPLE

In the past, one did not normally think of technological change within the quality control function as adversely impacting or significantly displacing personnel. However, it is clear that some of the largest productivity gains because of the computer will, in fact, derive directly and indirectly through automated test/computer-aided process control; on-line, real-time, computer-based quality information systems; and a myriad of computer-controlled production/inspection equipments.

If we look at the situation only a few years into the future, remote data collection devices, in some cases coupled with automatic inspection and measuring equipment, will furnish inspection data to our own and our vendors' Management Information Systems (MIS). Reference will be made to data banks of past dispositions and failure analyses, to determine—or at least recommend—disposition of defective material. Quality reports will be integrated into a common, company-wide MIS. Much of the routine work done today will have disappeared; therefore, some people's jobs may become obsolete.

It is, therefore, important that those people affected be considered. These include clerical personnel, inspectors, statisticians, test technicians, and even quality engineers.

The potential impact on personnel should be identified during the planning phase of a project. If applicable, the union should be contacted and a jointly prepared resolution derived. In any event, the usual actions should be considered: retraining, transfer, downgrading, early retirement, and so on. Good management requires that no effort be spared to prevent and solve personnel relations problems.

Pitfall to Avoid: Don't keep potential personnel dislocations to yourself. Contact the personnel or industrial relations department as soon as a problem becomes apparent, even if it is a year or two away. These problems often take considerable time to solve.

HOW TO COLLECT QUALITY DATA EFFICIENTLY

Every company—regardless of size, wealth, or business—collects quality data. Systems range from simple manual systems to on-line, real-time, computer-controlled procedures complete with message switching, process monitoring, and other complex techniques.

The company with no formalized data collection system is not necessarily in a dangerous position for the future, but it could be. Just how much volume is enough to warrant a formalized data collection system is a moot point. It is generally conceded that it's better to have some system regardless of how low the volume may be—if only to identify quality problems, ensure accurate records, and be able to spot trends for timely corrective action. The availability of low-cost computers has made such systems economically viable even for the small firm. The following checklist indicates symptoms of inefficient data collection.

Symptoms of Inefficient Quality Data Collection

√ Does your present system provide late, inaccurate comparisons of actual QC costs and hours to standard costs and hours?

√ Do supervisors keep their own records?

√ Are reports arriving too late for any corrective action that might be needed?

√ Is there friction between departments because errors cannot be pinpointed?

√ Are delivery dates unmet?

√ Is product quality falling below acceptable levels?

√ Do internal and/or external communication gaps exist?

√ Are there obvious discrepancies in production and QC reports?

√ Are production yields known?

√ Is it possible to prepare a quality cost report?

√ Do you know who the top ten problem vendors are?

√ Are data on engineering changes available?

√ Have you achieved optimum balance of direct and indirect labor productivity?

√ What percent of inspector time is spent in clerical work?

√ Have you achieved optimum equipment loading or are some pieces of test equipment overloaded while others stand idle?

√ Do you have excessive downtime on measuring equipment?

√ Are scrap and rework costs collected?

√ Is your calibration recall program in control?

√ Do you make decisions based on quality reports currently available, or have these reports lost credibility?

√ Are warranty costs collected and disseminated?

The need for timely product quality information is essential for effective control of quality.

Case in Point: One firm introduced an integrated on-line failure reporting system coup that combined incoming inspection, assembly test, and field failures. Cycle time was slashed by 15 percent and quality costs by 10 percent a year after introduction, because of faster feedback and corrective action.

Figure 11-2 shows the breadth of coverage of the quality information system. The outputs of such a system typically include:

● vendor rating
● defect failure report summaries
● product yields
● quality rating on outgoing product
● rework/scrap loss reports due to defects
● costs of acceptance

- costs of prevention
- warranty reports
- customer complaint summaries
- status position of solution of major problems

It is not necessary to wait until quality data can be integrated into the company's existing data processing system in order to test and demonstrate the usefulness of a quality data system. Time-sharing computer services can be purchased at reasonable cost to show what advantages, if any, will result from detailed analysis and reporting of quality data. The companies that sell this service are also able to provide assistance in creating the system and often have already available programs and report formats that can be adopted easily to quality records. A trial system created by this means need not attempt to include all the quality data available; detailed results for one or two functions and/or products will serve to illustrate what can be accomplished.

HOW TO DESIGN A COMPUTER-BASED QUALITY INFORMATION SYSTEM

The design of an effective quality information system requires much thought, planning, and consultation. The work of developing a computer-based system is typically organized into five phases (Figure 11-3). During phase 1, the scope, objectives, and parameters of the system are established. Phase 2 includes flow charting, forms design, report definition, and computer software design. Phase 3, implementation and operation, may be done in selected process areas so that programs and data handling techniques can be debugged. Manual reporting should be maintained in parallel. In phase 4, the overall operation of the system is evaluated. Output reports are initially held to a minimum to permit data verification and to minimize later reprogramming. As confidence is gained in the new system, the total family of output reports can be released for program-

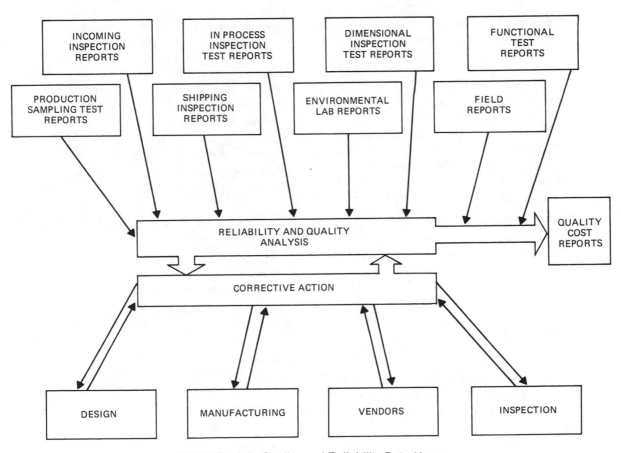

FIGURE 11-2. Quality and Reliability Data Usage
Courtesy of Canadian Marconi Company.

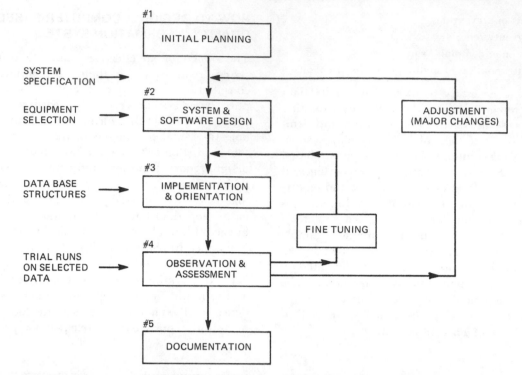

FIGURE 11-3. The diagram outlines the five phases in the development of a computer-based quality system, which produces reports that are useful, accurate, and timely. Courtesy of Canadian Marconi Company.

ming. This phase must continue for the life of the system if quality reports are to continue to be meaningful and useful. Finally, in phase 5 the system is documented. Instructions on operating, maintaining, and understanding the system are prepared both in QC and EDP technology.

The following fundamental factors must be considered during the development of the system:

- Clearly delineate purpose, functions, and objectives of the system.
- Secure solid approval and backing of top management.
- Contact all prospective users (general management, purchasing, manufacturing, engineering).
- Determine system input and output data requirements to satisfy users. The practicality and economics of recording each desired data element must be given serious consideration.
- Design versatility into the system. Information must be available in specific time periods and in any order.
- Ensure flexibility. Each major category must be alterable to add special and new reporting groups.

- Identify scope of proposed system including altered and unaltered interfaces.
- Provide meaningful defect categories. Separate defect types into broad categories to take advantage of the Pareto analysis technique.
- Select output format(s). This will also help determine input data requirements and reporting form content.
- Consider use of tabular, graphical, histogram, and Pareto presentations.
- Ensure reports highlight critical information such as unusually poor yield. Use dashes, asterisks, or spacing to draw attention.
- Provide for management summaries, detail reports, and exception reports. Exception reports are of particular value in failure investigations.
- Define information system constraints such as development costs, operating costs, date system is to be operative.
- Determine how often reports are needed and who needs copies.
- Ensure adequate training of appraisal personnel to familiarize them with the new codes, definitions, and input forms.

Caution: A danger in information system design is too much system too quickly. Many operations have failed dismally because of an attempt to create the ultimate system at the initial cut. Many companies take four or five years to develop a system. The most practical way that the required effort at any one time can be decreased appreciably, and at the same time provide for manageable segments of a total system design, is to break the effort into segments. Consider vendor operations, detail part quality, assembly, test, and final product quality as natural subdivisions.

Pitfall to Avoid: Quality control people are systematic and highly organized. However, EDP professionals have a lot to offer and maximum use should be made of their expertise during system definition. The QC persons' job is quality control; the EDP person's area is data processing.

LET WORD PROCESSORS TAKE ON TEDIOUS TASKS*

Quality control procedures are typically among the most thoroughly documented within a company's operating structure. Because quality procedures define responsibilities and operating methods of various groups, extensive interdepartment coordination is required to develop practical and effective procedures that satisfy management's quality policy objectives. This interdepartment participation in the quality program impacts procedural change activity as organizations, responsibilities, and expansions occur. The quality department, as coordinator and planner of the total quality system, must be responsive to change, and assure that procedure manuals describe an up-to-date operating system.

Quality program plans are normally developed as governing documents for specific product lines. Since their purpose is to integrate the control mechanisms for a given program, they usually reflect standard company process controls and acceptance criteria modified to accommodate unique product or customer quality control requirements. The quality engineer's task is to determine when standard process controls are adequate and when modified controls are neces-

---

* Based upon the article "Up Your Documentation," by J. K. Carpenter, *Quality Progress*, April 1979.

sary. The secretary retypes 80 percent or more of existing documentation for each new program, about 15 percent of modified existing documentation, and maybe 5 percent new material. All the material is subject to retype after each management and customer review.

Inspection work instructions or acceptance test procedures are structured to prescribe inspection equipment requirements, inspection methods, and acceptance or rejection criteria. It's this last item—criteria—that is most essential to maintain consistent and thorough inspections. Many times the criteria elements appear as a supplemental checklist to be marked off by the inspector as each verification takes place. Whatever the format or usage point, criteria elements are the most volatile control mechanisms because they are constantly amended by assembly, test, and customer feedback corrective-action loops. Quality documentation systems must be sensitive to these feedback loops and capable of timely response.

All of these documents require original typing, review, correction and issuance, followed by a second wave of changes (retyping) and reissue, due to engineering, customer, technological, or other changes. Properly managed, a word processor system can be a cost-effective method of implementing these changes. Word processors are computers programmed specifically for information processing, instead of the more familiar data processing functions. They apply the computer's inherent labor-saving features to written information tasks—and therefore significantly reduce the quality dollars spent maintaining documentation systems.

The principal advantage of a word processor—and the main reason quality costs are significantly reduced—is the ease with which documents can be edited during original development and subsequent change activities. The word processor displays text as it is typed on the keyboard, automatically shifts to the next line when the right margin is reached, and corrects errors when the typist backspaces and strikes over the incorrect text. Changes are simple—from inserting a sentence to deleting a paragraph or moving the margins. Once copy is shown correctly on the screen, information is transferred to the computer's memory, and the printer prints out one or more copies. It means typists can work at rough draft speed with perfect results.

Since documents are stored on the memory

disk files and recalled at will, repetitive typing is eliminated. Text is typed once and revised or used as often as necessary. This is extremely efficient during interdepartment procedure or program plan development. Some firms have found it useful to store standard process control instructions and criteria in paragraph files, then build unique product quality plans from the paragraph library by using search and merge function keys. Other proverbial time-wasters—changes to index pages and revision control notations on unaffected pages of revised manuals—can be updated by simply recalling the document, inserting the changes, and reprinting while the typist goes on to new work. Many other functions such as centering, justification (all the next perfectly aligned on the right side as well as the left), superscript or subscript, deletions, and underscoring are all handled by touching a key.

Checklist of Word Processor Considerations

√ Is the extra speed justified in terms of current and projected workload?

√ Can sufficient benefits and cost savings be enumerated in order to justify acquisition?

√ Has the nature of the workload been examined in terms of document length (number of pages)? (This will determine required memory size.)

√ Have personnel been kept informed of equipment acquisition and rationale?

√ What is the level of change and revision? An acceptance test procedure typically is changed two-and-a-half times prior to reaching stability.

√ Will word processing be physically and/or organizationally centralized?

√ Does the selected equipment have sufficient antiobsolescence features?

√ Are the number of key operations to use a particular feature minimized?

√ Will software upgrades be provided during the life of the machine?

√ Are graphics or arithmetic routines necessary?

√ Has adequate personnel training been accomplished?

√ Has a service contract with guaranteed minimum downtime been negotiated?

√ Has a special clean, quiet segregated work area been assigned?

√ Have adequate measures been taken to prevent file wipe-outs and data security?

√ Has a proper disk filing system been developed to ensure prompt retrieval?

√ Has configuration control been implemented over such key documents as test procedures, technical manuals, etc.?

Pitfall to Avoid: Word processors are frequently a status symbol for the QC manager and his or her secretary. It's important to realize this when considering a system. A typical secretary spends only a fraction of the day using a typewriter. It's sometimes hard to pin down the dollar savings or advantages. In the typical office situation, the biggest savings are speed (how much do you really need?) and convenience (do you really care if the secretary has to type the letter twice?)—and they're hard to quantify. If the system does save 20 percent of typing time (net), and if your secretary only types 20 percent of the time, the net saving is really very minor.

PUT STATISTICAL ANALYSIS ON THE SHOP FLOOR

A shop floor computerized statistical analyzer can provide a complete statistical analysis of a production lot from sample data. This can be accomplished without the need of a statistician or quality control expert to work out complex formulas from the gathered data. It is all computed and printed out by the machine.

Caution: In certain situations it may actually be an advantage to manually plot control chart points. It gives a better "feel" for the process.

The analysis involves an extensive list that typically includes the following:

• the capability to handle either English or metric data

• a measuring mode of either the actual, maximum, minimum, or total indicator reading or nominal

• both minimum and maximum tolerances values as dialed in on the thumb wheels or data entry terminal

• the total number of workpieces measured

• both minimum and maximum measured values within the sample

• the sequence number and measured value of each workpiece with the out-of-tolerance values indicated by an asterisk or other means

- the difference between the minimum and maximum measured values
- a complete pictorial histogram of the measured sample with optimum display arrangements
- the average of all measured values
- the standard deviation of the measured values
- the range of three standard deviations that will include 99.7 percent (normal distribution) of all pieces within the lot
- a true statistical estimate of the percent under and over tolerance in the lot being sampled
- a total percent out-of-tolerance based on the normal distribution computations
- the fit factor of the sample data, which is a measure of normality
- a discretionary analysis with or without any stray pieces in the sample

While computers have been doing this type of analysis for years, the microcomputer provides a very economical stand-alone unit that functions in the hands of an inspector and produces a complete analysis on a real-time basis without any external programming. It provides a very powerful tool to allow the shop to quickly act upon the analyzed data. It is right on the shop floor—not lodged in a central computer facility.

Since the introduction of inexpensive computers, electronic control charts have been available to even very small companies. With currently available measuring instruments, direct input of measurement data permits automatically generated statistical evaluation of processes.

Example: Figure 11-4 is a representation of some automatic process. Materials flow into the system, are acted on, and an output leaves through the outlet pipe. The output is under pressure and is at a high temperature. Both of these parameters must be maintained at specified averages and within statistical control.

In the example of Figure 11-4 A–D (analog to digital) converters change the analog transducer measurements of temperature and pressure into digitally coded equivalents. At specified intervals (for example, every sixty seconds), the computer signals that the data at that instant is to be stored. When four or five measurements of temperature and pressure (a subgroup of data) have been accumulated, the computer generates $\bar{X}$ and R data and tests that data for statistical control. Exception messages can be typed out on a printer and/or alarms activated to signal out-of-control conditions.

LOOK INTO VOICE DATA ENTRY

Although computers have cut the cost of organizing and analyzing quality control data, keying in data is still a slow, costly process requiring substantial human effort.

When manually recorded data is routed to off-line terminals for keying, up to four people handle each piece of information before production problems can be detected. If data is entered directly from work stations, inspectors must be specially trained in keying. Regardless of whether inspectors write or key in data, their hands, eyes, and attention are temporarily lost to the nonproductive task of data entry. Other inherent problems include:

- not real-time
- possible transposition errors
- illegible handwritten entries
- provides, after the fact, yield trend data
- minimal verification of data prior to computer input
- documents lost in transit

Voice Data Entry (VDE) eliminates these expensive and productivity-limiting constraints.

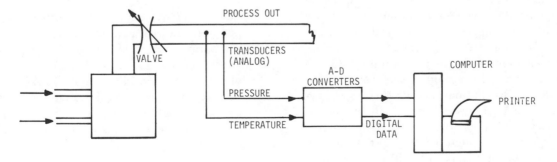

FIGURE 11-4. "Real-Time" Quality Control

Voice data entry equipment is a speaker-adaptive, real-time, isolated-word recognition system. The entire system is programmable. Individual words or the whole vocabulary and syntax structure can be changed, if required. The voice system requires training for individual users and/or words. The system automatically adapts to the voice characteristics of any single user, simply by the user speaking each desired word of the vocabulary to be used several times to provide a reference set of features. The system stores in memory an individual reference set of word features for each word in the vocabulary and for each talker in the system. Once the system is trained, new words spoken into the device are compared with the stored references and a "closest fit" is selected for the recognized word. A "no decision" or reject occurs when none of the characteristics of the word in the reference memory is close enough to the spoken word.

A VDE system speeds throughput by enabling QC personnel to enter data during, not after, product inspection. Because hands are always free to examine the product, and since speaking is faster than keying, operators spend less time entering data and more time controlling quality. Inspection cycle reductions of 50 percent are not uncommon.

Training the VDE system to understand an operator, regardless of dialect or language, takes less than an hour. In operation, spoken words and numbers are immediately displayed, ready for verification at a glance. If an error appears, it can be corrected or deleted. User manuals that come with the system give step-by-step instructions for use.

Case in Point: One quality control operation at a multinational can company requires that pull-ring lids be placed in gauges. All data entries are made by voice. Speaking into headsets, workers communicate directly with the company's main central computers. Spoken data is displayed for immediate verification, and then transmitted to the computers with a single voice command. In addition to eliminating data sheets and keying, the VDE system actually helps the inspectors do their jobs. The system prompts inspectors through correct test sequences and automatically identifies out-of-spec products by means of a REJECT light and a beep. Company engineers report that, while increasing quality control throughput by 40 percent, VDE systems have also reduced manufacturing costs by speeding detection of faulty containers. Each system paid for itself in less than a year!

Pitfall to Avoid: Don't expect miracles overnight. Like all production innovations, constant two-way communication is required during the introduction phase. Expect some initial resistance.

MICROCOMPUTERS REVOLUTIONIZE GAUGING

Early electronic gauging systems dealt primarily with analog signals. In the 1960s, digital electronics became more popular, allowing very high resolution-to-range ratios. Whereas an analog meter value is broken down into eighty gradations over the total measuring range, digital electronics allow a breakdown of the total measuring range into 4000 parts, providing much greater precision for the same measuring range. With the microcomputer it is possible to routinely combine analog signals in a complex fashion to achieve results that were heretofore achieved only by expensive specially engineered analog computing systems.

Microcomputer systems perform the same function as analog computer systems but are developed via software only. This means that hardware remains the same and engineering and fabrication costs are significantly reduced. Finally, microcomputers combine these signals in a far more accurate fashion. Analog computers typically experienced severe fall-off in accuracy as the complexity of the signal combinations became greater. Today's microcomputers can handle very complex signal combinations with no reduction in accuracy.

Case in Point: A machine shop inspection supervisor required a simple gauging unit for comparing a workpiece bore diameter to a master setting. Traditionally, the firm used air gauges for precise, accurate work. While relatively low cost, the air gauge required a constant supply of dry, clean air—utilizing energy and increasing operating costs. The supervisor found a competitive electronic gauge that was simple, did not lose precision near the ends of the scale, and had a wide selection of scale ranges. The unit was also easy to read and could be tied into a computer-controlled quality reporting system. After two months experience, all new procurements shifted to the electronic plug gauge. It was determined that pretax returns on investment exceeded 30 percent.

Case in Point: One application of a digital height gauge was in a tractor plant that used approximately sixty-five digital gauges for quality control of surface plates. The previously used regular-height vernier gauges were slow and cumbersome and one needed a magnifying glass to read them. Also, the numbers on vernier gauges wore off.

The electronic gauge has a bright digital readout and eliminates both the vernier and Cadillac gauges that were needed before. The Cadillac gauge costs almost as much as the digital unit, so three gauges were replaced with one, since the digital gauge is both English and metric. The firm has cut gauging time by at least 67 percent and has saved between $75,000 and $100,000. Downtime is also nil, even though they are used on a three shift basis.

ELECTRO-OPTICAL SYSTEMS ARE HERE

Electro-optical systems, which are able to "see," have been under development for several years. They have been attracting particular attention recently because of their potential application in test and inspection for automatic assembly. Already, vision-based systems can match human operators in on-line ability to inspect, sort, gauge, and recognize many patterns in real-time. Moreover, these noncontact systems often perform inspection and assembly-related tasks faster, more reliably, and at a lower cost than is possible with human operators.

The principle of operation for an electro-optical system is very similar to that of a photographic camera, although the actual hardware and its use are quite different. An electro-optical system retains a lens, but the one-time-use film has been replaced by a permanent and reusable electronic image sensor. At the same time, a computer has been added to give the camera system limited decision-making capability. In contrast to a traditional camera that permanently preserves the image, an electro-optical system is designed to continuously detect the changing or static image from the object of interest as detected by the sensor. The system uses the computer to interpret successive images and generate useful control signals. A typical block diagram is shown in Figure 11-5.

Current electro-optical technology can solve many practical problems, even though the vision technology is relatively new and much theoretical development work is still needed. Nevertheless, electro-optical technology's practical achievements are impressive so far. See Table 11-1.

Case in Point: Electro-optical dimensional-measurement capability, which can measure parts up to ± 0.001 inch accuracy, was used effectively by a spark plug manufacturer.

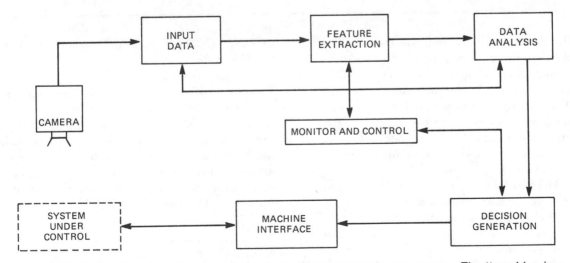

FIGURE 11-5. In the closed loop control scheme the camera acts as a sensor. The "machine interface" block is system's interface with the real world.

TABLE 11–1. Electro-Optical Systems Capabilities

Functional Capability	Applications	Industries
Dimensional measurement	• Parts measurement (length, height, diameter)	• Precision parts, thermometers, bearing length, electronic components
Parts grading, sorting, inspection	• Size • Surface roughness • Shape recognition • Flaws and defect detection	• Metal parts, food stuffs • Metals, wood, plastics • Multiple parts feed • Food, pharmaceutical
Presence or absence	• Labels on containers • Holes in parts • Tool in fixture • Complete set	• Pharmaceutical, chemical, food • Discrete parts fabrication • Machine tool, transfer machine • Electronic, pharmaceutical, food
Verification	• Correct alignment • Correct label • Correct component • Bar code reading • Character recognition	• Chemical, pharmaceutical, semiconductor, electronic
Deviation	• Alignment (welding) • Wear (tool) • Error (registration) • Adjustment (positional)	• Pipe, transportation, robotics • Parts machining, fabrication • Printing, labels, currency, stamps • Semiconductor, wire bonders, laser trimmers
Location, orientation, positioning	• Robotics • Automatic assembly	• Robotics • Automotive, major appliances, material handling

The electro-optical system was used to view and determine spark plug electrode gap at product rates of up to 900 pieces/hr. One precaution that had to be taken in this application was ensuring that the spark plug was always presented to the camera in the same orientation. With the acquisition of this machine, inspection personnel were reduced from five to two.

The field of view, measurement accuracy, working distance resolution, programmability, environmental conditions, expected cost savings and processing speed are the main factors to be considered when evaluating an electro-optical system for a particular application.

AUTOMATIC TESTING AND QUALITY CONTROL*

There are two basic reasons for performing any type of testing: (1) customer relations (goodwill, continued sales, warranty) and (2) internal efficiency (high yields, low rework/scrap costs). Because testing can account for 5 to 20 percent of manufacturing costs and 30 to 50 percent of the cycle time, automatic testing deserves attention. Automatic Test Equipment (ATE) has been cred-

* Material in this section, including figure, is based on K. Kivenko, "Some Quality Assurance Aspects of Automatic Testing," *Journal of Quality Technology,* Vol. 6, No. 3, July 1974.

ited with reducing the number and skill level of test technicians, increasing test integrity by eliminating human subjectivity, and accomplishing tests for which the quantity and speed were beyond the scope of manual methods.

Automatic testing, like manual testing, involves stimulation, measurements, switching, control, evaluation, diagnosis, and recording. Unlike manual testing, automatic testing performs most of these functions under the control of a computer or other device following a stored program sequence. A block diagram of an ATE system is shown in Figure 11-6.

There are several key points to keep in mind if you're thinking about purchasing an ATE system. Among the major considerations are the following:

Test Specifications

With the use of ATE, a new factor enters the testing specification picture. The ATE must be given precise instructions, including precise tolerances for measurements. The machine is not capable of looking sideways at a meter reading or changing its measurement instrument to get a better an-

swer. The current lack of precision, typical of specifications in manual testing situations, becomes very evident when quality engineers seek to convert such specifications into ATE computer software programs.

Product Testability

A decision to utilize ATE in the factory impacts the design of a product. Adequate test points, physical layout, and input accessability must be considered. Such considerations require the close cooperation of the product designer and the QC engineer during the earliest practical phase of product development.

Diagnostics

Unless appropriate diagnostic and repair capability is provided, rejected assemblies (and production costs) can start accumulating at a startling rate. The subject of fault diagnosis deserves more consideration than is generally given to it. A great deal of theoretical material has been published, but many of the basic assumptions are in practice

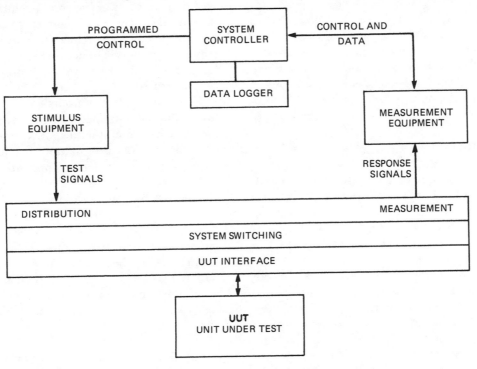

FIGURE 11-6. Block Diagram for Automatic Testing System: Connections between equipment and the unit under test are made using remotely controlled switching devices so that testing may progress from one condition to the next.

untenable. Multiple faults are a particular problem. Another important aspect of fault diagnosis that is rarely touched upon is the problem of diagnosing assemblies that have been incorrectly made. If it is assumed that there is an infinitely large number of wrong ways of making such an item, then the task is formidable. Fortunately, many of these faults are predictable. If they cannot be prevented economically, they can at least be anticipated. This may involve a specific automatic testing process to verify some aspects of manufacture before applying energy to the unit under test, since otherwise catastrophic damage might occur. Here again, the adequacy of test access will determine whether or not ATE can be used.

Programming and Software

The programming effort is of major importance. Programming consists of four basic phases:

1. analysis and program design
2. coding assembly and/or compilation
3. validation
4. demonstration

The test-requirements analysis effort usually accounts for 40 to 50 percent of the total programming effort. At this phase the parameters to be tested, methods of test, test point/connector requirements are analyzed, and problems with corresponding solutions should be identified. After the concept has been reviewed by a competent team, a detailed test design should be prepared and documented.

Documentation

The detailed test design is usually documented as a flow diagram. The flow diagram form is much preferred to a tabular listing, especially for diagnostic testing, because of ease with which the testing sequence can be tracked in this form. The flow diagram describes each test in the sequence in which they occur, the stimulus and measurement requirements for each test, special switching to connect or disconnect interface equipment, test limits and tolerances and the consequences of "high," "low," or "go" branches. The flow diagram is usually written in English to allow persons not familiar with the ATE to follow the test design logic. When complete, the flow diagram serves as a detailed description of the testing function as it will be performed by the ATE.

The program itself should be assigned a name and control number, be dated, and the author be identified. The part number and revision letter of the unit under test must also be given for configuration control purposes. Liberal use of explanatory comments is desirable to permit understanding of the program. This is particularly important during production when the manufacturing group is pretty well left to fend for itself and engineering changes are abundant.

Human Factors

Communication between the ATE and the test operator is an important consideration particularly if low-skill level personnel are utilized. Accept/reject status should be made evident through the use of green/red lights or similar means. A check should be provided in the event an incorrect tape or wrong adaptor is accidentally loaded, and the possibility communicated to the operator via a control panel or teletype.

Pitfall to Avoid: A statement that "Test #3 Failed Pins XXXX" is meaningless to a nonskilled operator. Specific component replacement data or detailed instruction to the operator is what counts in the production environment. Operator intervention should be kept to a minimum because human errors may be introduced and costs increased.

Utilize test data print-outs only when its use is justified by in-house needs or contractual requirements. Yield data should be accumulated, however, since such information is vital for cost estimating and problem identification purposes.

Corrective Action

Appropriate failure analysis and statistical work are more important in automatic testing than in manual testing because a larger fraction of the total test cost will be devoted to diagnosis and retest. Timely correction of defects or design deficiencies is necessary to ensure that the ATE pays its way.

Case in Point: A manufacturer of disk drives purchased an expensive ATE system. Although test time was in fact reduced, repair costs stood at the same level as before. Many retests had to be run for three or four repaired units, increasing set-up costs and subtracting from expected cost savings.

EQUIPMENT UTILIZATION

Another computer application area concerns machine utilization. Most quality managers assume their measuring equipment performs at approximately 80 percent efficiency. The fact is that most quality managers do not have a good feel for the actual equipment utilization in their plants. If accurate records were kept on measuring equipment utilization, most plants would find they are probably operating in the 35 to 60 percent range. The problem is that accurate records are not being kept; therefore, these managers are operating under a false assumption. High machine downtime is a cause of production bottlenecks and therefore of increased inventory, undue overtime, and degraded quality.

Cost-effective electronic monitoring systems are now commercially available to accomplish these tasks. Several manufacturers, recognizing the need for informing management of the utilization of their capital equipment, have developed low-cost, easy-to-install microprocessor-based monitoring information systems. These data collection and monitoring systems include all of the parameters necessary for measuring and controlling equipment utilization.

There are several analytical measures of equipment utilization. Each of the indexes serves a specific purpose. Tha Production Index (PI) is a measurement of the effectiveness of the support functions and the reliability of the machine. A low PI indicates extensive set-up time, delay, or maintenance.

$$PI = \frac{\text{Logged Production Hours}}{\text{Total Logged Hours}} \times 100$$

The Availability Index (AI) is a measure of the time the machine could have operated during logged hours. Nonmaintenance hours are compared to total logged time. A high availability index indicates a low requirement for maintenance and repair time. This is a function of both the reliability of the machine and the quality of its maintenance.

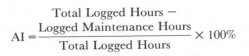

$$AI = \frac{\text{Total Logged Hours} - \text{Logged Maintenance Hours}}{\text{Total Logged Hours}} \times 100\%$$

The Utilization Index (UI) is a measure of capital equipment usage. The production and set-up hours are both considered normal functions of machine operation and are added in computing the index. This total is compared to the maximum possible number of hours that the machine could have been used (168 hours for a 7-day week), even though the equipment is seldom scheduled for the entire period. For every hour change in the combined total of production and set-up time, the UI changes 0.6 percent.

$$UI = \frac{\text{Total Production Hours} + \text{Logged Set-Up Hours}}{168 \times \text{Number of Weeks}} \times 100\%$$

Table 11-2 is an example of how these indexes can create the awareness of measuring equipment performance and thereby facilitate their management and control.

These indexes can provide the facts and figures needed to define problem areas that are decreasing equipment utilization. They can tell you if the corrective action taken to solve utilization problems is effective as well as the degree of effectiveness. Only when management is adequately informed, can attention be directed to improve or alleviate problem areas that result in nonoptimum operating levels.

Machine Tool	INDEX PERCENTAGE		
	PI	AI	UI
Ditmco	67.5	95.0	40.5
GR1796 ATE	67.7	100.0	41.8
Optical Comp.	50.0	75.0	29.8
Rel. Test Chamber	87.6	90.0	51.6
CMM	12.5	100.0	31.9
Anechoic Chamber	23.5	52.9	23.8

Although these performance measures are conceptually quite simple, they do require an accurate time log that categorizes total available machine time into the four basic categories. Because of the administrative workload, measurement and evaluation of equipment utilization are often abandoned or ignored.

For each machine or group of machines being monitored, reports are available that provide real-time operational status such as running, loading, preventive maintenance, etc. This information is displayed on a video monitor at all times. Management is now aware of whether any given piece of equipment is up and running or down, and for what reasons.

TRY PROGRAMMABLE CONTROL FOR ASSEMBLY AND TEST OPERATIONS

A Programmable Controller, or PC (not to be confused with a Personal Computer), is a software-based equivalent of a relay panel. Its primary purpose is to provide a rudimentary form of logic for determining the operating sequence of a machine or process. However, a relay panel is a specific-purpose control. Changes to its control sequence can be time consuming and expensive. A PC, on the other hand, is a general-purpose device. One model can be programmed to control a variety of machines, and programs can be changed easily for new jobs or changes in production routines. Moreover, a PC tends to be more reliable than complex relay panels and is smaller and more easily installed and maintained.

Early PC models, like their relay-panel counterparts, performed only logic-based sequencing functions. Many modern PCs still do only that. But some PCs now perform many duties that cannot be duplicated by relays and, in fact, they perform many minicomputer functions such as:

- simple arithmetic calculations
- data comparison
- setpoint manipulation
- solution of mathematical functions (sine, xy, ex)
- equation solving
- analog-to-digital conversion

Because the PC was designed primarily as a digital reprogrammable sequence controller, it was not well suited to dealing with analog input signals. Many test stands that depended mostly on inputs from analog transducers could not effectively exploit the advantages of PC control and traditionally relied on relay logic or hardwired electronic controllers. But subsequent improvements in PC operation, mainly in the form of ability to process inputs from analog transducers as well as arithmetic capabilities make the PC attractive for test applications too.

Programmable controllers today control assembly lines as well as assembly-related test sta-

tions. Their functions include inspection and gauging of automotive engine pistons, hot-engine testing and measurement of exhaust emissions, measurement of transmission gear backlash and selection of proper shims for optimum gear spacing, simultaneous assembly, and testing for manufacturing defects of automotive transaxle transmission components. Moreover, these functions are automatically performed more reliably, faster, and at a lower cost than is possible with relay logic or manual control.

This combining of assembly and test operations is a definite trend today. The reasons are economic. Because the cost of product rework grows geometrically with the degree of completeness of assemblies, early detection of defects can result in considerable cost savings in terms of both labor and material scrap reduction.

Case in Point: A PC and a microprocessor were teamed up by a manufacturer to assemble and test six-way transmissions for a major automotive body manufacturer.

A finished transmission pops out in less than 3–4 seconds from a continuous loop assembly line. Another 6.8 seconds are required to functionally test the transmission off-line. The list of defects that can be detected during testing is exhaustive and includes internal transmission misalignments, open solenoid cells, broken shafts, excessive drive torque, and missing parts.

The assembly line consists of automatic assembly stations and manual loading stations. The line is controlled by several programmable controllers that take over after the transmission housing is manually placed on a work pallet. As other components—such as bearing, shafts, solenoid assembly, drive dogs, and a retainer—are added automatically, their position is checked at every step. Off-line, a programmable controller controls the transmission test stand. Because the transmission is tested under dynamic conditions and requires measurements of rotation speeds, the PC scan rate is an important consideration. The builder of the assembly line avoided scan rate complications and chose to interface a microprocessor ahead of the PC to act as a measurement device. Also, the microprocessor was more suitable to processing the digital speed data gathered from shaft encoders.

The PC share of transmission testing consists of proper setting up of different test conditions including sequencing, part positioning, control of motor acceleration and braking, and valve operation. When the required test conditions are reached, the PC commands the microprocessor to initiate the measurement and test data evaluation cycle.

The actual testing measures rotation speed of various transmission components under different operating conditions. For example, shafts are tested at selected torque levels; motors are tested at certain speeds; and system response is tested by the rate of velocity increase after the brakes are applied and then released. The microprocessor monitors the outputs of a number of shaft encoders that are mounted on different parts of the transmission, measures the different velocities, and compares the data in real-time to constants stored in its memory. This particular system had a payback period of eighteen months.

COORDINATE-MEASURING MACHINES AND THE COMPUTER

Manufacturing has been using Computer Numerical Control (CNC) machines for years. The machines can produce complicated parts at a rapid rate. Usually a first piece-inspection is required before production can continue. With the conventional methods of layout inspection, several hours can elapse before first-piece acceptance, thus tying up expensive production equipment. Hole locations, contours, and surfaces of castings have always provided problems to the inspector, especially when the datum is a nonexistent line in space. Further, the skill level required for conventional inspection methods is in short supply in today's labor market.

The CNC Coordinate-Measuring Machine (CMM) provides a solution to these problems because drawings can be laid out in true-position dimensioning using the same coordinates that are used to inspect the part. To program a CMM, the programmer indicates which elements of the workpiece should be inspected, what the computer is to calculate, and what information should be printed out. Most systems use a high-level easy-to-learn language such as BASIC, so that the operator can readily get familiarized with computer operation and modify programs. Modular programming is utilized so that selected parts of the program can be modified, expanded, or exchanged without difficulty. The program modules are generally stored on diskettes, which are integrated with the computer and can be quickly recalled by means of a push button on the control panel.

The computer software used for three-dimensional measuring techniques permits the computation of a large number of metrological parameters and their interrelation. Edges, straight lines, planes, circles, cylinders, cones, spheres, and other basic elements can be determined, as well as symmetry, graduated circle, intersection of axes, point of intersection between axes and plane, and the line of intersection between planes. For example, two holes could be probed and the computer would calculate the true distance between centers or the degree of parallelism of a line between centers compared with an edge of the work piece. The data can be evaluated either in Cartesian or polar coordinates. Inspection results are displayed on a video monitor or high-speed printer. They can be further processed through spherical programs so that histograms, trends, and other quality control information can be obtained.

To use the machine the inspector places the work piece on the table, usually on a set of riser blocks called for by the work-piece process document. It is not necessary to square the work piece with the axes of the table; it is only necessary to inspect a few surfaces, holes, or bores to determine the specified plane of reference. The machine will automatically provide the same results that would have been obtained had the work piece been perfectly square with the table. The saving in set-up time is typically 0.5 to 1.5 hours. The inspector then keys in the work-piece part number and the fact that he or she is ready to begin. The computer verifies that all is in order and prints out a set of basic instructions, such as which probe will be used first and where the inspector is to begin. The process continues step by step with the computer able to compare any steps to determine any critical dimensional relationships. The instructions also tell the operator which probe to use and whether to use it in a vertical or horizontal mode.

Each step of the way, the operator follows the instructions that appear as each preceding gauging step is completed.

In summary then, the benefits of a CNC coordinate-measuring machine are:

- high measuring accuracy
- low set-up time
- reduced inspection time
- improved inspection consistency
- lower inspector skill level required
- elimination of computational errors
- automatic data capture and analysis
- enhanced process and manufacturing control
- elaborate holding fixtures not required
- improved production machine utilization
- integrated NC philosophy

Caution: A sophisticated inspection approach utilizing a computer does not come without some effort. Adequate time must be allowed for training. It is necessary to write a software program for each piece to be inspected, and the basic cost of the unit itself is a major capital investment when compared to a few manual gauging tools. When properly applied, however, a CMM can show returns on capital employed in excess of 25 percent.

LOOK INTO COMPUTER SOFTWARE QUALITY ASSURANCE

A significant fraction of a modern operating system's products consists of computer programs, many of them complex. Yet the assurance sciences have devoted the lion's share of their attention to computer hardware. This may be due partly to a lack of appreciation for the complexities of programmimg and partly to a lack of awareness of the impact of programming on total system effectiveness. Many consider programming to be a relatively straightforward job that could not cause reliability problems. Of course, this feeling is not shared by the programming community, which spends a great deal of time correcting functional problems but has been slow to adopt many of the disciplined approaches of reliability and quality control that the hardware QC and reliability field has pioneered and proven.

Example: Consider the events leading to the spectacular failure of America's first interplane-

tary probe, *Mariner 1*. The *Mariner 1* Venus probe and its *Atlas Agena B* launch vehicle traveled a flight path that was controlled by signals sent from a ground computer to a guidance computer aboard the spacecraft. Tracking was done by ground radar. After a short period of time, ground radar lost contact with the vehicle and began a wide-angle search for it. Simultaneously, the radar sent a signal to the computer telling it to ignore the wide-angle search. Unfortunately, a symbol was missing in the computer program: There was no bar above an "R" in one of the flight equations, telling the computer to ignore additional input until radar contact was reestablished. Because the computer was not told by the program to disregard the wide-angle search, it sent signals to the vehicle, causing it to nose downward. Having no alternative, the Range Safety Officer had to push the destruct button. Millions of dollars literally went up in smoke because of a software quality problem.

Down on earth, computer software reliability isn't any better. Errors in medical software have caused people to lose their lives. And software errors cause a constant stream of social dislocations because of false arrests, incorrect bank balances or credit records, fouled class schedules and school grades, lost travel reservations, or long-delayed payments to needy families or small businesses. Similar programming oversights have occurred in industry, costing millions. Clearly, computer software integrity is at least as important as hardware reliability.

It is true that computer programs do not suffer reliability problems as a result of wearout mechanisms or overstress. They do suffer from event-dependent failures. Hardware quality assurance professionals recognized years ago that many hardware failures were also event-dependent and could be prevented through application of assurance/prevention techniques such as design review, standards, FMEA, engineering testing, and prototype runs.

The five common types of software errors are:

1. Logical errors: incomplete or erroneous method used to obtain the solutions.

2. Coding errors: listing incorrect or incomplete addresses, transposition of digits in operand, transcription errors, and so on.

3. Input device errors made in the program preparation for input.

4. Changing the target machine (for example, Fortran compilers on different machines generally have slight differences).

5. Mathematics errors in specifying the problem: They are inadequate, insufficient, or do not cover all cases. (This problem will occur when the degree of mathematical fluency required for the problem is beyond the capabilities of the programmer.)

Typical figures indicate that on average, about 30 percent of the software effort is spent on analysis and design, 20 percent on coding, and a full (usually unplanned) 50 percent on checkout and test.

Before attempting to quality assure software, it is wise to define at least in broad terms what is meant by a "good" program. The key characteristics are:

The program is adequately specified and documented.

The program is under configuration control.

Mathematical calculations are correctly performed.

The program is logically correct.

There is no interference between program entities.

The program is intelligible.

The program is easy to modify.

The program is easy to use.

Take this study one step further from the general characteristics to more detailed attributes and once again you'll hear some familiar words. For example, the description of "The program is intelligible":

Consistent coding techniques are set up and followed.

Symbolic names and labels are clear and meaningful.

The program is easy to follow.

The real-time constraints of a program are clearly identified.

This is clearly akin to existing hardware quality assurance criteria involving the audit or preparation of any work instruction document—a shop order, purchase order, test specification, or test procedure.

The following tasks are suggested as major elements in the development and implementation of a computer software QA program.

Software Quality Assurance Planning

Effective software quality assurance must be properly planned. These plans should be included in the total quality assurance program plan. Such action establishes a recognized quality assurance position with respect to involvement in the development of the software. The quality assurance plans should be developed in conjunction with the software development personnel and receive approval of the project manager. The plan should identify each major software area of involvement by quality assurance, describe the effort to be accomplished, and identify applicable procedures.

Procedures

Develop procedures for software quality assurance efforts to support the plan as necessary. Procedure development should be accomplished in conjunction with the software development group. The procedures should allow for some flexibility in establishing the quality assurance detail tasks.

Subcontracted Software Development

The selection of a software subcontractor requires as much or more care than the selection of a hardware subcontractor. This is because software is nearly always on the critical path and second sources are not a meaningful alternative late in a project's life. A pre-award survey should help ascertain the subcontractors resources (personnel, facilities, financial), experience, quality control procedures, past performance, documentation standards, and other factors relevant to the work to be done. The degree of pre-award effort will be determined by cost, schedule, and complexity. After contract award, subcontractor quality assurance software efforts can be monitored through a software quality assurance program plan that describes the tasks, identifies applicable procedures and acceptance criteria, establishes responsibilities, and schedules the effort.

Standards

Standards must be applied to software in the areas of label usage, symbolic names, special symbols, size of program segments, amount of commenting, symbol usage in flow charts, conventions for subrouting linkages, register usage, and so on.

Such standards are just as critical to software quality control as they are to physical product.

Organization and Management

It is desirable to apply one or more techniques to software development that will increase confidence that a program will execute as it is intended to. Some possible techniques are:

1. establishment of a project schedule including milestones
2. structured programming
3. top-down design and very thorough design review
4. hierarchical structuring
5. chief programmer team concept
6. defensive coding
7. use of highest-level language feasible

Software Specification

In order to ensure that the ultimate programs will perform their intended functions, early agreement must be reached on the following, via a specification:

1. Definition of the objective(s) desired.
2. The specific functions to be performed.
3. Estimated time required. It is an important index to the programmer; it often tells the degree of research and testing needed.
4. The product environment (hardware, operating system, etc.) and the limits on resources (memory, storage media, etc.).
5. The expected level of performance (speed).
6. The reliability requirements (error tolerance).
7. The maintenance and support needs.

This task is considered an important reliability tool. Features in the released software that do not function according to expectations are errors. Therefore, the customer must realize that being specific at this point is imperative, if the ultimate product is to be responsive to company needs. There should be no incomplete, conflicting, or uncertain terminology; this only leads to problems later in the software development process.

Design Reviews

Design reviews for software are similar to hardware design reviews. These reviews are beneficial to allow insight into the system design and system testing and to strengthen the interface with the software development group and the user. Preliminary evaluations should also include the testing of real-time programs in nonreal-time to ensure that all possible program sequences are properly executed. This is followed by real-time execution—where further debugging must be minimal because it is difficult, costly, and time-consuming.

Software Testing

Software QA measures in this area should include:

a. Analysis of software requirements to determine testability.

b. Review of test plans for compliance with appropriate standards and satisfaction of performance specifications.

c. Review of test requirements and criteria for adequacy, feasibility, and satisfaction of requirements.

d. Review of test procedures for compliance with appropriate standards and satisfaction of performance requirements.

e. Control of tapes and test procedures to assure proper validation and release.

f. Monitoring of tests and certification that test results are the actual findings of the tests.

g. Review and certification of test results and reports.

h. Ensuring that test-related documentation is maintained to allow repeatability of tests.

i. Assuring that any support software and computer hardware used to develop software are themselves acceptable and maintained.

j. Testing the effect of noise on interrupt lines and other hardware/software interactions.

Reporting of Software Test Discrepancies

Formal software test discrepancies should be documented on a form agreed to between the software development group and quality assurance. The format should properly identify the test, test step, observation, resolution information, and proper signatures. Existing data collection forms may be appropriate for this task; they should at least be considered. The data collection system should be capable of handling field (operational) problems.

Corrective Action

The data forms should be held open against the software until proper corrective action is taken to resolve the discrepancy. After such action is taken, software retest should be accomplished to verify that the action taken resolves the discrepancy and that new bugs have not been introduced.

Documentation

Software should be supported by program listings and user manuals. For example, listing documentation should include a listing of source statements, including all comments, machine codes for all instructions and data, and label and symbol tables. The program header may contain the following information: name of program, author, date, issue and revision, purpose, related programs and data bases, general description of logic used, hardware configuration, memory required, timing, and method for loading and running. In addition, high-level flow charts or decision tables or an equally concise presentation of logic flow should be considered. Also, a software spec (separate) including the standard items just mentioned, equations used, references for math or logic, scaling information if not F/P floating point, arithmetic, units of major variables, implicit approximations, shortcomings or noncompliances, and any peculiar effects is very desirable.

Configuration Control

The object of configuration management is to assist in the control of costs and reliability of a software system. To do this, configuration management focuses on three areas: identification, control, and accounting.

Identification determines the exact nature of the problem, the method of solution, and the goals before any actual coding begins. The assumption is that complete and clear information produces a cohesive and reliable product. The *control* procedures provide for changes that will occur in the system. These procedures guarantee communications channels to keep all people involved in the project abreast of changes. Again, the assumption is that clear and complete information will yield a reliable product. *Accounting* provides visibility of the project's progress through a series of reviews, software documentation, and product validation.

The importance of configuration management is that it attempts to integrate the user, the administrators, the code developers, and the certification people. A side benefit of configuration management is that it provides for software filing other than on the programmer's desk (see list that follows).

BASIC ELEMENTS OF A SOFTWARE CONFIGURATION CONTROL PROGRAM

1. Obtain authorization to use the completed computer program for production work.

2. Compile the computer program data package:

   - program description of abstract
   - source deck
   - technical reports, user's manual
   - sample input deck (standard problems)
   - sample output (standard problems)

3. Deliver data package to central computer file.

4. Verify that source deck is fully operational by running standard problems and checking results.

5. Place computer code under restricted access control and issue instructions to destroy all copies of source decks/tapes and files other than the central file master copy. Identify computer program by a specific number (similar to a part number) and revision code.

6. Process all production use on master copy through central file.

7. Restrict any change to the computer code except through documented change control process.

8. When authorized by management, provide a single copy of the production tape to the authorized programmer for revision, but do not allow any production work on anything except the master copy.

9. After the revision is proven to be acceptable, obtain management authorization to replace the master copy with the revised master copy. Repeat steps 2 through 6.

10. Retain a history file of each master copy revision. Prepare a release or approved-for-use record for each program.

REFERENCES

Andresev, N. "Programmable Control for Assembly and Test Operations." *Assembly Engineering*, July 1980.

Carpenter, J. K. "Up Your Documentation." *Quality Progress*, April 1979.

Connors, J. F. "The Benefits of Microprocessors in Production Equipment." *Electronic Packaging & Production*, May 1979.

Curry, S. Y. "Strategies for Successful Computer Utilization." *Automation*, Jan. 1973.

Gettleman, K. "Coordinate Measuring Determines Functional Value." *Modern Machine Shop*, June 1978.

Gula, G. G. "Future Trends in Quality Techniques." *Quality Progress*, June 1973.

Henderson, J. T. "Automatic Assembly Documentation." *Assembly Engineering*, June 1978.

Holguin, R. "Today's News—Today; A Must in Shop Corrective Action." *IQC*, June 1965.

Kivenko, K. "Some Quality Assurance Aspects of Automatic Testing." *Journal of Quality Technology*, July 1974.

Schwartz, M. "Anatomy of a Microcomputer." *Machine Design*, March 11, 1976.

Whisman, D. "Effective Product Defect Reporting." *Quality Progress*, Feb. 1970.

12

Procurement Quality Control,
or
How to Save a Bundle

In these days of material shortages, rising prices, increasing product complexity and reliability, and international competition, the need for an effective supplier quality control system is essential. The cost of purchased materials can run as high as 90 percent of the factory cost depending on the nature of the product and business. A rejected shipment at incoming inspection can have major adverse consequences on assembly lines, inventory levels, and delivery schedules.

In order to ensure an orderly flow of purchased parts to the assembly area, a planned approach to procurement quality control is required. Control is defined here as the comparison of output against some standard, and feedback for corrective action. This control must commence during product development and follow through to field usage.

The ultimate objective of a Procurement Quality Program (PQC) is to procure material that so adequately conforms to purchase order quality requirements that there are virtually no surprises at the receiving dock; vendors feel part of a team; and PQC costs are optimized.

Important: Vendors ought to be chosen by their ability to be competitive and provide statistical evidence of quality control.

In Japan, the pressure put on suppliers to improve the quality of their own materials is intense and persistent. Japanese manufacturers work with suppliers to find out why problems arise and to help solve them. They even conduct seminars for employees of supplier companies. The message is simple, "If you follow these steps, you will learn to meet our requirements." Given the long-term relationships between suppliers and customers in Japan, suppliers cannot refuse or take lightly such assistance and advice.

A reliable supplier base is the hallmark of a successful enterprise. This chapter provides the methodology for building and retaining this important base.

WHY PROCUREMENT QC PAYS OFF

Procurement quality control costs in terms of salary, capital equipment, travel expenses, and a variety of other ways. The benefits, however, usually far outweigh the costs. Here's why:

- The inventory impact because of a rejection of an incoming lot can be enormous. The cost of the parts might be small, but the inventory that cannot be assembled or shipped is usually very large when valued at 1 to 3 percent per month carrying costs.

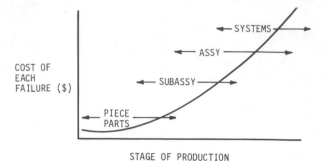

COST OF
EACH
FAILURE ($)

STAGE OF PRODUCTION

FIGURE 12-1. The Cost of Correcting a Failure Increases as the Complexity Increases.
Courtesy of Canadian Marconi Company.

- The cost each time of 100 percent screening of parts to find the few good ones is wasteful and expensive.

- Defective material entering the assembly area can be expensive to rectify and repair (see Figure 12-1). The higher the level of assembly, the worse the cost impact.

- Sales may be lost because of an inability to deliver on time because of purchased part quality problems.

- End product performance or reliability may be degraded if parts/components of marginal design or quality are utilized.

- Subassembly and assembly yields may sink too low for economic production, thus reducing profit margins. For instance, if purchased parts going to assembly are 0.5 percent defective on average and there are sixty parts per assembly, yield will be 75 percent. If the defect rate rises to 3 percent the yield will be less than 20 percent (see Figure 12-2).

- The costs of incoming inspection, material review, and source surveillance can add a major burden to the QC budget. The better you manage and control vendors, the less these costs will be.

- Valuable purchasing effort is wasted handling rejections, tracking shipment, and invoicing status, and sending telegrams.

- Late identification of planned vendor product line discontinuations do not allow time for stocking, redesign, or negotiation.

- Poor quality parts can inflate warranty costs. In most cases approximately 50 percent of field failures are due to faulty components.

- In extreme cases, defective purchased items can lead to equipment safety breakdowns resulting in loss of life, injury, or damage to property. This, in turn, can result in costly product liabil-

ity actions against the manufacturer and its supplier(s).

BUILD RELATIONSHIPS WITH PURCHASING

The purchasing department is under constant pressure from many directions. General management wants inventories kept low; production wants parts yesterday; and everybody watches purchase price. In addition, late engineering releases, inflation, internal audits, and government regulations don't make the job any easier. The individual buyer is expected to perform many tasks (see Table 12-1) during the course of the day. Given this background we can expect buyers to resist any additional restraints imposed by QC. Procurement QC, to be effective, must aid purchasing rather than hinder it. This can be accomplished as follows:

√ Supply purchasing with timely quantitative and qualitative data on vendor performance for their use. It is surprising how few purchase orders will be placed in the face of negative information.

√ Provide quick and accurate service to purchasing in the quality control area. This service can be in the form of timely quality surveys to make new vendors available, swift corrective action to put unacceptable vendors back in good graces, and periodic technical support.

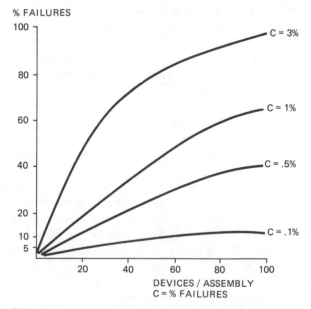

FIGURE 12-2. Percentage of Assembly Failures Versus the Number of Devices/Assembly
Courtesy of Canadian Marconi Company.

TABLE 12-1. Buyer Activities

1. Locating sources	11. Attend in-house meetings
2. Obtaining quotations	12. Dealing with accounting
3. Responding to vendor queries	13. Processing nonconforming material reports
4. Analyzing quotations	14. Chasing missing information
5. Selecting sources	15. Idle time, waiting time
6. Negotiating price/delivery	16. Processing engineering changes
7. Preparing purchase orders	17. Vendor surveys
8. Expediting, follow-up	18. Meeting vendors/representatives
9. Dealing with paper work	19. Training, reading trade literature
10. Filing, recordkeeping	20. Value engineering activity

√ Deal with special situations. There are situations in which purchasing, because of sole-source or delivery problems, may be forced into dealing with a less than desirable vendor. Quality control can aid purchasing and still assure product quality by adding or increasing source inspection, adjusting the receiving inspection plan, or conducting a vendor quality conference. It is this type of action that makes quality control an integral part of the procurement team.

√ Provide prompt service to purchasing on quality problems. This can be accomplished either by placing a person physically in the purchasing department if your organization is large enough, or by placing your own offices adjacent to purchasing, for easy access.

√ Ensure timely and coordinated disposition of nonconforming material. Rejection of material causes more grief to purchasing than it does to quality control. QC must provide *effective* costs (purchase price + unplanned inspection + material review + . . .) to purchasing. If this is not done, the low bid will be the sole purchase criterion.

√ Work jointly with purchasing on follow-up material discrepancy and corrective action reports. The company that assigns a clerk the job of insisting on getting vendor replies within the prescribed time, only to file them when they arrive, isn't achieving anything. Buyers should identify the most serious problems and concentrate corrective action effort on them.

√ Keep purchasing informed. Although direct communications between buyer and seller quality functions assists planning, understanding and communications, purchasing must be advised of informal agreements, quality status, problems, and quality achievements, otherwise buyers may be occasionally embarrassed and lacking information that may be useful in negotiations with the vendor.

√ Provide purchasing with up-to-date approved vendor lists (a list of disapproved sources may be a legal problem).

Promptly process material through incoming inspection. Slow processing means assembly lines don't get needed material, and this generally reflects poorly on purchasing. In addition, slow processing may mean the loss of trade discounts (typically 1 to 2 percent) in those companies that pay vendors only after material acceptance.

When purchasing recognizes that quality control is there to help, the cooperation will flow, and you can do your job more effectively and under more pleasant conditions. Vendor quality control must promote good relations with purchasing without compromising product quality.

In essence, a good procurement quality control program will supply timely information to purchasing on vendor performance, provide prompt responses to purchasing's quality problems, be flexible in defining quality requirements, and be an integral part of the procurement team.

HOW TO GET THE VENDOR ON THE TEAM

Vendors are merely extensions of your own factory. Suppliers are team members, not adversaries. A QC department that works closely with suppliers and purchasing can make a very valuable contribution to profits, customer service, and inventory control.

Case in Point: One European marketing vice president observed, "When I visit a U.S. customer, I am allowed to present my product and then out I go. When I recently visited a Japanese customer, on the other hand, I was told we would meet with a group of four people—which turned into a group of ten. I was told we would probably be there for an hour, but we were there for four hours as they questioned and probed me for information on what was happening in other areas and with other manufacturers.

"All the time I was speaking they were taking notes frantically. After I finished, they had a discussion to ensure that they had all the necessary information. I was then asked to tour their factory and make suggestions and recommendations to improve their product."

Quality will result when a sound and mutually profitable long-term relationship is established between seller and buyer. Here are some ideas:

√ Explain the requirements of the job from a technical, quality, and schedule perspective.

√ Spell out your quality standards and expectations in clear, no-nonsense terms. Explain how you will be accepting the product.

√ Prepare clear, unambiguous procurement drawings after discussion with vendors. Always inform suppliers of the intended application. Relate specification requirements to real needs and avoid excessive frills.

√ Get to know key individuals and build relationships; this will help when you want corrective action.

√ Provide engineering or other technical assistance when required.

√ Hold "vendor days" at your plant; let suppliers see how their product is used.

√ Streamline communication channels.

Case in Point: One U.S.-based manufacturer of aircraft was a very large number of small suppliers. In order to simplify the interfaces with them, a set of streamlined procedures are utilized. Special information packages and forms are prepared for these suppliers covering shipment documentation, source inspection, and handling of nonconforming material. Additionally, a telephone "hot line" was set up for these small suppliers that answered their business and commercial questions.

√ Assist in failure analysis.

√ Feed back quality results for corrective action, cost reduction, or product improvement.

√ Advise vendors of upcoming workload whether up, flat, or down.

√ Negotiate a fair price; if a traditional vendor is high, work together to bring costs down.

√ Make your test facilities available when working on common problems.

√ Try not to consume more than 15 to 20 percent of your supplier's productive capacity.

√ Call supplier conferences to explore specifications, future needs, value engineering, R & D. You'll probably learn as much as you disclose.

√ Give achievement awards: supplier-of-the-year plaques, letters of merit. Your vendors will appreciate it.

REVIEW SUPPLIER INVOICES

It is customary for the accounting department to reconcile receiving documents, the purchase order (PO), and a supplier's invoice before making payment. Several errors can occur, such as:

● Unit price on invoice is greater than PO price.

● Quantity shipped is greater than that ordered.

● Quantity received is less than that invoiced.

● Part number on invoice is different from that on PO.

● A precious metal or other surcharge has been unilaterally added to the invoiced price.

● The invoice is not in correct currency (e.g., Canadian vs. U.S. funds).

● Federal sales tax has been added, although it is not applicable.

● The invoice was mailed to the wrong address.

● Freight costs have been included although PO stated fob point was buyer's dock.

From a quality control point of view, some interesting observations and conjectures can be made. First, these errors—which are referred to buyers for resolution—upset buyers and waste their time. Second, delays in paying suppliers doesn't make them happy. Finally, suppliers who are sloppy in invoicing (their source of funds) just may be sloppy in manufacturing or quality control.

Procurement quality control can offer some very valuable assistance in improving invoice quality using established QC disciplines. The main benefit to purchasing is more time to spend on important matters such as source evaluation, negotiation, and so on. Also, the corrective action may just rub off on the vendor and purchased part quality once it is realized you are a professional organization.

Here are the steps:

- Establish invoice defect categories applicable to your business.
- Collect "defect" data for two or three months.
- Evaluate data so as to identify most frequently occurring reconciliation problems and most frequently offending suppliers.
- Take corrective action.

Case in Point: A manufacturer of industrial safety equipment was faced with a serious problem of overshipments by suppliers. This increased inventories and space, consumed much time in accounting and purchasing, and raised communication (telex, twx, long distance) expenses well over budget. A joint QC/purchasing evaluation pointed out that (1) PO did not in fact have an overshipment clause, and (2) only sixteen suppliers caused 95 percent of the occurrences. After adding the appropriate clause, sending a letter to the senior management of the sixteen companies, and refusing to pay several invoices until they were corrected, the problem virtually disappeared. It was estimated that savings were in excess of $1000 per month.

KNOW THE SOURCE SELECTION CRITERIA

It is instructive to review what factors most interest purchasing executives in the selection of sources. Generally, the selection criteria used are as follows:

1. Plant loading and capacity
2. Responsiveness
3. Quality controls
4. Quality of management
5. Capital and special equipment
6. Plant condition and housekeeping
7. Financial stability
8. Labor force
9. Previous schedule and quality performance
10. R & D technical competence
11. Systems and procedures
12. Paperwork: custom forms, C of Cs, test data, handbooks, manuals, reports

13. Location: freight costs, transportation
14. Satisfied customers

Caution: Treat "satisfied customer" lists with skepticism. Check them out for validity, relevance, and accuracy.

One could write a long diatribe on the importance price should play in source selection. The following quotation sometimes seen in QC managers' offices says it all.

It's unwise to pay too much but it's worse to pay too little. When you pay too much, you lose a little money—that is all. When you pay too little, you sometimes lose everything, because the thing you bought was incapable of doing the thing it was bought to do. The common law of business balance prohibits paying a little and getting a lot—it can't be done. If you deal with the lowest bidder, it is well to add something for the risk you run, and if you do that you will have enough to pay for something better.

John Ruskin
(1819–1900)

Purchasing must buy from the lowest, *responsible, responsive* bidder. PQC can help point the way.

Any award of purchase order will, of course, depend on price, modified by the fourteen parameters defined in Table 12-2.

Pitfall to Avoid: The PQC system must include *all* purchased items, although different approaches may be required. For instance, capital equipment is often purchased without a PQC involvement. Table 12-2 lists a typical set of procurement clauses for this class of purchase.

Case in Point: A buyer for a medium-sized pharmaceutical firm obtained five quotes. In evaluating the bidders she considered quality of management and housekeeping as deciding factors in the placement of the order. Her decision was based on the simple fact that when supervisors are first-class leaders, workers also will exhibit these same standards. During her plant surveys she was impressed with the second-lowest bidder and discouraged at management attitudes by the low bidder. Poor housekeeping, indicative of poor quality maintenance procedures and management practices, clinched the decision.

Case in Point: The subcontracts manager of a major aircraft manufacturer selected the

TABLE 12-2. Typical Capital Equipment Procurement QC Clauses

1. Final system acceptance will be after installation and successful testing at Buyer plant.

2. Warranty to start after acceptance of equipment at Buyer plant. This includes components which are part of the system but not manufactured by the seller.

3. Buyer reserves the right to visit seller's facilities when deemed necessary to review progress, design features, and/or proof-out activities.

4. Operating/Service manuals and parts list shall be part of the data package accompanying equipment shipment.

5. A copy of the detailed proof-out test data results shall be forwarded to Buyer with the shipment of the equipment.

6. By acceptance of this order, Seller agrees to inform Buyer immediately of any proposed changes that may affect input power, size, weight, performance, capacity, or other specified requirement of the item on this order.

7. All equipment(s) covered by this order shall have UL approval prior to shipment from Seller's plant.

8. The operator training course shall be held at Seller's plant. A maximum of five Buyer personnel will take the course detailed in Seller's proposal.

9. Digital readouts shall be in imperial units with touch-switch conversion to SI metric units.

10. Seller agrees to provide spare parts for ten years at prices contained in Seller's cost proposal adjusted for escalation.

- Engineering-critical items requiring extensive quality assurance
- Long lead-time items
- State-of-the-art, high-technology parts
- Scarce materials
- Large capital equipment purchases
- Sole sources
- Part numbers with high engineering-change activity
- Major tool design, tooling, or qualification test effort
- Computer software subcontracts
- Items recently switched from a make to a buy
- Items with high price escalation rates

Case in Point: An alert PQC engineer noticed rapid price increases of a component over a period of a few months. After a brief check at incoming inspection revealed increasing reject rates, he visited the usually reliable supplier. His on-site review quickly identified the cause of the problem. The supplier's raw material vendors had escalated their prices. The supplier in turn skimped on various tests and inspections in order to minimize price increases. After some discussion and minor price adjustments, reject rates returned to their former levels. Despite the slight increase in price, net costs were reduced 5 percent because of major reduction in reject rate.

MAKE OR BUY POLICY: A FUNDAMENTAL CONTROL POINT

Make or Buy is the decision-making process concerned with manufacturing or processing in-house versus purchasing an item or service from an outside source. Make-or-Buy decisions must be based on a considerable number of factors, many of which are not susceptible to straight cost analysis. Such decisions, except when concerning relatively minor matters, cannot be the responsibility of any one department or group.

The Buy decision is generally the easy way out. The cost can usually be determined in advance and included in the selling point. Unfortunately, if everything is bought and assembled, the product may not be salable because of the lack of quality control in manufacture, or the final selling

high bidder (7 percent higher than low bidder) based on quality controls and labor force. The low bidder simply could not demonstrate effective controls over product quality. His labor force was not stable or well trained and had a history of labor and strike troubles.

CONCENTRATE ON THE FEW

The Pareto principle applies to the procurement function as well. A PQC function that concentrates on the critical few will increase its cost effectiveness. The following list provides a clue into where potential quality problems lie:

price may be too high. Buying permits lower investment in facilities, smaller labor forces, lower plant cost for building and upkeep, and less space, insurance, supervision, and so on. Buying permits specialization, test/manufacture by the most efficient equipment, lower inventories, scheduling of deliveries as required, and competitive bidding.

The Make decision requires capital equipment, personnel, material, supervision, and, in varying degrees, overhead, maintenance, management attention, and other indirect costs. "Making" returns immediate control of quality. It also may provide work for idle equipment or personnel, utilize scrap material, shorten delivery time, permit use of a part that outside suppliers are not able to produce, permit experimentation, promote flexibility on new designs, ensure continuity of supply, train personnel for more complicated operations, cost less than purchased items, and keep design information secret.

Quality control has an important role to play in the make-or-buy decision. Quality control can usually provide valuable insight into the problems faced by the current vendors and the actions required to prevent recurrence. In some cases procurement problems are not the fault of the vendors, yet a company may erroneously decide to proceed with manufacturing a part in-house.

Case in Point: A manufacturer of general aviation aircraft instruments had severe quality and delivery problems with its supplier of illuminated front control panels. With production schedules constantly jeopardized by an inadequate supply of panels, the firm's management leaned toward making the parts itself. The QC engineer on the make/buy committee pointed out that the supplier was faced with working to procurement drawings that were unclear, ambiguous, and unrealistically toleranced. It was also pointed out that a constant stream of engineering changes further complicated the issue. Based on these facts a detailed review of the situation convinced management to clean up the engineering drawings and to work more closely with the supplier.

At times, QC may itself be faced with a make/buy decision. When should a firm purchase its own equipment, rather than go "outside" for testing? Among the factors to consider:

√ *Distance to laboratory.* How much time is lost in travel to that lab and waiting for tests to commence? Consider all the individuals who at various times will need to make the trip to witness tests. Include not only test personnel but also quality and reliability people, as well as project personnel.

√ *Schedule control.* Can outside facilities be made available when required? This can be crucial when a critical certification or qualification test program is to be scheduled.

√ *Number of sources.* If a number of acceptable test facilities are available, the schedule and cost problem is usually reduced. Conversely, a sole source can mean high costs and potential schedule conflicts.

√ *Loading.* Relatively continuous loading tends to favor the Make decision. Erratic or low-level loading favors the Buy decision.

√ *Space.* Test facilities such as an environmental lab take up significant amounts of space. If space is at a premium this factor can weigh heavily in favor of a Buy decision.

√ *Personnel.* The availability of trained personnel is an important consideration, as is their loading. Intermittent test loading can mean idle time/overtime cycles for highly paid test technologists.

√ *Capital costs.* Test facilities usually don't come cheap. A financial justification should be prepared whenever possible because management has many alternative uses for its limited capital resources.

√ *Psychological factors.* Perhaps the most important factor favoring an in-house laboratory is the number of tests that should be done (various development tests) but that aren't done due to distance and delays. For too many firms, a qualification test is the first test; a failure is catastrophic. Early developmental tests would have shown the weakness in time for redesign.

Case in Point: A medium-sized manufacturer of marine radar systems had a marginal case regarding the purchase of a random vibration test facility. At the suggestion of the QC manager, two other divisions of the corporation and several local firms were approached. Based on a very conservative estimate of their total test needs the facility was acquired. It made a tidy profit in its first year of operation.

REVIEW PURCHASE REQUISITIONS

Once the desired standard has been set, the procurement phase begins with the generation of a material requisition. The review of purchase requisitions by quality control personnel can be cost effective. Unfortunately, in many companies this activity is an "end-of-the-line" function, occurring just before or even after a supplier commitment has been made. All too frequently this review degenerates into a meaningless formality. To be effective, place emphasis on hardcore technical and quality control matters with priority on expensive and/or engineering-critical components. Management by exception is vital. Some of the items worth checking for include:

√ A clear and accurate definition of the part to be procured including type, grade, and class and applicable drawing number and revision letter. If you use a vendor's catalogue and specifications, watch for the notation "Subject to Change Without Notice."

√ The requirement for certified test data on all precision or expensive parts when satisfactory testing upon receipt is neither economical nor possible. Don't count on certifications of compliance to provide assurance of anything.

Certification   B.A.D. Corporation

This is to certify that to the best of our knowledge the materials delivered are in accordance with requirements.

Rush M. Out
Chief Expediter

√ The requirement of approval samples for such items as castings, extrusions, etc. Test coupons representative of the production lot should be used anywhere where destructive testing can be meaningfully avoided.

Case in Point: A manufacturer of process control equipment for the petrochemical industry used a complex multilayer printed circuit board in the main controller unit. Such boards require rigid quality assurance because once components are mounted on defective boards, the entire assembly may have to be scrapped. An alert PQC analyst noted that the artwork for the board did not contain a test coupon that could be cross-sectioned and microscopically evaluated. Evaluating multilayer board without a properly designed test coupon is like trying to wash your feet with your socks on. The artwork was amended and a potentially very costly problem averted. The estimated minimum saving was $175 since one of the boards would have had to be destructively tested.

√ Adherence to the company's approved component sourcing list. Don't leave vendor selection up to the distributor.

√ Adherence to the company's approved special processing (heat treat, welding, painting, etc.) source list.

√ Packaging and shipping instructions consistent with part fragility.

√ Identification of sources with poor or unacceptable quality histories.

√ Insertion of special QC terms and conditions (e.g., serialization, date coding, quality program requirements, test procedure approvals, first article approval, source inspection) as required.

√ Configuration control over vendor tooling. Many a batch of purchased items has caused severe pain to the buyer because of the lack of vendor configuration control. Procedures must be established to control vendor drawings, tooling, numerical control (N/C) programs, automatic test tapes, artwork, molds, etc., to ensure compatibility with engineering changes. Such procedures must include provisions for the identification, accounting, and periodic audit of vendor-retained items.

EMPLOY VENDOR SURVEYS WITH DISCRIMINATION

A vendor quality survey has become an accepted, if not always effective, fact of industrial life. This type of survey follows a general pattern: a visit by one or more functions almost always including quality control personnel, the answering of a series of questions on a questionnaire form, and a tour of the facility for the purpose of verifying by actual observation the correctness of the answers given in the questionnaire.

Sometimes surveys are an excuse for a quality manager to get out of the office. Sharp PQC engineers have successfully managed to schedule surveys during the Olympics, the World Series, and the Super Bowl. Clearly, vendor surveys and plant visits need appropriate management and control.

Important: Surveys must be tailored to the situation to take into account vendor size, nature of purchased commodity, and nature of procurement.

A properly conducted survey by trained personnel can be an important element of a PQC program. Typically it can:

- establish a level of confidence in the vendor's capability.
- screen out obviously unacceptable vendors.
- provide time to work with the vendor on known deficiencies.
- prevent development of quality problems.
- allow review of supplier's progress and milestone achievements.
- supplement inspection and testing.
- build relationships with vendor personnel.
- assist preplanning for source and/or receiving inspection activity.
- audit continuing quality competence.
- provide early warning of management shuffles, layoffs, bankruptcy, or strike.

Detailed survey checklists are available in many existing texts. Listed following, however, are the items that generally have the greatest bearing on final performance.

√ Does the vendor have written procedures for inspection, test, and process control?

√ How are customer quality requirements flowed down to vendor engineering, production, and QC?

√ Do engineering, manufacturing, and quality have good working relationships?

√ How does the vendor handle suppliers?

√ Are nonconforming material review practices centered around corrective action?

√ Is the plant in a growth or slowdown mode?

√ Are stockrooms clean and orderly?

√ Is vendor's quality information system adequate and used?

√ Are housekeeping and material handling practices adequate?

√ Is the plant operating at overcapacity?

√ Are the engineering depth and resources consistent with nature of procurement?

√ Is test and measuring equipment adequate in terms of quantity and technical requirements?

√ What is the tenure of company officers?

√ Do QC personnel appear technically competent and aggressive?

√ Is the QC-to-production personnel ratio realistic?

√ How are engineering and purchase order changes controlled?

√ Is there a final packaging and invoicing check prior to shipment?

Case in Point: The motor is a costly part of an elevator system. So when purchasing found a supplier bidding 25 percent less than existing suppliers, interest was high. Because of the safety-critical nature of the part, a quality engineer and a senior buyer surveyed their facility. They found:

1. a poorly defined quality system and organization
2. lack of calibration control
3. chaotic production and quality planning
4. inadequate contamination control procedures
5. lack of process control (e.g., welding)
6. no material certifications
7. lack of adequate test facilities

The vendor was advised of the findings but refused to take corrective action. His bid was deemed to be nonresponsive.

Evaluate vendors fairly and appraise them of survey results. This often points out communication breakdowns. The vendor has a right to know what the comparative quality position is because it predicts the future of his or her firm and employees. Common benefits are derived by working together. It is equally important to commend vendors for a job done well.

Surveys usually involve out-of-town travel and the time of several personnel. Accordingly, surveys should be selectively applied.

Consider these checklist items:

√ unit cost and total purchase order value

√ contractual complexity

√ engineering criticality (safety, performance, reliability of purchased item)

√ previous quality history of supplier

√ type of item procured (piece part, subsystem, computer software, etc.)

√ nature of item (custom part or catalogue item)

√ schedule considerations

Note: Vendor survey costs can be reduced by visiting several suppliers in a geographic area. Larger corporations establish central survey headquarters in various regions of the country. This arrangement also permits economical follow-up for source inspection and surveillance when required.

PURCHASE VENDOR SURVEYS AND SURVEILLANCE

Several firms will provide a range of source inspection, quality survey, expediting, and purchasing services at out-of-town locations for a fee. The potential benefits include:

- Reduced costs for air fare, lodging, meals, and car rental.

- No pensions, insurance, vacation time, sick leave, holidays, or other company-paid employee fringe benefits.

- Faster surveys because of on-site representatives.

- Lower costs if survey report for firm of interest is already in data bank.

- Expertise because of the large pool of available resources.

- Psychological advantage of having an on-the-spot representative.

- Payments only for work performed if for a half day or a few months.

- Improved productivity of quality personnel because of reduction in time lost in traveling to suppliers' plants.

Cautions: The use of purchased quality services must be on a case-by-case basis. For instance, when proprietary data or high technology is involved a company would probably use its own employees. Complex subcontracts may require so much briefing that a direct visit may be the only way out. The quality of personnel assigned to your job may not reflect your company image, or worse, may cause a deterioration in vendor relationships. Motivation, ethics, and loyalty are other problems that must be considered by the user of purchased quality services. Like any man-agement tool, this service must be used at the proper time and with the proper care.

DON'T FORGET DISTRIBUTORS

Distributors are firms that stock standard components and materials for sale to local manufacturers. They are useful when lead time or low purchasing volume preclude direct purchase from a vendor (manufacturer). Some different approaches to vendor quality are required when dealing with a distributor:

√ Ensure distributor is a vendor-authorized franchised distributor.

√ Check records for purchase date, vendor name.

√ Audit storage, shelf life, and preservation practices.

√ Ensure that quality controls, however limited, are adequate enough that you get the right part.

√ Ensure that adequate testing is performed by your incoming inspection.

QC VALUE ANALYSIS INPUTS CAN BE CRUCIAL

Value analysis offers a useful tool for achieving reduced product costs. In theory, value engineering changes should not adversely impact product reliability, quality, or safety. Unfortunately, in practice the integrity of a purchased item can be degraded if adequate change controls do not exist. As an absolute minimum, quality control should be a member of the change evaluation committee to ensure that due consideration is paid to compliance with functional requirements.

Case in Point: A vendor submitted a significant cost reduction proposal that would have replaced gold plated connector pins with a special process developed by the vendor. QC evaluation of the proposal resulted in nonacceptance because:

- The wear characteristics of the new process were below minimum requirements.

- The metals in the new process were not compatable with the pin material and would have caused a long-term reliability problem.

- Control procedures for the new process were found to be inadequate, lending to large lot-to-lot variations.

BEWARE OF DROP-SHIPPED ITEMS

Drop-shipped items include items going to erection or installation sites, parts going directly to distribution warehouses or to service agencies, replacement items ordered directly, and items sent directly to customers in order to minimize costs and test duplication. The basic concern, regardless of the form of the problem, is how to ensure the quality of items shipped directly from vendors to customers. In the customer's view, the product manufacturer is responsible for all shipments, including those shipped directly from a supplier.

In any drop-ship case, the possibility exists that unsatisfactory quality product may enter the supply channel because it is not subject to the types of control normally exercised over material used in in-house production. Some possible solutions:

√ Have all such material sent to a central site where it can be examined as though for production.

√ Utilize source inspection and acceptance procedures.

√ Employ vendor surveillance and certification.

√ Perform hardware audits throughout the distribution flow, including dealer and service stocks. (A related problem, which the audit program helps address, is the practice by some service agencies of substituting lower-quality, lower-cost replacement parts for qualified ones.)

√ Submit test data to product manufacturer in parallel with the drop-shipment.

In a given situation, combinations of all or some of these five approaches may prove most effective, perhaps coupled with dated stock, stock return allowances, and other service quality incentive programs. Whenever the programs fail and installers, service groups, or customers identify defective drop-shipped items, or when the controls uncover an unsatisfactory level of quality anywhere in the supply channel, the company must react positively and rapidly in correcting the problem. Such reaction may be complicated by questions of ownership of material, work that may have been done on or with the item, and the quantity and geographic dispersion of items involved. Nonetheless, the company's reputation may be at stake, as well as the potential for product liability claims and, in some product situations, action by a national consumer product safety agency or commission.

Proper control of drop-shipped items can re-

duce customer complaints dramatically and must be carefully planned.

Caution: Engineering- or safety-critical parts should not, in general, be drop-shipped.

USE SOURCE INSPECTION FOR SPECIAL SITUATIONS

Sometimes it is economical to visit suppliers and perform acceptance at source. This may be necessitated by lack of suitable buyer measuring equipment, the need for in-process or preseal controls or simply coordination of test methods. The development of personal relationships between buyer and seller is also enhanced. Source inspectors may also be called to perform other useful duties such as production status tracking, expediting, hand carry of material, and so on.

See to it that your people are properly informed on the requirements before going out on a job. There is nothing that will ruin your reputation more quickly with a vendor than having a vendor give your so-called expert an indoctrination course. Give the source person a packet containing the purchase order, quality requirements, drawings, and engineering specification before he or she leaves, so the person can show up on the scene fully prepared.

Incoming Inspection: The Forgotten Land

A key step in the procurement cycle is the acceptance of the part into inventory. Some manufacturers have found vendor certification schemes to be cost effective. Others employ source inspection extensively. Still others depend heavily on specialized test and evaluation houses. Nearly every firm has some form of in-house incoming inspection. Regardless of acceptance technique, the basis and criteria for acceptance between buyer and seller must be coordinated and well understood. Lack of communication has probably caused more unnecessary costs and trouble than any other single factor.

Incoming inspection is vital, but all too often it becomes a place rather than a function. Pareto's principle provides a sound basis for economical incoming inspection management. Operationally, this means that a small percentage of all part numbers make up most of the purchase dollar. It implies that a few vendors of the many will receive most of our purchase dollar; most important, it implies that a few part numbers will account for a large percentage of the problems. A good vendor quality information system will point the way.

Over the last few years, the question, "Do we need incoming inspection?" has been replaced by, "How much testing is enough?" Test equipment manufacturers point out that although devices are supposedly 100 percent tested under ambient conditions by suppliers, problems can occur because of human error, test discrepancies, incorrect branding, inadequate storage, or transportation damage.

The amount of incoming inspection/test will depend on the nature of the part, past vendor history, the criticality of the part in its intended application, and the nature of the characteristic. One must attempt to balance risks so as to minimize overall costs. Sampling plans such as MIL-STD-105D along with a classification of defects attempt to achieve this objective.

Incoming inspection effectiveness can be increased:

√ Develop a good integrated closed-loop failure reporting system.

√ Censure closer cooperation between production test and incoming test.

√ Run indoctrination sessions to increase the understanding of the role of incoming inspection in the production cycle.

√ Have reliability engineering give incoming test sufficient data to make a preliminary test plan before historical data is available.

√ Include classification of characteristics on drawings for vendor and incoming inspection planning.

√ Carefully control test methods and the inspection work instructions. In many cases, the responsibility for their validation, if not preparation, should be given to the designer or a test engineer.

√ Make the incoming test plan an integral part of the production test plan.

√ Review the physical location of incoming inspection with the aim of integrating it more closely with the production process.

√ Perform failure analysis of assembly failures leading to corrective action in the form of a change to the procurement drawing, incoming inspection test procedure, or source inspection.

Even a properly staffed and well-equipped incoming test function can be rendered ineffective if use-as-is material review dispositions occur more than 20 percent of the time. MIL-TFD-41 (see reference at end of chapter) provides excellent guidance here. A decision to get tougher on rejecting when the stockroom gets a little ahead on a part vitiates the purpose of specifications. Another important aspect of incoming inspection operations is special test equipment and procedures; have engineering assist in their development and prove-out, otherwise inappropriate tests may incorrectly reject good material or inadvertently accept bad material.

USE OF AQLs

In the U.S., POs or contracts embody agreed levels of AQL (Acceptable Quality Level). These AQLs, once agreed on, unify the parties on the sampling to be used and provide a basis for adjudicating disputes. Under this approach, many U.S. manufacturers tend also to view the AQLs as tolerable limits; efforts have even been made to standardize AQLs.

In contrast, the Japanese take the view that the AQLs tend to reduce the incentive for quality improvement. Hence, while for contract purposes they may quantify AQLs, their real purpose is to find the best vendor, not merely one whose AQL is competitive.

The reasoning behind the Japanese view is evident from two major imperatives of consumer product reliability. In the first place, component failures have been the major cause of field failures (and of in-house fall-off rates). Secondly, the number of components in, say, a color TV set runs to over one thousand. Such numbers can convert component defect rates of the order of 0.1 percent into set yield rates of less than 40 percent. For example, the reliability of a simple assembly with 100 parts would be:

RELIABILITY FACTOR OF EACH PART	OVERALL RELIABILITY OF THE COMPLETE ASSEMBLY
99.7%	74.0%
99.0%	36.6%
98.0%	13.2%
96.0%	1.7%

This multiplying effect has been a factor in the Japanese use of ppm (parts per million) as a unit of measure for component quality.

In the design qualification stage, components are overstressed, and environmentally tested to bring their weaknesses out into the open. In addition, there must be a strict discipline of discovering the precise failure modes so that corrective action can be taken. Subsequently, during production, defects at the ppm level can be dealt with only on an automated sorting basis. Clearly, for defect rates in the ppm range, the AQL concept is useless.

WHAT TO DO WITH INCOMING INSPECTION REJECTIONS

Rejections must be handled with extreme caution. If improperly dealt with, a rejection can result in major confrontations with purchasing, material control, manufacturing, and vendors. It can also upset delivery schedules, inflate work-in-process inventory, and increase production costs. The resolution of rejections requires a practical, down-to-earth systems approach. Poorly managed QC rejections are made up of misunderstandings and "standing on principle." Sometimes you have to rise above principle.

The first thing to do is confirm the validity of the rejection. All too often incorrect drawing issues, uncalibrated test equipment, or faulty test procedures are the true cause. The second step involves determining the degree of severity of the nonconformance. If it is minor, perhaps it can be accepted as is with a report sent to the vendor. If it must be reworked, repaired, sorted, or returned, then other affected functional units must be informed so that cost and schedule impact can be ascertained.

If manufacturing absolutely needs some parts and the replenishment time is excessive, 100 percent sorting may be in order. Purchasing would be given the task of negotiating the cost of sorting, debiting the supplier for the balance returned, and ensuring prompt replacement. Since improvement for the future is also required, PQC must provide the vendor with a test/inspection report documenting the nonconformances with a request for corrective action.

This direct liaison with the vendor is important for several reasons:

- It establishes a technical communication channel for promptly resolving quality problems.
- It demonstrates to the supplier's management that you are serious about purchased product quality.
- It shows that you are fair in your resolution of quality problems.

Case in Point: A major equipment manufacturer purchased electroplated mechanical parts from a small local firm. A contamination problem in her plating baths had gone undetected until receipt by the manufacturer, whose more sophisticated equipment did detect the contamination. A process engineer assisted the supplier in correcting her tanks and improving her technical controls. An inexpensive rework procedure was also jointly devised so that the rejected lot did not have to be scrapped.

- It avoids embarrassments, wasted time, and degraded relations.

Case in Point: A supplier of a high technology state-of-the-art part was notified by telex of 100 percent failure of his shipment. After one telephone call it became clear that the buyer's incoming inspection department did not have the proper test equipment or expertise to make the highly complex measurements.

- It develops mutual cooperation and diminishes defensiveness.

VENDOR CORRECTIVE ACTION: A TRICKY JOB

An interesting side effect of corrective action programs is that when solutions have been developed astutely, many problems, instead of requiring separate solutions, have disappeared with one corrective action. This interdependence is commonly discovered when correcting the cause of an apparently "internal only" nonconformity results in the disappearance of a field failure whose source was unknown. For this reason, many highly successful programs start with eliminating nonconformities associated with purchased material and correcting the sources of nonconformities while moving step-by-step through the manufacturing process.

Obtaining corrective action on purchased material involves dealing with a large set of complex variables associated with the dozens, hundreds, or thousands of vendors. Most vendor corrective action systems turn into paper mills. Some companies even measure their success by the volume of paperwork generated. If you are caught in the paper mill—sending letters to vendors on each discrepancy and getting answers in return—then the corrective action system is ineffective. Some play the game to satisfy the customer, but remember the vendor quickly learns his role in the game. He has a list of standard excuses (not corrective action) and picks the one that most nearly fits the situation without relation to the actual facts. Examples:

- "Our final inspector has been informed."
- "The guilty employee has been fired."
- "It must have been damaged in transit."
- "We've tightened up on inspection."
- "Our supplier sent us defective material."
- "We were working to an old issue of the drawing."

When engaging in corrective action make sure that a direct communication link is established between the buyer QC and vendor QC. Dealing solely through purchasing and the vendor's marketing operation or sales representative is ineffective. Something is always lost in the translation, if there is any translation. Make sure, though, that you keep purchasing fully informed—something may be going on that you don't know about.

Be flexible and initiate corrective action that will be effective. When dealing with suppliers on routine problems, a standard CAR form is usually used for convenience. When you really want vendor corrective action this form is supplemented with a letter or telex and possibly a phone call to the VP or president of the vendor's firm by your director of purchasing and yourself. For chronic problems or safety-related defects a high-level face-to-face meeting in which each item can be discussed and agreements made may be the only effective means of communication. Alternatively, that portion of the quality subsystem that is failing can be identified by analyzing the types of defects, and an audit of that quality subsystem can physically demonstrate to the vendor the reason for the failures. This approach has great impact and is very effective in getting verification that a problem exists.

When a vendor is not producing up to requirements, let him know in clear terms, backed up by facts. Remember, he is depending on the orders your company places. You are merely giving him a fair appraisal and a chance to straighten out. To do otherwise would be an injustice to the vendor. Don't decide to discontinue business with a vendor without confronting him with your performance appraisal. Give him a chance to defend his products and improve, if required. Many outstanding vendors are developed when they understand the rules of the game. Conversely, when you are convinced that all reasonable effort has been expended, and the performance standards are not being attained, it is your responsibility to see to it that this vendor is eliminated as a source of supply.

Pitfalls to Avoid: Check your facts before you request vendor corrective action. Have you read the purchase order? Is an AQL specified? Have mutually agreed test methods been established? Did purchasing issue any waivers? Are your procurement drawings ambiguous? Is there any evidence of shipping damage? When was your test equipment last calibrated? Were sampling plans, arithmetic calculations, and data recording properly accomplished? Does test data correlate with vendors?

HOW TO DEAL WITH A SOLE SOURCE

The sole source is an almost inevitable fact of modern industrial life. A sole source means tough bargaining, continuous price pressure, and, more often than not, a certain amount of nonresponsiveness and even arrogance. While every attempt should be made to avoid sole sources, the modern PQC manager must learn to deal with this situation and make the appropriate contribution to company goals.

First of all, QC must be aware of who the sole sources are and what's happening back at home base.

Case in Point: A buyer source inspector rejected an entire lot of packages used in the pharmaceutical industry. Unknown to her, her company was in delicate negotiations with the sole source firm regarding a multiyear contractual arrangement. The vendor increased his price because of the "rigid enforcement of specifications." Eventually this supplier priced himself out of the market, but the short-term damage was not welcomed by purchasing management.

A second important point is that corrective action activity with sole sources requires unusual tact, diplomacy, and patience. The most effective negotiating points are:

- Suggest that better in-process controls will decrease high quality losses and increase the vendor's market share and profit.
- Point out that continuing rejections, sorting, source inspection costs, and such are making his "effective" cost very high and inviting the attention of senior management.
- Advise him that product liability claims can extend to suppliers.

Buyers have their own list of negotiating tools, but the job is never easy and it is full of pitfalls for the unwary.

The last point is simple—PQC should help purchasing identify and develop alternate sources and/or suggest acceptable substitutions. An aggressive approach by PQC can be an invaluable aid to a buyer trying to keep assembly lines flowing.

CERTIFY YOUR VENDORS—SAVE MONEY

The concept of vendor certification is not new. This topic has been discussed in many conferences, and a number of papers have been written on this subject during the past decade. Yet, the application of this philosophy has been restricted; as a result, a brief restatement is required because it is clear that a vendor certification program can simultaneously reduce quality cost, improve vendor quality, and decrease inventory carrying expenses.

A certification program reduces (a) receiving inspection costs, (b) the quality losses in the plant that may be attributed to excessive percent defective in vendor material, and (c) material review and corrective action costs.

Certification can be performed at not only the raw material level, but also the component, the subsystem, and the system level. A certification program can be employed during any stage of this cycle and sometimes can be referred to as a product certification. Hence, certifications can be directed to either a given product or for all products that a given supplier produces.

A vendor is eligible for a certification program if it falls into one of two categories: current suppliers who have exhibited consistently good quality performance, new vendors who have established acceptable performance.

This program is carried out in five steps:

1. Select vendors eligible for program.
2. Initiate precertification program discussions (ensure vendor understands obligations).
3. Initiate a trial program.
4. Terminate trial program; start formal program.
5. Maintain spot checks and feedback to vendor.

Case in Point: A Japanese motorcycle producer has carried the vendor certification process to the limit. Component parts from all the firm's vendors are now so compliant with drawings (defect rates measured in parts per hundred thousand or per million) that there is virtually no incoming inspection. There is also no *hedging* of stocks—ordering excessive quantities because of expected poor yield—no earlier-than-required deliveries to compensate for expected rejections, and no large safety stocks to deal with quality problems.

Deliveries are made twice daily so that component inventories and storage space are minimized. As a direct benefit, work-in-process inventory is reduced and process/quality problems can be more readily seen (Figure 12-3).

This Kanban system (often referred to a "just in time") of inventory control is made possible because of the "lifetime" business relationship between buyer and seller.

There are several important limitations of certification programs:

- They are not generally applicable to distributors.
- The cost of incoming inspection may be very small because of automation or simplicity of part.
- Vendors may have several plants with nonuniform quality controls.

- The administrative burden is more significant than is often recognized.
- Some engineering-critical parts must be 100 percent tested because of the very high consequences of an "escape."
- The ownership and, hence, quality policies of the vendor may change without advance notice.
- Quality managers are often not willing to take the risks involved.
- Returns and warranty claims are very difficult to apply once parts have been paid for and accepted into inventory.
- Inadequate storage, mislabeling, packaging errors, freight damage, mishandling in receiving, or other environmental factors may degrade parts after departure from vendor's plant.
- Value engineering changes may be covertly introduced into the part by the vendor.

VENDOR RATING: LOOK OUT FOR TRAPS

When a firm has a large number of vendors some sort of vendor rating system is required. Some systems stick to quality ratings while others attempt to consolidate quality, price, and delivery performance into one rating. Here are some guidelines for running a vendor rating system:

√ Stick to what you know best—quality ratings. Purchasing generally has excellent visibility on other commercial factors. Besides, purchasing decisions are rarely made solely on the basis of such a simplistic tool as a rating figure or strictly on past performance.

√ Realize accuracy limitations. A vendor rating usually has some degree of inaccuracy and therefore should not be used as an absolute measure of performance. The rating should be considered merely a means of taking a massive amount of data and reducing it to a manageable form. The apparently poor-performing vendors require further investigation to determine their true performance. Never eliminate a vendor from your approved list without a detailed investigation.

Case in Point: A thorough investigation of a poor-performing vendor revealed that the procurement drawings supplied were ambiguous, the PO used the required due date rather than the date quoted by the supplier, and buyer-supplied material was deficient.

√ Watch out for built-in errors in the ratings. One point very often missed is that of omitting source inspection results from the rating. Not

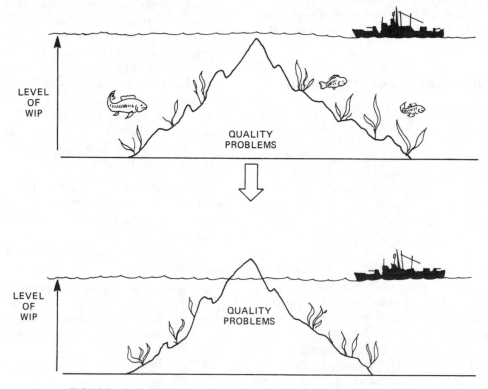

FIGURE 12-3. PQC Benefits on WIP and Problem Identification

infrequently, the source inspector rejects 100 percent, rework is accomplished, and then the receiving inspection results look excellent. The real facts are that the source inspector is controlling the vendor's quality and the vendor must not be rewarded.

√ Avoid rating formulas that are unduly complex. Keep your rating simple and make your data-capturing mechanism compatible with the size of your business. The most accurate rating system is often a simple percent acceptance ratio.

√ Don't automatically computerize the rating. A manually prepared report may be quite adequate for most purposes.

√ Ensure that ratings are considered in purchasing decisions. A special report should identify those vendors with totally unacceptable quality performance.

√ Organize the data so that it is easy to use and understand. Provide sorts by vendor (alphabetically), by commodity, and/or by buyer.

√ Distinguish between distributors/wholesalers and manufacturers when the same part number is available through both channels.

√ Ensure that report users understand the theory behind the system. Provide suitable comments where required.

Case in Point: Fifty pieces of a complex item were 100 percent inspected and eight defectives were found (that is, 84 percent good). Another simpler part, also a quantity of fifty, was sample-inspected using MIL-STD-105, and the entire lot was rejected (0 percent good) based on the sample information.

√ Provide current rating information. Old data is simply not useful to purchasing. Besides, they may have placed another order while you were still preparing the report.

√ Ensure that suppliers are appraised of their ratings when their performance is unacceptable or a downward trend is indicated. Exceptional vendor performers should also be advised—it won't hurt the QC cause within their firms.

CHOOSE OUTSIDE TEST LABS CAREFULLY

For a variety of reasons, a firm may need the services of an outside test laboratory. Some of the more common of these reasons are:

- A new firm has limited resources (all testing must be done outside).
- Laboratory space or equipment cannot be justified for tests that are seldom required.
- Testing capability can handle small units but not large assemblies.
- An in-house laboratory has an excessive workload.
- A firm is unable to find or keep qualified test personnel.

There is no test that some lab cannot do more cheaply than another, but price is only one criterion. Price *should* be considered, and very often one is required to obtain three quotes. Just don't base the selection (or allow the purchasing department to select) solely on price. QC must set an example in its own purchasing practices.

Before committing to a specific lab, talk to some users. Find out how often the lab work is not ready when promised or "bumps" customer tests. Speak with as many users as possible and don't be limited to those suggested by the lab. Try to protect against schedule delays by inserting penalty clauses in the purchase order for testing. Don't be surprised if the lab similarly seeks protection against your schedule delays.

Be sure to visit any laboratory being considered. Look around. Some signs of lax standards can be seen by casual observation, even by a nonexpert. Is there reasonable attention to personnel and equipment safety? Is the test area reasonably clean and neat? How are the instruments calibrated (in order that measurements can be certified for accuracy)? To what firm or agency are instruments sent for calibration? Ask to see some calibration records. Hopefully, the laboratory performs some types of calibration (checking its instruments against standards that are regularly sent outside for checking) while having other types of calibration done outside.

Seek an opportunity to speak not only with marketing personnel and laboratory management but also with test technicians, mechanics, and test engineers who will be handling your equipment. They will be setting up the test equipment and operating the laboratory's equipment during your test. How do you feel about their attitude toward the laboratory, toward their managers, and toward you—the prospective customer?

CHECKLIST FOR EVALUATING PQC

The items listed below usually provide a broad cross section of factors necessary to evaluate a PQC program fully:

√ Are vendor quality capabilities evaluated prior to placing an order?

√ Is quality-related information furnished to the vendor when a request for quotation (RFQ) is transmitted?

√ Are quality characteristics classified and AQLs established?

√ Are there special procedures for first-piece or first-shipment quality verification?

√ Is there a written quality plan for material acceptance?

√ Are disposition routines for discrepant material effective and timely?

√ How is regular quality information fed back to vendors?

√ Are vendor service activities (say, coordination of measurement equipment and practices) adequate?

√ Is there a vendor rating system?

√ Are present vendors certified to the greatest extent practical?

√ Are approved source lists available to buyers?

√ Do plant procedures adequately cover routing of purchased material through the quality control system?

√ Are failure analyses performed when required?

√ Does purchased part failure information from production, test, and field service form part of the PQC system?

√ Is there evidence that chronic quality problems are properly attended to?

√ Does a team approach attitude permeate vendor relations activity?

REFERENCES

ASQC Vendor-Vendee Technical Committee. "Procurement Quality Control: A Handbook of Recommended Practices." ASQC, 1969.

Behrens, W. H. "Procurement Document Reviews Move Upstream." *Quality Progress,* May 1969.

"How to Conduct a Supplier Survey." ASQC, 1977.

Hamblen, D. M. "Competent Purchase Specifications Help Assure Successful Product." *Computer Design,* May 1977.

Kivenko, K. "A Planned Approach to Procurement Quality Control." *Evaluation Engineering,* July/August 1979.

Johnston, P. E. "Electrical Component Selection." *Engineering Digest,* Sept. 1973.

McCoskrie, "Materials Test Measurements—Guideposts to Electronic Reliability." *Electronic Instrumentation,* Feb. 1972.

MIL-TFD-41 (Make it like the friggen drawing for once), unreleased specification, circa 200 B.C.

Shahnazarian, T. E. "Vendor Certification." *Industrial Quality Control,* April 1967.

"Why Purchasing Buys All That Junk." *Electronic Evaluation and Procurement,* Feb. 1963.

13

Shop Floor QC and the Real World

The shop floor is a complex environment. Quality control must deal with planned changes, tight delivery schedules, component shortages, and a host of other unplanned disturbances. The control of planned or unplanned changes is the underlying principle and the major substance of manufacturing quality control operations. As changes in planning occur, they call for careful evaluation and adjustment through planning, control, and coordination measures.

> If you can't find time to do it right, when will you find time to do it over?

Changes that create quality failures are by no means confined to management or to the individual worker's decisions. Therefore, they will not always be such clear-cut and noticeable phenomena as a change in raw materials or a change in manufacturing methods from milling to grinding. Many changes creep into the production system by virtue of time and production traffic. Metal wears not only on tool edges, but on checking surfaces, guides, sliding surfaces, bearings, handling devices, buffer pads, and a hundred other places. If one stands in a machine shop and listens, much of the variety of sounds indicates that wear is taking place.

The silent companions of wear in effecting changes are dirt and residue. Gradually they accumulate and build at "points of repose" much in the same way that a river bank collects debris in the quiet places behind the bends or below the rapids. Dirt composed of metal particles, lubricants, chemicals, small bits of the manufacturing materials moving through the line, and other waste material in the area can change the planned or designed paths of lubricants, wedge or throw moving parts out of alignment, trap moisture and chemicals to set up a corrosion process, or alter the direction and amount of fluids or solids flowing over a surface or into a process as originally planned.

Unplanned changes can be enormously expensive. It is evident that manufacturing and quality control engineers must work together to establish satisfactory process capabilities before production is initiated. The analysis of the results of carefully planned and conducted samplings of preliminary or trial operations allows useful prediction of future process capabilities. The actual verification of the adequacy of the process, however, can only be determined by sampling and evaluation under production line conditions.

Before you can increase productivity or improve quality, you must have stability and continuity in your manufacturing process. Management's job is to keep crises from developing on the production floor so that production people can focus their attention on quality and productivity (Figure 13-1).

This chapter shows you how to combine people, machines, and materials into a highly productive, competitive force.

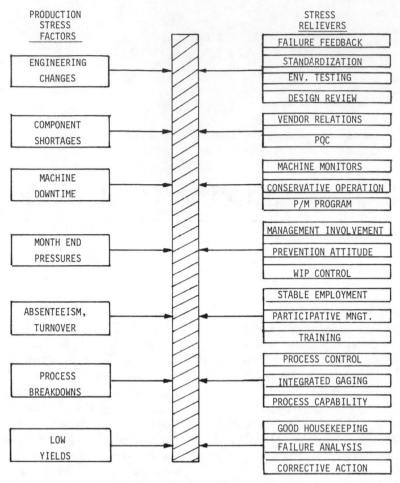

FIGURE 13-1. Balancing of Forces

IS THE WORK ETHIC GOING OUT OF STYLE?

There are many visible signs that the work ethic is being challenged. More and more executives retire while still in their fifties, dropping out of jobs in favor of a more relaxed lifestyle. In auto plants, absenteeism has doubled since the early 1960s, to 5 percent of the work force; on Mondays and Fridays, it commonly climbs to 15 percent. In nearly every industry, employees are increasingly refusing overtime work; union leaders explain that their members now value leisure time more than overtime.

Beyond that, an increasing number of people see no virtue in holding jobs that they consider menial or unpleasant. More and more reject such work even if they can get no other jobs. Young adults are particularly choosy; many have little interest in the grinding routine of the assembly line or in automated clerical tasks like operating an addressing machine or processing a payroll. Millions of workers under thirty may be too educated, too expectant, and too anti-authoritarian for many of the jobs that the economy offers them. Workers, particularly younger ones, are taking work more seriously. Young and old are willing to invest more effort in their work, but are demanding a bigger payoff in job satisfaction. Survey after survey asking working people to rank various aspects of work in order of importance consistently place "good pay" in a distant fifth, behind "interesting work," "enough help and equipment to get the job done," "enough information to do the job," and "enough authority to do the job."

A few enlightened employers have concluded that work, not workers, must change. In restructuring work, corporate experimenters have tried a number of productive and promising ideas. Some examples:

1. *Give workers a totality of tasks.* Confining, limited tasks increase boredom and turnover and decrease motivation and quality.

Case in Point: In compiling its telephone books, a telephone utility used to divide seventeen separate operations among a staff of women. The company gradually changed, giving each worker her own directory and making her responsible for all seventeen tasks, from scheduling to proofreading. Results: Work force turnover dropped, and errors, absenteeism, and overtime declined.

Case in Point: A man was buffing the carriage end-covers in a typewriter assembly operation. This job was interdependent with that of another man, who plated the end-covers. Both jobs were essential if the piece was to come out with a polished chrome finish; either man could ruin the work of the other. It was concluded that each man could quite easily learn the other's work. So each took total responsibility for half of the end-covers—not just for buffing or plating, but for the *total* finish on the parts. Now, instead of each person having the other to blame if work comes out poorly, they are in friendly competition to produce parts with a fine finish.

2. *Break up the assembly line.* A potentially revolutionary attempt at change is under way in the Swedish auto industry, where manufacturers are taking a number of operations off the assembly line. Some brakes and other subassemblies are put together by teams of workers; each performs several operations instead of a single repetitive task. In the U.S., auto firms have used the work team to set up a conventional engine assembly line. Foremen were given complete freedom to design the line, hand-pick team members, and use whatever tools and equipment they wanted.

3. *Permit employees to organize their own work.* Typical examples: Let scientists pursue their own projects and order their own materials without checking with a supervisor; allow shop workers to run their machines at the pace they think best; permit QC engineers to send out letters to dissatisfied customers with their own signatures, without review by higher-ups; encourage assembly operators to set up quality circles. Benefits in the form of increased productivity, better quality, and increased motivation will typically accrue.

4. *Let workers see the end product of their efforts.* Auto firms, for example, have sent employees from supply plants to assembly plants so they can see where their parts fit into the finished product. Some companies have also put assembly line workers into inspection jobs for one-week stints.

Case in Point: A sheet metal fabrication shop placed a welder in its final inspection department. His comment: "I see metal damage, missing welds, and framing fits that I never would have noticed before. This week has been a sobering experience."

5. *Let workers set their own hours.* In West Germany, some 3500 firms have adopted "sliding time." In one form of the plan, company doors are open from 7 A.M. until 7 P.M., and factory or office workers can come in any time they like, provided that they are around for "core time," from 10 A.M. to 3 P.M. and they put in a forty-hour week. Productivity and quality is up, staff turnover is down, and absenteeism has fallen as much as 20 percent.

The right work climate can be created in a number of ways: worker involvement in decision making, training managers and supervisors for a better understanding of employees, management willingness to accept suggestions regardless of where they come from, and letting employees know that they are respected as intelligent adults with helpful ideas. Talking directly with employees or conducting anonymous surveys is a very useful means for identifying problems standing in the way of productivity and cost improvement. Employees don't always understand management's objectives, and management really doesn't understand its employees. Smart managers are making dramatic improvements in productivity and cost savings simply by communicating with employees and satisfying employee demands for more freedom, more feeling of participation and personal responsibility, and more sense of accomplishment on the job.

Checklist for Redesigning Jobs for Total Responsibility

√ Identify the job that needs doing.

√ Let operators participate with supervisor in setting of goals.

√ Divide up or reorganize the job so that each operator remains fully accountable for a specific, challenging piece of work.

√ Provide the necessary training and familiarization with quality standards.

√ Design the job so that each person automatically knows if his or her work is good or poor. Provide go/no-go gauges, sensors, and the like to provide quick feedback. If poor work slips through, can responsibility clearly be traced (even after a product reaches the customer) to the individual responsible for it? Can credit be ascertained and acknowledged?

√ Try to include tasks (such as machinery repair, replenishment of parts and supplies, inspection, recordkeeping) that a worker can do individually as part of the job. Must the worker get approvals before acting? If so, how can he or she be held responsible for ensuring that the service is accomplished?

√ Make it possible for a person to look at the finished product and state exactly what he or she contributed to it.

√ Give recognition and reward when appropriate.

√ Provide opportunity for operator to improve skills and obtain a promotion.

RAISE THE LEVEL OF QUALITY CONSCIOUSNESS

There are several relatively low-cost ways of raising the level of quality consciousness among employees. Keeping people alert and productive is one of the never-ending problems of managing a business. Even the best of workers need occasional reminders to keep them moving full-steam ahead. The management that relaxes its efforts to create and promote good employee attitudes leaves the door wide open for poor attitudes to move in and take over.

√ Try a poster campaign using a low-pressure, humorous approach.

√ Hand out pamphlets, available from several commercial outfits. Typical titles: "Good Enough Is Not Enough Today," "Quality Is Our Most Important Product," "Let's Start a War on Waste," "Zero Defects—A Goal to Shoot For," "The Quality Our Customers See" (they can be included in pay envelopes).

√ Post defect charts in selected work areas. Plot yield rather than scrap rate and don't pinpoint individuals. Remember you want to motivate, not criticize.

√ Exhibit scrap items in a central area with dollar signs attached.

√ Distribute favorable customer quality surveys, letters, quality awards, and reports to production, purchasing, and other supervisors.

√ Periodically show indoctrination films or videotapes.

Case in Point: One manufacturer of word processors purchased a 16mm copy of the film "If Japan Can—Why Can't We?" and showed it to managers, union representatives, and production employees. The effect was so penetrating that the film was discussed months after its showing. There was noticeable improvement in attitudes.

√ Clip out and circulate newspaper articles dealing with quality achievements of local firms.

√ Put quality slogans on internal stationery, forms, and pencils.

√ Run Zero-Defects or Quality days, hand out inexpensive give-aways, have the president speak on quality control matters.

√ Include quality oriented articles in the company Newsletter.

Observation: The indoctrination programs must be continuous and sincere. If employees perceive the programs to be simply a means of increasing short-term output, their failure is assured.

√ Try an "error-cause-removal" program. This consists of asking employees to identify existing or potential causes of defects. Suitably designed error-cause-identification forms are filled out by the employee and submitted to a quality enhancement committee, who check to see if the problem is a valid one. If it is a real or potential cause of error, they attempt to correct the situation promptly. If the problem is not a real one, or for some reason cannot be corrected, the employee is told why.

In either case, the employee knows that management is doing everything possible to ensure quality production by removing the potential causes of error. The employee must know that the organization cares before he or she will take interest.

√ Invite government officials, customers, and users to speak on the need for quality products.

√ Distribute a monthly or quarterly quality newsletter highlighting significant quality achievements, individual contributions, and reduced warranty costs. Try to link to increased sales, profits, and job security.

CREATE A CLIMATE OF ERROR-FREE PERFORMANCE

1. *Instruct employees as to the types of quality jobs they are expected to do.* Show what is acceptable, what is not acceptable, and why. Explain tolerances, dimensions, specifications, and standards. Be sure quality terms are clear. Give written as well as verbal instructions. Repeat instructions until you know that employees understand the quality limits of the job.

2. *Demonstrate new or different tasks to employees:*

● Make sure machines are adjusted, material up to standard, and the workplace orderly, clean, and well lighted.

● Always perform the job the right way when instructing a worker.

● Don't encourage workers to take short cuts.

● If an employee makes a mistake during try-out, analyze what he or she may be doing when errors occur and what defects appear most frequently. Discuss weaknesses with him.

● Give workers reasons for instructions or changes.

● Take enough time to stress quality pointers during instruction.

3. *Check that skills are correctly used.* In most cases, it isn't necessary to teach new skills to achieve error-free performance. Just make certain that skills are properly and correctly used. When faults are found, additional operator training can be scheduled and monitored until individual skill is developed.

4. *Create a framework for quality work.*

● Provide realistic work schedules.

● Provide adequate tools.

● Provide opportunity to make suggestions, to participate, to influence the work environment (ego involvement).

● Encourage the feeling that each employee's work is important; develop a product identity.

● Praise employee for above-average quality work.

● Provide good working conditions and reasonable hours.

Case in Point: A mechanic reported that a bearing in a blast machine was about to fail, and would ruin the shaft along with it. The foreman was advised that it must be corrected promptly. Not unexpectedly, the foreman, thinking of his monthly shipments, replied: "We can't take care of it now." Before they got the load out, the bearing seized. In the repair job, it was also found that the shaft was badly grooved and must be replaced. The stoppage was costly, as he had to get a new shaft by air from Boston at premium prices. The production target is not met despite heavy overtime expenditures. The foreman dare not put in his best efforts for the company, as he is judged by numbers only, not for avoiding shutdowns. The mechanic, after a few experiences like this, not wishing to be a troublemaker, just let machines break down and does his best to promptly repair them. Quality and productivity take a nosedive. Foreign competitors smile.

5. *Give recognition to quality performers.* In almost every group, one person will be found who takes great pride in his or her work. If this type of person can instill enthusiasm and this desire for excellence in co-workers, his or her value may well be worth more to the company than a dozen quality control people further along the production cycle.

Give the quality performer recognition without antagonizing the rest of the group.

DON'T FORGET THE STOREROOM

Control over stored material is one area all too often ignored by the quality program. Stores should be considered a basic control point in the normal process flow. Consider the following:

● Paints, epoxies, rubber, and adhesives have a definite shelf life.

● Semiconductor chips must be stored in dry nitrogen to prevent oxidation.

- Certain chemicals must be stored under controlled temperature conditions to prevent degradation of properties.
- Some electronic devices are sensitive to static electricity and must be stored in conductive packages.
- Some components are simply fragile and require special handling and packaging.

These are only a few physical considerations. There are other important factors.

Case in Point: A government audit of a small pharmaceutical firm revealed the following stores deficiencies:

- The material was not traceable to a lot number.
- Some material did not bear positive evidence of acceptance.
- The area was not clean and was open to anyone.
- Some material marked "reject" was intermingled with acceptable material.
- Stores personnel did not wear special gloves and smocks for handling the compounds as required by the regulations.

In order to set up a good stores control program, consider these points:

√ Identify and label age- or environmentally-sensitive material (Figure 13-2). Engineering and vendor assistance will probably be required to obtain the necessary information.

√ Limit access to stores to authorized personnel.

STORAGE CONDITION

R. Hum. % _____

Temp. _____

Special
_____

SHELF LIFE OF THIS
MATERIAL EXPIRES ON

INSPECTOR

FIGURE 13-2. Typical Shelf Life Label

√ Follow a first-in, first-out policy.

√ Keep the area neat, clean, and organized.

√ Lock up the stores room (this is also good inventory control practice).

√ Indoctrinate stores people in proper storage, preservation, and handling procedures.

√ Provide a means for identifying (including revision letter) material: Use tags, labels, bin codes.

√ Only allow material that has been accepted by QC in the stores. Provide separate quarantine stores for rejected or obsolete materials.

√ Periodically audit the stores for compliance with control procedures.

√ Provide a retest policy for functional or age-sensitive items stored in finished goods stores for extended periods.

Observation: Kit inspection can be a very cost-effective control vehicle depending on the complexity of your kits or parts. In essence, an inspector checks the kits as prepared by the storeman for such things as:

- completeness
- correct part numbers and revisions
- proper packaging and protection
- visual defects or damage
- adequate documentation

A good kit inspection operation can increase assembly productivity, cut wasted time, and decrease rejects.

CONSIDER THE WORKPLACE

The workplace is a home away from home. If it is claustrophobic, unpleasant, or unsafe, quality work will not result. The provision of suitable human-engineered employee workspace is a management controllable task. Here are the primary considerations:

- Enough space at workplace to keep tools, rejected parts, gauges, incoming work, and completed work in orderly arrangement.
- The right tools and measuring and instrumentation devices.
- Appropriate and well-designed fixtures that promote safety, quality, and productivity.
- Workplace laid out in a way to minimize effort handling and maximize operations efficiency.

- Unnecessary parts and equipment removed promptly, thereby promoting an uncluttered work area.
- Requisite reference data readily available as needed: blueprints, layout sheets, quality standards, critical dimensional values, assembly instructions, materials instructions, feeds and speeds.
- Proper light intensity, without glare or shadows.
- Workplace arrangement, heights of benches and chairs, and other work factors set up so as to minimize strain and fatigue.
- Controlled temperature and humidity, removal of fumes, vapors, and odors.
- Noise level at minimum, considering type of manufacturing involved.
- Aisles large enough to accommodate movement of people and work (tote boxes, trucks, conveyors).
- Adequate heating and air-conditioning, freedom from drafts.
- Adequate materials handling equipment to avoid operator strain and speed work flow.
- Periodic sweeping, cleaning up of spoilage and other floor debris; control sources of litter, catch metal shavings, use plastic tubs or pipes to catch and direct oil away from the workplace.
- Maintenance of generally pleasant work conditions (painting—preferably in color schemes, clean washrooms and break areas).

> If you clean up the factory floor, you tend to clean up the thought processes of the people on it, too.

THE ROLE OF THE PLANT ENGINEERING DEPARTMENT IN PRODUCT QUALITY

The plant engineering department is sometimes called the maintenance department, plant services, or even industrial engineering. The functions performed by this department have direct and indirect effects on worker attitudes, productivity, and product quality. The typical tasks of the plant engineering department include the provision of a clean and safe working environment with adequate utilities and preventive maintenance.

Case in Point: A manufacturer of cans for the fruit industry found itself with high prices and poor quality. The president of the firm assigned a task force consisting of sales, QC, and production the duty of finding a solution. After two weeks, the problems were very apparent, albeit surprising.

- Numerical control machines had a high downtime because of poor-quality repairs and no preventive maintenance.
- The physical facility was dirty with residual metal shavings all over the floor, a leaky roof, peeling paint, and filthy washrooms.
- A new machine had been improperly installed, causing a high degree of scrap and operator frustration.
- Fume hoods and blowers were inadequately serviced, causing operator headaches, fatigue, and illness.

It is essential that physical plant and equipment be well maintained. The modern firm must be particularly efficient with regard to plant layout, plant safety, and minimization of production downtime. All of these factors influence product quality.

Operations people have enough pressures from customers, regulatory bodies, suppliers, and corporate management, without having to worry about compliance with health, pollution, and safety standards, roof leaks, inadequate water pressure, or dirty floors. These tasks should be handled by plant engineering so that users can spend more time on production and cost reduction.

Plant engineering has a vital role to play, but the organization must be responsive, technically up to date, effectively staffed and managed, and sensitive to user needs.

WATCH MATERIAL HANDLING

Material handling is wholly a service function, yet it directly affects costs, quality, efficiency, inventory, and profits. Thus, it always should be subject to review and improvement. Further, a plant layout that does not consider material handling problems is likely to be unsatisfactory. When handling and layout are planned together, positive gains can be realized in cost, quality, safety, material flow, and general efficiency. When material handling is improved, it will yield the following benefits:

Reduce Waste. Breakage is frequently a high-cost factor. Proper material handling equipment and techniques can minimize this cost. Any items damaged must, of course, be repaired or remade, thus upsetting production schedules.

Case in Point: In one small metal-working plant, skid boxes were stacked high with parts ready to be moved from one production area to another. When the forklift operator started off with the boxes at excessive speed, parts began dropping off behind him in all directions. Discovering that he was losing a good part of the load, the operator stopped, backed up, collected the scattered parts, and restacked them.

Again he started up, at a slower speed, but struck a bump in the floor and again parts scattered. Another bump elsewhere and delivery of the parts was delayed a third time, all at mounting costs applying in three ways.

First, the operation took much longer than it should have. Paid to move the parts, the truck operator spent much of his time collecting the scatterings. Second, expensive parts had to be scrapped, and others were sent back for reprocessing. Third, because the load was late at the intended workplace, a machine and its operator had to stand idle until it arrived.

The solution was the posting and enforcement of a rule limiting the height to which skid boxes could be loaded and the speed of handling vehicles, and the smoothing of the bumps in the floor. Annual savings: $4800 minimum.

Use Labor More Efficiently. Production employees are paid to produce. Every unnecessary minute they spend handling material is a minute that could be applied to productive effort. Devise material handling techniques that reduce the number of times an item is handled, thereby reducing cycle time and possible physical damage.

Case in Point: A Japanese auto producer has initiated a major effort on standardization of in-plant containers. The reported productivity benefits include:

- 90 percent reduction of identification errors
- 95 percent decrease in counting time (count containers, not parts)
- minimization of forklift costs (some containers have own wheels)
- elimination of need for separate packaging
- better control of work-in-process (container size one-hour supply or less)
- reduced handling time (parts are easily inserted in container)
- 25 percent saving in space (containers designed to be safely stacked)
- minimization of transport cost (containers designed to fit future conveyors)
- less product damage (higher yields)

Improve Working Conditions. Efficient material handling makes for safe work conditions; it reduces employee fatigue and the number of plant accidents. Employees will be more productive when their personal comfort is improved.

Increase Productive Capacity. Modern material handling methods can smooth out workflow. In so doing, they can increase productivity, increase machine efficiency by reducing downtime, and improve production control.

Reduce Inventories. Inventories tie up more capital and require more storage facilities. Usually, the more efficient a material handling system, the smaller the level of work-in-process and finished goods inventory required.

Improve Space Utilization. Space represents money. Effective material handling techniques can optimize the use of space. For example, inventories can be better controlled, and, through planned package handling, pilferage can be cut.

Improve Distribution. Efficient material handling will decrease product damage in distribution and help ensure that customer delivery commitments are met.

Materials handling can eat up 10 to 25 percent of production costs—even more in some industries. Though handling expenses add little to product value, they can't be avoided. Unless the handling is smooth, safe, efficient, and economical—assuring delivery of acceptable material at the right time and place, in the right quantities —costs and inventory levels can become excessive.

WATCH YOUR NONCONFORMING MATERIAL

The proper control of nonconforming material requires that the material is removed from availability and formally segregated pending disposition.

Many operations have "hold" cages, locks, a formal list of personnel authorized to enter, and considerable space allocated. This occurs because they do not have the mechanism to dispose of the nonconforming material promptly. Since your primary concern is to keep from using this material in the product, decisions should be made quickly. If it sits around, it creates temptation.

√ Is defective material positively identified?

√ Do all personnel recognize this identification?

√ Is there a company policy that says anyone using such material for deliverable products will be disciplined?

√ Is there a procedure that states the method of handling this material?

√ Does nonconforming material sit around more than one day before being processed for disposition?

√ Do more than four people have keys to the restricted area?

PRE-EMPTIVE MATERIAL REVIEW: MATERIAL SUBSTITUTION CONTROL

Substitutions occur more often than QC managers care to admit or even know about. A substitute part or material is one that does not comply with an engineering parts list and/or a QC-approved vendor list. This can result in a lower-reliability part or a material or unknown quality or characteristics being used in production. The main reason is usually delivery lead time. The best way to control this is to document the substitution (Figure 13-3) formally and have engineering (or applicable design authority) approve its use after due evaluation and analysis. Material substitution

---

Material/Part Substitution Request

No: _____

Date: _____

Material: From: _____   To: _____

Assembly used on P/N: _____   Used on Name: _____

Product: _____   Contract No: _____

Originator: _____   Title: _____   Tel. Ext: _____

Reason for Substitution:

Evaluation (include constraints as applicable):

Approvals:

Engineering: _____   Date: _____

Safety (when required) _____   Date: _____

Reliability: _____   Date: _____

FIGURE 13-3: Example of Material/Part Substitution Form

should be formally covered by a QC operating procedure.

Case in Point: A manufacturer of programmable controllers could not obtain a ± 1% resistor in time to meet scheduled deliveries. A ± 5% resistor was authorized by the project engineer and sorted to the ± 1% level at incoming inspection.

Case in Point: The supplier of a plastic part went into receivership and could not supply the required brackets for a furniture factory. A quantity of brackets was made of aluminum sheet until a new supplier could be brought in. Since the plastic part was used solely for economic reasons, end quality was not impacted. In this case, the temporary substitution was approved by the chief industrial engineer.

CONTROL YOUR TOOLS, MOLDS, AND DIES

Fundamental to the effective control of manufacturing quality are the design, preparation, and maintenance of tools. Faulty tools, molds, and dies make it impossible to produce satisfactory production output. Many firms pay little attention to checking the quality of purchased or in-house produced tooling. An attitude seems to prevail that drafting and shop practices are either "infallible" or else so seldom off-standard that there is no need to question them. Any such reliance can be dangerous. Even first-piece inspection may be too late. Often defective product can be traced back to the tool. It should be obvious, then, that tools should be in top condition before they start cranking out parts.

Tool proofing is the process of validating tools for their intended purpose (making acceptable product). Typical of such tools are drilling templates, casting dies, injection molds, and machining positioning/holding fixtures. All tools that determine product compliance with drawings should be proofed before use. The usual steps are:

1. Tool engineer designs tool.
2. Drafting office prepares drawings.
3. Drawings are checked against part drawings.
4. Tool room or vendor fabricates tooling.

5. Tools are inspected against tool drawings.
6. Small quantities of parts are produced using the tooling.
7. QC inspects the parts against part drawing for compliance.
8. Acceptable tools are identified, marked as approved, dated, and registered in master log book.

Checklist for Efficient Tool Proofing

√ Make tool proofing a formal procedure, not an ad hoc inspection.

√ Tool inspectors must be of a high calibre because a mistake can be costly.

√ Tools must be properly stored and identified in a tool bin or storeroom.

√ Indoctrinate people to handle tools carefully and report accidental damage to supervision.

√ Periodically check tools for wear and tear, abuse and deterioration.

√ Flag engineering changes affecting part drawings to the tool designer so that corresponding tooling will also be changed.

√ Calibrate tooling used as a media of inspection, just as any piece of measuring equipment.

Pitfall to Avoid: With increased computer utilization in the modern factory, tooling is becoming less physical and more software-oriented. Numerical control paper tapes, diskettes, and magnetic tape are most common. The alert QC program must not overlook this opportunity at defect prevention. This is another example of where software quality assurance techniques are applicable.

KEEP YOUR INSTRUMENTS CALIBRATED

Lord Kelvin is said to have made the observation, "If you can't measure it, you really don't know very much about it." You can add to that: If you measure it and you haven't properly calibrated the measuring equipment, then you still don't know very much about it. And to compound the felony even more if you assume your calibration is accurate, and you proceed to measure under that assumption, you might believe your measurements to be accurate (with errors of measurement likely to show up later) and base judgments thereon. The latter could lead to rework, costly engineering changes, and warranty repairs.

Once in service, measuring gauges and test instruments require a formal program of rechecking, reevaluating, and recalibration to assure their continuing accurate performance. A recall system, whereby measuring devices are returned from production to recalibration and reissuance, should be employed for this purpose.

Aside from normal wear and tear, all equipment is subject to occasional accidental abuse. Time and environmental conditions also degrade all measuring devices. The following are typical types of deterioration:

1. *Temperature measurements.* Readings will drift because of degradation of the thermocouple or electronic components.

2. *Hardness measurements.* Readings will drift from wear of the indentation point.

3. *Gauges, calipers, micrometers.* False readings can be caused by wear of measuring surfaces.

4. *Vacuum measurements.* False readings are created by water vapor contamination of the mercury column.

5. *Electrical measurements.* Accuracy may degrade due to drift or degradation of electronic components.

6. *Pressure measurement.* False readings are produced by wear of bearings, fatigue of springs, or fouling of gears.

7. *Weighing systems.* False readings can be traced to wear or misalignment of pivots or mechanical linkages.

Pitfall to Avoid: In calibration, there is also a need to avoid the extreme, and thus accuracy needs to be established. It makes little sense (and becomes quite expensive) to establish high calibration accuracy figures if the subsequent tests are conducted under less than ideal conditions or if the customer doesn't care about the accurately measured parameter.

An accuracy figure should be set somewhere between the two extremes, recognized by all, and achievement of this objective attained by cooperative action between all parties involved.

Calibration recall permits the periodic review of equipment so that those equipments that have shown accuracy degradation can be reconditioned. Thereafter, recalibrated devices should be checked and reissued. Each industry and factory operation has its own production and quality requirements, so it is impractical to recommend useful general frequencies for the recall of gauges, equipments, and instruments. Achievement of proper control depends on:

1. Maintaining records on the length of use and corresponding amount of degradation of each measuring device.

2. Determining for each type of equipment, on the basis of engineering judgment and experience, the allowable time of wear before the equipment will drift beyond tolerances.

3. Maintaining a file or a computer-generated report to assure equipment recall at predetermined, scheduled intervals.

While eventually calibration intervals will depend on usage, equipment quality, operating environment, and other factors, initial intervals can be based on manufacturers' recommendations or your company's experience with similar units. Each unit should be labeled with a decal indicating date calibrated, initials of calibration technician, and next due date.

Look for these potential weaknesses in your calibration program:

√ The calibration standards themselves are not properly maintained (either in-house or from a subcontractor).

√ Calibration decals are not physically visible to the user or contain confusing information.

√ Tamper-proof seals are not used on adjustment knobs and screws.

√ Production equipments used for process control are not an integral part of the calibration program (this comment also applies to custom-designed inspection and test jigs).

√ Inadequate replacement parts are available to effect prompt repair of needed equipment.

√ QC personnel are not indoctrinated to handle and treat measuring equipments carefully or to report anomalies.

√ The communication among the calibration laboratory, engineering, and users is very poor.

√ Calibration procedures and standards are not in proper order. Find out if your calibration people are really calibrating or are "switching stickers" on you.

√ The engineering department employs uncalibrated test equipment yet they use this equipment to set product standards and tolerances.

√ Inadequate back-up equipment exists so that users refuse to have their equipment recalled for calibration. Sometimes it is easier to put calibration equipment on a cart and take it to line test equipment, instead of vice versa.

Far too often the calibration problem is taken to extremes, and large expenditures are made to protect against a very unlikely event. A much more significant problem is, in fact, the deficiencies to be found in test methods and inspection set-ups. This can be improved by a QC certification of measuring systems.

In practice, there is a scarcity of documented cases tracing customer quality problems to inaccurate measuring equipment. This is perhaps because:

1. The original engineering tolerances were excessive for the intended application.

2. The test equipment error must be in a direction that makes the product appear better than it really is.

3. The magnitude of the test equipment error has to be fairly precise—the worse the product, the less likely it is to be accepted through test equipment error, because the worse the product, the more precise (relatively) the test equipment error has to be.

4. The test technician or inspector may sense something is wrong because of experience.

5. A second parallel test station does not yield corresponding results and so suspicions are raised.

6. Subsequent tests further up the line catch the "escape" prior to the shipment to a customer.

Yet calibration in principle cannot be dropped:

● Customer or government auditors always look for out-of-calibration conditions because it is easy to do and does not require technical knowledge.

● The process of meaningful measurement is fundamental to effective quality control.

● Calibrated equipment is essential for making alignments and adjustments.

● Product specifications and tolerances must be established based on precise measurements.

● The political consequences of a QC escape caused by inaccurate measuring equipment can severely damage the integrity of the quality program.

● Good lawyers can use ineffective calibration programs very effectively in product liability suits.

Here are some ideas on how to make your calibration program cost effective:

√ Ensure that the engineering department uses calibrated equipment.

√ Calibrate only those equipments that are actually used to determine a value for acceptance purposes or for establishing process control.

√ Concentrate your calibration dollars on those equipments used for engineering-critical measurements.

√ Establish time (or cost) targets for the calibration laboratory (or vendor).

√ Combine equipment calibration with preventative maintenance.

√ Base calibration intervals on usage rather than a fixed interval where appropriate. This is relatively easy for instruments using electrical power; several current-integrating elapsed-time meters are commercially available.

√ Specify the lowest permissable accuracy equipment in test procedures and inspection work instructions.

√ Don't calibrate indicating dials and monitoring equipments if they are not depended upon for final measurements. Annual maintenance is usually more than adequate.

√ Don't calibrate over an entire range when in practice the equipment is used in a limited portion of the range. A special decal should be placed on the equipment when this is done.

√ Withdraw equipments beyond economical use from the calibration program and replace them. Also, don't calibrate surplus equipments.

It's time to retire an equipment from service when:

√ The annual maintenance cost approximates the annual depreciation cost of a new equipment.

√ The time between failures is so unpredictable that inspectors distrust the equipment.

√ New measuring equipments are available that would yield appreciable cost savings. (Some new instruments contain microprocessor computers that can also perform arithmetic calculations.)

√ The commercial availability of spare parts is dwindling.

√ It is technologically obsolete because of the greater accuracy, precision, and response time of new products. (Digital readouts are easier to read and less prone to reading errors than analog meter instruments.)

> If a measurement is worth making, it's worth making right.

BASIC QUALITY CONTROLS

The requirements that the finished product has to meet, along with the finished product inspection and test specifications, should be thoroughly reviewed during the development of the in-process inspections and controls. This review provides the quality engineer with the information needed to determine the type and degree of in-process inspection required at various stages of the manufacturing process or assembly operations. It also helps the engineer select the kinds of in-process controls that will prevent the manufacture of defective product and yield the best economic return. A periodic review of the planned inspection and tests should be made to assure that the levels remain economical in light of quality history. There are five basic types of inspection and test controls: operator inspection, 100 percent in-line inspection, first-piece inspection, patrol inspection, and in-process acceptance inspection.

Operator Inspection

In-process controls can be enhanced by requiring an operator, stationed at a machine or at a processing station, to inspect his or her own work. The operator must be provided with the proper gauges and instructed in their proper use. He or she should be trained in the required quality standards. Enough time should be provided in the work standards to allow the person to perform the inspection with reasonable care.

These are the advantages of operator inspection:

- The operator usually handles every piece coming off the line.
- He is thoroughly familiar with the item he is making.
- He is in a position to spot defects quickly and call for help to correct problems as soon as they appear.

Cautions:

1. Special care may be necessary for the operator to keep the records required for an effective inspection procedure.

2. It is sometimes difficult for an operator to spot his own errors.

Case in Point: The Japanese approach to quality-at-source related to color TV receivers involves extensive operator training, assembly conveyors designed to make it easy to disengage a set from the line, simple gauges to permit operators to quickly assess their own quality, a host of tools and sensors to prevent defects, and the broad use of morale-building quality circles. The principle of *jidoka*—making problems visible to everyone's eye and stopping the line if trouble occurs—is practiced extensively. Apparently it is exportable, as evidenced by the dramatic improvement in color TV set quality when an American firm was acquired by a Japanese organization. Before coming under Japanese management, the U.S. factory ran at a fall-off rate of 150 to 180 per 100 sets packed (1.5 to 1.8 defects per set). Three years later, the fall-off rate was down to 0.03. (In Japan, the fall-off rate is 0.005.) During the same period, the fifteen employees required per assembly line to perform line inspection and repairs were reduced to one. Quality attitudes, operator self-inspection, and good employee morale were major contributors to this startling enhancement of product quality and productivity.

100 Percent In-Line Inspection

Inspection or testing may be carried out on a 100 percent basis at designated points in the manufacturing line. Its purpose is to screen out items that either do not conform to quality workmanship standards or are not likely to pass the finished product inspection.

Advantages:

- It saves the cost of further processing of a product that is likely to fail final inspection and test.
- It provides data on quality performance that can be used to take corrective action.

Disadvantages:

- The in-line inspection function may become a routine step in the manufacturing line. Because the rejects are being screened out, there may be less emphasis on the prevention of defects and more acceptance of chronic problems.

- It tends to increase inspection costs.
- It is not 100 percent effective because performing 100 percent inspection does not guarantee that all of the defective items will be detected.

First-Piece Inspection

In first-piece inspection, several pieces at the beginning of every new run are inspected to determine whether the set-up has been properly made and whether the tooling is adequate. The samples should provide a complete check of the machine or operation set-up. If the machine has five spindles, for instance, samples should be taken from each spindle.

The advantage of first-piece inspection is that since the items turned out by a process or operation are evaluated at the beginning of the run, any necessary correction can be made before the run is started. This saves the cost of defective material that would be produced if the correction were not made. One disadvantage is that production must wait for inspection results, thus possibly increasing idle time. To really make this approach work, prompt inspection, using semiautomated or automated equipment, is required.

Patrol Inspection

The inspector patrols the operations at periodic intervals and inspects the items being produced. Since inspection is performed concurrently with the operation, patrol inspection can provide faster response than inspection after the item has been completed. When problems occur, the inspector can have action initiated to correct them before many defective items are made.

It is advantageous to use patrol inspection under the following conditions:

- When a process turns out a high percentage of defective products and requires frequent inspection.
- When the operator is unable to do a thorough job of inspection.
- When new or untrained operators are on the job.
- When there is a need to collect special detailed data on the performance of the process.
- When the process is erratic and there is a need to supplement the operator.
- When an audit of the process is required.

Disadvantages of patrol inspection:

- It is difficult to ensure a specific quality level unless significant sampling at machine or control charts are used.
- The inspector must carry gauges from machine to machine.
- The inspector may be diverted to a troublesome machine and remaining machines may be ignored.

In-Process Acceptance Inspection

This is the classic type of inspection. All the items made at an operation in a given period of time are inspected together as a lot. They must be inspected before they are approved for release to the next operation. The inspector takes a sample from the lot and if the lot meets the specified quality level, it is accepted and released to the next operation. If it fails to meet the required level, it is rejected and held for material review disposition.

In-process acceptance inspection provides several advantages:

- It makes it possible to control the quality level at each successive stage of the manufacturing process.
- It provides data to use in preparing performance reports to help pinpoint problem areas.

On the other hand, it also has some limitations:

- It does not prevent defects since the inspection is performed after the items have been completed.
- It delays the movement of parts from one operation to the next thus increasing manufacturing cycle time.
- It is not easily applied to continuous processes because of the difficulty of forming lots without disrupting the continuity of production.

Of the five types of inspection, none is completely effective by itself. An efficiently designed inspection system requires several of them in combination. How they can best be combined to serve particular needs depends on an evaluation of the following factors:

- The cost of each type of inspection.
- The type, amount, and availability of personnel each type requires.
- The history of quality performance. Has the process been in control in the past? If the process has given little trouble, inspection need not be as extensive as when the process has been frequently out of control.

- The type of process. Is it continuous, or can the items produced be collected and inspected in batches?

- The stability and the capability of the process.

- The nature of the product characteristics being controlled. Are the characteristics critical or minor?

Pitfalls to Avoid: Watch out for confusion, which results when inspection standards vary from day to day, shift to shift, or inspector to inspector. Don't wait to catch in-process rejects at final inspection; catch them earlier in the production cycle. Learn how to control quality of rework efficiently. Watch out for inspectors working to the "quota system." Control "recirculating" rejects by dotting items on each reject.

CONTROL SPECIAL PROCESSES

For the purposes of this text, we define a special process as one that cannot be fully evaluated without destructive testing and/or is extremely costly to rework/repair. A special process then requires in-process controls to prevent defects.

When direct inspection of operations is impractical, equipment settings, rates, speeds, feeds operator performance, and other conditions of manufacture are evaluated instead. Electro-plating can be taken as the classic example. Proper plating requires a trained operator (plater), a clean work area, and controls over current density, plating duration, and plating solutions. Although beta back scatter techniques are now available for nondestructively evaluating plating thickness, plating is nevertheless a special process because full evaluation still requires cross-sectioning and rework costs can be high.

Achievement of a single product characteristic may require many work operations. For instance, degreasing, chemical cleaning, surface treatment, priming, and painting may all be necessary to achieve a desired painted surface. Work control in such a case calls for detailed instructions for operation and checking of every stage and type of work necessary to prepare and paint the item.

Even so-called basic work operations may be prone to defects. For example, in chemical cleaning, too short an immersion time may leave parts dirty, while too long a time can cause corrosion or erosion damage. In priming and painting, coverage can be spotty with "holidays" or paint furrowing or "tear-dropping." Work instructions

usually should include descriptions or references to samples of adequate and inadequate work, so that workers know what is acceptable and unacceptable.

Sometimes both direct and indirect inspection of work operations is required for technical or contractual reasons. For example, inspections of both the welding process and the welded product often are necessary to assure that the product is of adequate quality. Similarly, it may be necessary to inspect the potting operation of an electronic component as well as the final potted product.

To control special processes, the following actions are required:

√ Identify your special processes.

√ Prepare a process specification.

√ Provide suitable environmental conditions.

√ Train and/or certify operators.

√ Provide operators with appropriate work instructions.

√ Delineate process control elements including frequency of checks and record requirements.

√ Provide periodic checks that require process controls are implemented and effective.

√ Use control charts.

DON'T LET THE WORK ENVIRONMENT REDUCE INSPECTION EFFECTIVENESS

When an inspector is wondering what she will say when the expeditor comes around, or how she will respond if the foreman of the brazing section sounds off again, or how she can keep the people from sales off her back, she doesn't have much time to think about quality. She's going to become confused and distracted. The more it appears to her that she is being left to bear the brunt of questions and complaints alone, the more confused and distracted she will become. Quality suffers as defects are missed in the confusion; indeed, the inspector may develop a subconscious bias in favor of letting borderline defects go by to alleviate pressures, aggravation, and stress.

The treatment of borderline cases will have a profound effect on product quality as it affects the attitude (quality consciousness) of the production work force. The disposition of borderline cases cannot be left to the inspectors; they must not be compelled to make the decision by default.

To assure the quality of the product, the quality manager must know that what is on the minds of the inspectors is quality. The inspectors must be looking for defects without a subconscious motivation not to see them. The prime task of quality control supervisors is to create an environment in which the inspectors can work without interference; the supervisor or an appointed assistant must absorb all inquiries, complaints, and exclamations.

The creation of a working environment favorable to quality would include other time-saving and confusion-minimizing features. For example, the inspector shouldn't have to chase around trying to find the latest drawing change. He or she should be able to be sure that any gauge issued is accurate.

The quality manager must take steps to protect inspectors from the ranting of irate production supervisors and the constant prodding of expeditors. The quality manager can arrange it with fellow managers that all inquiries and comments are to be addressed to him or his supervisors. It will be more effective if the arrangement is made the subject of a management procedure.

The quality manager should ensure that every inspector has quick and easy access to a quality assurance supervisor. It may be necessary to increase the ratio of supervisors to inspectors for this purpose. As a general rule it may be said that the ratio of supervisors to workers in all categories should be determined, among other considerations, by the frequency with which problems may occur.

The quality manager must see and be seen by the inspectors. The inspectors must know that they have a representative in management. Each inspector must be in the physical presence of the quality manager at least once a month; more frequently would be better. This can be effected by meetings to discuss problems, instructional seminars, or by the manager's presence on the line. Remember that front-line quality is in the hands of the inspectors; the manager and supervisors are there to plan, to instruct, to solve difficult problems, and to provide moral support.

TO SHIP OR NOT TO SHIP

The acceptance and shipment of knowingly below-standard product is a major factor in the success or failure of a quality program. Quality control will, in the long run, determine output quality levels by its attitude, behavior, and response to situations. If QC and general management are perceived to be weak, indecisive, and passive with regard to quality, then processes will not get better, yield will not improve, and warranty costs will not go down.

Consider the case where a batch of product is submitted for inspection. The last process in the sequence has for some reason gone out of control, and the batch does not meet specifications. Your company was counting on the revenue from this batch to meet budget. What do you do? In theory, there is no question of what to do—reject the batch since it does not comply with standards. In practice, production and marketing pressures may be very high in support of making the shipment anyway. Here are some approaches to dealing with the situation:

√ Stick to your guns and make production appeal to higher management. Since there will be a confrontation, make sure the reason for rejection is a major defect that affects safety or fitness for use rather than some unimportant parameter.

√ Call a materials review board. This board usually consists of engineering, QC, and sometimes industrial engineering. It's mission is to make a disposition on nonconforming material and to define corrective action. The MRB decisions are (at least in theory) technically based and help ensure that product quality requirements are not subordinated to cost or schedule considerations.

√ Use logic, reason, the physical sciences, market research data, or other neutral approaches to argue against shipment.

√ Ask marketing to obtain a customer waiver or deviation. This is usually an effective approach but obviously one that cannot be used very often. Be on the lookout for verbal authorizations to ship—get it in writing.

√ Cite customer requirements, legal codes, and product liability implications. Involve the contracts and legal departments if necessary to obtain additional guidance.

√ Negotiate the deficiency. Quality must sometimes be traded off against cost or schedule. The key is limit these trade-offs to minor or subjective issues. QC must demonstrate a willingness to be mature, broadminded, and business-oriented. Corrective action should be an integral part of any negotiation.

Pitfalls to Avoid: Don't turn these critical situations into interdepartmental wars. Properly managed, a ship/no-ship conflict can lead to better understanding and a stronger QC program. Avoid such archaic practices as red-tagging of machines, having QC physically stop machines, hiding discrepant material, or having strongly worded arguments out on the shop floor.

> The bitterness of poor quality remains long after the sweetness of meeting the schedule has been forgotten.

You are better to have a reputation as a strict (but fair) manager rather than try to give a break to everyone who has nonconforming material to ship. With rare exception, you (the QC manager) will be in more trouble later if the customer forces product rework or rejects the shipment. You won't get into real trouble for upholding quality, for insisting on rework, reinspection, or retest, even when it causes shipping delays. Severe criticism will occur when you yield to in-plant persuasions, promises, and pressures to allow the shipment of out-of-tolerance material.

WORK-IN-PROCESS (WIP) INVENTORY AND QUALITY CONTROL

Many manufacturing companies are in a serious price-cost squeeze and increasing attention is being given to control of internal operations to improve profits. One of the areas offering the greatest opportunity for improvement is WIP inventory investment. Figure 13-4 depicts the impact of a cost-effective quality program on WIP.

Work-in-process is the inventory of materials and components being worked on or waiting between operations in a factory. It exists to even out

ups and downs on the shop floor between operations when these operations cannot be fully balanced.

Waiting time accounts for 80 to 95 percent of the cycle. Clearly, the shorter the cycle time, the less the required inventory investment.

Excessively high WIP inventory can be an indicator of production problems. Design deficiencies, poor yields, and excessive rework all cause bottlenecks and inflate WIP. Even when high WIP is due only to poor production planning and scheduling, you can expect quality problems caused by shipping panics, high overtime, customer threats of cancellation, and other disturbances.

Case in Point: An electronic navigation system was experiencing a long manufacturing cycle because of excessive final test failures. These failures resulted in several days' troubleshooting and repair. After cajoling by QC, the engineering department provided test specifications so components and subassemblies could be tested before final assembly and test. The final results were greatly reduced failures at final test, a reduction of about 20 percent in the average manufacturing cycle, and a reduction in required WIP of 15 percent.

Quality control can be a major contributor toward providing improvements in cycle time and WIP inventory. By implementing a component standardization program, fewer different part numbers are required for stock. Each of the standard parts is typically available from at least two vendors and has a minimum of quality problems, thus decreasing the probability of shortages. The

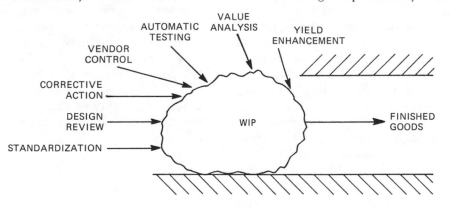

FIGURE 13-4. WIP Inventory and Quality Control

utilization of improved test procedures or measurement equipment, sampling, or automatic test systems can eliminate a bottleneck work center. Stringent process controls and corrective action help ensure more repeatable manufacturing that can lead to looser tolerances and higher yield. All of these actions lead to lower cycle time and hence reduced work-in-process inventory.

Reduced WIP can, in turn, increase profit by reducing operating costs. With large WIP on the shop floor there is a significant chance of incurring a high obsolescence cost. The lower the WIP, the lower the risk of large inventory write-offs.

Another potential cost that can be reduced with reduced WIP is process failures. If a process failure occurs early in a manufacturing sequence but is undiscovered until further down the line, a large scrap or rework cost may result. The less WIP that is accumulated between the point of failure and the point of discovery, the less that will have to be scrapped or reworked. Having a reduced cycle time also means that the causes for reduced process yields should be easier to determine.

CONTROLLING THE ENGINEERING CHANGE

Perhaps the most potentially disruptive factor in terms of quality, production costs, and scheduling is the engineering change. Product design changes affect every segment of the organization. Inadequately evaluated design changes can break sales, result in degraded product integrity and increased appraisal costs, inflate inventory, and raise havoc on the shop floor. The probability that a design change will result in one of these problems is greater when the product is complex and/or has a high production rate, and when a rigorous evaluation of the numerous side effects of the change has not been made. In order to minimize the effect of an engineering change, it should be consolidated, documented, and reviewed by representatives from manufacturing, QC engineering, marketing, and customer service.

A design change may affect one component, a group of components, or the total product. When a number of components are to be revised to meet the objectives of the change, the evaluation should consider all of the affected components at one time. If the evaluation is made piecemeal, the conclusion drawn from it may be erroneous. To illustrate the problem, consider a

situation in which three fabricated parts are changed and each part is considered separately. The cost and lead time for tooling and fixtures for the first two parts might be small, but the third part might have a significant cost or lead time. A piecemeal evaluation would result in production having to scramble to meet the scheduling impact in the tool room incurring an unnecessary cost increase in the process.

The date the design change will be incorporated is a very important piece of information that must be included in the change record. Production planning has to schedule parts. Purchasing has to ensure that orders are placed for timely delivery of materials and parts. Tooling and process methods have to be defined and made available by the necessary dates. New or revised inspection/test work instructions will have to be prepared.

Material control will be impacted because obsolete parts will have to be written off or disposed of at a substantial loss. Parts inventory not only involves parts in stock, but also parts that are in-process, on order and at dealer locations. Questions that should be answered in the inventory evaluation include: Can standard purchased parts be returned to the supplier for credit? Can parts on order be cancelled? Will there be cancellation charges? Can existing parts be reworked to meet the new requirements? Can parts be utilized on another product?

Interchangeable parts can be used as spares or in finished goods. In such cases, engineering should reduce the possibility of a swollen parts inventory by delaying the introduction of the design change. When a design change is mandatory, and inventory contains many noninterchangeable parts, delaying the introduction will not be a viable option, and consideration will have to be given to scrapping or reworking parts to salvage as much of the original cost as possible. Of course, such solutions ultimately increase the cost of sales and potentially impact product quality.

The following checklist will help ensure that the adverse quality effects of engineering changes are thoroughly considered, before implementation.

√ Is the stated reason for the change clear and accurate?

√ Is the change really necessary and cost effective?

√ Have the appropriate quality-level parts (and approved vendors) been used?

√ Will the input power, thermal dissipation, weight, or center of gravity change in a significant way?

√ Is test or other data available demonstrating that the change is really effective?

√ Does the change violate applicable customer, government, industry, or company requirements, specifications, or standards?

√ Have any new, critical failure modes or safety hazards been introduced as a result of this change?

√ Will the MTBF or maintainability of the equipment be significantly reduced as a result of the change?

√ Have appropriate regulatory agencies been advised of the change?

√ Is this change properly classified? (A class II change is one in which form, fit, interfaces, performance, reliability or weight is not significantly affected.)

√ If change is class I, has unit been reidentified in accordance with configuration control procedures? (Interchangeability and the impact on spares must be considered.)

√ Does the nature of the change require that product qualification be redone in whole or in part?

√ Is the effectivity point of the change clear? What is the disposition of existing inventory?

√ Are units in the field affected by the change? If so, will appropriate modification bulletins, technical manual changes, mod kits, and the like be prepared and distributed?

√ Does the change affect inspection work instructions or acceptance test procedures? Will units require retest and/or reinspection as a result of the change?

√ If a new special process is being utilized, has this process been qualified?

√ Is tooling, special test equipment, or field support equipment impacted by this change?

√ Does the change request accurately and clearly define the required change?

√ Will the drawings be updated immediately or for the next factory order?

√ Is there an alternative better way of satisfying the reason for change?

FACING MONTH END WITHOUT FEAR

Month end can be a hectic time in a manufacturing company. In some companies, 80 percent of shipments are made in the last week. These shipments are crucial to meeting the required monthly profit levels. The pressures on production and QC during this period are enormous. This causes an increase in production errors and inspection escapes, increased stress and conflict, and excessive overtime costs coupled with decreased productivity.

Case in Point: A manufacturer of control consoles was so hard pressed to make monthly targets that a partially complete unit was shipped to a customer. It was subsequently rejected, but the short-term objective had been achieved. In the long run, such practices can only lead to decreased market share and profitability. In addition, the interruption of the natural flow creates a vacuum in the initial stages of the following fiscal period, and it may well be marked by idle time, low productivity, and decreased efficiency. Together with the overtime premium paid in the preceding period, this practice can only add to manufacturing overhead without any corresponding benefit. Once initiated, this uneven balance of resource application is difficult to correct.

The only real solution is an intermediate or long-term one involving a formal production control system supported by management. Such a system, usually computer-based, permits manufacturing management to have early visibility on shop capacity, work center loading, procured part status, job progress, and conflicting shop orders. The result is a smoothed production flow that will decrease inventory, improve schedule performance, and increase product quality.

Until such a system is in place, QC must take defensive actions—otherwise they will end up being the scapegoat for missed deliveries, since final test/inspection is at the end of the line. These defensive actions are somewhat political in nature, but they are necessary for survival and can help force management to speed up the introduction of a modern, integrated production control system.

- Log in work orders into final test by job number, part name, quantity, and date.

- Keep track of your output—this information will be needed at the quarterly witch-hunts and purges.

- Charge work orders with legitimate idle time at the beginning of the following month—this will get management's attention.
- Try your best to meet the peak demand; work overtime if really required—this will also receive management scrutiny and lead to questions.
- Borrow QC people from receiving inspection, field service, product audit, or other divisions to help you deal with the overload.
- Ask for more test stations to deal with month-end tidal waves—this also will drive management to look at fundamental scheduling problems.
- Consider part-time temporary help such as re-

tired ex-employees, homemakers, technical school students.

√ Hire more people if economically justifiable. If employees are multiskilled they can be loaned to environmental test, calibration laboratory, repair, or engineering if workloads temporarily fall.

√ Attend production planning meetings so that you know of the upcoming load. Make your capacity position known—it helps to have established unit test (or inspection) times including set-up time, expected yield, and troubleshooting time.

√ Include suitable subliminal notes on uneven scheduling in status reports to management.

REFERENCES

Betz, G. M. "Production Liability." *Production Engineering,* Nov. 1979.

Caplen, R. H. "A Practical Approach to Quality Control." London: Business Books Ltd., 1969.

Goldstein, R. "Failure Review Board—A Management Tool for Producibility and Profit." *Quality Progress,* June 1976.

Harvey, R. E. "Quality Assurance Is More Than Just Testing." *Iron Age,* Jan. 14, 1980.

Hayes, G. E. *Quality Assurance: Management and Technology.* Capistrano Beach, California, Charger Productions, 1974.

Hughes, C. G. "The Role of Statistics in Measurement." *Electronic Instrument Digest,* Sept. 1970.

Juran, J. M. "Japanese and Western Quality—A Contrast." *Quality Progress,* Dec. 1978.

Kivenko, K. "Managing Work-in-Process Inventory." New York: Marcel Dekker, 1981.

Kivenko, K. "Stop Killing Your Electronics Parts in OEM Production." *Evaluation Engineering,* Nov./Dec. 1971.

Skinner, W. "Production under Pressure." *Harvard Business Review,* Nov./Dec. 1966.

Weiser, B. "Human Factors' Effects on Reliability." *Industrial Quality Control,* Dec. 1965.

14
Corrective Action in Quality Improvement

It is often stated that the real payoff from a quality system comes from its ability to implement quick and effective corrective action. The quality program must first have the ability to identify problems and thereby seize cost reduction opportunities. Many tools exist for identifying quality problems—Pareto analysis, control charts, error cause removal, statistical analysis—to name just a few. Other techniques, such as failure analysis, designed experiments, cause-and-effect diagrams, and stress testing, are available for isolating quality problems to root causes in order to identify required corrective actions.

The ability to implement corrective action in a timely manner is perhaps the one acid test of a quality control program. Because corrective action involves changing the status quo, it must be "sold." Persuasion, sensitivity to political and environmental factors, negotiating skills, as well as technical competence are essential to run an effective quality improvement program. The Japanese regard *all* problems as important. Quality means error-free performance. Their concept of zero defects is a good example. If you do an economic analysis, you will usually find that it is advantageous to reduce your defect rate from 10 percent to 5 percent. If you repeat that analysis, it may or may not make sense to reduce it further to 1 percent. The Japanese, however, will reduce it to 0.1 percent and then to 0.01 percent. The Japanese regard defects as treasures. So few of them turn up that each can be studied individually and

mined for the information it contains about the remaining bugs in the production process. This obsession for quality has been enormously successful and is living proof of the value of well managed quality improvement efforts.

What does an effective corrective action/quality improvement program provide? Here's a partial list:

- improved product yield and reliability
- reduced manufacturing time span and in-process inventory
- the ability to anticipate problems
- identification of design weaknesses
- constructive inputs to design decisions
- correction of test equipment deficiencies
- identification of organizational problems
- supplier corrective action
- improvements in maintainability
- increased customer satisfaction

The primary reason for seeking corrective action is to promote quality, to make good parts, and to avoid the consequences of quality failures. This chapter deals with the important subject of quality improvement.

SOME OBSERVATIONS ON PROBLEM SOLVING

In a manufacturing environment the quality control function has the constant task of problem solving. In recent years, problem solving has become a subject of formal study for modern management. In general, it is known as a search-and-discover type of activity. Much of the critical effort in problem solving is in determining the source of a problem.

In most problem solving, there is an "apparent" problem that seems to be self-evident and in need of immediate attention, and an underlying real problem that is masked by layers of misinformation and symptoms. Symptoms can be misleading. A medical problem, for example, may have symptoms that are real or imagined, and that proceed from many sources. Just as its key aspect will be identified by a correct diagnosis, so, in other kinds of problem solving, the real problem will be identified by analysis (Figure 14-1). If the problem has more than one basic element, the analysis will determine the relative importance of each. Good results are only possible when the problem is correctly identified and defined. Much managerial time and effort can be wasted in working on the wrong problem.

No matter how technically involved a problem may be, the first effort of every problem solver in approaching a problem is generally a heuristic ef-

fort that does not follow a particular systematic procedure. We explore different approaches and learn by trial and error. Each time we learn more about the problem, that information is fed back into our total knowledge of the problem, and it influences our selection of the next approach to the solution.

A useful definition of a problem is that it is an undesirable situation. It can either be a change from a standard behavior in quality control terms—or it can be the need to invent or discover a new method of doing something that will be an improvement over the present undesirable method. You must have a mental picture of the structure of a problem. One such picture reveals the structure as a chain of cause-and-effect phenomena or events. Event "a" causes a change from state "A" to state "B." In turn, event "b" causes state "C" to happen, and so on. This is illustrated in Figure 14-2.

In the case of a problem situation, the structure is expanded to show several chains. The undesirable or problem situation is a newly established chain that deviates or is different from the original or desired situation. This is shown in Figure 14-3. It can be seen in this illustration that the oc-

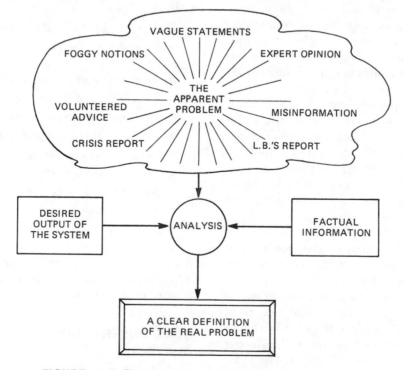

FIGURE 14-1. The Apparent Problem and the Real Problem
Courtesy of Canadian Marconi Company

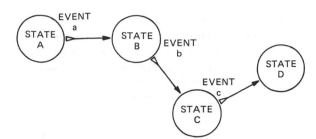

FIGURE 14-2. Problem Structure
Courtesy of Canadian Marconi Company.

currence of event "b'" instead of event "b" caused a deviation from the desired chain of events.

Table 14-1 provides a troubleshooting checklist that will help you stay on the right "chain."

HEAD OFF PROBLEMS: USE YOUR INFORMATION SYSTEM

Every QC system generates significant amounts of quality data. This data is usually (but not always) processed to provide such information as:

1. vendor performance
2. assembly and subassembly reject rates
3. yields at key processing stages
4. breakdown of defect causes
5. production quality costs
6. warranty costs

Other sources of problem intelligence include:

1. Failure to pass contractually required tests, such as environmental qualification, reliability demonstration, or safety.

2. Poor field performance, as evidenced by an inability to meet specifications or inadequate reliability. Field engineering reports may be accompanied by outspoken customer complaints.

3. Repeated field requests for spare components or assemblies when the attrition is in excess of the predicted failure rate.

> Those who cannot remember the past are condemned to repeat it.
>
> Philosopher George Santayana

This data can also be sorted to provide sorts by part numbers, specific time frames, failure location, generic subassembly, component type, and failure classification. All too often, this information accumulates dust on some manager's desk. The information can be used in problem solving and corrective action. Such information can also be used to project trends and head off problems.

Case in Point: A quality engineer for a computer peripherals company reviews subassembly failures on a weekly basis. The data is generated by computer and formatted for easy scanning. After reviewing the weekly failure summary report, she spots a certain printed circuit-board assembly with a growing failure rate trend. The quality control engineer sees the failure cause as internal short circuits in the board. She has the art-

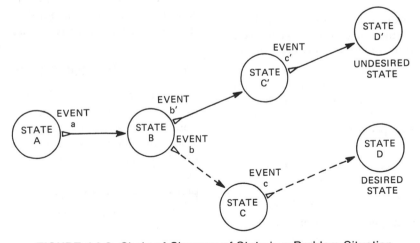

FIGURE 14-3. Chain of Changes of State in a Problem Situation
Courtesy of Canadian Marconi Company.

group of people, is used throughout the construction and use of C & E diagrams. To obtain the greatest results from the brainstorming, all members of the group participate equally, and no ideas are criticized in any way.

There are five steps in the construction of a C & E diagram:

1. Identify the effect.
2. Establish goals.
3. Construct the diagram.
4. Write down the causes.
5. Incubate the diagram.

Step one. Identify the effect for which causes will be sought. This sounds simple enough, but in fact, is often so poorly done that much time is wasted in the later steps of the process. It is critical that the effect (problem) be stated clearly and concisely. All too frequently, causes are identified and eliminated, only to find that the problem still exists.

Effect statements may be arrived at via a number of routes, but the most common are: (a) consensus obtained through brainstorming, (b) one of the "vital few" on a Pareto chart, and (c) sources outside the group.

Step two. Establish goals. The importance of establishing realistic, meaningful goals at the outset of any problem-solving venture cannot be overemphasized. Problem solving is not necessarily a self-perpetuating endeavor. Most people need to know their efforts are doing some good in order for them to continue to participate in any process. Therefore, the goal should be stated in terms of measurement related to the problem, and must include a time limit. An example would be, "A 50 percent reduction in the defect rate by September 1." This, of course, assumes a good understanding of the existing situation before setting a goal. How does one know when a 50 percent reduction is achieved when the baseline is unknown?

Step three. Construct the framework upon which the causes are to be listed. The effect is placed in a box to set it off from all the other words that will appear on the diagram. Then a horizontal arrow is drawn pointing to the box. This horizontal line is called the *process line,* or the spine of the "fishbone." Its function is to focus attention on the effect being studied (see Figure 14-5). Three to six smaller "bones" are then added to the horizontal line. The purpose of these smaller lines is to connect the major causes to the effect. They serve to group the subcauses as they are written, and connect them to the related major causes. The diagram should be constructed on a chalkboard or on large paper, visible to all members of the group.

Step four. Write the causes on the diagram. It is frequently difficult to know just where to start in listing causes, so an effective method is for the person making the diagram to write several fairly universal major causes at the ends of the smaller lines (see Figure 14-6). An easy-to-remember starting formula is the 4 Ms: Manpower, Machinery, Methods, Material. The important thing is to use words that have some significance for the people making the diagram. The group leader then asks each member, in turn, to suggest a cause. It is of utmost importance for the leader to allow only causes to be suggested. It is very easy to slip into analysis of possible solutions before all the probable causes are listed. As the suggestions are made, they are written on the appropriate branch of the diagram. Again, no criticism of any

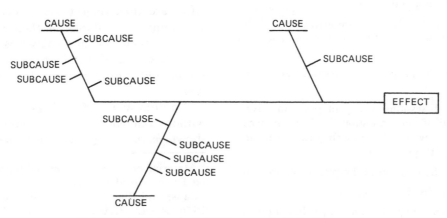

FIGURE 14-5. Basic C&E Diagram (with Subcauses)

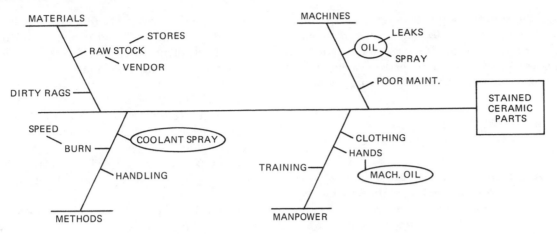

FIGURE 14-6. Completed C&E Diagram

cause is allowed at this stage of the activity. All ideas are welcome, because even ideas that eventually turn out to be false causes may serve to provide ideas leading to the true causes.

Step five. Incubate the diagram. It is usually a worthwhile delay in the process to let the diagram remain on display for a few days so everybody involved in the problem has an opportunity to add suggestions.

The group then critically analyzes it in an attempt to identify the most likely true causes. It should be noted here that another result of the incubation period is that the members of the group are less likely to remember who suggested which cause. It is, therefore, much easier to criticize the ideas and not the persons who suggested them.

It is important to keep the diagram simple. For instance, in Figure 14-6 a second generation diagram can be prepared to examine machines. Poor seals that may be due to wrong lubrication or wear may be sub-subcause of an oil leak.

Pitfall to Avoid: The C & E diagram should not be needlessly restricted to problem solving. In fact, this tool is equally useful in the identification of those factors that cause a desired effect. As frequently happens in nearly every process, some results are more desirable than others. The tragedy of this situation is that all too often the good results are attributed to chance, when in reality they are the result of some variation or change in the process. Stating the desired result as the effect and then seeking its causes can also help identify undiscovered changes that have favorably influenced production costs, yield, or other important parameters.

REGRESSION AND CORRELATION*

Regression analysis is a study of association among variables and is a powerful problem-solving tool. We try to find out how the average change in one variable is associated with a given change in a second. For example, one might want to estimate how an increase of a given number of inspectors in a department will affect the output as measured in physical units.

In manufacturing quality control we are interested in relationships between variables for several reasons.

First, many tests of quality involve destructive evaluation of product. If nondestructive tests are highly correlated with destructive tests, then it may be more economical to substitute the nondestructive tests for the destructive ones. (For example, hardness is sometimes used as a substitute for tensile strength.)

Second, by knowing the factors that are important in producing variability in quality, we can, by controlling those factors, control the variability of the entire product.

Third, application of regression analysis involves the establishment of control limits for quality characteristics having time trends. This arises, for example, when the quality characteristic is produced by a tool or die that wears with time. This wearing of the tool or die produces the time trend in the process average that might result in a sample value outside the control limits even

---

* Material in this section is based on J. D. Jordan, "Regression Analysis is Applied to Improve Product Quality," *Industrial Engineering*, Mar. 1981.

though the shift in process average is acceptable. Control limits that reflect the time trend can avoid the erroneous out-of-control indication.

Regression analysis hypothesizes some functional form for the relationship among variables such as:

$$Y = b_0 + \sum_{i=1}^{n} b_i X_i + \epsilon$$

where Y represents the variable of interest (dependent variable) and the Xs are the variables we wish to use in describing Y (the Xs are the independent variables). The b_i's are coefficients of parameters relating the X and Y values, b_o is a constant that may be thought of as a scale transformation factor, and ϵ represents the error or difference between the actual value of Y and the value predicted by our function. These errors are usually assumed to be normally distributed with a mean of zero and some variance that is constant over the range of X and Y values.

Other functional forms are possible; for example, Y may be related to different powers of the X_i's (say X_i^2 or perhaps the logarithm of X_i. Plotting paired observed values of Y versus X_i usually provides some indication of what functional forms to reasonably hypothesize.

With the hypothetical functional form and observed values of the Y and X_i variables, the problem is then to determine values of b_o and the b_i's that do the best job of describing Y in terms of the X_i's. Various techniques for accomplishing this are available, the most common of which is ordinary least squares.

The ordinary least squares approach gives values of b_o and the b_i's that minimize the sum of the squared errors between the actual Y values and the values given by the function. The equations for the b_o and the b_i's are in terms of observed Y and X_i values.

Unfortunately, there is no assurance that the formulas yield values of the b_i's that correctly and accurately describe the relationships between the X_i's and Y. Various statistical tests may be used to determine if a particular b (that is, b_k) is sufficiently different from zero to conclude that the corresponding X_k and Y are related. The value of b_k is then used in estimating that relationship. Other statistical tests or indices may be used to judge how well the functional relation and the observed data correspond (fit).

Developing a satisfactory function may involve repeated trials with different combinations of the X_i variables, or perhaps even different forms for the hypothetical function. Once satisfactory results are obtained, this function can be used to predict values of Y for given values of the X_i's or it can serve as a guide for modifying the X_i's to attempt to achieve some desired value of Y.

Regression and correlation analysis excels when the problem is not well understood, when you have dozens or even hundreds of variables that might in some way bear on the problem, and when you don't know where to begin looking for an answer. In short, it's a method to use when you're completely baffled. The method is superb for tracking down the reason for quality problems when trouble stems from some apparently innocuous and unsuspected factor.

Case in Point: In one case the time of day that a part was machined influenced the percentage of parts able to meet blueprint tolerances. In the afternoon, sunlight shining through a skylight caused uneven thermal expansion in the machine tool, throwing tolerances out of limits. Parts machined in the morning or on cloudy days were more frequently in-tolerance.

A regression/correlation analysis typically proceeds in several steps:

1. Define the extent of the process. Put boundaries on the problem. And in cases of material failure, "process" means any aspect of material supply or fabrication that may have an influence. The best way to identify limits is to ask, "Where does the process start and where does it stop?"

   You have to assume that some parts are good and some are bad. This technique will do nothing unless there are some successful specimens (or at least specimens indicating a tendency toward success) to serve as a basis for comparison.

2. Define all variables in the process. Think carefully before making judgments concerning whether you think a variable is important or not. In one study of plating failures at an industrial plant, the company chemist tried to talk the analyst out of monitoring a certain ingredient in the plating bath. That ingredient, according to the chemist, couldn't possibly play a role in subsequent plating blemishes. But the ingredient was monitored nevertheless, and it

proved to be a significant factor in the failures.

3. Determine methods for evaluating each of the variables. Determine in what manner and how often they will be measured. If you must measure temperature, for example, decide whether you need a strip chart recorder or whether measuring at specific intervals is sufficient. If a process is turning out bad electrical switches, and parts for the switch are turned out on any one of three presses, keep track of which press has been used to produce each part.

4. Derive a method for tracking the product through its entire manufacturing cycle. Assign numbers to assemblers or people on the production line if you must.

Case in Point: A manufacturer of coffee urns found that for some mysterious reason, 20 percent of the urn spigots leaked. A study showed that spigots produced by the regular work force were acceptable. All of the defective ones came off the production line when a particular relief person filled in at a specific station.

It turned out that he was not using an air hose to blow chips out of a machined valve component. Instead, he was tapping the component on the edge of his work table to dislodge chips. The tapping caused small nicks that made the valves leak. This simple study increased product yield 20 percent!

Pitfall to Avoid: Don't try to reconstruct something that happened in the past unless you can recover all of the data. For example, you're not likely to be successful if someone asks you to find out why parts made six months ago have failed (unless the same process is being used to produce them today).

After you've accumulated complete statistical information, you may have to apply some sophisticated statistical reductions to get meaningful results.

An important question is how long you must study a process before you can be confident that some finite number of measurements (samples) represents what happens over the long run. This question is crucial in a regression/correlation study, and it is answered by a branch of statistical mathematics dealing with confidence levels. Given a set of some finite number of measurements exhibiting some specific spread or statistical variation, this class of mathematics tells the probability of a limited number of measurements being representative of the entire process.

One commonly applied test of this type is called the Student's "t" test. It works well if you have data that conforms to a normal distribution. Sometimes, however, distributions are not normal, especially when human adjustment and correction are involved. Experience has shown that the chi-square test is superior in this situation.

Whatever the statistical process used, there is a need to validate the conclusions. The only way to do this is to make changes in a process to see if they actually make a difference in outcome. The data, especially after the first preliminary runs, may set you off in the wrong directions. But after enough runs for a good statistical base, meaningful information begins to emerge. It is clear that information about one or more variables that are related to X may be most helpful in predicting Y. The power behind regression analysis lies in the fact that the proportion of the variance accounted for by the regression and the strength of the relationship (correlation) can be calculated.

Caution: The benefits of employing statistical methods can be substantial. The essence of successful application is knowing the problem. If the problem is thoroughly understood, technical help can be obtained to find the solution. Statistical methods have to be recognized for what they are, valuable tools, but ones that must be used with a great deal of care and professional judgment. Those who attempt to substitute mathematical formulas for informed judgment are doing themselves and their organizations a profound disservice.

DESIGN OF EXPERIMENTS

There is a frequent need to evaluate through experiments the effect of design or process changes, changes in calibration point, or the use of second source/substitute materials. Statistics can assist not only in assessing the results of experiments but also in formulating the design of the experiments themselves. Methods have evolved whereby more than one experiment may be undertaken as one. For example, the use of factorial designs, Latin squares, and analysis of variance enables evaluation of more than one factor within the structure of one series of experiments; it also permits effective removal from experimental results variability attributable to specific factors that are not the primary subject of the experiment.

The essential feature of the statistically designed experiment is the simultaneous consideration of a large number (sometimes all) of the possible causes for a product or process problem. It can categorically rule out most of the possible causes after a limited number of experiments. This means that the major source of trouble can be more and more closely pinned down until it is finally isolated.

The approach often makes use of, but never depends on, hunches and guesses in problem diagnosis. If the initial hunches happen to be right, the time for the experiment may be cut down; if the hunches are wrong, as often happens, the experimenters' efforts are not held up until a new hypothesis can be formulated. Because statistical design can impartially evaluate most or all of the causes of a problem, it is a completely objective device.

Finally, acceptance or rejection of hypotheses and consideration of alternatives can be evaluated in terms of known confidence levels. The risk of a wrong decision can be reduced, for all practical purposes, to almost zero.

Usually, the time involved in problem solving by statistical methods is relatively short. It is not impossible for a single week's investigation to turn up an answer that has been eluding a company for years. Quick problem diagnosis, leading to quick cure, cuts the expenses of a high-cost operation, and the savings quickly pay back the initial costs. The process does not disrupt production; only minor interference is usually necessary. The experiments can be brief; the tests often involve only a relatively small number of units; and tinkering with operating methods on the line and with product specifications is kept to a minimum.

The theory and practice of statistical design of experiments rest on a series of simple logical propositions:

1. Every effect has one or a number of possible causes.
2. When there are many possible causes, the major portion of the effect usually comes from one or just a few causes.
3. These few major causes are not constant in their activity; they produce variation in the end product (the effect).
4. Therefore, if variations in the end product are analyzed and related to their possible causes,

one factor (or part of the total variation) may be expected to show up as being more important than the others, and the unknown cause may be associated with that particular factor.

Case in Point: After a final polishing operation, a company experienced an excessive rate of rejects. Polishing followed plating, and too often the hand-held polishing wheels exposed the base metal. Plant supervisors were certain that the difficulty stemmed from variation in skill among the several polishers and/or some inherent differences in the cloth from which the polishing wheels were made.

Believing that the supervisors' hypotheses were reasonable, the quality engineer assigned to the problem decided to begin by determining, with a given statistical confidence level, who were the least and the most successful workers; then a study could be made of their different polishing habits, the results of which would be incorporated into a training program. In addition, the engineer planned to compare polishing wheels in order to see if variations in their material bore any relationship to work quality.

For statistical validity, it was necessary to run a short test during which a random mixture of different parts were issued to each polisher, and each person used one polishing wheel. The results of this test showed no significant difference among operators.

Freeing his mind of all preconceptions about the problem, the quality engineer now decided to look at the plating process to consider the total variation in plating thickness in terms of three of its factors: (a) from time to time, (b) from plating tank to plating tank, and (c) within a tank. Parts were identified for a short period according to the side of the tank and tank number in which they were plated and the hour when the plating was done. A small variation in plating thickness showed up in the hour-to-hour figures and in the tank-to-tank figures, but none of the parts plated on the righthand side of the tanks had the plating polished off, while many of those from the lefthand side had thin plating and had been rejected for exposure of base metal. Therefore, something that correlated with within-tank variation had to be controlled to move the variation in thickness toward zero.

Discussion with the plating foreman brought no clues. Anode to cathode distances and electrical potentials had all been balanced when the tanks were installed. It seemed desirable, therefore, to observe the plating procedure. The only nonsymmetrical feature seen was a hand valve on a pipe on the righthand side of each of the ten tanks. This pipe carried steam along the length of the tank at the bottom on the right, across the front, and back on the left, rising up and out. The steam kept the plating solution warm, which was necessary for good results.

A reason for the polishing difficulty now became clear—a reason that fitted the observed facts. The steam must be hotter on entering the tank than on leaving it, so that the right side of each tank was warmer. Since warm water rises, a counterclockwise circulation of the plating solution must have been created. That meant that the plating particles coming from the anodes were in a rising current on the right side and in a falling current on the left. The articles hanging on the left side of each tank, therefore, received less thickness of plate. The steam valves were then closed. Parts from both sides of all tanks were polished. None was rejected.

The solution to the problem was relocating the heating coils in the tanks in order to avoid a circulation that would affect plating thickness. Thus, a major quality problem told on itself in less than one week. The answer unfolded as soon as the quality engineer insisted on an entirely objective approach, unbiased by what the management thought to be the crucial factors—operator skill and/or polishing wheel differences. The payoff: annual savings in excess of $35,000.

It seems particularly important to note that the usefulness of statistical designs is not limited to problem situations. They can be applied to situations in which products and processes are adequate, but not as efficient or economical as they could be. Through the use of statistical experimental designs, companies have a relatively quick

and inexpensive way to find out objectively where improvements can be made and what the specific improvements ought to be.

PARETO ANALYSIS, MONEY, AND TIME*

The Pareto distribution has long been used to identify the vital few defects. However, when losses are translated into dollars, nonrecurring costs considered, and time factored in, the picture can change drastically.

For example, suppose that the incidence of defects on a particular unit of product has the distribution shown in Table 14-2. The defects have been listed in the order of frequency of occurrence and identified by letters.

The picture is clear in this Pareto distribution. Only three defects (A, B, C) are responsible for 75 percent of all the defects that occurred. These appear to be the vital few.

Should we then attack defects A, B, and C? The answer is yes, *but only if our objective is to reduce the total number of defects (or the average number of defects per unit).*

Attacking defects A, B, and C may not really help us if they have a minor impact on the *quality dollar losses.* It makes more sense to management to assign a monetary value to each of these defects to give a truer picture of the costs of the defects.

Our simple Pareto distribution of one dimension (defect frequency) takes on another dimension (annual dollar losses). The new distribution may look like Table 14-3.

Defects E and G have now moved up, while A and B have moved down. Defects C, E, and G account for almost 80 percent of all quality defect dollar losses. It would seem that these are the defects against which we should utilize our resources.

It can be a difficult task determining the dollar values for each of the defects; most accounting systems have not been adapted to quality cost reporting. Even if only rough estimates are available the results can be fruitful.

At this point we may encounter some serious logistics obstacles that are not usually considered in the customary Pareto approach. The nature of defect C is such that it would take at least five

* Material in this section is based on H. Pitt, "Pareto Revisited," *Quality Progress,* Mar. 1974. Courtesy of the American Society for Quality Control.

TABLE 14–2.

DEFECT	PERCENT OF ALL DEFECTS FOUND
A	32
B	29
C	14
D	7
E	6
F	6
G	2
H	2
I	1
J	1
Total	100

years to remove that defect. We may have to re-design a critical machining operation at a cost of $150,000, to say nothing of assigning three full-time engineers to the project. Eliminating defect C looks less optimistic.

Which of the defects, then, should get our attention? Should we tackle a problem whose solution will yield $45,000 in one year of effort, or should we attack one that will yield $300,000 in five years of effort? Our impatience to get visible returns for our investment in a *reasonable period of time* may not be selfish or impractical at all. The cultural and political environment in Western industry being what it is, long-term projects may simply not get the continuing direction and sustained enthusiasm that are needed for successful completion. (In a sense, this is one of the significant differences in the Japanese approach.)

There is another dimension that can be added to this intriguing approach to decision making.

TABLE 14–3.

DEFECT	ANNUAL LOSS	PERCENTAGE OF TOTAL LOSS
C	$ 300,000	34.7
E	$ 250,000	28.9
G	$ 130,000	15.0
B	$ 45,000	5.2
D	$ 45,000	5.2
A	$ 35,000	4.0
H	$ 20,000	2.3
F	$ 20,000	2.3
J	$ 10,000	1.2
I	$ 10,000	1.2
Totals	$ 865,000	100.0

We should be able to assign some *probability of success* to our venture, knowing what we do about the nature of the defect, the validity of the loss estimate, and the expertise of our human resources. In short, we can impose an element of *risk* on our project.

What we have done is to recognize the realities of what the Pareto principle truly implies in its implementation. Profit and return on investment are, after all, the ultimate objectives of an industrial enterprise.

One simple way of making sense out of this is to develop a Pareto Priority Index (PI) that effectively combines all the parameters so that realistic decisions can be made. One such possible PI could be:

$$PI = \frac{\$ \text{ Value} \times \text{Probability of Success}}{\text{Time to Recover Value} \times \text{Investment } \$} \times 100$$

Let us assign times, investments, and probabilities to each of the defects and then calculate the PI. The results are shown in Table 14-4.

It now appears that defects A, B, and E should receive priority. Defect C seems to have fallen out. During the five years that the project team is working on defect C, losses have accumulated to $1.5 million. With a probability of success of only 65 percent, the potential recoverable losses are $195,000 a year, but this would not begin to be realized until the end of five years. Since it cost us $150,000 to solve the problem, substantial savings won't show up until the seventh year. It's probably not worth waiting that long, when you consider the rapid changes in policy, products, personnel, and technology that take place today.

ANALYZE YOUR FAILURES

Most failures can readily be traced to root causes by simple production line troubleshooting or physical observation. Sometimes, however, the root causes of failures can be elusive. In these instances a comprehensive analysis of the failure is in order; this often involves a rigorous evaluation of the failed part or subassembly, typically including such elements as:

1. Depotting or delidding by chemical, abrasive (sand blasting or dental drill), or other means to permit visual examination.

2. Microscopic (optical) or SEM (scanning electron microscope) examination to magnify de-

fects for better understanding of failure mechanisms.

3. Spectographic and other tests to identify unknown materials and contaminants.

4. X-ray or PIN (particle impact noise) tests to locate foreign objects or loose particles.

5. Cross-sections of materials to expose faults not apparent from a top view.

6. Stress testing, such as vibration or temperature, in order to more clearly highlight the failure mode.

7. Thermal evaluation using thermometers, infrared guns, or liquid crystals to study heat flows and to detect hot spots.

8. Leak tests to determine the hermeticity of a device.

9. Chemical tests to determine chemical concentrations, pH and other properties.

10. Physical tests for such parameters as tensile strength, strain, hardness, adhesion, fatigue strength, etc.

11. Nondestructive testing such as ultrasonic testing, magnetic particle, and holography to detect voids, blowholes, cracks, discontinuities, and surface displacements.

12. Gauges and other measurement devices for making accurate readings of dimensions, roundness, and squareness.

Often these equipments will not be available in-house and the work will have to be subcontracted. There are numerous independent laboratories available for this purpose listed in various trade directories.

Regardless of the equipment, the failure ana-

lyst must be technically competent and be familiar with the theory of failure mechanisms relevant to the particular industry. The end result of a failure analysis is not simply a report stating that a contaminant caused some component to fail; the analyst must be willing to visit the scene of the crime to determine how the defect was caused so that it may be prevented.

Case in Point: During production of a complex digital processor intended for satellite usage, a number of failures of a certain integrated circuit (flat-pack) occurred. All failures were observed during electrical test of the subassembly at −20°C.

The failed devices were sent to the failure analysis laboratory where microscopic inspection and microprobing disclosed that there were open circuits in these devices because of cracks in the integrated circuit chips. These chips had been mounted in their metal packages via an epoxy pedestal. The analysis appeared rather straightforward: "Thermal mismatches in coefficients of contraction between the chip, epoxy, and metal package developed high stress at −20°C which resulted in cracks. Sufficient recurrence of this problem might have resulted in a change to a different part manufacturer. One might have even gone to extensive sophisticated ion probe or Auger analysis in order to characterize the materials involved."

Luckily, the pragmatic analyst did some extra-laboratory fact finding. The parts

TABLE 14-4.

DEFECT	ANNUAL VALUE ($)	TIME TO RECOVER (YEARS)	INVESTMENT ($)	PROBABILITY OF SUCCESS	PI
C	300,000	5.0	150,000	.65	26
E	250,000	2.0	50,000	.80	200
G	130,000	3.5	80,000	.60	28
B	45,000	1.0	10,000	.85	383
D	45,000	1.5	15,000	.50	100
A	35,000	0.8	5,000	.70	613
H	20,000	2.5	8,000	.95	95
F	20,000	1.5	10,000	.70	93
J	10,000	2.0	4,000	.40	50
I	10,000	1.0	6,000	.80	133

failed sometime after incoming test but either before or during the −20°C electrical test. He first visited the module fabrication area and found that the flat-packs were cemented to plastic spacers before installation. The adhesive used hardened in a few seconds. The analyst asked the assembler what would happen if a flat-pack became "set" with improper alignment. The assembler then demonstrated how it was sometimes necessary to remove a flat-pack with an x-acto knife and then reposition it for proper alignment. Repeating this action showed that prying almost always caused cracked chips. This was the true cause of failure, and corrective action was now clear. Since the average cost of just one failure was $100, the $20-per-hour analyst had achieved a payback period measured in hours!

External consultants may also be useful in failure analysis:

Case in Point: A manufacturer of oil rigs was experiencing a severe vibration problem. The exact source of the vibration could not be located. A consulting engineer with many years experience in vibration problem solving was called in. Using her expertise and sophisticated test equipment, the root cause of the vibration was identified. Although the bill was $1000 per day for two days plus expenses, she had quickly isolated a problem that had eluded company engineers for weeks. With the source identified, appropriate design changes were implemented and the problem solved.

Caution: Company engineers may resent calling in consultants. Ensure that you thoroughly evaluate the situation before insisting that a consultant be utilized.

Failure analysis is a necessary QC activity if true cost-effective corrective action is to be implemented. The results of a properly conducted failure analysis ease in-house acceptance for quality improvement. A documented failure analysis report containing charts, test data, microphotographs, x-rays, and the like is also very convincing evidence for a vendor to take corrective action.

Figure 14-7 shows a sample summary analysis report form.

HOW TO DOCUMENT CORRECTIVE ACTION AND GET RESULTS

A written corrective action request should be organized in terms of a well-defined purpose. Once the purpose has been determined, the final form of the document should be designed to accomplish that purpose. A reader should not have to go through an entire report to determine whether or not it is relevant. A concise, logical format can be structured around four basic questions:

What?

The title or subject should answer the "What?" question clearly and at once. It must be so clear that the reader cannot possibly misunderstand at this point.

Why?

The statement of a purpose or the outlining of a problem should justify the writing of the report. Your report should immediately relate to the reader's interests or needs. Some words are more useful than others. "Unless" implies a warning. "Unfortunately" sounds the knell of doom. State that a customer complaint, poor yield, technical problem, or safety hazard has necessitated the need for corrective action. Try to avoid implying that it is a QC department problem. Show how QC can help solve the problem rather than try to get the engineer to admit fault, laxity, or poor judgment.

So What?

If he or she is still with you after "What?" and "Why?" the reader's next thought will be "So what?" You have looked into the matter, gathered the facts, and investigated the problem. Now, you should state in no uncertain terms what you have learned that must be passed on to the reader. This is the place for conclusions.

The wise quality engineer or manager will distinguish between conclusions, based on facts, and suggestions, based on these conclusions. The former are actualities, the latter are tinged with the color of the writer's opinions.

FAILURE ANALYSIS REPORT

			FR-		

PART D - FAILURE ANALYSIS				MO	DAY	YR

ITEM	NAME			SYMBOL	P/N	S/N
	HOURS	MFG.	DATE MFGD.	LOT/TYPE/OTHER		

DIAGNOSTIC ANALYSIS	ANALYSIS METHODS, TESTS, RESULTS AND OBSERVATIONS
DESIGN REVIEW	ANALYSIS OF ITEM DESIGN IN REGARD TO FAILURE
APPLICATION ANALYSIS	ANALYSIS OF ITEM APPLICATION IN REGARD TO FAILURE AND RATINGS
BACK-GROUND	SPECIAL INFO AND HISTORY FROM OTHER ANALYSES, RELATED REPORTS
CONCLUSIONS	MANNER AND CAUSE OF FAILURE
ACTION AND COMMENT	CORRECTIVE ACTION AND STATUS

PREP BY:	APP BY:	ORG:

FIGURE 14-7. Failure Analysis Report Form
Courtesy of Canadian Marconi Company.

Therefore?

If the reader agrees with your conclusions that something can and should be done, the next question will be "What should be done?" This is where you make your recommendations. You should give your reasons for the steps you advocate. You might even explain why you have not suggested certain other, more obvious courses.

A written request for corrective action should have these attributes:

√ *Clarity.* Carefully organize facts, use good prose, employ charts and visual aids.

√ *Tact.* Avoid irony, satire, and sarcasm. Your objective is corrective action. Stay away from QC jargon and symbology, unless you are sure the reader is comfortable with it.

√ *Accuracy.* Be careful of rounding off, state your assumptions and explain interpolations and extrapolations, identify information sources.

√ *Significance.* Interpretations should seem speculative or contestable; stick to the subject.

√ *Proper approach.* Tailor your presentation to the reader's existing level of information and attitudes.

√ *Emphasis.* There are two ways of giving emphasis in a report: by place and by space. Emphasis of place gives emphasis to those matters that deserve precedence by placing them first. Emphasis of space is given to an item by the amount of space devoted to it. You should use the emphasis of place to gain the interest of the reader, and the emphasis of space to gain his or her support.

√ *Intellectual Honesty.* Facts must be scrupulously weighed and a distinction drawn between facts, opinions, and hypotheses. Lack of QC bias must be obvious to the reader.

√ *Conciseness.* Conciseness does not consist in using few words, but in covering the subject in the fewest possible words that will express what is in the quality engineer's mind. Use charts, graphs, and appendices to reduce data and eliminate clutter.

√ *Completeness.* Provide proof of adequate research, favorable/unfavorable findings and fairness. Have all pertinent questions likely to arise in the reader's mind been answered? Quality people tend to forget the impact on other departments when assessing a situation.

Pitfalls to Avoid:

1. Don't let writing corrective action reports become an empty ritual. One of the hazards of formalized reporting is that the writer may give the procedure equal importance with the substance of the report, and it can continue to flourish even after the substance has shrunk to almost nothing.

2. Don't forget Mr. Pareto. Raise corrective action requests for problems of consequence. Consider the nature of the defect, the proportion of parts defective, or the frequency with which the defect has occurred previously.

3. Select the most important target—usually the person responsible for giving or getting final approval—and aim the report directly at him or her. Then use the letter of transmittal to tailor the report to lesser targets.

HOW TO INTRODUCE CORRECTIVE ACTION

Corrective action is not useful until it is implemented. Moreover, the problem is not usually solved just by communication of the decision. Follow through to the conclusion so that modifications to the solution can be made as new information arises.

Almost always, and especially in management, the solution is implemented by and through other people; they must have motivation and good communication to implement it effectively, especially when it is innovative. Here are some pointers:

Involvement

People will work hardest on problem solutions that they themselves have helped generate. This means that the people who have to carry out a solution should be involved in the decision-making process.

Ideally, involvement begins with the problem definition and follow-up with every systematic step. It becomes a team effort. The person with the overall responsibility for solving the problem should be flexible enough to incorporate the other persons' views and ideas into an integrated problem solution.

An understanding of the reasoning behind the corrective action requirement will allow those affected to carry out the intent when a variation of action is called for.

Pitfall to Avoid: Involvement must be sincere to be effective. A manager who is pushing through her own ideas for a problem solution may ask for help, but in reality may be trying to get others to work with her ideas. She won't succeed. The Japanese call this involvement process "ukezara," which means "preparing the plate for the food."

Communication

Often a problem solution will be carried out by people who are unfamiliar with all that went into its development, and its successful implementation will depend on their doing exactly what is intended. Communication for implementation is effective when:

1. It is understandable to those who will implement corrective action.
2. The means of communication are varied to suit the situation. This includes some combination of face-to-face discussions, meetings, telephone, letters, forms, sketches, samples, and photographs.
3. The action people are informed.

Most complaints about communications have to do with underinforming. For this reason, copies of the required corrective action should go to all those who need to know about it. At the same time, those who have no need whatever to know about it should be excluded from the list.

Phasing

Major changes must be introduced gradually. When a major corrective action affects the work-life of a group of people, the rate of change (or information flow) may be too great for them to accommodate. Their defense against this is to resist the change (quality improvement) or to drop out in confusion.

Example: A manufacturer of solid state telephone exchanges observed what appeared to be a classical vendor-date-code semiconductor failure trend. Components analysis might show repeated internal overstresses of the transistor. The date code theory could not be validated. A circuit analysis was performed with negative results. The assembly and its test equipment were next checked for high-voltage transients with similar results. The answer in this case proved to be inductive transients generated by a buzzer inadvertently used for continuity testing of a functional assembly. Further investigation disclosed that the buzzer had indeed been borrowed from the wire harness testing area (where its application was less

critical) when the authorized nondestructive tester was returned for calibration.

Appropriate corrective action would be to purge the entire assembly and test area of buzzers and other uncontrolled continuity checkers and replace them with a nondestructive tester sanctioned by the component engineering department and controlled by the metrology department. The approved continuity tester should then be made a company production standard.

Concurrent with purging the destructive testers, a commitment and schedule for the purchase of safe devices must be obtained from management, or many vital areas in the plant will be incapacitated by the purge. Recommendations necessitating purchase of required material will be meaningless unless approved and scheduled by management. The affected department may not be budgeted for the corrective action regardless of how worthy it may be.

The previous example illustrated that:

- The problem source was identified only after obvious potential causes were eliminated.
- Corrective action must be costed, scheduled, and committed if it is to be effective.
- Implementation will not be easy. The difficulties in getting approval to scrap and replace existing testers, negotiating a new company standard, and educating personnel to use it probably will be the hardest part of the corrective action phase.

"We must bear in mind, then, that there is nothing more difficult and dangerous, or more doubtful of success, than an attempt to introduce a new order of things in any state. For the innovator has for enemies all those who derived advantages from the old order of things while those who expect to be benefited by the new institutions will be but lukewarm defenders."

Niccolo Machiavelli
THE PRINCE

Feedback

The nondefensive quality engineer is never absolutely certain about a solution and seeks feedback about its defects during implementation. This enables improvement of the solution when new information arises through feedback.

CORRECTIVE ACTION FOLLOW-UP

The purpose of corrective action follow-up is two-fold: to verify implementation as intended and to determine the effectiveness of the corrective action. The first step is usually established via inspection records or some type of configuration verification system with records or other documentary evidence of the required corrective action. In some cases, visual observation makes the change obvious (like painting all surfaces red rather than black). The second step usually compares the inspection and/or test rejection rates or the field failure rates before and after the corrective action. Four basic types of results may be looked for:

1. Complete elimination of the discrepant condition.
2. Partial elimination of the discrepant condition to the point of recognition of product improvement.
3. Insignificant change of the discrepant condition and continuation of the same failure rate.
4. Actual worsening of the failure rate indicating that the corrective action not only failed to correct the condition but caused it to become worse.

Verification of corrective action is performed analytically or by test rerun. It is general practice to designate a discrepant condition that has occurred two or more times as being repetitive. The number of occurrences of the discrepant condition usually is easily defined and generally accepted. The determination of what constitutes a repetitive condition is based on establishing a sufficient number of compatible circumstances among reported discrepancies. In comparing discrepancies for repetitiveness the number of compatible circumstances may be one or more. For example, if ten pieces of equipment were damaged last week because they were dropped, it could be a repetitive condition on two counts: time and failure mode. If all had the same drawing number, this would make three counts. If all occurred in the same location, it would make four counts; if on the same shift, five counts; if by the same person, six counts.

It is possible to slightly reverse the nature of the individual counts and logically conclude that the related counts did not constitute a sufficiently strong relationship and the condition is not considered repetitive. This would be the case if it were observed that ten pieces of equipment, hav-ing different drawing numbers, were damaged during the past year, in all work locations, on various shifts by different people.

A closed loop failure reporting, analysis, and corrective action system requires follow-up to close the loop (Figure 14-8). The main concept is that each failure is monitored through the reporting, analysis, and corrective action phases to determine if the corrective action was effective. If not, new analyses may be performed and new corrective action recommended and initiated. In other words, the process progresses until corrective action is obtained. This is the closed-loop feature. Successively higher levels of management are involved on a strict time schedule until permanent, effective, and economical corrective action is obtained or until the manager with full profit-and-loss responsibility decides that nothing more is to be done. The net effect of this approach is that, although any level of management can take such corrective action, only the top executive can stop it from being taken.

Another aspect of follow-up is the use of regular reports to management after preliminary failure analysis, after further analysis, and at periodic intervals (cumulative reports). Management interest in effective corrective action makes the difference in the results obtained.

Nothing in the world can take the place of persistence. Talent will not; nothing is more common than unsuccessful men with talent. Genius will not; unrewarded genius is almost a proverb. Education will not; the world is full of educated derelicts. Persistence and determination alone are omnipotent.

Calvin Coolidge

CORRECTIVE ACTION: THE NUTS AND BOLTS

The degree to which discrepant conditions are corrected depends on the effect of the discrepancy on performance and the cost and time required to correct the discrepant condition. Thus, goals should be set for (1) the total number of failures (per unit produced, per unit time, or whatever), and (2) the number of repetitive failures.

Having identified a set of problems, priorities must be established. Except for legal, safety, or contractual deficiencies, the emphasis normally

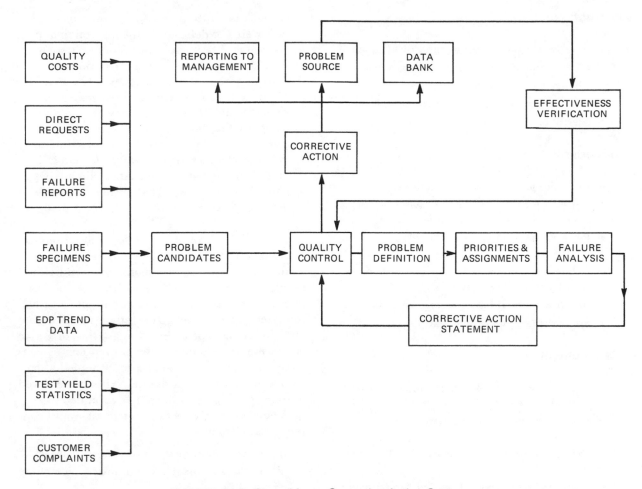

FIGURE 14-8. Closed-Loop Corrective Action System
Courtesy of Canadian Marconi Company.

would be on financial gain. It is thus recommended that problems be ranked by their dollar value—that is, the potential gain or loss to be achieved through the solution of each problem. This encompasses effect on customer relations and good will.

The second ranking is based on two time frames: the estimated time required to solve the problem, and the schedule to be met if the solution is to have a useful impact.

The third ranking is a function of your corrective action capabilities. Problems requiring more resources than management has allocated should not be undertaken until parity is achieved. This is not to suggest that only tailor-made problems be accepted to show a good score; rather, like any successful business, it is wise to recognize the difference between a demanding contract and one that assures bankruptcy.

After you accept a series of problems, consider them, and decide on priorities, activities should be scheduled and various action items assigned that will contribute to the solution of each problem.

Caution: Product quality is not some etherial aspect of goodness; it is making the product according to the print; or, in the case of processes, it is keeping yield and rework in line with management standards. The classic example is the common incandescent light bulb. Here, the QC objective is to keep the operating life within engineering limits so as to promote continued replacement sales. Without question, the technology for extending bulb life is known but not implemented for business and commercial reasons. Be sensitive to this in your corrective action activity.

Once the problem has been analyzed, corrective action can usually be grouped into four main categories: instructional, procedural, management, and design.

Instructional

- Improve personnel training and certification
- Increase quantity or quality of supervision
- Change QC operating procedures
- Eliminate work instruction error or omission
- Clarify quality standards

Procedural

- Add additional QC control stations
- Improve process planning to avoid omissions, eliminate errors, and control work sequences
- Protect stored parts against oxidation or contaminants
- Debug processing and test equipment and associated procedures before use
- Improve material handling and protection
- Strengthen configuration controls

Management

- Provide better work environment (lighting, ventilation, material flow, work area)
- Reduce employee fatigue, stress, and dissatisfaction
- Define acceptable yield, clarify quality objectives
- Authorize acquisition of needed capital equipment or tooling
- Provide adequate resources
- Consider impact of unrealistic schedules on product quality

Design

- Correct drawing and specification errors or ambiguities
- Improve product design
- Adjust tolerances
- Use better-quality parts and materials
- Change processes
- Control procurement sources for critical parts

Sometimes, however, the required corrective action may be subtle.

Case in Point: A manufacturer of marine radios found high field-failure rates in the first thirty days of service. Investigation re-vealed that although in-plant quality controls were not deficient in the inspection and test sense, infant mortality failures (that is, time dependent) of various electronic components were not being detected. It was decided to include a temperature cycling test. The thermal stresses caused weak components to fail but did not overstress good components. Two weeks after introducing this special screening test, early-life field failures virtually disappeared. Approximate net annual savings: $40,000 at current sales volume.

Normally the corrective action will be separable into two phases, remedial and long term. Remedial effort provides a response to an individual problem without searching for root causes (say, screen a rejected lot and retain only good units). Long-term corrective action attempts to isolate and overcome root causes. Long-term corrective action may be likened to fire prevention, as contrasted to the fire-fighting aspect of remedial corrective action. Both kinds of activity are required in today's complex industrial environment.

A good corrective action statement would contain these elements:

1. A description of the investigation conducted.
2. A clear statement of the ultimate cause of the problem.
3. Assemblies, parts, or material involved in the corrective action.
4. Request for a purge of the defective item from stock, assembly, and/or distributors.
5. Engineering-change requests specifying recommended changes in materials, components, processes, tolerances, and design.
6. Analytical and test data validating the recommended changes.
7. The actions required to correct the cause of the nonconformance and thereby preclude recurrence.
8. Evidence that a cost-benefit analysis justifies corrective action.
9. Identification of the department or vendor responsible for taking corrective action.
10. Effectivity point by date, lot number, or serial number.

Involve only those people who are immediately affected. The manufacturing VP doesn't want to be notified every time a Corrective Action Request (CAR) is issued, neither does the quality manager, since he or she has supposedly placed the job in responsible hands. Also, lower-level managers may feel you've gone over their heads, which is not at all good for interdepartmental relations. Higher management should be involved only when their participation is crucial to the solution or resolution of an important problem.

It is, however, recommended that the quality manager—briefed by the quality engineers—call top management into conference once a month and summarize what has been done and what dollar amounts have been saved. You may also choose to point out what has not been done and why.

A well-organized, planned approach to corrective action will achieve permanent, clearly defined, positive results.

SOME COMMON FAILURES OF CORRECTIVE ACTION SYSTEMS

The following are some of the most prevalent reasons that quality corrective action systems fail to achieve objectives.

Setting of Arbitrary Standards. If QC demands corrective action based on unsupportable AQLs, subjective opinions on what a good yield should be, or open-ended workmanship standards, then opposition defenses will be based on "experience," "It's good enough," and "Why should they (the customer) get more than they pay for?"

Haphazard Data Collection and Processing, Retrieval and Analysis of Failed Hardware, and Gathering Intelligence to Identify Failure Circumstances. Of the many pitfalls leading to ineffective corrective action, the substitution of subjective judgments for systematic data collection and analysis ranks close to the top of the list. Speculative opinions will invariably fill the information gap when data collection and analysis are lacking.

Lack of Management Commitment. Personnel assigned to diagnostic activities are aimlessly interchanged with their potential contributions unfulfilled. The loan of key specialists may be refused, with interdepartmental funding problems serving as effective roadblocks to progress. Management interest is minimal and short-lived and financial restrictions are severe.

Poor Timing. Unless the failure is safety related or costing you a bundle, be careful when you ask for corrective action. For instance, asking a production manager for corrective action on some noncritical matter at month end will probably not meet with much success.

Lack of Cost-Effectiveness.

Case in Point: A manufacturer has an order for 100,000 widgets. With her present equipment, they cost 71¢ each, but with a 14 percent defective rate. A quality engineer has suggested corrective actions that have a nonrecurring cost of $4000 and will raise the variable cost to 75¢ per unit. The breakeven fraction-defective Pb is found by equating:

$$\frac{100000}{1-0.14} \times 71\text{¢ to } \$4000 + \frac{100000}{1 - \text{Pb}} \times 75\text{¢}$$

Solving, we find that Pb is 5 percent. If it is felt that the tightened controls will improve the yield to 95 percent or better, the corrective action should be implemented, otherwise the lower yield should be tolerated.

Misinformation. Make sure you're using the latest drawing revisions, applicable contract provisions, and accurate data sources before you ask other departments or vendors to correct a situation.

Unwillingness to Take Responsibility. Errors do occur in QC. Inspectors misinterpret drawings, test methods may be inaccurate, measuring equipment can be out of calibration or defective, QC control points can be poorly located. If QC does not sometimes accept responsibility for defects and take on corrective action obligations, then other functions will display similar attitudes.

Failure to Distinguish Management-Controllable from Operator-Controllable Defects. The basic criteria for operator controllability are:

1. Operator knows what to do and
2. Operator knows what he or she is actually doing and
3. Operator can regulate
   (a) himself or herself—by exercising skill or
   (b) the process—by adjusting variables

Situation is management-controllable if any one of above is not true.

Corrective action for operator-controllable errors usually includes better training, more supervision, improved work instructions, motivational programs, foolproofing techniques (locating indexes, holding fixtures), and redundancy (countdowns, interdependent operations). Management-controllable errors that constitute the vast majority of errors usually require significant technical, financial, diplomatic, and negotiating skills. The resolution of management-controllable errors is often time-consuming. Quite often the true nature of a problem is not immediately apparent.

Case in Point: A rash of soldering defects was traced to three new soldering operators. The quality engineer wrote up a report and considered the matter closed since the workers were transferred to other duties until their soldering training was complete. The QC manager, however, considered this a management-controllable defect. How did untrained people get assigned to production before training? How come the potential problem wasn't detected earlier? Was training the total solution? Could plant lighting, component solderability, or product design deficiencies also be contributing?

Management must take responsibility if:

1. Equipment, tooling, or work environment is not adequate for the work involved.
2. Schedule constraints are such that people are rushed, pressures are high, and overtime is excessive.
3. People are not properly trained and/or certified.
4. Engineering specifications, work instructions, and quality standards are missing, incomplete, or ambiguous.
5. There is no quality "culture" in the company.
6. There is no commitment to quality improvement or corrective action.
7. Supervision is inadequate.
8. Operators are not treated with respect.

Case in Point: A medium-sized manufacturer of shoes was having trouble with his new, expensive sewing machines. The operators were spending a lot of their time rethreading the machines, a serious financial loss. The astute quality manager made the key observation that the trouble was common to all machines and to all operators. A few tests showed that it was the thread that caused the trouble. The shop owner had been purchasing poor thread at bargain prices. The loss of machine time had cost him hundreds of times the difference between good thread and what he had been buying. Better thread eliminated the problem. Only management could make the change. Even a heroic effort by the operators would not improve machine uptime, production efficiency, or yield.

Too Many Cooks in the Kitchen. If follow-up has been poor and if the inspection records cannot be tied in to the corrective action procedure, there may be too many people involved. It is recommended that one individual be made responsible for implementing corrective action. This person can keep inspection reports in constant review, decide when previous inspection history justifies the issuance of a CAR, or when the proportion of defectives in a lot of parts manufactured for the first time is so high as to demand immediate investigation. He or she can follow up and compare inspection reports before and after and prepare monthly summary reports. In a large organization, the analyst may need assistance. In a small organization, it may be a part-time occupation for a nominated individual. In any case, the issuance and follow-up of corrective action requests and the necessary coordination should be somebody's business, not everybody's.

Working on Problems with Uncorrectable Causes. These include, but are not limited to:

1. Chance variation inherent in physical, chemical, and metallurgical processes.
2. Electrical, hydraulic, and pneumatic power surges or failures.
3. Machine malfunction (not due to misuse or poor maintenance).
4. Tool breakage (not due to misuse).
5. Items processed through multiple processes—or departments—if positive responsibility cannot be determined. The potential for this type of situation should be minimized.
6. Failure to establish standard(s)—applicable to minor workmanship errors, process control levels, yield limits—to control minor nonconformances not requiring individual corrective action. These recommended standard(s) would specify the level of nonconformance permissible

(before corrective action must be taken), describe criteria for determining that level, and provide for the accumulation and maintenance of data for monitoring processes and obtaining corrective actions as dictated by collective analyses, trend reviews, or other suitable means.

Overreaction to Problems. If every defect requires corrective action, if everyone nit-picks, and reasoned discrimination is absent, don't expect anyone to take you seriously. Crying "wolf" too often reduces the impact you will need when a serious matter needs corrective action. Perhaps inspectors and supervisors hold the belief that every rejec-

tion calls for a corrective action request. Check your procedures to see exactly what they say. If it's possible to interpret them in this manner, better tighten the phrasing to remove the ambiguity. Indeed, you might add a paragraph specifying when a corrective action request is not to be made.

Lack of Market Knowledge. Make sure that what you're working on has a future. Don't make the mistake of demanding costly corrective actions on products that are vitually obsolete or will be discontinued. Check out the situation before you spend a lot of money on troubleshooting and analysis.

REFERENCES

Caplan, F. *The Quality System.* Radnor, PA: Chilton Book Co., 1980.

"Corrective Action and Disposition System for Nonconforming Material." MIL-STD-1520A(USAF), U.S. Government Printing Office, March 21, 1975.

Fuller, D. "How to Write Reports That Won't Be Ignored." *Machine Design,* Jan. 11, 1979.

Goldstein, R. "Failure Review Board—A Management Tool for Producibility and Profit." *Quality Progress,* June 1976.

Jordan, J. D. "Regression Analysis Is Applied to Improve Product Quality." *Industrial Engineering,* March 1981.

Lipinski, T. "Tracking Down Elusive Causes for Failure." *Machine Design,* April 3, 1975.

Pitt, H. "Pareto Revisited." *Quality Progress,* March 1974.

Quigley, P. E. "Quality Control Used to Forecast Product Problems." *Industrial Engineering,* March 1981.

"Reliability Reporting Guide." ASQC, 1977.

Tarver, M. "Systematic Progress Analysis: An SQC Tool." *Quality Progress,* Sept. 1974.

15

Evaluating the Performance of the Quality Program

The objectives of the quality program are many and varied. This makes the evaluation of its performance a complex task, but it is a task that must be accomplished on a regular basis. It is similar to the monthly, quarterly, and annual evaluation of financial achievement and controls.

The major warning signs of an unhealthy quality program include:

- frequent customer complaints
- recurring quality problems
- high scrap, low yield, high prices, loss of competitiveness
- poor employee attitudes
- chronic use of nonconforming material
- excessive quality costs
- high rate of missed deliveries
- large number of engineering changes
- growing warranty costs
- unproductive interorganizational conflict

There are several techniques for assessing the quality program. Some are quantitive; some are qualitative. Some involve the product; others deal with processes and workmanship. In still others, quality costs are the primary tool; often, the topic of interest is control so that a system audit is appropriate. Here are the main methods used for evaluating quality system performance:

1. walks on the shop floor
2. employee attitude assessment

3. review of quality program status
4. evaluation of nonconforming material controls
5. quality system audit
6. process audit
7. product audit
8. ratio analysis
9. quality cost analysis
10. customer complaint review
11. corrective action effectiveness
12. armchair self-appraisal

This chapter will show you how to find out where you stand.

> Evaluating the overall performance of the quality program is the ultimate feedback loop.

TAKE A WALK ON THE SHOP FLOOR

Getting out of your office and walking around the shop floor will reveal a lot about your quality program if you keep your eyes and ears alert. Look for these tell-tale signs:

√ Rework and repair operators with heavy physical backlogs are indicative of a high level of nonconforming material.

√ Bulging scrap bins tell you that your profits are far from optimal.

√ Heated debates between production and QC

point to problems with quality standards, personnel training, or interdepartmental interfaces.

√ If operators complain that work pace is too fast, tools are inadequate, overtime is high, or interruptions are excessive then you can expect product quality to be lower than it should be.

√ Expeditors and stock chasers madly running from one work center to another breaking setups, splitting batches, identifying material shortages, or introducing engineering changes tell you that nothing stands in the way of delivery.

√ Massive congestion on the shop floor points to disorganized release of work orders and associated schedule pressures. Typically, bags, boxes, crates, and pallets are stacked in every nook and cranny, and general chaotic conditions are readily apparent.

√ A deterioration in the physical appearance of stock, either because of dust, hasty bagging and tagging, corrosion, or deterioration of age-sensitive material is a sure sign of a quality control system on the skids.

√ High machine downtime or excessive machinery repairs are leading indicators of a potential quality problem.

Case in Point: The president of a Quebec manufacturer of snowmobiles took a group of visiting Norwegian customers on a plant tour. Within thirty minutes he had made the following eye-opening mental observations:

1. Test technicians spent significant time scrounging around for appropriate test equipment to complete set-ups.

2. Assembly operators strained to read small-sized blueprints in an inadequately lighted area.

3. A welding machine produced 50 percent rejects because of inadequate maintenance.

4. Machinists complained that lubricating oils were not available at the work center, necessitating machine shutdown and a visit to a central stores area.

5. Mechanics clocked up idle time because of nut, bolt, and washer shortages.

Two months after the tour, productivity was up 6 percent, yield 4 percent and shop capacity 8 percent because of the incorporation of corrective measures.

Such informal periodic visits can tip you off to impending problems, usually faster than any organized technique. These visits are also motivational since it shows production and QC personnel that management is really interested in what goes on out on the shop floor. Be positive; when performance is good, say so.

DO YOU INFLUENCE EMPLOYEE QUALITY ATTITUDES?

Without the proper quality atmosphere, many of the best quality systems and techniques may prove useless. Employees must know the importance of quality and how their performance can impact the quality of the goods or services being produced. The degree of quality awareness that employees have will determine the quality of the product. You, as quality manager, have an important role to play in forming quality attitudes. The more times you can answer yes to the following dozen questions, the better shape your quality program is in. If you answer no to six or more, major surgery is in order. The situation may, in fact, be terminal.

√ Does someone explain to each worker exactly what is expected in his or her job, quality wise?

√ Is there close cooperation in improving quality involving supervisors of departments that supply or receive components from one another?

√ When work is rejected, are the workers concerned made aware of what is wrong and what they can do to improve?

√ Is each department provided with a list of defective work that they produced in a given week or month so that actions can be taken to prevent recurrence?

√ Are operators praised for exceptional quality achievement?

√ Do you have a system for getting suggestions from your workers on how to improve quality? (Do operators participate in planning for corrective action?)

√ Are regular talks held with each worker regarding the quality of the work he or she is doing?

√ Are workers aware of the cost of defective work in their department?

√ Are examples of good and bad work displayed for workers to observe?

√ Do you have an effective method for encouraging pride in workmanship?

√ Is each worker acquainted with the relationship between quality workmanship and job security?

√ Do your employees understand the value placed on quality performance when they are considered for raises or promotions?

CALL PERIODIC QUALITY PROGRAM REVIEWS

Periodic informal quality program reviews, involving incoming inspection, quality engineering, reliability, product test, quality audit, and representatives from purchasing, engineering, material control, and production can have enormous benefits. These include:

- improved communications among quality control sections
- acquisition of useful information to quality management
- constructive interaction between QC and other functions
- voluntary agreements, not grudging submissions
- better decision making
- improved understanding of other people's problems
- avoidance of adverse "surprises"
- a breakdown of barriers among departments

A typical agenda would cover the following topics for a newly introduced product line:

Agenda: Quality Program Review (Product XXX)

1. Program organization, QC team, and responsibilities
2. Equipment design status
3. Measuring equipment design/certification program
4. Environmental test program
5. Top five problem areas
6. Procured item control
7. Configuration control
8. Use of statistical techniques
9. Workmanship level
10. Special process control
11. Failure history, results of failure analysis
12. Material review activity

13. Corrective action status
14. Quality costs
15. Activities requiring management action

CONTROL YOUR NONCONFORMING MATERIAL

The management of nonconforming material in many ways reflects the overall state of health of the quality program. Nonconforming material must be clearly identified, physically segregated, and promptly and effectively dispositioned. Future corrective action is the ultimate objective.

When pressures build up to produce and deliver, they can conflict with quality. In such situations a group meets to decide the fate of the nonconforming material. This group is often called a Material Review Board (MRB). The MRB's primary purpose is to obtain corrective action in the most practical manner. The MRB is no place for purists, idealists, theoreticians, or academicians.

In principle, an MRB should never make an exception. What it should do is change the drawing/specification (if called for), then rejudge the previously nonconforming material. In this way, the company's intentions can grow to be more clear and exact, rather than becoming a hodgepodge of exceptions. Careful, judicious, down-to-earth decision making is required.

A well-run MRB ensures that engineering, purchasing, and production people know that corrective action and defect prevention are the cornerstones of the quality program. The basic idea is to say what you mean and to mean what you say.

When material is found to be nonconforming, it should be examined by competent quality control personnel to determine if the nonconformance should be dispositioned as:

1. *Scrap.* Nonconforming material that is not usable and cannot be economically reworked or repaired. Scrapped material should, where practicable, be conspicuously and permanently marked to preclude its subsequent use in production. Don't forget about salvage possibility or precious metal reclamation.

2. *Rework.* Nonconforming material that can be subjected to a planned manufacturing process that will restore all nonconforming characteristics to the requirements of the purchase order,

specification, drawing, or other approved product description.

3. *Return to supplier* (if applicable). Don't forget corrective action.

4. *Use as is.* Material with minor nonconformances determined to be satisfactory for its intended purpose.

5. *Repair.* Nonconforming material subjected to a planned manufacturing process designed to reduce but not completely eliminate the nonconformance (say, welding a cracked casting).

6. *Standard repair.* A technique for repairing a nonconformance, developed and approved by methods, engineering and possibly the customer, when it has been demonstrated that the technique, properly applied, will result in an adequate and cost-effective method for dispositioning the nonconformance.

Pitfall to Avoid: Don't forget to include instructions for reprocessing material after repair in the standard repair or other repair procedure. These instructions would include the requirement for necessary inspection/test during and following reprocessing. Before any repair action, a determination must be made that the repair will be cost effective, relative to other disposition alternatives.

7. *Lot screening.* If sampling has been employed, it may be possible to screen the balance of the lot to keep production lines rolling. In the case of purchased parts, it may be possible to reclaim some or all of this cost from the vendor, if prior agreement is obtained.

Just how inefficient a poor material review system can be is exemplified by the findings of a management audit in a Southern California aerospace firm. Among the highlights:

1. Continuous or periodic disposal action had not been taken on obvious scrap material.

2. Not all material was ordered scrapped by QC (or other authorized personnel) leading to dispositions with a high probability of error.

3. Rejected material was not traceable to stores inventory records.

4. Material from quarantine stores was occasionally requisitioned by material control.

5. Material that should have been returned to the vendor for failure analysis was in the quarantine store.

6. Obsolete and surplus material was found in quarantine stores.

7. Some parts were scrapped that could have been economically repaired.

8. Simple cannibalization and normal industrial salvage procedures were not in evidence.

9. Some material could have been used for test jigs, experiments, training, defect displays, etc.

10. High-cost components that failed on the assembly line could have been returned to suppliers for credit or warranty repair.

In order to ensure that the material review system meets its intended objectives the following guidelines must be adhered to:

- When the pressure is on, watch out for someone rejecting an item into MRB just to get "off the hook."

- "Change to follow" is not an acceptable disposition. A change authorization number must be referenced on the nonconforming material report. Engineering changes should not be made solely to permit the acceptance of material.

- Every attempt must be made to charge legitimate rework/repair costs back to the vendor. In any event, rework/repair activity should be kept to the minimum consistent with schedule and other needs. Keep vendors informed of nonconformances even if your firm decides to absorb rework costs.

- All dispositions must be accompanied by a brief written explanation of the technical merits behind the disposition.

- The analysis of nonconforming material should go into sufficient depth as to find the underlying causes, thus permitting effective corrective action. A very professional approach is required.

- Return nonconforming material to vendors whenever practical. If not watched, over the years your firm will be the dumping ground for marginal parts and materials. The return of this material counteracts this.

- Continued use of use-as-is dispositions obviously contaminates the MR system. Recurring problems must be adequately dealt with via vendor corrective action, changed drawings, or other suitable measures.

Case in Point: A medium-sized manufacturer routinely passed below-specification materials through the costs of paperwork, material review, meetings, materials handling, storage, and the like, hoping to recoup greater remunerations from a markdown sale than from scrapping or reworking defectives now. This led to inflated inventories until the write-down had to be taken. In this company, profits were made in inventories, causing taxes to be paid with cash against profits in work-in-process or finished goods inventories that subsequently proved to be of dubious value.

- Follow-up on corrective action is an essential part of the MR system. If progress becomes stalled on a significant problem, next higher-level supervision must be notified. Watch out for slippage of verbal promises for necessary drawing or specification changes, for corrective actions or for failure analysis. Even written or posted schedules and due dates have to be watched for slippage. Don't let the project engineer or designer risk the engineer's job. Tighten the number of follow-up calls and memos that are initiated. Be aggressive. All this is part of doing an effective corrective action job.

TAKE AN INDEPENDENT LOOK: AUDIT THE QUALITY SYSTEM

A *quality system audit* is an independent review to verify by examination and evaluation of objective evidence that applicable elements of the quality system have been developed, documented, and effectively implemented in accordance with specified procedures.

An auditor must understand the control process. The basic structure of the control cycle, intrinsic to an audit, includes identifying the control subject, defining the unit of measure, establishing standards, measuring and comparing actual performance against a standard, and taking action on the differences. The auditor must also have a reasonable understanding of accounting and finance. With this financial perspective, he or she can review quality requirements to assure that compliance and effectiveness are achieved at optimum cost. The auditor must do all these things with tact and diplomacy.

A well-performed quality audit can benefit quality control operations by:

- Calling attention to the need for changes in company policy adversely affecting product quality.
- Citing examples relating to the breakdown of operational controls.

- Pointing out specific areas for cost avoidance or cost reduction in purchasing, production, or materials handling.
- Suggesting improvements to manufacturing or QC operating procedures.

Case in Point: During review of nonconforming material reports at receiving inspection, an auditor found that many batches of nonconforming product had been accepted. Each accept decision was based on the precedents established by prior decisions. In essence, the formal engineering drawings were by-passed by local tradition. Corrective action resulted in a change to the drawings and tightened nonconforming material review procedures.

- Highlighting the need for new policies, procedures, systems and organizational forms needed to strengthen controls.
- Commenting on the validity, completeness, and accuracy of the management information system used in the factory decision making and control processes.

Case in Point: In one audit of a failure reporting system, the auditors were able to learn, within hours of commencing the audit, that at least 65 percent of the computer-generated reports were in need of some change. At least half the reports were of no value to QC or manufacturing management whatsoever, and the balance were too frequent, failed to utilize exception criteria, were too widely distributed, and contained serious accuracy discrepancies. This resulted in a corporate policy change whereby users were to pay for computer services used instead of allocating the cost to a general administrative fund. The number and the nature of reports were drastically altered, and operating efficiency was enhanced.

To be effective, an audit must be a planned and systematic activity. Management must recognize the potential worth of the audit and then provide a firm policy backing the audit function. In doing so, management has the right to expect that each auditor has gathered sufficient background information about the area to be audited to determine the key quality assurance requirements applicable to that area.

```
┌─────────────────────────────────────┐
│ READY, FIRE, AIM!                    │
│                  QC Auditor's Syndrome│
└─────────────────────────────────────┘
```

Poorly prepared audits, which waste several individuals' time, often produce more aggravation than results. It is, therefore, imperative that the auditors be allotted enough time to prepare before conducting an audit. During this preparation period, the auditors, in conjunction with management, must establish the objective of a particular audit. Is the auditee a new plant, and is the purpose of the audit to evaluate how well company quality requirements are understood? Is it to ascertain whether a work area is following procedures? Is it to determine how well the auditee has incorporated and implemented corrective actions resulting from previous audits?

GROUND RULES FOR QUALITY AUDITORS

1. Should an audit reveal extensive nonadherence, no hasty conclusions should be reached before the following possible reasons are eliminated:

- Procedure is not practical.
- System is not understood.
- System is not up to date.
- No procedure is available.
- Supervision is inadequate.
- Verbal changes of system were not documented.
- System does not cover all alternatives.
- System is not coordinated with all functions concerned.

2. No audit is meaningful without a corrective action and follow-up mechanism. Getting to facts is only the first half of an audit program. The savings and improvements are derived from corrective action. An auditor should be prepared to listen to alternative corrective action solutions proposed by the auditee.

3. Never generate an audit report without a postaudit meeting. The postaudit meeting is also a good time to discuss the forthcoming written reports, including when a reply will be due, and what is expected in that reply. The reply should include, as a minimum:

a. a restatement of each open item or finding

b. a determination of the cause of each

c. a description of the verifiable corrective action to be taken or that has been taken

d. a schedule of implementation for each one

This coordination activity is sometimes referred to as "massaging."

4. Avoid matching your opinion about the effectiveness of a control or the need for an additional control with operating management. Normally, such a position can be avoided by providing, through normal auditing techniques, satisfactory evidence that a control is not effective and should be corrected or that an uncontrolled area should be placed under control. It is absolutely essential that solid evidence be developed and produced in support of the auditor's position.

5. Don't give the impression of being arrogant or authoritative. The whole operation can turn into a very negative experience with the participants trying to outwit each other. It may be very difficult to convince the auditee that the auditor is there to help, but the attempt should be made. The first step is to establish the climate of the audit in a pre-audit with the auditees, at which it should be pointed out that audits should be two-way situations, benefiting both the auditee and the auditor.

6. Audit reports must be timely and scrupulously accurate both in facts and perspective. Language should be simple, clear, and concise. Reports should have a consistent structure including executive summary, foreword, statements of purpose, scope, findings, observations, and recommendations. Trivia should be avoided. Ask what the effect is to put the seriousness of the discrepancy in proper perspective.

Don't nitpick. Out-of-calibration equipment just can't be the most serious problem 90 percent of the time.

7. Avoid asking leading questions, which tell the auditee what the auditor is looking for and allow the auditee to answer or evade questions. Questions should be prepared so the auditee is forced to answer from his knowledge, not the auditor's. This also applies to those off-the-cuff secondary questions that follow the primary questions prepared for the audit. (It is often necessary to talk to the people who do the work to verify that certain requirements have been transmitted to the work area. Make sure that supervisors know this is part of normal audit procedure.)

8. Maintain an awareness of employee atti-

tudes. Poor attitudes caused by internal griev-
ances can cue the auditor that potential quality
problems might exist in that particular area. In
this case, the auditor may wish to delve a little
deeper than planned to be sure a problem area is
not overlooked.

9. Audits must be constructive. Too often the
auditee is overwhelmed with faultfinders who tear
down, but do nothing to rebuild. Give credit
where credit is due.

10. Schedule your audits. Surprise audits may
have the benefit of spontaneity, but they breed ill
will. Besides, without an appointment the auditee
could have a visitor, be at a meeting, or be on vacation. Although scheduled audits may permit
the auditee to "houseclean" prior to an audit, remember that the object is to obtain corrective action. The professional auditor will be able to
recognize if a control has been established as a
showpiece.

THE PROCESS AUDIT

The control of process operating conditions is essential for uniformity of product. At times, processing conditions are changed (either planned or
unplanned), which may detrimentally affect
product quality. As a result, auditing of operating
instructions is essential to minimize the effects of
variability of processing conditions on product
quality.

The process to be selected for an auditing procedure would be primarily left to the discretion of
the quality control engineer and/or manager of a
facility. However, as a guide, the following is a list
of checkpoints that should be considered during
the selection of process audits.

√ Is it a process you are having trouble with? An
  audit is especially useful if good product quality
  was experienced before the time of trouble.

√ Is it an erratic process? If this is the case,
  changing processing conditions may be contributing to the problem.

√ Is it a process having a direct affect on product
  quality and/or subassembly with no complete
  built-in control available? An example of this
  would be plating in which the plating conditions affect the final quality characteristics of
  the plated part. Even though some tests are
  performed, it does not completely explain the
  total plating characteristics.

√ Is it a relatively new process?

√ Is a purely random selection of processes to be
  audited?

√ Is it a process where postinspection/testing is
  not feasible to determine if process controls
  were effectively followed?

Prior to auditing any given process, the quality
control engineer should obtain the applicable
standard work instructions or specifications. The
characteristics of the process to be audited and the
levels and tolerances of the operating conditions
would be obtained from these instructions. Examples of characteristics include:

types of tools or instruments

machine speeds and feeds

pressures

temperatures

cycle time

solution concentration

electrical power requirements

As part of preparation for the audit, team
members or other planners should prepare checklists when appropriate, to serve as the minimum
definition of the audit scope. Checklists should
never serve as "blinders" to the auditors but can
help ensure that key items are not overlooked.
Table 15-1 shows a typical process audit checklist.
Checklists provide an audit trail for future audits
and are, when completed, objective evidence of
audit findings.

The quality control engineer should establish a
plan for sampling the conformance of a process to
standard practice. Under no conditions should
auditing be initiated in a department without the
department supervisor being first notified by
quality control. The advance notification period
must, however, be judiciously chosen.

The frequency of the audit should be based on
a *minimum* of two checks randomized over more
than one shift. The purpose of sampling over
more than one shift is to ascertain whether or not
consistency exists from shift to shift in either
meeting or not meeting the standard practice requirements.

A case can be made for using professional auditors to do process (and procedure) conformance
audits for ensuring more consistent results and reduced audit time. An equally strong case can be
made, however, for rotating nonprofessional
membership on the audit team. The latter alternative serves to educate the auditors, and second-

TABLE 15-1. Typical Process Audit Checklist (Wavesoldering)

Procedure Section-   Quality Audit Checklist
Procedure Title-   Wavesoldering PX 6.46.01.11.02

Yes   No

1. Is bar solder used per QQ-S-571; SN63 Alpha Vaculoy (type S)?
2. Is soldering flux in accordance with MIL-F-14256?
   (Alpha Metals 711 or 811; Kester 1544)
3. Do unsoldered circuit boards comply with the solderability requirements of EIA Standard RS-178A?
4. Is solder pot, assembly pump, and machine cleaned every forty working hours?
5. Has solder bath been analyzed at least every month?
   Are objective test results available and do they evidence control?
6. Are all locally stored materials identified, accepted, and within shelf-life requirements?
7. Are goggles worn in the vicinity of the machine?
8. Is oil purging accomplished every sixteen hours?
9. Is preheating in the 160–200°F range?
10. Is solder temperature monitored and controlled (525 ± 50°F) (using a calibrated thermometer)?
11. Do completed joints comply with the QA provisions of PX 6.46.01.11.02?
12. Have inspectors been certified and annually recertified to MIL-S-46844?
13. Are soldered boards cleaned per PX 6.46.01.13.02 within eight hours?
14. Are all control and measuring equipment calibrated and within expiration dates?
15. Are divisional anti-static handling procedures followed in this area?
16. Are the MIL-S-46844 visual standards used in inspection decision making?
17. Are maintenance checklists completed per Appendix 1 to PX 6.46.01.11.02?
18. Have adequate rework controls been established?
19. Does an adequate IWI exist?
20. Are heat-sensitive components adequately protected?
21. Is area clean and well organized?

Courtesy of Canadian Marconi Company.

ary corrective actions often take place in their own areas because of what they have seen. It also can reveal "pet" problems that might escape the professional auditors, and it encourages acceptance and involvement by the audited areas. These last two results occur particularly when the team includes a key representative of the area being audited. The rotating team concept is even more effective when the chair is permanent and is also a professional quality auditor. Product conformance audits are typically better done by professionals.

Document the results of the audit on suitably prepared forms. While the audit emphasis is on determining control, you will gain supporters by documenting any evidence of noteworthy commendable quality system activities—those efforts that go beyond control requirements in promoting quality and safety.

Upon completion of the audit, summarize the data and give a comprehensive report to the production supervisor involved. Corrective action should be taken promptly. If for any reason it is impossible or impractical to take corrective action, the results should be immediately submitted to the quality control manager.

THE PRODUCT AUDIT

The product quality audit is used to determine the actual level of quality that the customer will receive. Audit findings tell you something about inspection effectiveness and production quality. It is usually much easier to convince people of the need for corrective action when they can be shown that defects are being delivered to the customer.

The product audit normally samples the output of manufacturing by examining products from the finished goods area that are ready for shipment to customers. This sample, although very small, is random, and experience has shown that the information obtained in this audit is indicative of what customers find when they receive the products from which the samples were taken.

The product audit department is typically in an area remote from manufacturing, staffed with top labor-grade people, and it usually reports to the quality control manager. (In theory, product audit should report to general management to ensure an unbiased evaluation.) Since this area operates on a small sample basis, the pressures for output are less severe and a more careful, thorough reinspection can be performed.

Upon receipt in the audit area, the product is unboxed and checked for proper documentation and accessories that should accompany it, such as instruction books, warranty sheets, and power cords. It is also wise to ensure that the "Tested OK" tag or other appropriate documents are attached and have been properly stamped by inspection and test personnel. Check also for proper labeling, marking, and packing. This part of the audit duplicates the initial customer response as he opens the carton, certainly an important time for a favorable customer opinion.

After unboxing and visual inspection, the product is subjected to an operational test if applicable. This test is to the same requirements originally used by manufacturing, using either the production test procedure or preferably the customer acceptance test method when it is available. However, being performed in a different area, by a different technician and with a different set of test equipment, this operation allows several types of problems to be uncovered. This duplicates the customer performing his own receiving inspection tests. Such things as test equipment calibration, test procedures, or differences in test limits are possible areas of discrepancies.

Bonus Benefit: If audit tests are performed using the maintenance manual, you get the extra advantage of validating its accuracy and adequacy.

After this test, the equipment would be partially disassembled and subjected to a complete reinspection for adherence of workmanship standards manual, and to any important dimensional requirements. Here again, any deviations are noted by the operator performing the inspection. The product audit department discrepancy list can be quickly reproduced and sent back to the particular production area for followup action. The important point is that the information is transmitted back quickly to the source so the proper action may be taken promptly. The product under audit is then reassembled and retested to ensure that no errors were made in the inspection and reassembly process. After this final test, the audit technician attaches a new "Tested OK" tag (or similar form) displaying an acceptance stamp. At this point, the product audit department assumes the responsibility for product acceptance. The equipment is repackaged and returned to finished goods for storage and shipment.

Case in Point: The QA audit department of a nuclear valve manufacturing company subjected a valve to the same test as utilized by the customer. Discrepant results were observed. Upon further investigation, it was learned that the customer acceptance test procedure was deficient and did not accurately measure the relevant parameters. The customer was informed and agreed to change test procedures, thus saving needless dispute.

There are some important factors that must be considered when setting up an audit activity:

- The increased cost of audit personnel, space, and test equipment. Sometimes you can spare yourself the cost of duplicating test equipment by using the equipment of your repair department.

- The disruption to monthly revenue when audit samples are taken. If your end product has a low unit cost, this is not significant. You also have to decide what to do if you discover a critical or safety-related defect on a sample.

- The range of products that must be tested by the limited audit staff.

- The production rate, which can vary from 1 per month to 100,000 per month.

- The sample size (certainly an audit of only one sample should be avoided, because of the high risk of misleading conclusions). It should, however, be recognized that an audit measures more than the quality of a product type only; it reflects on the total effort of a producing department.

- The relative complexity of different products. A "possible error count" can be developed for each product based on number of operations, parts count, series failure rate, or other appropriate technique. Thus, what may appear to be a very small audit sample is, in fact, a sizeable statistical sample when evaluated in terms of effort measured by possible errors.

- The need for prompt feedback of defect information and orderly status reporting.

RATIO ANALYSIS: AN EARLY WARNING SYSTEM

The benefits of ratio analysis were discussed in Chapter 3. Some specific ratios (and their trends) that are especially helpful in measuring quality system performance are:

Internal

- repair/rework hours as a percent of direct labor hours

- appraisal costs as a percent of total factory labor cost

- operating profit as a percent of sales

- return on capital employed

- inspector absenteeism/turnover rates

- percent yield of key operations

- scrap costs as a percent of production cost of sales

- incoming inspection rejection rate(s) for major commodity groups

External

- market share ratio

- warranty as a percent of sales

- order book/billings ratio

- repeat order index

- accounts receivable turnover ratio

- field MTBF as a percent of target MTBF

- order cancellations as a percent of orders booked

- cumulative sales (this year) as a percent of corresponding cumulative sales (last year)

Ratios can be misleading if either the numerator or denominator has significantly changed in nature or scope. Also, some of the ratios are not 100 percent correlated with quality levels, so that changes in ratios may not necessarily mean your quality program is unhealthy or healthy. However, taken as a group and combined with other measures of product quality, your chances of awakening to a false alarm are very small indeed.

QUALITY COSTS

When all is said and done, the quality program must present itself as a cost-effective vehicle for attaining company profit and growth objectives.

Quality systems are in need of measurement and evaluation. The quality costs in terms of real dollars are the most effective and realistic measurements as well as programming tools. The four phases of introduction and application of *quality costs* are:

Phase I
definition of quality costs
identification of the cost elements

Phase II
construction of the system that produces the cost figures

Phase III
application of the quality cost system as a quality improvement and cost reduction tool

Phase IV
trend reporting and relative measurements, maintenance and administration of the quality cost module

Quality cost is the tool that permits management of the quality control function to occur in a businesslike manner. Return on investment and justification of personnel and equipment can be expressed similarly to any other manufacturing function.

Comparison bases are an important part of operating and application of the system and should be selected with care. Because of great differences in businesses, and sometimes even differences among departments, it is advisable to evaluate the advantages and relevance of the various bases, and select the most meaningful one(s).

1. *Labor Bases*
standard direct hours
standard cost of labor input
total labor (including burden)

2. *Manufacturing Cost Bases*

standard cost of output

shop cost of output

actual operating cost

3. *Sales Bases*

net sales invoiced

cost of sales at standard cost

4. *Unit Bases*

total number of units manufactured

total units processed

total units shipped

The primary task is determining the present level and how it compares with past performance and targets and reviewing the trend of the quality cost applied to the selected base(s).

Caution: Extreme care must be exercised when departments and companies are compared, or even a single department is compared with the company average. The diversity of factors—such as degree of automation, material content, unit value of product, age of facility, batch sizes—may render comparison completely irrelevant, if not misleading.

Are quality costs really known? Some costs may be reported with reasonable accuracy, but often many go undetected. Many costs are lost in variances and standards or are absorbed in the cost of manufacturing. Proper identification, isolation, and tracking of quality costs can spotlight problem areas and focus attention where needed. All too often, standards have built-in higher rates. These rates become a way of life, and there is little incentive or pressure to decrease the reject rate. Other times a firm just keeps making enough product until orders are filled without really knowing how much material was rejected, destroyed, or otherwise lost for various quality reasons.

Sometimes, quality cost reports are generated but are of little use because of their structure. The reports must have a sound basis and be part of the goals and objectives of all departments directly impacting quality. The data base of the quality cost report must be identified. It is important to determine how the report is being used, its credibility, who receives the report, and what actions are taken. The frequency of the reporting must be predetermined and strictly adhered to. Modifica-

tion and updating of cost reports as organizational changes, product introductions, and so on occur must closely follow. All cost reports must be signed by responsible individuals and indicate full list of distribution.

The real values of the quality cost system applications are threefold:

1. Providing general trends that measure the effectiveness of quality management.

2. Providing quality cost composite values.

A typical breakdown of the quality dollar by a large corporation might be:

5¢	Prevention
25¢	Appraisal
60¢	Internal failure
10¢	External failure
1.00	

3. Pin-pointing problem areas. Both high failure values and appraisal costs can be quickly identified.

Table 15-2 shows a sample cost report format that satisfies the three previous applications.

Acid Tests

(a) Are quality cost improvements incorporated into departmental goals (other than the QC department)?

(b) Does management feel the quality cost report is accurate and a valuable management aid?

(c) If unfavorable trends appear in the quality cost report, does management initiate an investigation?

An interesting exercise for the operations research minded: Devise a mathematical model relating detection/prevention costs and failure costs to product quality/reliability. The model can be used to find the optimum level of total quality costs. You can then compare your current position against this theoretical level.

FREQUENT CUSTOMER COMPLAINTS CARRY A CRUCIAL MESSAGE

Business complaints are unavoidable. Perhaps the customer is using your product incorrectly and has exceeded its intended application. The customer may be trying to return an obsolete product or reduce inventory. It may be company policy to accept these items as returns for "quality" rea-

TABLE 15–2. Sample Quality Cost Report

Product Line or
Department _____   QUALITY COST REPORT   Date _____

	$	%	$	%	$	%	$	%	$	%
Prevention										
1. A. Quality Planning (QC Eng. type work)										
B. Process Quality Control (PC Eng. type work)										
2. Instruction writing—Test, Insp. & Proc. Cont.										
3. Qual. Assur. Equip.—Design & Develop.										
4. Quality Training										
Total Prevention										
Appraisal										
1. Incoming Test & Inspection										
2. Laboratory Accept. Testing										
3. Laboratory or other Meas. Service										
4. Inspection										
5. Test										
6. Checking Labor										
7. Set-up for Test & Insp.										
8. Test & Insp. Material										
9. Quality Audits										
10. All Others*										
Total Appraisal										
Failure										
Internal										
1. Scrap										
2. Rework										
3. Scrap & Rework—Fault of Vendor										
4. Material Procurement										
5. Factory Contact Eng.										
Total Internal Failure										
External										
1. Complaints										
2. Product Service										
Total External Failure										
Total Failure										
TOTAL QUALITY COSTS										

Courtesy of Canadian Marconi Company.

sons. The particular nature of your business will dictate what guidelines you need to use to determine if a real problem exists in this area. However, there are some general steps that can be taken to analyze the customer complaints situation.

Look for trends when the total quantity of customer complaints has changed from previous months, quarters, or years. This information may be expressed in terms of dollars, percentage of output or sales, or number of units. Data must give a consistent measure from period to period. For example, dollars alone would not be a meaningful measure if the sale volume has increased significantly from period to period. However, those dollars converted to a percentage of sales would enable the examiner to determine if customer returns have increased over time. Try to categorize the returns into one of three major categories:

1. design-related
2. conformance-related
3. nonquality-related

The first category refers to returns that were within product specifications when they left the plant, but failed to meet the customer's needs. This may have been caused by a functional failure, premature wear-out, or other design-related failure. This category of returns points the way to additional investigation that may lead all the way back to the drawing board. Perhaps the product specifications were not stringent enough for the application, and a higher-grade item is required.

The quality-of-conformance category includes those items that failed to meet product specifications. An adverse trend in this category should lead toward additional investigations into the test/inspection department, quality engineering group, or manufacturing department. There is a host of reasons why a nonconforming product may have been shipped. Failure to detect the defects is the most obvious. There should be a formal system to address the causes of nonconformance. Generally, a committee or group made up of representatives from the various departments involved is the most effective. As a minimum, have the quality engineering department investigate the leading causes of nonconformance. Inspector training, misinterpretation of specifications, and differences among test methods may be other reasons for the shipment of nonconform-

ing items. The key is to have a formal system to monitor customer returns and to initiate investigations when unfavorable trends appear.

Case in Point: After investigating a dozen customer complaints, it was found that nine of the field failures were caused by a particular relay. A check of items in stock indicated an 80 percent reject rate (caused by corrosion of electrical contacts). All stock in assembly and service centers was purged and replaced with relays from another source. The customers were told the reasons for the failures and the corrective action taken. A subsequent check of the relay supplier indicated that his quality system had broken down with a change in company ownership.

Reasons for nonquality related returns include shipping damages, purchasing errors, excessive inventory, and obsolescence. This category generally catches all the miscellaneous reasons for return of products that are considered acceptable quality-wise. Damage caused by customer mishandling would fall into this category. However, failure of a product to meet normal shipping stresses may be a quality-of-design problem.

It is a fact that only a fraction of customers take the time to formally complain. More often than not, they just switch to another manufacturer. So when you do get a complaint, treat it as important, critical information. Responsiveness to complaints is an attribute that customers value highly.

There are several ways an alert QC manager can find a potential or actual field problem before it reaches crisis proportions. Here are a few of them:

- *Accounts receivable.* Delays in payment can reflect a customer cash shortage or customer unhappiness. In about 50 percent of the cases performance shortfalls, incoming inspection failure, and open CAR's are the underlying causes of a receivable that extends thirty days or more beyond the due date.

- *Inactive accounts.* You may find that sales have lapsed because the customer, having a grievance, did not give you an opportunity to adjust it. A letter, a phone call, or a personal visit may be instrumental in identifying the customer's rationale.

- *Credit notes.* An examination of credit/debit

notes often reveals an underlying quality problem.

- *Spares orders.* A high level of spares orders for a particular part number may indicate a quality problem or part misapplication.

   Caution: Spares orders sometimes represent a significant source of profits. Before getting too involved with this data source, check with marketing.

- *Customer quality representatives.* Informal contacts with customer survey teams or source inspectors can provide valuable insight into user quality problems.

- *Surveys.* Questionnaires to be answered by users or potential users of the product can reveal problem areas.

- *Trade shows.* A display of products to a select group of users can obtain preference information.

- *Field trials.* Consumer panels and in-use testing of new products can determine the appeal and performance of new products or design changes.

- *Panels.* User or dealer advisory panels meet regularly to discuss quality and user problems.

Answer these questions to see if frequent customer complaints will be a problem in your company:

1. Is there a formal system to collect and consolidate complaints?

2. Is there a formal program to investigate customer complaints?

3. Are these responsibilities assigned to organizational units?

4. Are adverse trends in the number and severity of customer returns flagged for management attention?

5. Is analysis being performed to identify any patterns that may exist in the type of complaints, products involved, or component failures?

6. Can you categorize the complaints as design-, conformance-, or nonquality-related?

7. Are complaints being reviewed with engineering, manufacturing, inspectors, foremen?

8. Are periodic summary and trend reports sent to management and marketing?

YOUR CORRECTIVE ACTION SYSTEM: HOW EFFECTIVE IS IT?

Corrective action distinguishes a QC system from an inspection system. Do you have a QC system?

√ Does the system provide for prompt detection of inferior quality?

√ Is adequate action taken to correct the causes of nonconformities in products, facilities, and procedures?

√ Are analyses made to identify trends toward product deficiencies? Is corrective action taken to arrest unfavorable trends before deficiencies occur?

√ Is there a method of documenting each discrepancy (vendor, in-house, and field) so that its characteristics may be recorded and compared with others?

√ Does a quality engineer investigate discrepancies; classify them as to seriousness, cause, and responsibility; and require resolution through formal means?

√ Does a capability of failed parts analysis exist to determine the underlying reason for failure and eliminate it?

√ Does corrective action extend to suppliers' products?

√ Is there a review and disposition, by a representative board, of all defects that cannot be reworked to drawing configuration?

√ Is a "top ten" problem list an integral part of the division or general manager's weekly meeting?

√ Is there a capability for retraining operators who are having difficulty with specific techniques?

√ Does the system provide for prompt action when requested by a customer?

√ Does the system define the responsibility for performing follow-up reporting of each phase of corrective action?

√ Are data analysis and product examination conducted on scrap or rework to determine extent and causes of nonconformities?

√ Is the effectiveness of corrections reviewed, and are they monitored later?

If your overall approach to corrective action passes these criteria with high marks, it will, in the long run, reduce waste of resources, permit the productive use of manufacturing personnel and facilities now dedicated to producing nonconforming product, and reduce both internal and external failure quality costs in dramatic increments.

Don't limit your activities to complaining or hypothesizing. Get deeply involved. Good corrective action is not easy, but it can make or break the quality control effort.

TRY QUALITATIVE ANALYSIS

A qualitative analysis of your quality program can be performed right at your desk. It is subjective, but it is based on the consolidated evaluation of a complex set of variables. If you can't pass this test you don't need the more sophisticated approaches to tell you where you stand.

1. Is your boss happy with the performance of the quality program? (Does the QC manager participate in the bonus plan?)

2. Is quality control an integral part of the management team?

3. Does engineering, purchasing, or marketing periodically seek guidance or consultation from quality control?

4. Is QC meaningfully involved from product definition through to customer usage?

5. Is the quality image of your company consistent with your objectives?

6. Is there a good working relationship between manufacturing and QC?

7. Do engineers, operators, and supervisors respect and understand what the company's quality goals are?

8. Has the quality program actually helped control product quality (reliability, safety) and reduced costs through its prevention and improvement activities?

9. Have you been able to attract top technologists, engineers, and managers to your department? (Alternatively, have QC people gone on to bigger and better things?)

10. Does your department have a solid reputation for innovation, statistical expertise, and technological depth?

11. Are you and your people regarded as ethical, hard-working professionals with a meaningful mission?

12. Can you really influence the quality of design and conformance of your products or services? (Conversely, are conflicts and frequent management intervention required to make the right things happen?)

If each question were worth up to five points, would you rate more than forty-five points? more than fifty?

Another way of looking at your situation is to put your department into one of five fundamental classifications.

1. *Infancy:* "We don't know why we have problems with quality." Quality improvement activities are not organized: main activity is fire-fighting.

2. *The dawn:* "Is it necessary to have chronic quality problems?" Short-term problems are attacked, but the QC budget is inadequate.

3. *Enlightenment:* "Management commitment is helping us." Corrective action is effective under the leadership of a professional quality manager reporting to top management.

4. *Maturity:* "Defect prevention is a routine part of the quality program." All functional departments support the quality objectives and quality improvement activities are formalized.

5. *Wisdom:* "We know why we do not have quality problems." Quality costs are minimal and optimized; QC manager is on board of directors or is an officer of the company.

Where do you stand?

REFERENCES

Crosby, P. B. "Measuring Maturity." *Quality,* Aug. 1980.

Kivenko, K. "Surviving the Operational Audit." *Production Engineering,* June 1979.

Lindgren, L. H. "Auditing Management Information Systems." *Journal of Systems Management,* June 1969.

Marash, S. A. "Performing Quality Audits." *Industrial Quality Control,* Jan. 1966.

Van Dine, H. A. "Quality Auditing—Familiar Land Explored." *Quality Progress,* Nov. 1980.

Wachniak, R. "Ten Commandments for Quality Auditors." *Quality,* 1980.

White, B. "Quality Fitness Test." *Quality,* March 1981.

Williams, C. D. "How You Can Optimize the QC Function in Your Firm." *Industrial Engineering,* March 1981.

Wilson, M. F. "The Quality Your Customer Needs." Collins Radio Company, DOC. 523-070665-00181R, 1968.

Index